MARCEL BREUER
Building Global Institutions

MARCEL BREUER
Building Global Institutions

Edited by
Barry Bergdoll and
Jonathan Massey

Lars Müller Publishers

In memory of Robert Gatje (1928–2018),
for his contributions to the architecture of Marcel Breuer & Associates
and to the research for this volume.

6 Introduction: Bureaucratic Genius

18 **I SAINT JOHN'S ABBEY**

34 Marcel Breuer and the Invention of Heavy Lightness
Barry Bergdoll

64 **II UNESCO**

80 Architecture and Mediocracy at UNESCO House
Lucia Allais

116 Marcel Breuer: Structure and Shadow
Guy Nordenson

140 **III PRECAST PANEL**

154 From Garden City to Concrete City:
Breuer and Yorke's Garden City of the Future
Teresa Harris

180 Atomic Bauhaus: Marcel Breuer and Big Science
John Harwood

202 **IV NEW YORK**

222 Architectures of Opportunity at Breuer's Bronx Campus
Jonathan Massey

252 **V FRANCE**

272 Modernism as Accommodation
Kenny Cupers with Laura Martínez de Guereñu

292 Breuer's Ancillary Strategy: Symbols, Signs, and Structures
at the Intersection of Modernism and Postmodernism
Timothy M. Rohan

318 **VI GLOBAL BREUER**

348 Postface: The Marcel Breuer Digital Archive
at Syracuse University
Lucy Mulroney

359 **Acknowledgments**
360 **Biographies**
361 **Index**
367 **Credits**

1 Marcel Breuer's Massachusetts registration card, 1946

Introduction: Bureaucratic Genius

What is the nature of architectural authorship? How do a designer's distinctive hand and eye interact with institutions and their processes—with corporate and government clients, engineers and other collaborators, or even colleagues within the same firm? How did modern architecture change during the mid-twentieth century as corporations, universities, and bureaucracies both within and beyond government scaled up and took a leading role in shaping societies around the world?

These questions are central to architectural history, and they come up with particular richness in the case of Marcel Breuer, the Hungarian-American architect known as a "form-giver" of modern architecture. As one of the first students at the Bauhaus—Germany's legendary crucible of modernism in the arts, architecture, and design—and subsequently an influential teacher there and at Harvard's Graduate School of Design, Breuer in the first part of his career epitomized modernism in furniture and architecture. In subsequent designs for research labs, corporate and government headquarters, university facilities, churches, housing estates, and museums, Breuer gave shape to the postwar world throughout North America as well as in Europe, Latin America, and elsewhere. Through close readings of key Breuer buildings, the essays in this volume examine these transformations in modern architecture and the world it instantiated.

In the past decade, Marcel Breuer's architecture has enjoyed a stunning comeback. While Breuer's tubular steel furniture was already ubiquitous in his own lifetime and has been in houses and cafeterias ever since, his architecture had fallen out of fashion and, in a way, out of view even before his death in 1981. A decade after his death, the *New York Times* published an article on the ubiquity of the cane-seated, cantilevered, tubular steel "Cesca" chair available in nearly identical versions at every price range, and even now every day brings more Breuer chairs into the resale marketplace.[1]

But even more dramatically than for almost any other of the masters in what Alice and Peter Smithson once called the heroic period of modern architecture, Breuer's reputation sank to a nadir with the rise of postmodernism.[2] This was precipitated by Breuer's involvement in the late 1960s in a controversial, and ultimately scuttled, scheme to build a tower over Grand Central Terminal in New York; and the sinking of his reputation was advanced further by the publication of the popular antimodern polemic from the barbed pen of Tom Wolfe, *From Bauhaus to Our House* (1981), in which Breuer was often front and center in the satirical put-down of high-modern utopian earnestness.

As an architect, Breuer disappeared from the scene just as an architecture of ornament and historical reference was staged by a new generation of postmodernists in the false fronts of the 1980 Venice Architecture Biennale's Strada Novissima, a prelude to the Whitney's first controversial expansion project, in which Michael Graves thought to subsume Breuer's famous inverted ziggurat into one-half of a postmodern façade collage. Even Breuer's obituary in the *New York Times* by Paul Goldberger on July 2, 1981, dwelt at length on the former Bauhaus master's fall from grace before it went on to detail his myriad achievements in furniture design and architecture, as well as to list the numerous awards his practice had garnered since the 1950s. In the first line of the obituary Goldberger offered a phonetic rendering of Breuer's name for those who might not know how to pronounce it, let alone pronounce it with respect. Sadly, a major exhibition of Breuer's work in preparation at the Museum of Modern Art, seen perhaps as a corrective to rising postmodernism, opened a few weeks after Breuer's death. In it, Christopher Wilk set a new standard of historical research and consolidated Breuer's reputation as a furniture designer in the 1920s through 1940s, even as his project eschewed any presentation of his later work as an architect of prominent building complexes everywhere from Washington, DC, to numerous American university campuses to the commanding Whitney Museum on Madison Avenue.[3]

Yet even before the Metropolitan Museum decided in 2015 that the easiest way to "rebrand" the former Whitney Museum, now home to exhibitions organized by the Met's Department of Modern and Contemporary Art, was to dub it the "Met Breuer," the architect was enjoying popularity among fans of mid-century modernism. In recent years Breuer has become a

p. 294/2

staple in everything from modernist lifestyle magazines, where his American designs—houses in particular—appear with a steady drumbeat, to renewed academic interest in the intersections of America's post–World War II architectural modernism with the rise of American corporate culture and international hegemony. Even Breuer's institutional architecture has ridden the coattails of this renewed appreciation for precisely the architecture that had been the object of critique in the postmodernist polemic. There are now two lengthy monographic studies chronicling his architecture from the early Bauhaus years in Germany, where Breuer joined the experimental school near the end of its first year in Weimar, to the postwar decades in New York, during which his office became one of the most prominent representatives of American postwar prosperity and dominance on a world stage, exporting even architecture around the world, from Argentina to Afghanistan, from Australia to Lake Zurich. By the early 1960s, with the rise of jet travel, Breuer was one of the new globalists of the Pax Americana.

Marcel Breuer: Building Global Institutions opens the subject to a current cohort of architectural historians whose approaches to the study of institutions and to architectural practice suggest new interpretations of a career by now well documented but under-analyzed. Working catalogs of Breuer's production have appeared in the years since the Breuer firm's papers, deposited at the Syracuse University Libraries—an archival tale related here by Lucy Mulroney—were first given a repertory and opened to researchers. In 1998, Joachim Driller's doctoral thesis on Breuer's residential architecture—always more widely admired than his institutional work—was published in German with a comprehensive catalog of the built and unbuilt house designs that dominated Breuer's career, from his immigration, first to London and then to the United States in the 1930s, until the mid-1950s. Driller's work appeared in an English translation in 2000, and one year later a comprehensive monograph by Isabelle Hyman combined a catalog of work by Breuer and his associates in all aspects of architecture and urban design with a biography of the peripatetic architect. Breuer left his native Hungary as a teenager to study art and design, first in Vienna and then in the Weimar Bauhaus. He practiced in Berlin, Zurich, Budapest, and London in the late 1920s and early 1930s before accepting a position in 1938 at Harvard. In 1946, after a dramatic break with Walter

Gropius—a rift later mended—Breuer moved to New York on the brink of a postwar building explosion. His practice grew exponentially—not from metropolitan commissions but with the simultaneous arrival of two major institutional commissions in 1953: UNESCO headquarters in Paris and St. John's Abbey.[4] With the fundamental shift in the nature of Breuer's practice from private residential clients to institutional work, the very nature of his engagement with the political, economic, and social context of his adopted United States changed as radically as did the nature of his architectural design.[5]

This is the subject of our book. Eschewing the aim of completeness that would guide a *catalogue raisonné,* our authors —drawn from among the most incisive scholars working on twentieth-century modernism—focus on projects that open onto interpretive questions relevant to the broader trajectory of modern architecture at mid-century. By interleaving their essays with generous visual portfolios, however, we introduce readers to the full range of Breuer's major institutional commissions, including some that are little known or that are even newly recognized, such as Breuer Associates' large-scale proposals for the development of the coastline south of Bordeaux in France during that country's state-led encouragement of vacation communities in the mountains and at the seaside. By further opening the archive and situating Breuer's practice within a rapidly transforming postwar world, this volume suggests paths forward for research into a rich and extensive corpus of buildings and documents generated by a practice that grew rapidly from a handful of drafting staff in a Manhattan brownstone to an office occupying several floors of a midtown building over the course of three decades of global practice.

The group of authors gathered here emerged from the final phase of a seminar co-taught by the volume editors at the Syracuse University School of Architecture in 2010 at the invitation of Dean Mark Robbins. The course was held in the Breuer archives at the university library, giving the students a rare opportunity to work directly with a paper-based archive, as novel for them as an approach to primary research as it was an exposure to drawing formats now rendered productively unfamiliar by the rise of computer-based drawing and design. While the students completed individual research projects in the archive—largely unstudied Breuer projects such as the designs for a commercial center, El Recreo, in Caracas, Venezuela, or the unbuilt project for a new Episcopalian cathedral in Burlington, Vermont—collectively the seminar was tasked with conceiving a small exhibition, thus adding a curatorial and exhibition design component to the curriculum of historical research. For the final review of the seminar, a group of historians interested in the period but not necessarily versed in Breuer's career was invited to Syracuse to review the proposals for the content and design of the exhibition. The discussion that ensued in the review, which brought together most of the authors in the current volume, was so lively and stimulating that the idea of gathering the group together to produce a book of essays on Breuer's larger meaning for postwar American architectural culture seemed self-evident by the end of the meeting.[6]

Particularly stimulating was the shared sense that two tendencies were converging. On the one hand, numerous moments in the discussion addressed the resonance of Breuer's formal approaches to and attitudes toward certain contemporary practices in the broad re-engagement with postwar modernism through influential practices from OMA, notably in the Porto Opera House, to Diller Scofidio + Renfro, both in their acupunctural renovation of Lincoln Center and in new work such as the Broad Museum in Los Angeles, commissioned in 2010. At the same time, it was clear that growing numbers of architectural historians were engaging with Breuer as they reconsidered the relationship of architectural practice to institutions of the period—what we might call the mid-career reevaluation of the stakes of mid-century modernism.

Research on Breuer has become exponentially easier with the creation of the Marcel Breuer Digital Archive. This pathbreaking initiative, completed by the Special Collections Research Center at the Syracuse University Libraries with funding from the National Endowment for the Humanities, has made almost all the drawings, photographs, correspondence, and papers of the Breuer firm available online. The digital archive combines the core collection of office records at Syracuse with material from other major repositories, including the personal papers of Breuer donated by his widow, Constance Breuer, to the Archives of American Art in Washington and available in microfilm copies at regional centers, as well as holdings at the Bauhaus-Archiv in Berlin and the archives at Harvard University's Graduate School of Design, where Breuer taught for nearly a decade. Robert McCarter's monumental monograph on Breuer, published in 2016, is the first fruit of the new remote access made possible by the digitization project, although it remains largely formal and descriptive in its appreciation of Breuer's accomplishments in so large a spectrum of building types and national contexts.

The expanded access afforded by the digital repository coincides with the resurgence of interest in Breuer and his work. As this book has been assembled over the last five years, it is clear that not only has Breuer's reputation largely been rehabilitated, even if not all share in the newfound enthusiasm for the legacy of brutalism or (for those who worked with Breuer) accept his relationship to it. Certainly Breuer's centrality to any evaluation of American architecture of the 1940s to 1970s is clear. A solid scholarly apparatus for the study has been assembled, not only in the scholarly monographs by Driller, Hyman, and McCarter, already mentioned, but also in the contributions of the key associates in Breuer's practice, thus providing not only invaluable firsthand insights into the work of a major creator of architectural form but also a portrait of a model of practice in a period when the American architectural office became something of a global model.

Breuer's office was unusual in that he set up a series of relationships with individual partners who played key design as well as supervisory roles in major projects. Two of the key actors have left us memoirs of their time with the firm. Herbert Beckhard worked hand-in-hand with author David Masello to publish *Architecture without Rules: The Houses of Marcel Breuer and Herbert Beckhard*, which collated work that had been done with Breuer together with Beckhard's own subsequent independent practice—a decision that ruffled certain feathers for taking on the mantle of a designer who had spread his coattails to collaborate in parallel with a group of talented associates. This was all the more timely as its appearance in the mid-1990s coincided with a moment when the modest scale of many of Breuer's houses, particularly in the Northeast, threatened them with demolition. Alongside his own large-scale institutional work, Beckhard was to renovate and expand a number of key Breuer houses, notably Breuer's own first New Canaan house, in a vocabulary developed from Breuer's own residential language.

On the other hand, longtime associate Robert Gatje, a great help to the authors in this volume as he has continued to be engaged with the historical memory of an office in which he spent several decades (notably in the years in which offices were maintained in both New York and Paris), has left us with a lively account of Breuer's career and with precious insights into the design practices and daily life of the Breuer office (*Marcel Breuer: A Memoir*, 2000). Although more discreet in imparting firsthand knowledge, Isabelle Hyman, it should be noted, began her working life as a secretary in the Breuer office before studying Renaissance architectural history. She therefore approaches Breuer's practice both from an insider's perspective and with the objectivity and methods of a trained art historian in her 2001 monograph, *Marcel Breuer, Architect.* At the same time, preservationists, notably those brought together in the local and national chapters of Docomomo, paid particular attention to Breuer. Exhibitions on modernism celebrated his work in, for example, Litchfield, Connecticut, and on Cape Cod—locations vaunted for their place in American tradition but in which Breuer had also honed a form of modernism that found considerable traction with progressive clients in the 1940s and 1950s.[7] Of the exhibitions that built on this popularity, only the widely circulating Vitra Design Museum exhibition on Breuer sought to take on his career as a whole.[8]

The authors brought together in this volume are interested not in returning to a celebration of Breuer's work on the residential scale, something given a huge boost by his selection as the first designer, in 1948, for one of MoMA's three influential houses in the garden immediately after World War II, but rather in examining the institutional work and its context in the wake of the commissions for UNESCO headquarters in Paris and for a master plan for the church and university campus of one of the world's largest Benedictine houses, St. John's Abbey and University in Collegeville, Minnesota. With perhaps the exception of Victoria Young's study of St. John's in relation to the liturgical movement that swept the Roman Catholic Church prior to Vatican II and in which St. John's played a leading role, few have set out to study the institutional turn in Breuer's practice in relation to the changing institutional landscape of the United States in the pathbreaking decades of globalizing shifts, from World War II through the Cold War.[9]

It was precisely in this increasingly important nexus between increasingly numerous international corporations, new networks of scientific research between an enlarged government apparatus and a burgeoning American university culture, and the founding of international organizations seeking peace amid the threat of a new scale of warfare (made possible by those very industrial and scientific forces) that Breuer's American architectural language took form. This was a world at a very far remove from the fragile Weimar Republic Bauhaus in which Breuer had been trained, and thus it seems appropriate to leave behind something of the ideology of America as inheritor of the Bauhaus and to seek, rather, to understand Breuer's architecture in relation to the distinctively American globalized reality of the 1950s to 1970s.

This group of essays emphasizes the immediate stakes of Breuer's practice rather than focusing on the continuity of the modernist project independent of local and national politics so dear to the modern movement's early historian-critics, some of whom, like Sigfried Giedion, were closely associated with Breuer. The strongest recent scholarship has situated architecture within the nexus of a study of institutions, networks, and discourses. Addressing these interpretive approaches in regard to Breuer, who worked in precisely this milieu from the 1950s to the end of his career, these essays focus as much on institutions as on the charismatic lead architect as a sole author. Indeed, what and where is agency in the work of an office called "Breuer," a surname that was also shorthand for an ever larger office staff and a cohort of key collaborators integral to producing the work? The growth of the firm paralleled the scaling up of institutions in the postwar era, yet the business was not a corporate firm in the style of Skidmore, Owings & Merrill (SOM). Unlike the big corporate firms that blossomed after World War II, Breuer's was a large studio, with the founder involved at some level in every project. The nature of that practice, as much as the formal resolution of individual projects, is central to the ways our authors interpret the churches, laboratories, office buildings, museums, university buildings, and manufacturing facilities designed by Marcel Breuer and Associates. Breuer honed an immediately recognizable architectural signature out of group effort, creating a distinctive office style. In this he was as different from peers such as Eero Saarinen, who spoke of the "style for the job," as he was from the corporate approach of SOM, since the hands of individual collaborators can often be assessed—notably, for instance, that of Hamilton Smith, whom Breuer even credited as co-author on the cornerstone of the Whitney Museum of American Art.

As in Breuer's office, each of the authors here makes a distinctive contribution. Collectively, these essays illuminate the back-and-forth between architect and client at a time when his modernism was no longer avant-garde but not generic either. Further, they show how the design, construction, and occupancy of Breuer buildings were testing grounds for emerging modes of complex architectural authorship and distributed agency. Could we say that "genius bureaucrat" sums up this position, as Lucia Allais advances in her reading of Breuer's work as part of a team at UNESCO that found both process and form in the new modalities of transnational bureaucracy? Others, such as Barry Bergdoll, see the stronger guiding line of a single "initiatory genius" in the realm of form-giving, notably in the continuities and ruptures from Breuer's Bauhaus training and International Style lightness to his work in the weighty aesthetic sometimes called brutalist—a term that Breuer would hardly recognize. Teresa Harris, fresh from several years leading the Breuer digitization project, sees an important cauldron for future ideas in Breuer's exhibition project, the Garden City of Tomorrow (1936, with his British partner F. R. S. Yorke), which contained not only an idiom for reinforced concrete but also a catalog of institutional types for an urban center in a world of rapidly changing realities. Hers is the only essay to focus on Breuer's experience before his immigration to the United States, but she suggests that Breuer's exposure to the debates on modernism and tradition, urban and suburban, in interwar Britain was just as consequential for his development as the Bauhaus. That interwar experience also honed a model of collaborative practice that was to be expanded in Cambridge, Massachusetts, in association with Walter Gropius as he formed the ideals that would lead to the Architects' Collaborative. Through a masterful reading of Breuer's engagement with the structural capacities of reinforced concrete through projects generated in collaboration with different engineers, Guy Nordenson shows how the changing nature of his professional collaborations modulated Breuer's stance toward modernist principles of structural expressiveness and tectonic truth.

Most of the essays here read Breuer's institutional work as much from the perspective of the institution as from that of the architect, raising the question of authorship within the expanding postwar military industrial complex. By situating the precast concrete panels that enclosed most of Breuer's government, university, and corporate laboratory buildings in the trajectory of architecture for "big science," John Harwood tells a hidden history of negotiation among professionals with different stakes in the vast flow of research funding. His reading of projects in Brookhaven and La Gaude shows how their back-and-forth with scientists and bureaucrats led the Breuer firm to monumentalize the high cultural status and stakes of postwar scientific research by integrating mechanical services into building façades. Jonathan Massey takes us to one of the many campuses on which Breuer was to work in this period, exploring not only the ideas and aspirations that gave form to New York University's expanding uptown campus in the Bronx but also following the vicissitudes of its rise and decline as reflections of the period's changing stakes of urban growth. Here architectural history is not only a tale of heroic form-giving but also a study in the limited capacity of form to advance institutional strategies amid unpredictable economic and demographic changes. No less a trajectory accompanies Breuer's foray into the overcharged world of French large-scale state-subsidized housing in the creation of ZUPs, or zones of prioritization for urbanization, at the edge of the Basque city of Bayonne in a case studied by Kenny Cupers with Laura Martínez de Guereñu. Because of the ways that the Breuer ZUP adapted ingeniously to change, we can see modernism not as a canon of forms but as accommodation—as a process of adjustment to conflicting demands and changing circumstances. This group of essays concludes by challenging the commonly drawn distinction between late modernism and postmodernism. Timothy Rohan generates a perceptive and subtle reading of Breuer's "ancillary structures," products of the architect's tendency to precede a building with a sign tectonically related to the daring engineering and formal expression of the institution behind. Situating these works in relation to the modernist search for a new monumentality and the growing culture of advertising, Rohan reintroduces them as anticipations of the signage that Venturi, Rauch and Scott Brown foregrounded in their postmodernist works of a few years later.

    The volume ends with Lucy Mulroney's history of the Breuer archive at Syracuse University, shedding light on its genesis and underscoring its potentials for future research. Indeed, the new capacity for data analysis to exploit the digital archive for new kinds of interpretation—image analysis and comparisons, geographical and social network analysis, studies of office practice—suggest that these essays are the leading edge of new horizons of research opened up by digital media and methods. The translation of the Breuer papers—long housed in file boxes, flat files, and aluminum tubes—into a linked network of machine-readable data opens the history of modern architecture to the questions and practices of digital humanities, such as distant reading, geospatial analysis, and visual analytics. Much as his buildings mediated the emerging formats of postwar global governance, scientific research, and corporate organization, so Breuer's archive may prove a medium for new convergences of twenty-first-century knowledge and power.

1 Elaine Louie, "The Many Lives of a Very Common Chair," *New York Times*, February 7, 1991.
2 Alison Smithson and Peter Smithson, *The Heroic Period of Modern Architecture* (London: Thames and Hudson, 1981).
3 Christopher Wilk, *Marcel Breuer: Furniture and Interiors* (New York: Museum of Modern Art, 1981).
4 Barry Bergdoll, "Breuer as a Global Architect," in *OfficeUS Agenda*, ed. Eva Franch i Gilabert, Amanda Reeser Lawrence, Ana Miljački, and Ashley Shafer (Zurich: Lars Müller Publishers and PRAXIS, 2014), 149–59.
5 Robert McCarter, *Breuer* (London: Phaidon, 2016).
6 The exhibition *Marcel Breuer and Postwar America* was staged the following year, February 15–March 29, accompanied by a small brochure. See http://chengsnyder.com/projects/marcel-breuer-and-postwar-america.
7 In 2003, Rachel Carley organized the exhibit *Modernism in Litchfield* at the Connecticut Historical Society in Litchfield. In 2006, Peter McMahon organized an exhibition on Cape Cod modernism in Wellfleet, now developed in the study by Peter McMahon and Christine Cipriani, *Cape Cod Modern: Midcentury Architecture and Community on the Outer Cape* (New York: Metropolis, 2014).
8 *Marcel Breuer: Architecture and Design*, exhibition catalog (Weil am Rhein: Vitra Design Museum, 2003).
9 Victoria Young, *Saint John's Abbey Church: Marcel Breuer and the Creation of a Modern Sacred Space* (Minneapolis: University of Minnesota Press, 2014).

The scheme Breuer developed with F. R. S. Yorke for a "Concrete City" encompassed compelling designs for large housing, civic, and commercial structures. But it was not until 1953 that Breuer's firm got to complete major institutional buildings. One was a new abbey church and campus expansion for the Abbey of St. John the Baptist in Collegeville, Minnesota.

After considering a dozen distinguished candidates, including Breuer's former partner Gropius, the brothers of this large Benedictine community selected Breuer to create an architecture serving and symbolizing the Catholic liturgical reform they had led since the 1930s. In the church, which was dedicated in 1961, Breuer established a "spiritual axis" that led worshippers beneath a giant bell banner into an intimate baptistery, then below a deep balcony into the expansive nave toward the altar and abbot's throne. In contrast to a traditional Latin cross configuration, the trapezoidal plan turned the nave into an auditorium in which seats and pews surrounding the central altar promoted lay participation in the service.

This generous space was enclosed by folded concrete walls, developed with engineer Pier Luigi Nervi, and it was lit by a giant screen of hexagonal stained-glass windows. Inspired by Gothic cathedrals, Breuer and his clients created a modernist sacred space through structural, architectural, and aesthetic innovation. The church was the linchpin of an ambitious master plan—a "Comprehensive 100-Year Plan"—for a modern university campus, including a modernized cloister, dormitories, and a new library that complemented the church to create an entry plaza for the campus. The sculptural concrete form-making heralded in banner and church recurs in the precast concrete panel façades and in the library's freestanding staircases and giant branching column.

1 St. John's Abbey Church, Collegeville, Minnesota, USA, 1953–61, vestibule space with staircase to balcony
2 Reviewing St. John's plans, left to right: Subprior Father John Eidenschink, Abbot Baldwin Dworschak, Hamilton Smith, and Breuer
3 Sketch perspective of church and proposed monastery cloister
4 Night view of Bell Banner and St. John's Abbey and University library, Collegeville, Minnesota, USA, 1964–66
5 Sketches for Bell Banner
6 Sketches for Bell Banner
7 Side façade of church and Bell Banner
8 Bell Banner and church
9 View from chancel
10 Interior of the church with balcony looking across the main body of the nave
11 Preliminary plans of church with annotations by Breuer, Robert Gatje, and Hamilton Smith, November 1, 1953
12 West elevation and longitudinal section drawings, October 4, 1957
13 Main floor plan drawing, October 4, 1957
14 View of the nave and sanctuary from the balcony
15 Stair in library
16 Library reading room
17 Site section drawing showing library and church
18 Drawing of library column details, May 15, 1964
19 St. John's Abbey and University, campus master plan drawing, 1954
20 St. John's Abbey and University, Residence Hall II, Collegeville, Minnesota, USA, 1965–67, perspective rendering
21 Residence Hall II, precast window units

1

2

3

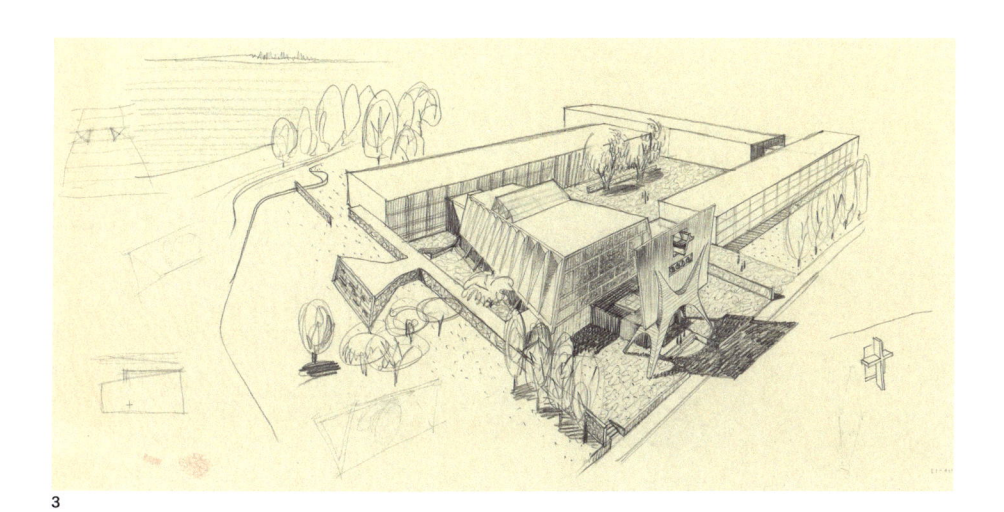

4

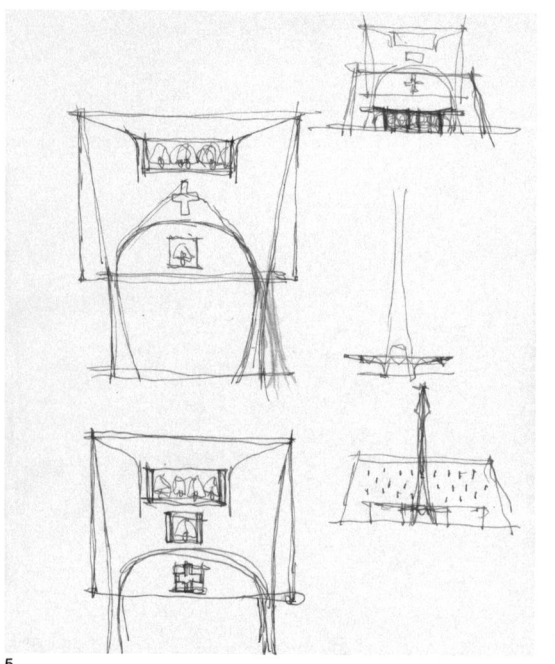

22 | I SAINT JOHN'S ABBEY

5

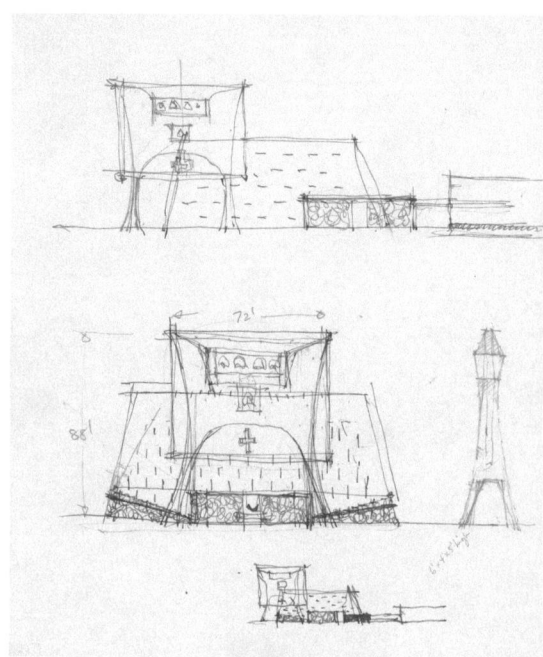

6

7

8

I SAINT JOHN'S ABBEY

10

I SAINT JOHN'S ABBEY

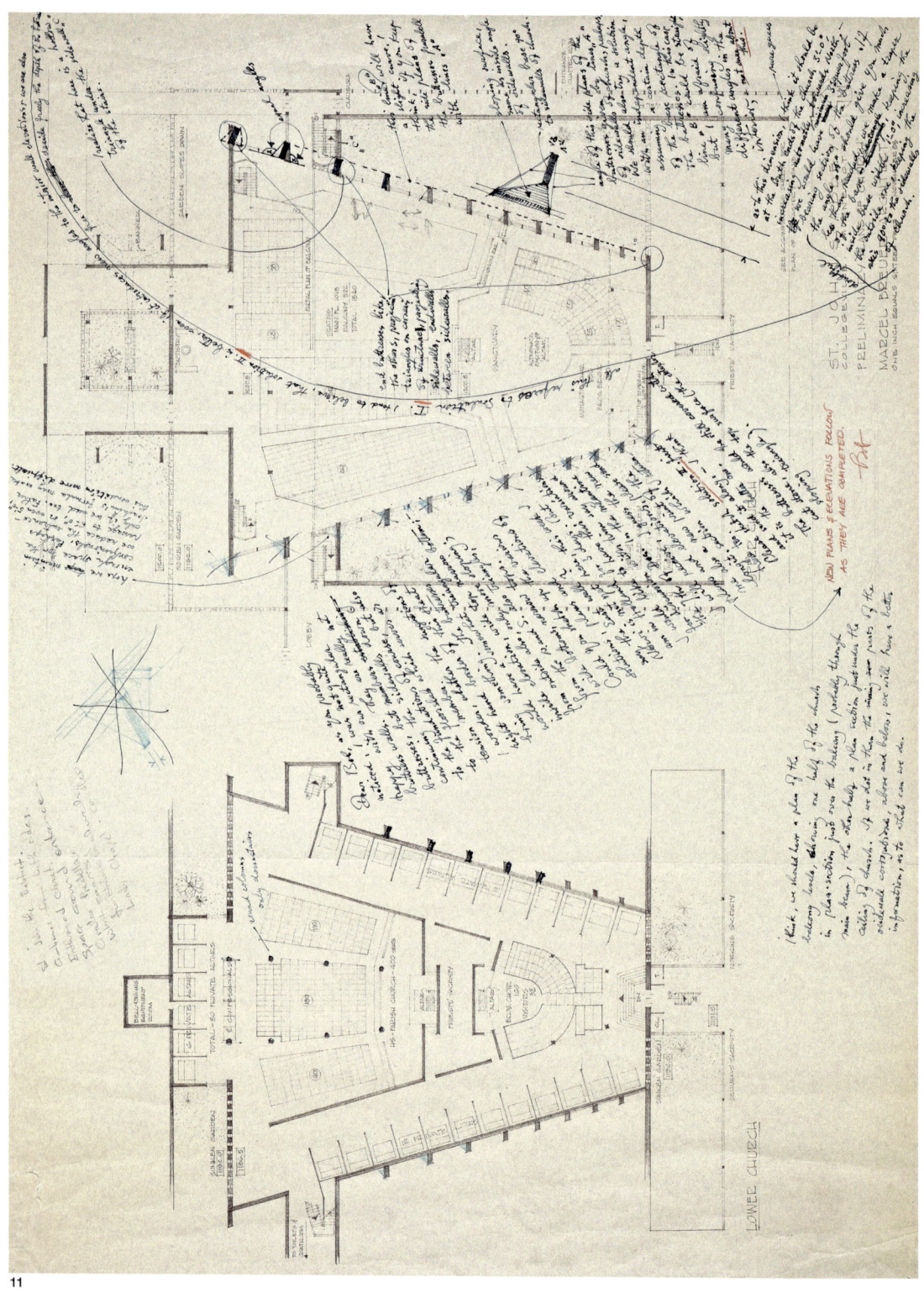

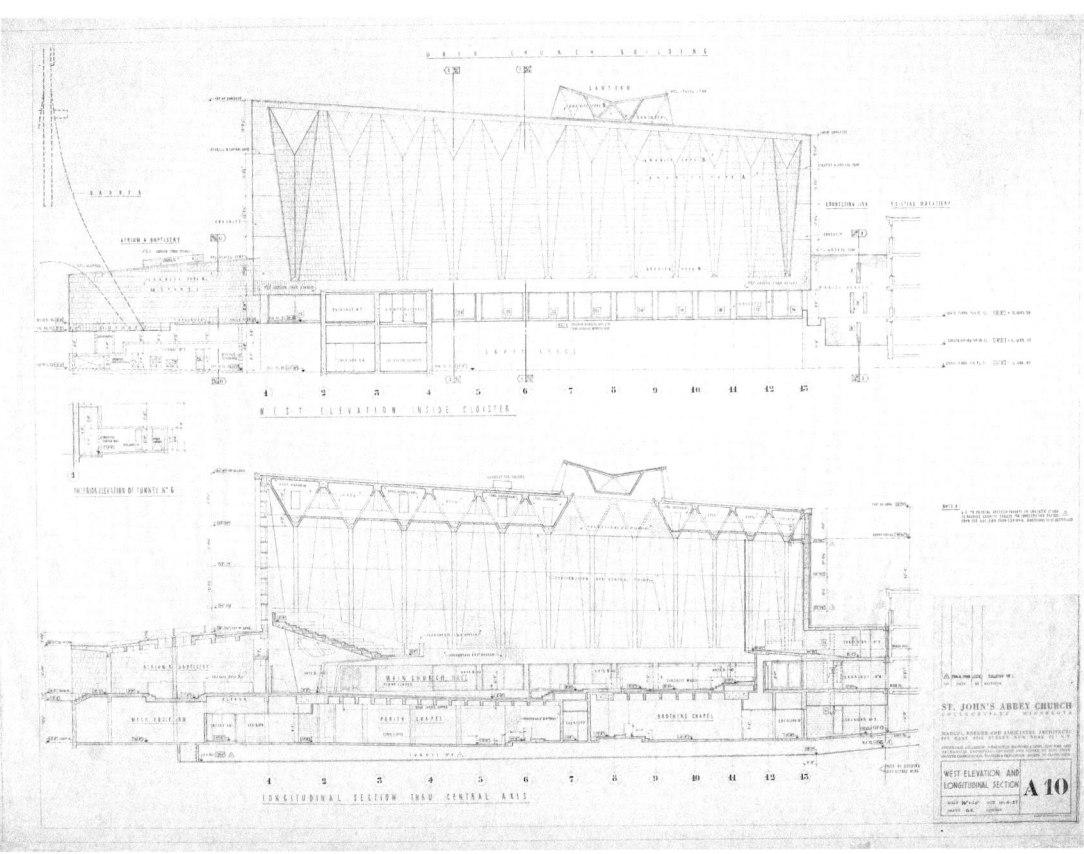

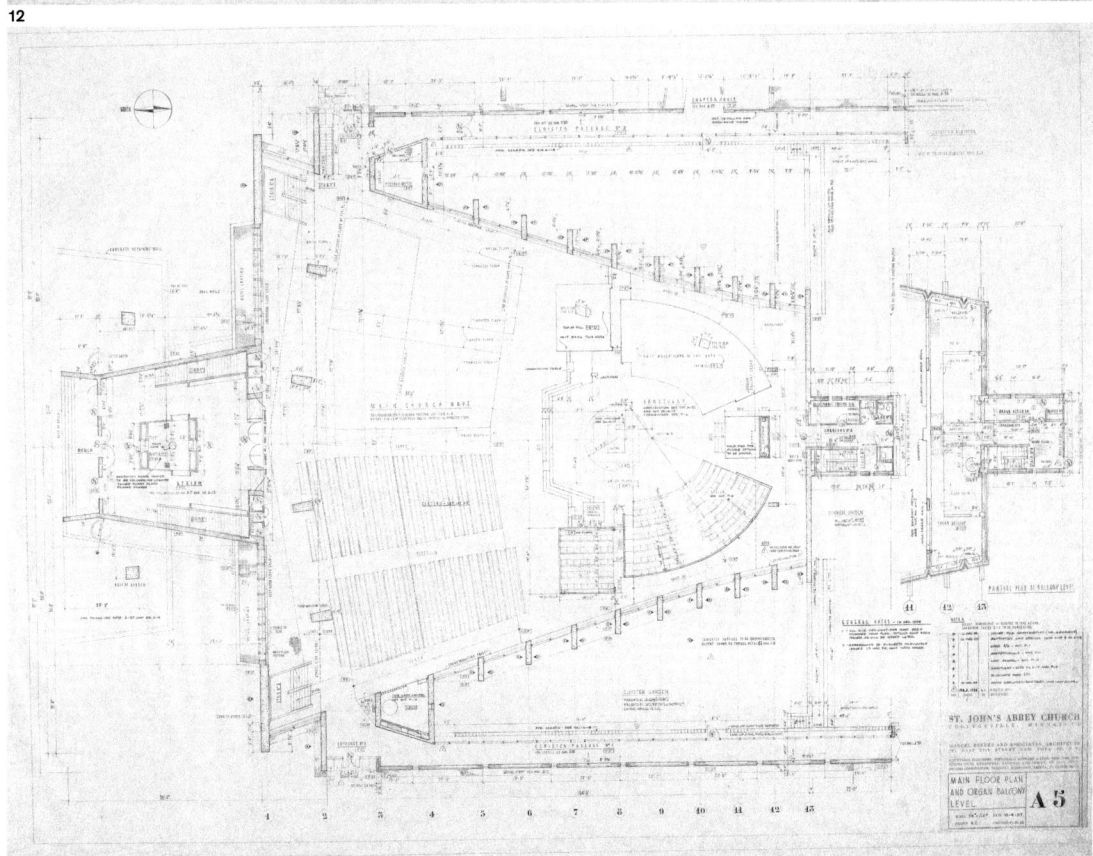

12

13

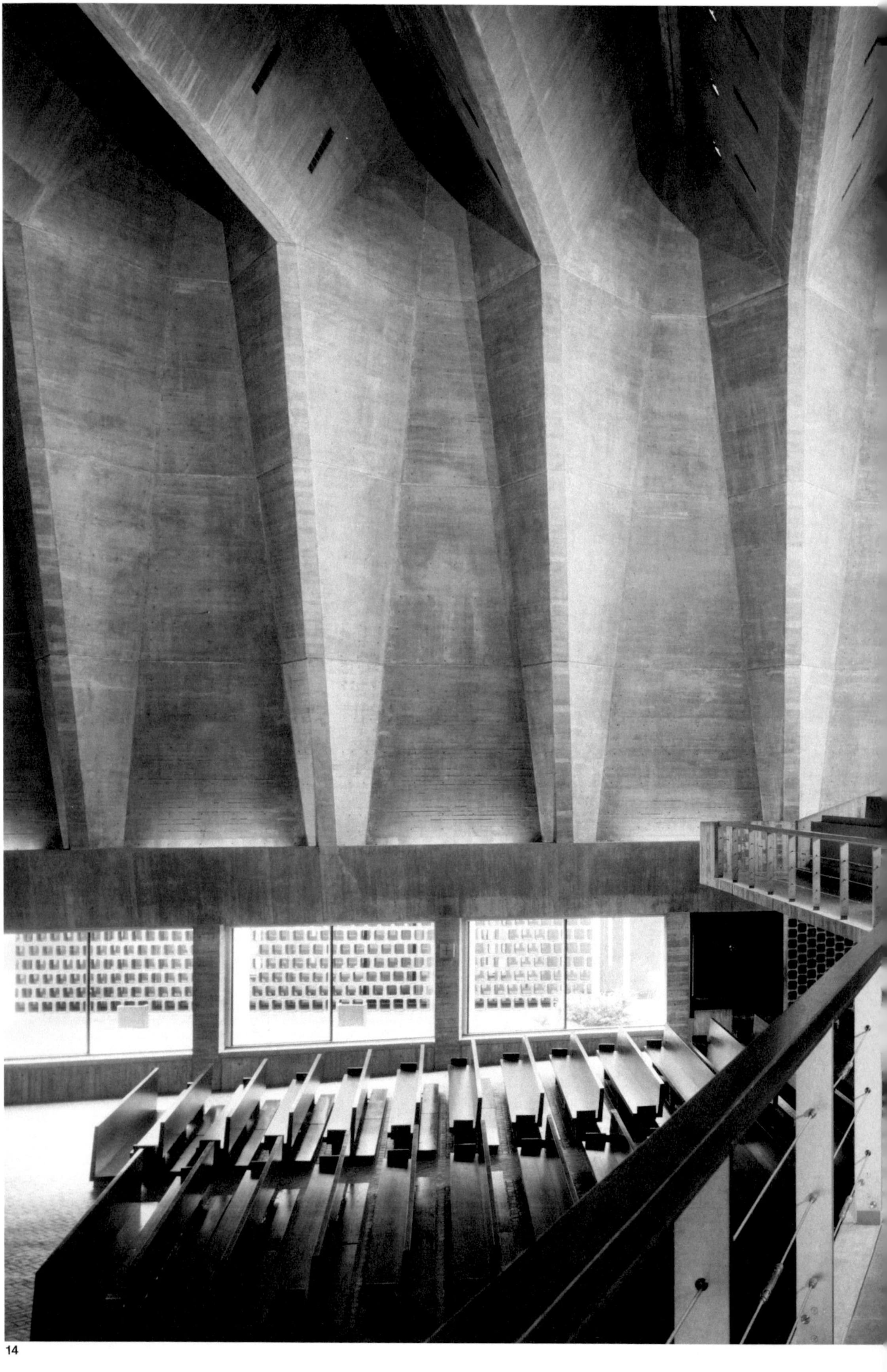

29

I SAINT JOHN'S ABBEY

15

16

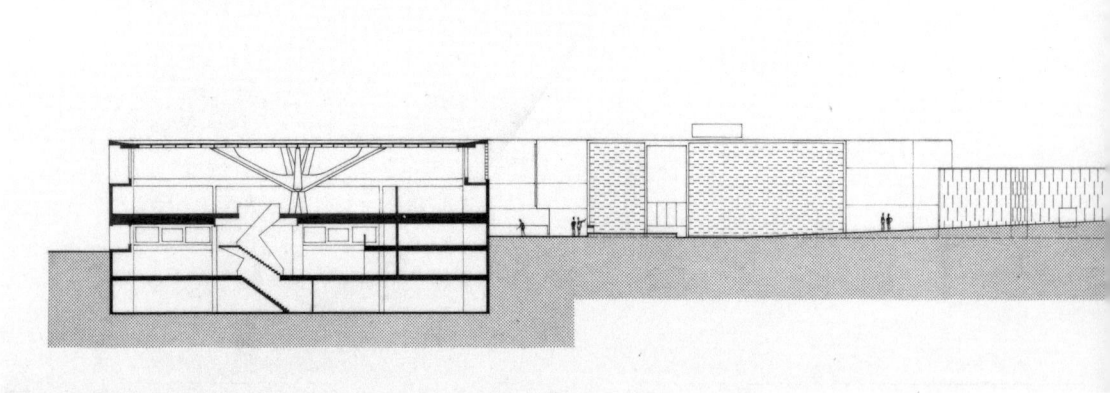

17

18

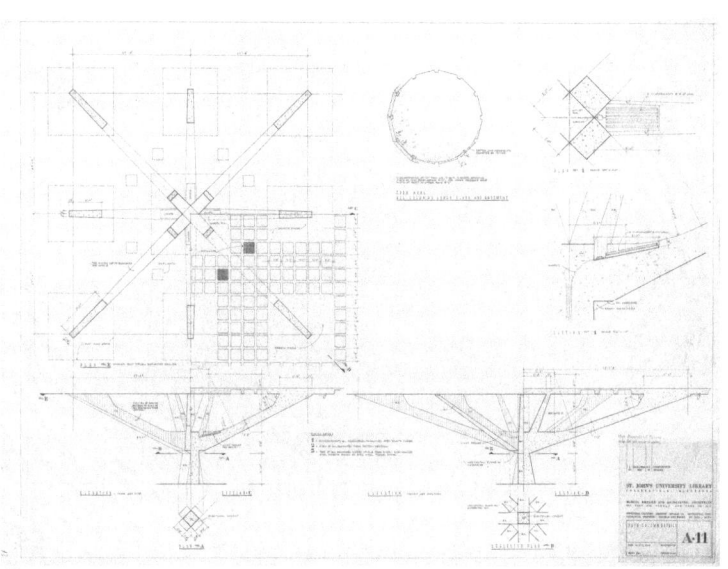

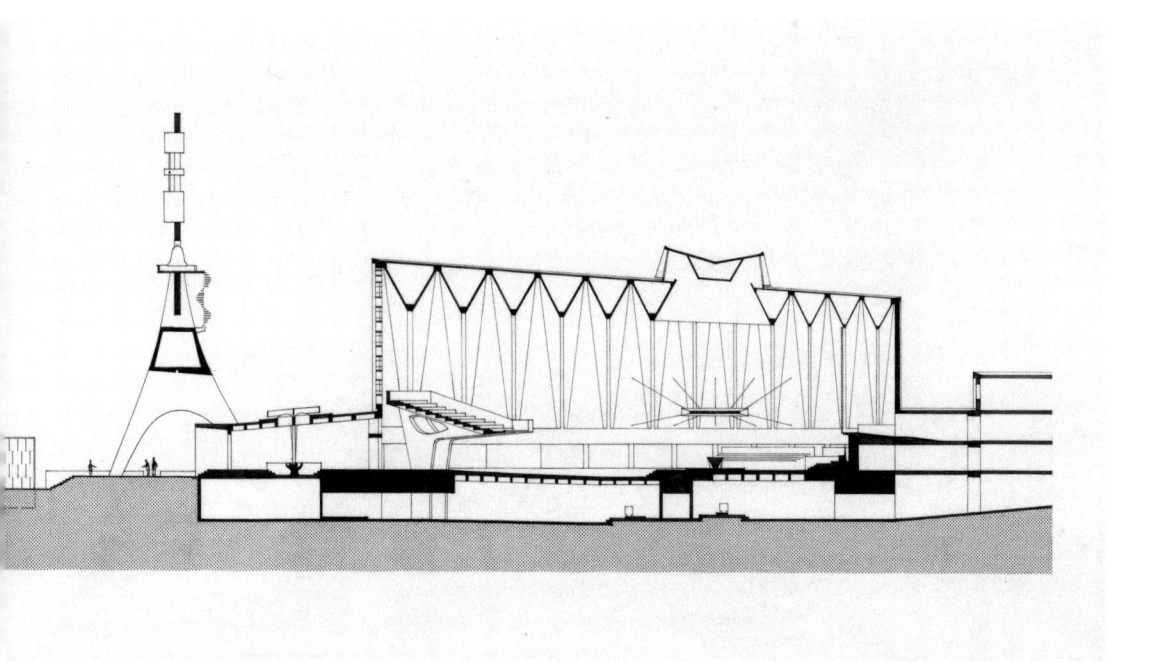

I SAINT JOHN'S ABBEY

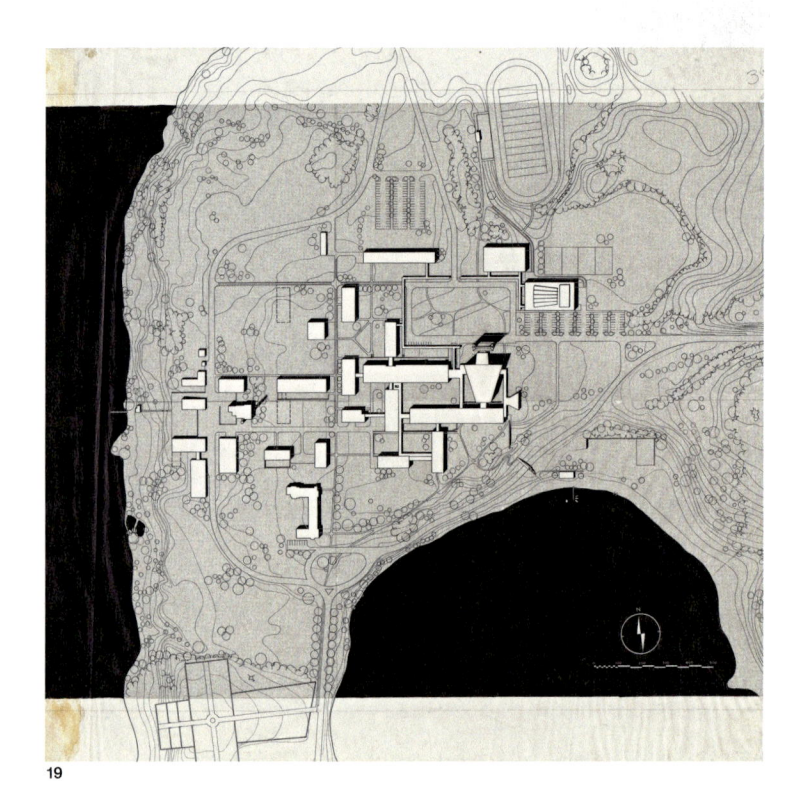

19

20

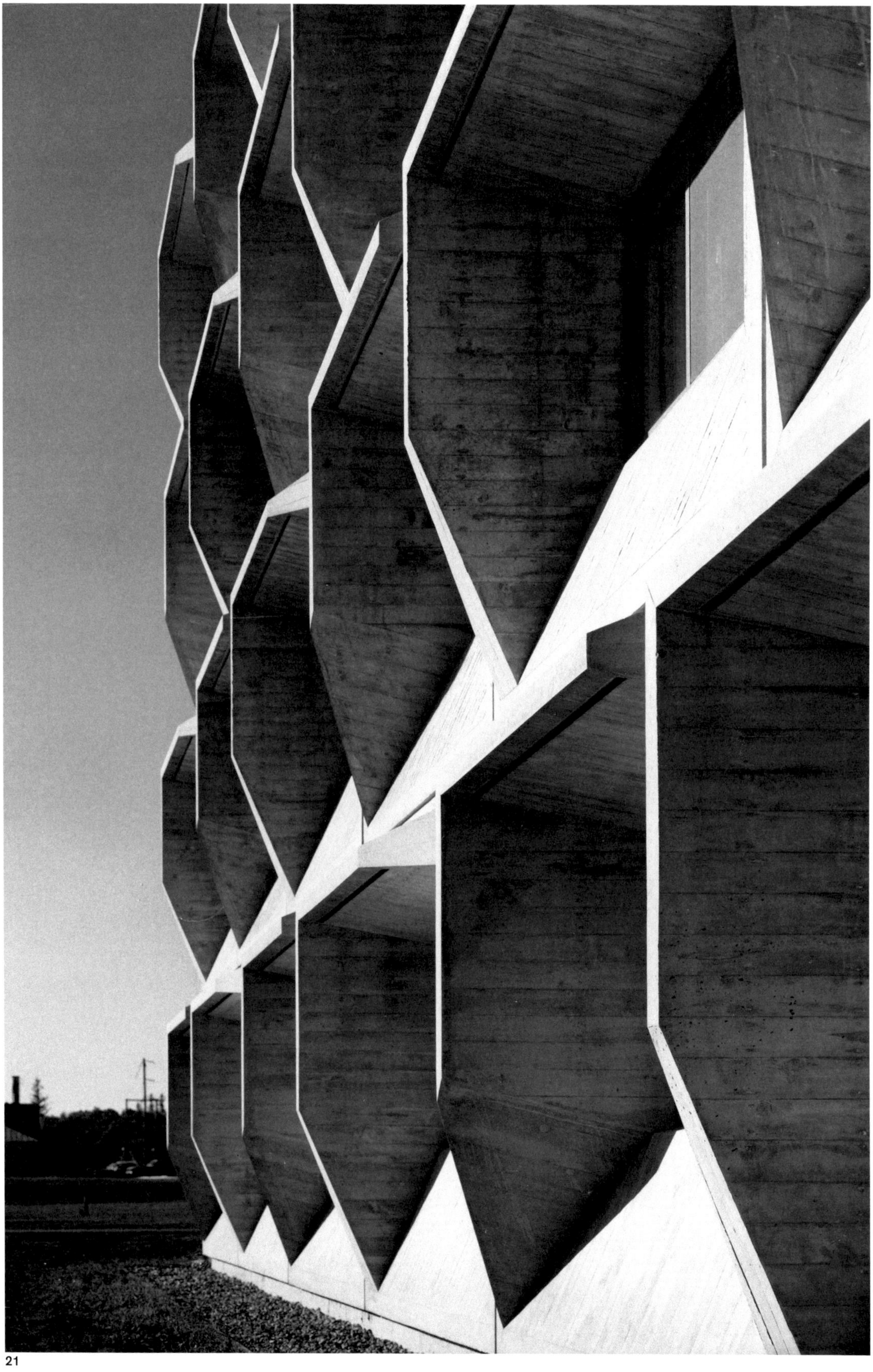

1 *ein bauhaus-film fünf jahre lang* (a bauhaus film five years long), poster reproduced in *Bauhaus*, no. 1, December 4, 1926

Marcel Breuer and the Invention of Heavy Lightness

Barry Bergdoll

Marcel Breuer's devotion to the lightweight, even the weightless, was heralded in his determined search for new and ever more minimized forms for furniture during his years as a student in the Weimar Bauhaus and even more so once he became master of the furniture workshops at the Dessau Bauhaus. Lightness was celebrated—advertised even—in a photomontage published in December 1926 in *Bauhaus,* the magazine begun when the school moved into the new buildings designed by Walter Gropius and Adolf Meyer. For the school's auditorium, Breuer designed folding chairs —as flexible as the space itself. For the Bauhaus's new magazine, he designed a poster advertising a purely fictive "Bauhaus film," one that would telescope five years of design exploration into an implied cinematic time lapse epitomizing a radical commitment to progress [1]. In the film, humankind would progress within five short years, 1921 to 1926, from being ensconced in a massively heavy and symbolic wooden throne with woven seat (the "African chair," as it was later dubbed) to sitting on chairs ever lighter in their membering and materials.[1]

Between the ages of nineteen and twenty-four, Breuer had moved rapidly from an interest in the folkloric to an uncompromising devotion to the present, even—with this fictive film—to a projective futurism. In 1926, his most recent chair design embraced the use of tubular steel, which he could bend rather than hammer into a form that resembled more the ease of a drawn line in space than the careful craft of carpentered assembly. The sitter was now cantilevered over a void on a stretched canvas or leather seat rather than firmly placed on four stolid legs. The chair enclosed a large space in its linear frame, the whole of it so lightweight it could be picked up and moved with ease. An imminent reality (indicated in Breuer's fanciful poster as "19??") for this concept chair was projected, although it was an open question as to when

2 Whitney Museum of American Art, New York, 1964–66, front elevation on Madison Avenue

physical chairs would be supplanted by a supportive column of pressurized air summoned from the floor, the physical object replaced by an invisible force, one making sitter rather than maker in charge of height and posture. "Every year things are going better and better," the poster announced. For a moment Breuer even seemed ready to relinquish his authorship rights, claiming that the chair was designed as much by larger forces as by any individual author. The poster declared—in all lowercase letters in Bauhaus font—that the film's author was, in fact, life, which demands its rights ("das leben, das seine rechte fordert"), while Breuer, the cameraman, recognizes those rights ("der diese rechte anerkennt").

But the next step would not be as effortless as Breuer predicted. While it would not be until the 1960s that the use of hydraulic pistons in office chair design became common, it was a matter of months before Breuer was entangled in authorship disputes over this tubular steel invention and plagued by protracted financial disagreements over the concept of the cantilevered tubular steel chair and whether he personally or the Bauhaus collectively held the rights.[2] The paradoxes of design ingenuity in serialized production were laid bare, but Breuer remained committed to the pursuit of lightness. After he moved to Berlin in 1928, he set out to translate his aesthetic from furniture to architecture. His realized work was largely confined to interiors, as well as to a radical proposal for an interior of total transformability and openness in the installation *House for a Sportsman,* shown at the German Building Exhibition of 1931 in Berlin [3]. In competition entries for large public buildings—notably a design for a hospital with 1,110 beds at Elberfeld drawn up with a former student, Gustav Hassenpflug, for a 1928 competition—he continued experiments with his "Bamboo" housing. That project, whose aim was to house members of the Dessau Bauhaus, had begun with the cantilevering of seemingly

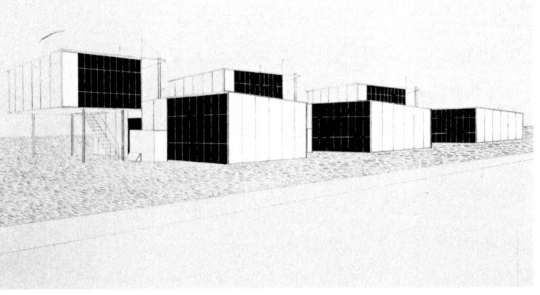

3 With Gustav Hassenpflug, Haus für einen Sportsmann (House for a Sportsman), German Building Exhibition, Berlin, 1931
4 With Gustav Hassenpflug, competition entry for a hospital with 1,110 beds, Elberfeld, Germany, 1928–29, photograph of lost model
5 "BAMBOS," project for Bauhaus younger masters' housing, Dessau, 1926, perspective view

weightless volumes above the ground to create an architecture that might float as effortlessly as a woman seated on a column of air [4,5].

The Bauhaus tradition of making, of crafting radically new versions of familiar items was well established. It arose from the exploration of the properties of materials and innovative training in issues of visual perception in the preliminary course developed by Johannes Itten and retooled by László Moholy-Nagy. But now a third element was announced: an interest in mathematical calculations from the realm of engineering, something Breuer encountered firsthand on visits to the Junkers aircraft factory in Dessau. Some have speculated the encounter with lightweight aluminum furniture used in the assembly hall might have been a decisive influence. But if we extrapolate into the future that Breuer so poignantly designated with question marks on his imaginary film poster, what did it hold for this Hungarian exile who was to wander between 1933 and 1937 from Zurich to Budapest to London and finally to Cambridge, Massachusetts, in search of a career, while Hitler's reign in Germany was making Berlin an untenable home for the Jewish-born Hungarian? By 1938 he had settled in at Harvard and into a small joint practice, side by side once again with Gropius. A decade later his fledgling practice in New York would be given a huge boost by his decision to exhibit a model house in the Museum of Modern Art garden, and then a few years later there would be a whole new scale to his work realized at UNESCO in Paris and at St. John's Abbey in Collegeville, Minnesota.

By the 1960s, Breuer's New York office was at the height of its invention of new architectural approaches. The images of his work that circulated most widely in the press during that decade were of monumental buildings, buildings either clad in large blocks of stone or having exteriors of exposed reinforced concrete rather than in the wooden idiom he and Gropius had developed for houses. Perhaps none was more iconic than the Whitney Museum of American Art (1964–66), described repeatedly in the press as a kind of "fortress" for art [2]. From "floating on air" to a "fortress" —how can one address this radical reversal of the valence of the metaphors, the seeming paradox of a career with a radical change of heart? How could this architect who had made the pursuit of lightness the sine qua non both of his personal aspirations as a designer and, in a sense, of the very nature of modernity in turn become one of the greatest form-givers of the aesthetics of weightiness we associate with the popularity of poured-in-place and precast concrete, and with International Brutalism as it developed in the 1960s and 1970s?[3] It would be as though Mies van der

Rohe, famous for his adherence to *beinahe nichts,* or almost nothing, were to turn to granite cladding for his frame skyscrapers of the 1960s. My title phrase, "heavy lightness"—an oxymoron lifted from Shakespeare's *Romeo and Juliet*—is meant to suggest that, despite marked visual shifts in character between Breuer's early work in Europe and his American work after he immigrated to the United States on Gropius's invitation in 1937, both the material and structural experiments and even a pursuit of lightness continued, in transmogrified ways, throughout his decades-long career. It is worth backtracking to trace that evolution.

Had it been finished but a few months earlier, the thirty-year-old Breuer's earliest freestanding building, the Harnischmacher House of 1932 [6], would no doubt have gained a place as a youthful masterwork of the International Style, just then being defined by Henry-Russell Hitchcock and Philip Johnson in their canon-making Museum of Modern Art exhibition, catalog, and especially their influential book of that same year. Here was a lightweight volumetric box on a frame of steel and reinforced concrete raised on *pilotis* above its sloping site in the villa district of Wiesbaden overlooking the ponderously neoclassical spa buildings in the valley below. The house, moreover, embodied Le Corbusier's five points of a new architecture, revealing the impact of Breuer's short stint in Paris between his time at the Weimar Bauhaus and his return to Dessau. The structure perhaps also reflected the influence of the Weissenhof Siedlung (1927), in which Breuer's furniture was prominently displayed in Walter Gropius's model house immediately adjacent to Le Corbusier's buildings. The Harnischmacher House signaled that Breuer was already moving toward his own synthetic architectural language distinct from that of Gropius.[4]

6 Harnischmacher House, Wiesbaden, Germany, view from garden, 1932

Even more striking in the Harnischmacher House design's cultivation of sharp contrasts is the legacy of the Bauhaus Vorkurs—the influential preliminary course—in which students were sensitized to contrasting textures, materials, forms, and even *gestalt* theory of patterns of perception to develop an approach to making that was freed of composition, relying instead on the physicality of making. Breuer's marked taste for strong contrasts—between open and closed, grounded and projected or even levitating, between parallel and perpendicular, between glazed and open—are all prominent, even if the material diversity he would later cultivate had yet to triumph over the purity of white, if one judges by the handful of surviving black-and-white photographs of this house, which was lost to World War II bombs. The main volume was flanked by raised porches, themselves studies in contrasts. A two-story porch set perpendicularly to the main mass could be protected from sun or rain by outdoor curtains. These shades perhaps reflected the extended influence in the German-speaking world of Gottfried Semper's ideals of the textile origins of spatial enclosure, an influence reinforced perhaps by Breuer's first marriage, to Martha Erps (1902–77), who studied in the Bauhaus weaving workshops and, like Breuer, had worked on the furnishings of the Bauhaus exhibition house of 1923.

By 1934, Breuer had developed an intellectual position to sustain his artistic explorations. In it, his interest in contrasts was extended from the autonomous art work to the stakes of modernizing life. It was something no doubt set in motion by his own rootlessness as the rising threat of the Nazi regime led him to depart Germany for an extended tour through Morocco, Spain, and Greece, where he focused especially on traditional architecture and villages. I have previously written about the embracing of the freestone structural wall, something left as a garden contrast in the landscaping of the Harnischmacher House but developed with a whole new sense of hybrid materials, construction, and textures in a temporary structure in England—Crofton Gane's Pavilion for the Bristol Agricultural Fair of 1936 [7]. To turn to such an explicit display of traditional masonry reflected more than interest in the increasingly present vernacular in the contemporary work of Le Corbusier, as in the Villa Mandrot that Breuer had visited on a bike trip with Herbert Bayer through the South of France, or that of Alvar Aalto. It was also a direct political response to the challenges of the 1930s.[5] Decades later, in a 1972 interview with István Kardos for Hungarian television, he would say that he was primarily interested in "farmhouse architectures," notably "the old traditional farm buildings of the Arabs and Berbers," something he had repeatedly mentioned as he explained to historians that his work was based in an authentic expression that Bauhaus method could share with unauthored barns and farmhouse architecture, something abundantly clear to him in a deliberate play on words in German: *Bauhausarchitektur* versus *Bauernhausarchitektur,* or Bauhaus versus Farmhouse.[6]

7 With F. R. S. Yorke, Gane Pavilion, Royal Agricultural Show, Ashton Court, Bristol, England, 1936

But this was no position of nostalgia, as he had explained in one of the rare moments when he penned something theoretical—a 1934 speech before the Swiss Werkbund. He proudly reprinted that speech, "Wo Stehen Wir?," in the first monograph of his work, *Marcel Breuer 1921–1961,* published in 1962. The lecture made it clear that much more was at stake. Modern architects have a natural affinity with the authenticity that speaks to the traveler who finds a native tradition. These are "places where the daily activity of the population has remained unchanged," he explains, even while acknowledging that such places are fewer and farther between than in the past and that imitation of such building patterns is thus not only out of the question but ethically and politically untenable:

> The modern world has no tradition for its eight-hour day, its electric light, its central heating, its water supply, its liners, or for any of its technical methods. One can roundly damn the whole of our age; one can commiserate with, or dissociate oneself from, or hope to transform the men and women who have lost their mental equilibrium in the vortex of modern life—but I do not believe that to decorate homes with traditional gables and dormers helps them in the least. On the contrary, this only widens the gulf between appearance and reality and removes them still further from that ideal equilibrium which is, or should be, the ultimate object of all thought and action.[7]

All neotraditionalisms firmly rejected, Breuer's fascination with new technologies and new materials, including even working with sandblasted glass as a type of lens in his installation of the *Werkbund* exhibition in Paris's Grand Palais in 1930, was aimed at reconciling progress and tradition, or at the very least bringing them into dialogue. Strikingly, in 1962 he included a deliberate double exposure, or overlay of two photographs, as the frontispiece to the retrospective part of his monograph: a photograph of his most recently completed work, the IBM Research Center at La Gaude in the South of France, superimposed over a view of a nearby town. Here, the heavy precast concrete façade supporting heavy loads on great muscular Y-shaped treelike piers, or treelike columns, as they are called in the project description, is collaged with the freestone masonry of the rustic village [8].

8 Collage of detail of IBM La Gaude with the village of La Gaude, France

From 1937, when he arrived in the United States, until 1946, when he left New England for New York City, Breuer had been based at Harvard, teaching and practicing architecture in and around Cambridge in collaboration with Gropius. There, Breuer's interest in developing a dialogue between the modern expression of materials such as steel and glass, new techniques such as steel-frame construction and cantilevered spaces, and new experiences such as transparency and changing views and—surprisingly enough—vernacular tradition, notably with fieldstone walls and, ultimately, with experimental adaptations of American timber construction, notably of the timber balloon frame, had taken on a new intensity. Soon much of his attention was focused on aluminum—until it became too expense and rare during the war—then concrete, and finally plywood. Breuer's was an attempt to complicate and enrich not only the modernist vocabulary but the modernist project as a whole, consonant with Le Corbusier's development in the 1930s. But it was not until he had gone into exile in England, a country where modernism was viewed with enormous suspicion, that Breuer embraced the heavy stone wall as a constituent element of a new collage of materials and structural techniques. It was the first opening of his architecture to more ponderous sculptural effects played off against the quest for light volumetric floating solids, and it was to remain a lifelong interest, notably in his design for an unrealized ski resort in the Tyrolian Alps in Austria [9].

This interest in the vernacular formed the key to his quest for an architecture that could embrace at once an authenticity of identity and region with a frank acceptance of the facts of modern life, a position of realism through the deliberate juxtaposition of opposites that is especially apparent in the early works of his new American career, such as his own house in Lincoln or the Hagerty House at Cohasset, Massachusetts, both coauthored with Gropius in 1938–39 [10]. In these houses, heavy, self-supporting walls of fieldstone—in his own house slightly curved—were juxtaposed with the American balloon frame, with its volumetric and material lightness, to great effect. For Breuer, who was following a line developed in this period by Sigfried

9 Model for a winter sports hotel (unexecuted), South Tyrol, Austria, 1937
10 With Walter Gropius, Hagerty House, Cohasset, Massachusetts, 1938–39

Giedion in his influential *Space, Time, and Architecture* (1941), American wood-frame construction (particularly the balloon frame, which had rapidly made the United States the master of both machines and western expansion) was evidence of American no-nonsense engagement with the everyday facts of life.[8] It constituted an attitude of readiness that seemed able to meet the Bauhaus masters halfway. Breuer had by 1942 sought to transform this great American given, a sort of constructivist objet trouvé in the Corbusian sense, into a type of prefabricated construction, proposing an alliance between modern design and industry with a belief that this was to realize the manifest destiny of American production set in motion by the invention of the balloon frame. As Breuer explained three decades later in his interview with Kardos, the house was for him always the ideal laboratory for future larger-scale projects and thinking. The Chamberlain Cottage, he acknowledged, became the most famous of his scores of houses: "The house represents the modern transformation of the original American wooden building. It has only one large room and a kitchen and bath, but in my opinion it was the most important of all [of my house designs], and had perhaps the greatest influence on the development of American architecture" [11].[9]

11 With Walter Gropius, Chamberlain Cottage, Weyland, Massachusetts, 1940

In relation to Breuer's shift toward a more weighty and sculptural aesthetic with the adoption of a heroic engineering, it is important to note that in another interview Breuer referred to the triple-ply plywood truss of buildings, such as his own dramatically cantilevered weekend house in New Canaan, Connecticut (1947), or the Chamberlain Cottage, as a kind of reinforced concrete.[10] Here he had sought to abandon American stud frame and infill in favor of a construction in which the rigidity of the frame and the space-making capacity of the infill could be united in a single composite material. His own house was, in essence, a great habitable space truss of reinforced plywood, where the orientation of the slats increased the tensile strength of the individual sheets of plywood, making the whole into a type of engineered frame. From that frame he even attempted to project a second expansive balcony supported by "tension cables of standard marine rigging."[11] In an unrealized project for a prefabricated wooden house to be called the Plas-2-Point house, developed with Harvard students, Breuer upended the balloon frame by making the floor and roof mirror triangular truss constructions on the analogy of an airplane wing, with the occupiable frame within rendered rigid by a skin of plywood panels treated with a new Monsanto product that would add strength to the sheets, the whole "acting only as a tension member"[12] [12–13]. If in the years during and immediately following World War II Breuer engaged in intense material and structural research in both individual houses—especially his own in New Canaan and in Wellfleet on Cape Cod—and in prototypes for prefabrication, within a few years his work was to change valence and scale entirely as public buildings came to occupy the time of office staff.

In the early 1950s, Breuer's career took a distinctly different turn. It was not just because of his move from New England to New York City, which was emerging as a kind of world capital—particularly with the construction of the United Nations complex during his first years in Manhattan, along with a whole new string of corporate headquarters along Park Avenue. The change was also due to the shift of his office from a small architectural studio, concerned largely with individual house clients, to a growing partnership of architects working on whole complexes of buildings.[13] Two unexpectedly ambitious commissions came his way in 1952–53: one to rebuild one of the largest Benedictine abbeys in the world and the other to build a second complex of buildings for the United Nations, this time in Paris to house the newly created United Nations Educational, Scientific and Cultural Organization (UNESCO). These projects were to catapult Breuer into a whole new mode of practice; almost overnight he became one of a new type of American architect emerging in the 1950s—a global designer and an architect of institutional identities.

Each project has recently been the subject of a monograph that establishes the detailed planning and construction histories, so what is of interest here is to witness the extent to which they became commissions in which Breuer's relationship to engineering, to materials, and to a new visual balance between heavy and light was catalyzed.[14] As the two projects developed in the early 1950s in close juxtaposition, even in tandem, these two idealistic

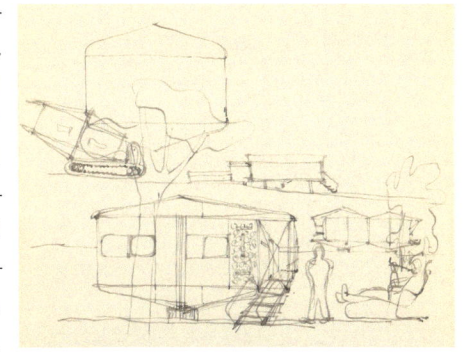

12 Plas-2-Point House, 1942, sketches
13 Plas-2-Point House, 1942, photograph of model built by students outside Robinson Hall at Harvard

and ideologically charged institutions of supranational governance afforded unprecedented opportunities to give form to recent calls for a "New Monumentality," one that would not betray modernism's fear of empty symbols and historical rhetoric, even as architects sought to counter a perceived lost communitarian and psychological depth in design. This was the call already formulated during the war, by Sigfried Giedion, Josep Lluís Sert, and the exiled French painter Fernand Léger, as "Nine Points on Monumentality" (1943). It was a highly influential effort to reconcile symbolism and emotional response for architecture, both from its nineteenth-century academic banalization and from its recent discrediting in fascist rhetoric. It also addressed the challenges of making democracy durable in a postwar context and of building community through architectural means, which were linked together in the challenge to architects to find a new monumentality, one that, paradoxically enough, could place even modernism's fascination with Giedion, Sert, and Léger's call for "light elements," "mobile elements," and "animated surfaces" in the service of building places of celebration, of joy, and of renewed community focus.[15]

Opening a letter from a Benedictine monk in Collegeville, Minnesota, in mid-March 1953, Breuer could scarcely have imagined that within the next five years the design of a monastery church would make the Catholic Church a mainstay of his growing practice. It was certainly not apparent to him in England in 1936, when he had first expressed his aims to expand his practice beyond the domestic cell to develop a comprehensive architectural language that could embrace new materials and new needs for all the building types and programs of a modern city. This had been the ambition of his utopian Garden City of the Future, discussed in this volume by Teresa Harris. Although little published at the time or since, the lost model of this British project contained a veritable catalog of building types that would reappear decades later in Breuer's research for a language of public architecture, one that could be realized with a new freedom of concrete, often taken to the exterior as a frame that is also façade. The small amoeboid pavilion, for instance, had been developed in lightweight wood for the Ariston Club at Mar del Plata on the Argentine coast (1947–48). Even more consequential was his interest in a concrete exoskeleton frame, one in which the structure becomes highly expressive—the opposite of the tradition of the American balloon frame or the so-called Chicago steel frame, in which structure retreats to an invisible interior.

Equally foreseen in 1936 was the Y-shaped planned building that would make its productive debut in Breuer's career with UNESCO, a project he had won as part of an international team. That cohort included the Italian engineer Pier Luigi Nervi, who was to be a decisive influence on Breuer's post–World War II work, and the younger Bernard Zehrfuss, with the three men engineered into what Breuer called "an Arab marriage" by a team of international advisors to the UN led by Gropius.[16] Breuer, Nervi, and Zehrfuss had first devised a project for a site at the Porte Maillot, one in which for the first time muscular *pilotis* appear that simultaneously pay homage to Le Corbusier's unrealized Algiers project and his just completed Unité d'habitation in Marseille as well as to the structural work of Nervi. In their form, however, the *pilotis* also point to an awareness of Oscar Niemeyer's most recent Brazilian work, in particular the American Hospital in Rio de Janeiro, also designed in 1952. The new aesthetic of lifting a frame vigorously off the ground with expressive, treelike forms, V-shaped or branching, was being explored on both sides of the Atlantic; it would soon become one of the leitmotifs of Breuer's designs and one that would take his work ever more into dialogue with structural engineer form-givers, from Nervi to Paul Weidlinger. Here too the framed, glazed slab was to be the background for a figural form— a great thin-shell vault in Paris, touching the ground only at a few points, more like a handkerchief than a traditional masonry vault.

This was the type of structural experiment that Nervi, in his Italian work, was engaged in and that foreshadows the building that would later make Zehrfuss's fame: the CNIT at Paris–La Défense (1956–58). But by the end of the year the Porte Maillot project had run into major controversies and was on hold. In the meantime, the scene shifted back to Collegeville. By then, however, Breuer's "Arab marriage" might already have proven to be a union made in heaven, as in Nervi he found a real impetus to advancing his thinking. In many ways Nervi's work in *ferrocemento* (reinforced concrete) in the previous decade had led the Italian engineer to realize experiments in concrete with interesting parallels to Breuer's experiments with laminated sheets of plywood. In both cases the idea that sheets placed in alternating orientations produced great strength and that the material began to perform in unprecedented ways made it possible to mold it and to calculate thinner structures in ever lighter and, in the case of concrete, ever more complex forms.

At St. John's, the inadequacies of the existing buildings had become painfully clear by the early 1950s. In August 1951 the monks formed a building committee to consider ways of providing more adequate facilities for the aging members of the community. However, the committee soon became the venue for a discussion of the monks' dissatisfaction with the existing buildings, in particular the lack of differentiation—distinction, as they put it—between the monastery and its service buildings. After more than a year of meetings, the building committee submitted its final report to the chapter, proposing that the abbey name an "outstanding architect to study overall needs and prepare a comprehensive plan" for both the abbey and its college, which was growing by leaps and bounds in the wake of the GI Bill.[17] The only trained architect among the group, Dom Cloud Meinberg, a graduate of the University of Illinois's School of Architecture, was entrusted with drawing up a list of twelve names. The list would ultimately have reflected dual, if not immediately compatible, desires. For one thing, the monks were eager to create a monument to the great liturgical reform that had transformed practices and attitudes in the Catholic Church. It was a reform movement that had been spearheaded by St. John's beginning in the 1930s and that stood in contrast in many ways to the Latin cross–planned brick basilica that was the most prominent of the abbey's buildings, located on the shores of Lake Sagatagan. More remarkable than this liturgical modernity was the conviction, at least on the part of a vocal segment, that St. John's should make a contribution to modern architecture. As Hilary Thimmesh, then one of the youngest of a remarkably young cohort of monks, recalled, "Father Cloud Meinberg, himself an architect … cited … Abbot Suger's decision to renovate the Romanesque church of Saint Denis along the lighter but structurally riskier lines of the then new Gothic style. Cloud saw Suger's break with the past as historic precedent for Benedictine risk-taking in church architecture."[18] Yet the list of potential architects was ultimately, as is so often the case with search committees, an amalgam of the diverse desires held by the community. It included Catholic and non-Catholic architects, Americans, Europeans, and recent émigré masters whose work had often come into conflict with the architectural mainstream, as well as architects with considerable experience with buildings for worship and others who had never designed a church but who had experience in large-scale institutional planning. Among the twelve were some leading church architects: Thomas Sharp of Oxford; Barry Byrne, a former employee of Frank Lloyd Wright; Joseph Murphy of St. Louis, a leading designer of Roman Catholic churches; the Austrian Robert Kramreiter; the Germans Rudolf Schwarz and

A. Boslett; and Herman Bauer, from Switzerland. American modernists, who were mostly European émigrés with little or no experience building for the church—Richard Neutra, Walter Gropius, and Breuer—rounded out the list.

A letter that Abbot Baldwin Dworschak wrote to the architects was a remarkable manifesto of religious and aesthetic modernism and an open-ended invitation to enter into a period of mutual learning leading to the creation of a new Benedictine architecture: "The Benedictine tradition at its best challenges us to think boldly and to cast our ideals in forms which will be valid for centuries to come, shaping them with all the genius of present-day materials and techniques. We feel that the modern architect with his orientation toward functionalism and honest use of materials is uniquely qualified to produce a Catholic work. In our position it would, we think, be deplorable to build anything less, particularly since our age and our country have thus far produced so little truly significant religious architecture."[19]

Something of this determination had already been reflected by the abbot's predecessor, who in 1947 had commissioned Antonin Raymond, a modernist who had followed Frank Lloyd Wright to Tokyo to supervise construction of the Imperial Hotel and had stayed on to pioneer the use of exposed concrete construction in Japan, to provide powerful syntheses of Japanese tradition and Western aesthetic and technical innovations [14]. In St. Anselm's, completed in 1954 while the monks were still discussing the form of their new abbey in Collegeville, Raymond's brilliant use of a system of hollow folded plates of concrete to create a box of light on a dense urban site in the heart of Tokyo was evidence of the St. John's community's commitment to an experimental

14 Antonin Raymond, St. Anselm's Church, Tokyo, 1954

architecture that could give form to their liturgical modernity. It had parallels with the experiments—structurally even more advanced—in folded concrete that Nervi was developing in Italy and that Breuer was soon to experience firsthand in Paris. Abbot Baldwin explained that "the Abbey is one of the largest Benedictine communities in the world at this time … but … the design would need to be addressed not only to a community resident at St. John's but to the far-flung set of parishes and monastic foundations the abbey is in charge of in the Bahamas, Mexico, Puerto Rico, Kentucky, and Japan."[20] Here was an attitude resonant with Breuer's ideas of developing building prototypes rather than one-off designs.

Over the course of the next month the American architects in consideration visited for several days, living with the monks, sharing their meals, and meeting them in after-dinner discussions. The remarkably candid notes drawn up by Father Meinberg reveal that the monks were looking as much to enlist a temporary member of their community as to commission a design, all the more since the Rule of St. Benedict required them to build their own accommodations. The monks' description of Breuer is telling: "He is a very quiet man who makes no attempt to impress the client, remains calm, although he was evidently very much interested, and speaks only when he has something to say. It didn't bother him at all that much of his information came piecemeal, scattered and mingled with interruptions."[21]

Breuer was intrigued by the idea of the monastic cell as a building block, almost a module of design, although he did not mention the use of that idea in studies for housing produced at the Bauhaus—a place many in the 1920s saw as an avant-garde monastery—and in the numerous studies for prefabricated mass housing he had undertaken first in concrete in Berlin and then in wood frame as recently as his wartime housing done with Gropius at New Kensington, outside Pittsburgh. Meinberg noted that for Breuer "modern work … has now progressed into a second stage.… Mere functionalism was not enough. He was not at all opposed to functionalism—quite the contrary—but wanted more depth."[22] When asked about religion, Breuer responded that although he was not a Catholic—he claimed to be a Lutheran though in fact he was born Jewish and in adult life practiced no creed—and had not built a church, "the modern man in general has a great thirst for works of content, if you want, for the spiritual. He is looking for something that expresses more than pure functionalism, for a deepening of content."[23] "He talked about the integration of engineering and architecture, especially about the possibilities of working with a really creative engineer. Engineering was not used enough today, he said, 'as a demonstrative form.'" In explanation of what this meant, Breuer was said to have commented that in Gothic architecture, the way the weight was supported (the engineering) was actually the form of the church: "it demonstrated the engineering." When the monks asked Breuer about concrete, he replied that "modern architecture has not yet exploited reinforced concrete as a form," and he again referred to Gothic as an analogy, although he said he preferred the stronger, less fussy forms of the powerful Romanesque churches. "His statement that we should make use of as daring engineering as our theological and liturgical understanding demands, reveals an architect of the caliber we need," the monks concluded.[24] A marriage between the abbey's desire to push liturgical reform toward a greater sense of community participation (in advance of the Vatican II mandates) and Breuer's sense that the modern movement, in aligning itself with engineering, might take a step toward a new formal expressiveness was taking place. Not surprisingly, Breuer would soon call on Nervi to act as a consultant for the St. John's commission even as they were collaborating on UNESCO.

At UNESCO Nervi played a crucial role, not only in finding the dimensions of the vigorous, faceted piers that support the Y-shaped administration building, allowing structural forces to generate shape, but in creating demonstration pieces of the new concrete experiments. These mark the building as a progressive architectural practice for this new experiment in global politics. The two radically different entrance canopies demonstrate and monumentalize Nervi's experiments with what he called isostatic rib systems, as well as with inverted paraboloid shapes. But most consequential for Breuer's own later design vocabulary, and in striking contrast to the transparency of the great Y-shaped curtain walls with their (problematic) plate-glass sun-shading devices (discussed in this volume by Lucia Allais) were the great slanted walls, corrugated profile, and swooping grooved ceiling that Nervi developed for the Conference Building, where the formal expression was the direct result of experiments in hollow, folded plates of concrete [15]. Here was an expression of enclosed massiveness, even if the research was focused on minimizing the sections of rhythmic flows of concrete, as Nervi sought to balance the derivation of form from the progressive

15 UNESCO Conference Building, Paris, side elevation

refinement of structural calculations with an aesthetic expression for a structure that sloped inward as it rose and swelled with what was almost a modern, engineering type of entasis. Breuer, we can only guess, was entranced, as not only the design of the church at Collegeville but also many of his later masterworks, from St. Francis de Sales Church at Muskegon, Michigan (1964–66), to the Grand Coulee Dam Visitors Center (1972–78), are the direct result of this collaboration with Nervi in Paris. In Minnesota he would ask Nervi to work with him hand-in-glove on the design refinement.[25]

p. 320/2-1

For the next eight months the problem of designing and laying out a whole new monastery preoccupied both Breuer and the monks. Meinberg, who would serve as the conduit for liturgical advice to the Breuer office, set himself to studying medieval buildings, concluding ultimately that the Tuscan medieval cathedrals of the Arno valley, particularly those of Pisa and Florence with their detached baptisteries, were models. He consulted Erwin Panofsky's *Gothic Architecture and Scholasticism* (1951)—lectures originally delivered before a Benedictine college in Pennsylvania—as he sought a modern translation of its demonstration of Gothic's marriage of structural logic as a "parallel to the systematic and brilliant logic of the Scholastic Synthesis."[26] "The twentieth century Architect must accomplish a similar task, but his objective must be to form an architectural parallel to the glory of Christ in the liturgy," he noted. "But who can design such a church? Our age is full of obstacles to such an achievement. Most architects are still imitating styles of the past. Others attempting to break with the past become involved in materialist functionalism or produce novel designs which shock us out of the sterile torpor of imitation but which have little positive value in themselves. Neither type of structure is formed by the liturgy for which it is used."[27]

Breuer left it to two young designers in the New York office, Hamilton Smith and Robert Gatje, to work on translating the St. John's community's liturgical beliefs into a diagram for the layout of the monastery as the core of a master plan.[28] By the time they finished this diagram, dated July 2, 1953, Breuer was back in Europe, where the design of UNESCO was at a crucial juncture. At long last the issue of the site in Paris had been resolved. Even the debate over the introduction of a modern architecture of glass, steel, and concrete forms into the French capital's historic heart had been settled. The new structure would be on a prominent site, completing half of the semicircular *place* facing

16 UNESCO, Paris, aerial view looking south with École Militaire in foreground

Jacques-Ange Gabriel's mid-eighteenth-century classical École Militaire [16]. Modernism's relationship to tradition, as well as the symbolism of international organizations in local settings, was now being discussed on two fronts—Paris and Collegeville, secular and sacred.

UNESCO played a very real role in the evolution of Breuer's design for St. John's over the next few months. Although he took a side trip to Germany to study liturgical arrangements in buildings along the Rhine, from the great Romanesque Maria Laach Abbey to the recently completed works of Rudolf Schwarz in and around Cologne, Breuer in the end took more cues from the great Conference Building at UNESCO. It pointed the way toward giving form to the monks' desire for a wholly new space for worship in which the community of monks and the congregation could be brought into more direct connection and in which the sacraments were brought out of the recesses of the apse into the focus of the space and the ceremony. Marking up Smith and Gatje's drawing, Breuer made notes on details of plan relationships between the church and the monastic dwelling, as well as between different parts of the expanding college in the northwest quadrant of the diagram, but he zeroed in on the shape and the spatial planning of the great church. Smith and Gatje had drawn an extended, thin, longitudinal church, a sort of modernized Maria Laach nave, preceded by a separate baptistery. Responding at once to the desires for a new relationship between the monks and the congregation and to the lessons he was learning about disposing large crowds, hierarchically arranged but in working harmony in the various-sized assembly halls of UNESCO, Breuer sketched an emphatic equilateral triangle over the diagram. By the end of the month the triangle had become a trapezoid, precisely the form used for the Conference Building at UNESCO. As at UNESCO, this form had the advantage of holding large numbers of people and yet creating a sense of intimacy and a central focus. Seen from the choir space, the nave appears much shorter than it is in reality; from the nave the monks' choir is splayed into a panoramic view. This effect would be further enhanced once the three-dimensional form that could house this great, broad figure without compromising interior supports was worked out in an intense period of collaboration between Breuer and Nervi, whom the monks had endorsed as a collaborator for the structural questions during Breuer's August 1953 visit. Nervi immediately extended his experiments in achieving great spanning capacity and strength in folded plates of concrete, used both in elevation and to span the space, the whole tied together as an integral cage of buttress-like trusses. At UNESCO, the revealed concrete had lent gravitas. Here, Breuer was determined to clad the form in granite, both to help it withstand the harsh Minnesota climate and to emphasize a certain lightness in its whiteness; in 1954 he compared the form of the church to a tent, as Thimmesh recalls.[29]

On Nervi's advice, Breuer imparted many of the most successful aspects of the UNESCO assembly halls to the church, where a dynamic space of diagonals in all planes was affected. The ten great serrated buttresses of the UNESCO Conference Building in Paris were translated, at Collegeville, into twelve buttress-like walls perpendicular to the nave. Above, the nave's pleated folds increase in all dimensions—width, depth, and wall thickness—as they cross successively broader segments of the bell-shaped plan; in the course of design the strict straight line gave way to a subtle curve, "just enough to recede into infinity," according to Father Thimmesh.[30] The longest fold, immediately inside the front door, accomplishes a clear span of more than 135 feet, soars 15 feet from top to bottom, and has walls that vary in thickness between 6 and 8 inches. The effect of all this diagonal movement, enhanced by the floor, which slopes downward toward the altar, is a subtle telescoping of the space and a great dynamism of movement, which is impossible to read from the diagrammatic plan and most inadequately captured in photographs.

In Paris, Breuer emphasized the sense of organic wholeness and enclosure of this integral structural system by connecting it to the Secretariat by a low passage so that a sudden transition of scale takes place upon entering the Conference Building. Indeed, this is one of the most remarkable elements of the UNESCO plan—its feature of a meandering landscape over which the buildings emerge but in which movement runs through and beyond each individual element. The great transition of scale is accomplished by a deliberately informal asymmetrical juncture, a perhaps somewhat tense result of a lack of resolution between the formal gestures required by the site and Breuer's Bauhaus belief in asymmetrical planning. In Minnesota, guided by liturgical requirements and decorum, Breuer achieved a much greater richness of effect and embraced for the first time axial planning, which he was to use over and over again in his most monumental works of the 1960s: the Whitney Museum in New York and the IBM headquarters at La Gaude in the South of France, with its almost neo-Egyptian entrance sequence, or the headquarters of the US Department of Housing and Urban Development in Washington, DC. By then, Breuer had penned the introduction to a photographic essay on ancient Egyptian architecture celebrating the lessons to be learned from the Egyptian sublime scale for an aesthetic of modern concrete and institutional expression.[31]

The result was trumpeted by the editors of *Architectural Record:* "Breuer... has gone into an expression new to him—sculptural form of structure. Checked out by the brilliant Italian engineer Pier Luigi Nervi—whose career had begun in the 1920s in stadium architecture, notably with this municipal stadium in Florence—Breuer will bend a thin cowl of concrete into walls and roof over this monastic church, creased into folds for structural stiffness."[32] As had been the case with Le Corbusier's church for the Dominican monastery at Ronchamp, the architectural press found itself resorting to pictorial analogies for the first time in decades in an effort to explicate the form-giving of modern architecture in a new phase. Famed engineer Mario Salvadori was equally admiring of the Conference Building at UNESCO: "The conference assembly building is an extraordinary and imposing structure which looms larger than its size would suggest," he proclaimed in *Architectural Record.* "It consists of a solid corrugated front wall which folds at the top to become a slanting roof. The roof slopes down to a set of columns and rises again to the top of the back wall. The structure is monolithic and gives a feeling of tremendous strength and lightness. I consider this particular structure one of the masterpieces of the concrete age.... The corrugated front wall and roof give a plastic definition of space to the assembly hall which is entirely new in concept, completely correct structurally and extremely exciting visually."[33]

For years to come Nervi and Breuer would echo one another, expressing in almost identical phrases their joint conviction that it was the role of a new synthesis of technology and art to carry the incomplete miracle of Gothic further. Nervi, in his 1962 Charles Eliot Norton lectures at Harvard, suggested that the miracle was, in engineering terms, one of "replacing the equilibrium achieved by masses of masonry with the equilibrium of forces created by the interplay of thrust and counterthrust of slender ribs built with very good materials."[34] Breuer added the synthesis of architecture and sculpture, the fluid ways in which concrete was made and in turn made manifest the play of structural forces. "It can," he explained in a 1963 lecture at the University of Michigan, "reflect the stresses working in the structure with photographic truthfulness."[35] It seems also an echo of Nervi's lectures, in which he spoke of the need "to put the concrete where it works best."[36]

One of the most extraordinary features of this collaboration, and the vital feature that distinguishes the earthbound UNESCO Conference Building from the sacred space of St. John's Abbey was the decision to lift the folded plates in the air on a system of concrete piers that at once call to mind the buttresses of the Gothic cathedrals but is, in essence, a brilliant visual reversal of the system of loads in a Gothic cathedral. Bringing the clerestory of Gothic to the ground, Breuer extends the interior space of the church to lateral views into the modernist cloister gardens alongside the nave, in a horizontal complement to the vertical expansion of space. The transfer of the structural loads is accomplished through a continuous hollow edge beam, which also carries concealed uplights that make the dramatic capacity to hold heavy concrete aloft as awe-inspiring at night as during the day.

p. 27/12, 14

One of Breuer's earliest surviving perspective sketches for the proposed church is unmistakably a development of the UNESCO Conference Building. Breuer and his team now imagined the great pleated concrete walls of the world government's broad assembly building stretched to form the directional space of a church and fronted by a huge bell banner. It was at once a search for a modernist equivalent to the towers and domes of traditional Christian symbolism and a monument to the modern technological achievements of reinforced concrete. The banner was nothing less than a huge slab of concrete cantilevered upward to demonstrate its strength and rigidity, as well as its ability to provide heroic scale and form; it made a veritable highway sign of the new materials and structural principles deployed here. Even the form Breuer sketched in the revised plans for the chapter house late in 1953 comes directly from the structural experiments with reinforced concrete at UNESCO, where Nervi had encouraged his colleagues to develop great contrasts in form to express different functions —offices, assembly, reception. He had also called for them to demonstrate the full range of possibilities of concrete—a great open frame with cantilevered edges raised on massive *pilotis* for the curving Y form of the Secretariat slab, the inclined planes of the folded plates of the Conference Building (a theme carried over in the roof to create an even greater organic continuity of form and a greater rigidity of structure in its amazing creation of heavy openness), and, in between the two, the different entry canopies. These canopies are nothing short of small-scale showpieces displaying reinforced concrete's capacities. A slab held aloft on the side of the Place de Fontenoy and facing Gabriel's classical building, and a great sweeping saddle-shaped (or shell, some contemporary sources say) structure resting on only two points at the entrance form the plaza shared with the Conference Building. While Zehrfuss, the French partner on the team, would scale this up to a more monumental size a few years later to build the Centre National des Techniques, or CNIT, at La Défense (built between 1953 and 1958), Breuer thought to introduce it to America in the form of the monks' chapter house, a place of focused gatherings [17]. By the end of the long process of designing the church, Breuer had fully incorporated Nervi's aesthetic of concrete as he searched for an expression in which the supports and the banner would form a more flowing, harmonious whole, obscuring the distinction between support and span, as in the nave of the church. Perhaps the greatest difference—and here Breuer's Bauhaus training is clear—was Breuer's introduction of texture, which Nervi sought

p. 23/8

17 Project for chapter house at St. John's Abbey (unexecuted), 1953

generally to suppress to allow the form to have the smoothness of calculation rather than the contrasts of modernist collage.

Breuer would ultimately design some nineteen buildings at St. John's, although none of them achieved the international acclaim of the abbey church and monastery, celebrated first in a striking exhibition at the Walker Art Gallery, a display designed by Breuer himself in 1961.[37] Of these buildings, the only one to pursue further the theme of heavy lightness in ways that were to prove influential beyond Collegeville was the university library, today the Alcuin Library [18]. The exterior was of the utmost discretion; forming the northern edge of a great forecourt before the church, the library deferred in every way to Breuer's great sculptural group. It not only stepped aside to allow the road to sweep up to the Bell Banner, but it stepped down the hill so that what was in fact a multistory building appeared as a long horizontal box on the great plaza before the church. However, the real surprise comes within. Here, the great concrete waffle-grid roof slab, a monumental ceiling plane, floats above an enormous open interior space, 204 × 124 feet, and interrupted by only two supports. Inspired by Nervi's Palace of Labor in Turin, nearing completion as the centennial of Italian unification approached in 1961, Breuer designed a series of concrete trees that branch out to brace eight points on the roof [19, 20].[38] This was what Breuer saw as the great challenge of modern structure and materials. "Buildings no longer rest on the ground," he explained in *Matter and Intrinsic Form,* his 1963 University of Michigan lecture. "They are cantilevered from the ground up. The structure is no longer a pile—however ingenious and beautiful—it is very much like a tree, anchored by roots, growing up with cantilevered branches, possibly heavier at the top than at the bottom." He concluded with the

18 Library, St. John's Abbey and University, Collegeville, Minnesota, 1964–66, rendered elevation
19 Library, St. John's Abbey and University, interior
20 Pier Luigi Nervi, Palace of Labor, Turin, Italy, 1961

new demands for an architecture in which sculptural form and its space-making capacities would lead to a fundamental reevaluation of the modern movement's earlier refusal of the symbolic dimensions, which, as St. John's had told him, could not be separated from material realties. "With the rebirth of solids next to glass walls, with supports which are substantial in material but not negligent in structural logic ... a three dimensional modulation of architecture is again in view; the brother or lover of our pure space. Although not resting on lions or acanthus leaves, space itself is again sculpture into which one enters."[39]

Perhaps no building better exemplifies this newfound aesthetic of heavy lightness than the Whitney Museum of American Art, a commission that came in just a few months after Breuer's Michigan lecture. After only nine years in a new (Miesian or Philip Johnsonian) building designed for the museum by architect August L. Noël (of Noël and Miller, Architects) on West Fifty-Fourth Street, on land donated by MoMA adjacent to its own expanding museum being planned by Philip Johnson, the Whitney museum trustees decided in June 1963 to get out from under the shadow of their more famous neighbor and sometime rival and establish a new presence in the heart of the gallery scene on the Upper East Side. After interviewing I. M. Pei, Louis Kahn, Paul Rudolph, Edward Larrabee Barnes, and Philip Johnson, the trustees chose Breuer to create a building that could situate American art more prominently both on the grid of Manhattan and on the world map. Breuer, whose renown had been escalating along with his cultivation of an elemental monumentality since the commissions for St. John's and UNESCO, understood the challenge immediately.

According to Gatje's memoir, Breuer spent a weekend at home and then returned to work with a design for an inverted ziggurat, clad in flame-treated gray granite, that would loom mysteriously over the corner of Madison Avenue and East Seventy-Fifth Street.[40] Without violating any building or zoning codes, Breuer inverted the image of the famous setback skyscrapers of the 1920s and 1930s and of the white-brick apartment houses sprouting everywhere during the East Side's residential building boom, thereby creating a building that is at once of the urban fabric and decidedly singular. "What should a museum look like, a museum in Manhattan?" was how Breuer began his remarks when presenting the project to the trustees on November 12, 1963. "It is easier to say first what it should *not* look like. It should not look like a business or office building, nor should it look like a place of light entertainment. Its forms and its materials should have identity and weight in a neighborhood of fifty-story skyscrapers, of mile-long bridges, in the midst of the dynamic jungle of our colorful city. It should be an independent and self-relying unit"—he knew how to refer to their "annex anxiety" from Fifty-Fourth Street—"exposed to history, and at the same time it should have a visual connection to the street, as it deems to be the housing for twentieth-century art. It should transform the vitality of the street into the sincerity and profundity of art."[41]

Profundity of meaning and physical presence were the word of the day as the modernists of the 1920s retooled their program. Giedion had delivered his lecture series, titled "The Eternal Present: The Beginnings of Architecture," which celebrated the relevance of the weighty forms and symbolic aura of Mesopotamian temples, Sumerian ziggurats, and Egyptian pyramids, in 1957 at the National Gallery. He was also working on the page proofs for the publication of *The Beginnings of Architecture*, while Breuer was penning an introduction, entitled "The Contemporary Aspect of Pharaonic Architecture," for photographer Henri Stierlin's 1964 book on Egyptian architecture, *Living Architecture: Egyptian*.[42]

The experience of entering the Whitney is too well known to require recapitulation here. The itinerary takes one from the Madison Avenue sidewalk via a bridge announced by a cantilevered canopy, under the overhanging of the upside-down ziggurat, into a west-facing glazed lobby with a gridded ceiling of circular lighting fixtures. As much as this design resonated with the emerging minimalism in 1960s sculpture, Breuer was thinking largely in terms of the stakes of history and symbolism that had entered the internal critique of architectural modernism since the debates on monumentality in the mid-1940s. "Today's structure in its most expressive form is hollow below and substantial on top—just the reverse of the pyramid. It represents a new epoch in the history of man, the realization of his oldest ambitions: the defeat of gravity," Breuer told his friend Peter Blake in 1964 as the concrete frame was being poured for this reworking of Kahn's loft spaces of the Yale Art Gallery into a stacked temple of modern American art for a Manhattan street corner.[43] With exposed bush-hammered concrete fin walls to separate off his granite-faced, cantilevered sculpture, Breuer cut out the urban equivalent of the white box gallery so beloved by his contemporary minimalists and asserted the singularity of culture, creating a sense of aura to protect art from the nearby world of commercial culture and to create a sense of remove from the quotidian.

Designing with his associate Hamilton Smith and aided by structural engineer Paul Weidlinger, Breuer lifted his stepped cantilevered mass above a glazed recessed ground floor—the world of the sidewalk and the sales counter on an axis with the entrance, connected by a fixed-in-place drawbridge. He also inserted great panes of glass into the recessed stair tower between the inverted ziggurat and the midblock fin wall. Breuer clearly had an eye on what his former pupil I. M. Pei was doing in the recently completed and much-lauded Everson Museum in Syracuse [21] as he worked on the complex section of the negative space created by the excavation of the below-grade sculpture court, which would also form the moat separating the sanctuary of art from the hot-dog sellers of the sidewalk.[44]

21 I. M. Pei, Everson Museum, Syracuse, New York, 1961–68

Although in an early project he imagined glass panels providing an unobstructed view of this sunken sculpture garden, in the end he replaced these with a low parapet of granite, easily peered over by pedestrians, but carefully screening the skirts and shorts of the sidewalk pedestrians—as well as the cars on the street—from the abstractions on display below. The museum was becoming a complex, cubist spatial sculpture, replete in the initial design with a spiral stair connecting the lobby with the lower level (as Pei had used at the Everson), although this had to cede to a more conventional switchback stair after review by New York City's Buildings Department. The controlled dialogue between interior and exterior would continue in the stair, where what Kahn during this period called "servant spaces" were converted into the place of greatest connection between the ritual of museum visit and life outside. The great windowpanes of the other stair, enclosed rather than on display and taking visitors to the upper-floor galleries, provide changing views of the Madison Avenue streetscape with each switchback, the first in a series of staccato framed views that find their echo in the great neutral galleries once the visitor has discovered the function of the mysterious trapezoidal "eyelid" windows freely attached like ornamental brooches on the blocky exterior. To keep the great planes of glass from conflicting with the emphatic reliance on artificial light for displaying art, the trapezoids are angled outward to provide somewhat uncanny vignettes of the city and glimpses of sky, while avoiding any capricious play of light in the inner sanctuary. Breuer referred to them as "psychological"—and, in an even less auspicious choice of words, "a crutch"—a respite in any case from the viewing of art that was to be protected from that form of distraction aesthetic theorists in his Weimar youth had found such a challenge to the modern condition of art. At the same time, they have the uncanny effect of framing views of the city detached from quotidian experience.

Breuer and Smith created a building of deliberate contrasting experiences: a lobby based on the new ideal of flow and spatial excitement, in which architecture, large-scale public sculpture, and the city dialogued, while on the upper floors attention was focused inward. On the first two gallery floors the Whitney's equivocation between its roots as a club for the artistically initiated and its desire to open wide to the public and the new scale of postwar art was expressed by a counterpoint between soaring loft spaces and a sequence of rooms with warm wooden paneling and domestic modern furniture selected by Connie Breuer, the architect's wife, then working on interiors for the firm. The greatest uninterrupted expanse and loftiest ceilings were reserved for the fourth-floor gallery: a full 118 feet of clear space before the installation of the movable system of panels. It was as though not only ancient tradition but modern rivals had been turned on their head; here was a free span space like Mies van der Rohe's Neue Nationalgalerie [22] in Berlin but lifted high above the city. Mies's panoramic glass connection to the city is here replaced by the largest of Breuer's trapezoidal windows—the only one on the Madison Avenue front, p. 202/1–2 one that captures and pictorializes the façades across the street.

22 Mies van der Rohe, Neue Nationalgalerie, Berlin, 1962–68, interior

The Whitney Museum in an odd way returns full circle to Breuer's experiments with vision and viewing in his early Bauhaus days, as well as to the idea of levitating, sitting on air. Here it is an inverted ziggurat that floats over the open space of the lobby, at once not only set off by a bridge but also visually an extension of the sidewalk [2, 23]. The oxymoronic combination of heavy, hollow forms over transparent ground floors might even be said to be a turning into architectural space of Nervi's experiments with the folded concrete plates. In any case, Breuer had abandoned the youthful dream of the dematerialization of art for a commitment to the notion that an art of the experience of contradictions held in dialogue was the platform for engaging with and enriching life in the complex postwar world. Here was a temple of art that also engaged with the commercial streetscape of Madison Avenue, a balance between removal and connection that balanced equally the appearance of heavy with the engineering means of lightness. It was at once a unique building in Breuer's growing portfolio and a culmination of a research project under way for decades.

23 Whitney Museum, night view of entry bridge over the sculpture garden, looking south

1 On the African chair, see Christopher Wilk, "Marcel Breuer and Gunta Stözl, 'African' Chair, 1921," in *Bauhaus 1919–1933: Workshops for Modernity*, ed. Barry Bergdoll and Leah Dickerman (New York: Museum of Modern Art, 2009), 100–109.

2 This has been much commented upon. See, for example, Frederic J. Schwartz, "Utopia for Sale: The Bauhaus and Weimar's Consumer Culture," in *Bauhaus Culture: From Weimar to the Cold War*, ed. Kathleen James-Chakraborty (Minneapolis: University of Minnesota Press, 2006), 216ff.

3 Ruth Verde Zein, *Brutalist Connections* (São Paulo: Altamara, 2014), and www.brutalistconnections.com.

4 A number of surviving photographs are annotated as "designed with Walter Gropius," notably one in the photo archives of the Museum of Modern Art and one reproduced on the comprehensive website on Breuer's work by North Carolina Modernist Houses at http://www.ncmodernist.org/breuer.htm. However, none of the archival sources that I have consulted provide any evidence of Gropius's involvement. The house is also sometimes referred to as the Harnismacher House, an alternative spelling that appears notably in Christopher Wilk's important study, *Marcel Breuer: Furniture and Interiors* (New York: Museum of Modern Art, 1981), 110.

5 Barry Bergdoll, "Encountering America: Marcel Breuer and the Discourses of the Vernacular from Budapest to Boston," in *Marcel Breuer: Architecture and Design* (Weil am Rhein: Vitra Design Museum, 2003), 260–307.

6 "Transcript of an interview of Breuer by television interviewer István Kardos, 1972," Box 6, Microfilm Reel 5718, Breuer Papers, Archives of American Art, Smithsonian Institute, Washington, D.C.

7 Marcel Breuer, "Wo Stehen Wir?" (1934), reprinted in English as "Where Do We Stand?," in *Buildings and Projects, 1921–1961*, by Marcel Breuer, with captions and introduction by Cranston Jones (New York: Praeger, 1962), 269.

8 Sigfried Giedion, *Space, Time and Architecture: The Growth of a New Tradition* (Cambridge, MA: Harvard University Press, 1941), 269–76.

9 Kardos interview, *op. cit.* note 6, unable to read the original Hungarian, I am translating from the German version in the document in the Archives of American Art, Reel 5718, frame 508: "Dieses Haus vertritt die moderne Umgestaltung von Original amerikanischen Holzgebäuden. Es besteht nur aus einem größeren Raum und Kuch sowie Badezimmer, aber meine Meinung nach war veilleicht am Wichtigsten vor allen, und vielleicht hatte es die größte Wirkung auf die moderne Entwicklung der amerikanischen Architektur. [sic]"

10 Breuer, describing the house in a letter to his former English partner, F. R. S. Yorke, March 8, 1943, Box 45, Breuer Papers, Syracuse University Libraries, Syracuse, NY, cited in Isabelle Hyman, *Marcel Breuer, Architect: The Career and the Buildings* (New York: Harry N. Abrams, 2001), 334.

11 Breuer, *Buildings and Projects, 1921–1961*, 222.

12 See a reproduction of this diagram in Breuer, *Buildings and Projects, 1921–1961*, 248, fig. 88.

13 Barry Bergdoll, "Breuer as a Global Architect," in *OfficeUS Agenda*, ed. Eva Franch i Gilabert, Amanda Reeser Lawrence, Ana Miljački, and Ashley Shafer (Zurich: Lars Müller and PRAXIS, 2014), 149–59.

14 See Victoria M. Young, *Saint John's Abbey Church: Marcel Breuer and the Creation of a Modern Sacred Space* (Minneapolis: University of Minnesota Press, 2014); and Christopher E. M. Pearson, *Designing UNESCO: Art, Architecture and International Politics at Mid-Century* (London: Ashgate, 2010). See also Hilary Thimmesh, *Marcel Breuer and a Committee of Twelve Plan a Church: A Monastic Memoir* (Collegeville, MN: Saint John's University Press, 2011); and Colm J. Barry, OSB, *Worship and Work: Saint John's Abbey and University 1856–1992* (Collegeville, MN: Liturgical Press, 1993).

15 Sigfried Giedion, Josep Lluís Sert, and Fernand Léger, "Nine Points on Monumentality" (1943), in *Architecture Culture, 1943–1968: A Documentary Anthology*, ed. Joan Ockman and Edward Eigen (New York: Columbia Graduate School of Architecture, Planning, and Preservation, 1993), 29–30.

16 I have discussed this at greater length in "Into the Fold: Nervi, Breuer and a Post-War Architecture of Assembly," in *Pier Luigi Nervi: Architecture as Challenge*, ed. Carlo Olmo and Cristiana Chiorino (Milan: Silvana; Brussels: CIVA, PLN project, 2010), 87–115.

17 St. John's Abbey, "Report of the Building Committee to Community," March 3, 1953, copy in File 6, Box 70, Breuer Papers, Syracuse University Libraries, Syracuse, NY.

18 Thimmesh, *Marcel Breuer and a Committee of Twelve*, ix, n.12.

19 Abbot Baldwin, letter to architects, March 7, 1953, Folder 13, Box 2, Office of the Abbot, New Church and Monastery Building Records, 1952–81, St. John's Abbey Archives, Collegeville, MN.

20 Ibid.

21 "Notes and Observations on a Visit of Mr. Breuer to St. John's, April 20, '53," typescript, Folder 4, Box 5, Building Committee, Comprehensive Plans and Reports, St. John's Abbey Archives, Collegeville, MN.

22 Meinberg comment is from "Notes and Observations on a Visit of Mr. Breuer to St. John's."

23 Breuer comment quoted in "Notes and Observations on a Visit of Mr. Breuer to St. John's."

24 "Notes and Observations on a Visit of Mr. Breuer to St. John's," op. cit.

25 For the most recent, and thoroughgoing, documentation and analysis of the Breuer/Nervi collaboration on the concrete work at UNESCO, see Roberto Gargiani and Alberto Bologna, *The Rhetoric of Pier Luigi Nervi, Concrete and Ferroconcrete Forms* (Lausanne: EPFL Press, 2016), esp. chap. 9.

26 Rev. Cloud Meinberg, "The Monastic Church," lecture text, September 1953, St. John's Abbey Archives. See also Daniel J. Heisy, "Erwin Panofsky's Gothic Architecture," in *American Theological Inquiry: A Biannual Journal of Theology, Culture, and History* 8, no. 1 (2015): 41–48.

27 Meinberg, "Monastic Church," op. cit.
28 See Whitney S. Stoddard, *Adventures in Architecture: Building the New St. John's* (New York: Longmans, Green, 1958), 38–43; and Robert Gatje, *Marcel Breuer: A Memoir* (New York: Monacelli Press, 2000), esp. 87–92.
29 Thimmesh, *Marcel Breuer and a Committee of Twelve*, 1.
30 Ibid., 17.
31 Marcel Breuer, "The Contemporary Aspect of Pharaonic Architecture," preface to *Living Architecture: Egyptian*, by Jean-Louis de Cenival (New York: Grosset & Dunlap, 1964), 3–6, originally published in French as "Modernisme de l'architecture pharaonique," in *Egypte: Epoque pharaonique*, ed. Jean-Louis de Cenival and Henri Stierlin, in the series Architecture Universelle (Fribourg, CH: Office du Livre, 1964), 3–6 (bibliographically confusing, as the book appears sometimes under the name of the photographer Henri Stierlin, sometimes under that of the author of the accompanying text, Jean-Louis de Cenival). Breuer was very proud of the book and seems to have gifted it to clients. My inscribed copy was a gift from Professor Molly Nesbit of Vassar College, who inherited it from her father, who had served on the committee of the Episcopalian church in Rochester, New York, and had interviewed Breuer as the potential architect for their new church.
32 "A Masterplan for the Next One Hundred Years," *Architectural Record* (November 1961): 132.
33 Mario Salvadori, "UNESCO Headquarters, Paris, France," *Architectural Record* (February 1958): 166.
34 Pier Luigi Nervi, *Aesthetics and Technology in Buildings* (Cambridge, MA: Harvard University Press, 1966), 5.
35 Marcel Breuer, second annual Reed and Barton Design Lecture, presented at the University of Michigan, Ann Arbor, March 6, 1963, published as *Matter and Intrinsic Form* (Taunton, MA: Reed and Barton, 1963), unpaginated.
36 Robert Einaudi, "Pier Luigi Nervi Lecture Notes, Roma 1959–60," in *La lezione di Pier Luigi Nervi*, by Pier Luigi Nervi, Annalisa Trentin, and Tommaso Trombetti (Milan: Pearson Italia, 2010), 112.
37 "Marcel Breuer: The Buildings at St. John's Abbey, Collegeville, Minnesota," *Design Quarterly* 53 (1961).
38 This solution knew a great popularity at this moment, including Nervi's design of the Italian embassy in Brasilia, Ove Arup's design for a bridge at Durham University in the UK, and German Samper's SENA building in Bogotà.
39 Marcel Breuer, *Matter and Intrinsic Form: The Second Annual Reed and Barton Design Lecture* (Ann Arbor: University of Michigan, 1963), final page of printed pamphlet. The same lecture was delivered in November at Cornell University; a bound typescript of "Remarks of Marcel Breuer, December 4, 1963, Cornell University," is in the Avery Library, Columbia University, New York, NY.
40 Gatje, *Marcel Breuer: A Memoir*, 196.
41 Quoted from "Notes for M.B.'s comments at the Presentation of the Project on November 12th," Frame 431e, Reel 5729, Breuer Papers, Archives of American Art, Smithsonian Institution, Washington, DC. Cleaned up, these notes were later reused in many different publications and printed as "Breuer's Approach to the Design of the Whitney Museum," *AIA Journal*, April 1967, 67. They are reprinted in Tician Papachristou, *Marcel Breuer: New Buildings and Projects* (New York: Praeger, 1970), 14–16.
42 Sigfried Giedion, *The Eternal Present: A Contribution on Constancy and Change; The Beginnings of Architecture* (New York: Bollingen Foundation, 1964); Jean-Louis de Cenival and Henri Stierlin, eds., *Egypte, Époque pharaonique*, with a preface by Marcel Breuer (Fribourg, CH: Office du Livre, 1964). A later English edition of the latter was published under the title *Egypt* as the fourth book in the Architecture of the World series (Cologne: Benedikt Taschen, n.d. [c. 1995]).
43 "Upside-Down Museum in Manhattan," *Architectural Forum* (January 1964): 91.
44 See Barry Bergdoll, "I. M. Pei, Marcel Breuer, Edward Larrabee Barnes and the New American Museum Design of the 1960s," in *A Modernist Museum in Perspective*, ed. Anthony Alofsin (Washington, DC: National Gallery of Art, 2009), 107–23.

When Breuer received the St. John's Abbey commission in spring 1953, he was in the midst of working out a plan for the Parisian headquarters of UNESCO, the United Nations Educational, Scientific, and Cultural Organization. Whereas at the Benedictine abbey Breuer's firm had sole design authority, the UNESCO campus developed through a complex collaborative process that involved a changing mix of architects, culminating in a team that partnered Breuer with the Italian engineer Pier Luigi Nervi and the French architect Bernard Zehrfuss. The outcome was a complex of four concrete buildings adorned inside and out with artworks by leading modernist painters and sculptors, including Picasso, Miró, and Calder, as well as a garden designed by Noguchi.

The UNESCO complex is dominated by the Secretariat, a seven-story office building with a Y-shaped plan, lifted on giant concrete piers above a plaza. This building is joined to the trapezoidal Conference Building (sometimes referred to as the Assembly Hall after its grand interior auditorium), which is composed of folded-plate concrete, by a link structure that creates a casual site strategy played off against the strong sculptural form of the main building components. Nervi's contribution made the Conference Building and the hyperbolic paraboloid canopy entries to the Secretariat tours de force of modern construction technology.

The forms of UNESCO House were designed to participate in an array of communications media, while the sometimes tortuous generative process negotiated the tensions between two models of the architect: as individual creative genius and as organizational bureaucrat. While the architectural press disparaged the buildings as mediocre upon their completion in 1958, they became emblems of institutional modernism, and Breuer's emergence as the primary designer of the complex established his distinctive position among modernist architects as something of a genius bureaucrat.

1 Breuer with UNESCO design team in Paris office, 1953
2 Breuer-Nervi-Zehrfuss, UNESCO Headquarters, Place de Fontenoy, Paris, France, 1955–58, site orientation and axes drawing
3 View of construction site, Conference Building in foreground
4 Site plan and section drawings
5 Aerial view of site looking south from the École Militaire
6 Floor plan and office detail plan drawings
7 Lobby of Secretariat
8 Detail of sun protection elements, Secretariat
9 Wall section drawing of sun protection elements
10 Detail of exterior stair, Secretariat
11 View of exterior stair, Secretariat
12 Section perspective drawing and structural details, Conference Building
13 Longitudinal section drawings, Conference Building, May 31, 1954
14 View of plenary hall, Conference Building
15 Exterior of Conference Building
16 Delegates' lounge, center supports, and concrete bridge to projection room, Conference Building
17 Pedestrian entrance to Secretariat
18 UNESCO Headquarters, Building 4, 1960–61
19 View of Eiffel Tower from roof terrace of Secretariat
20 Concrete wall of the Conference Building and Secretariat seen from Avenue de Ségur

1

II UNESCO

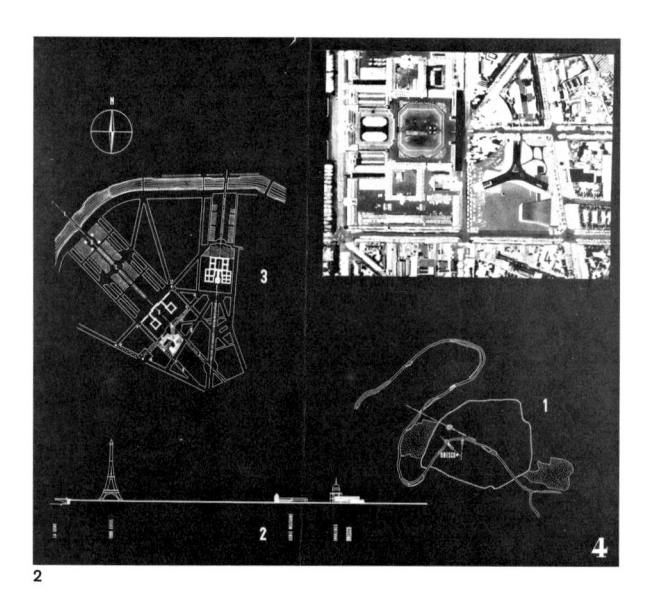

67

68   II UNESCO

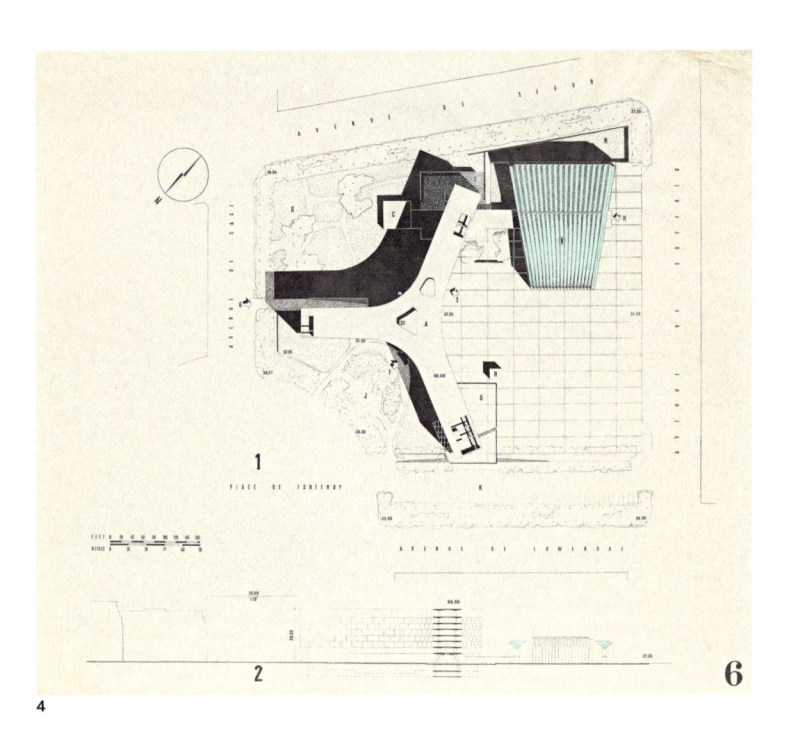

4

5

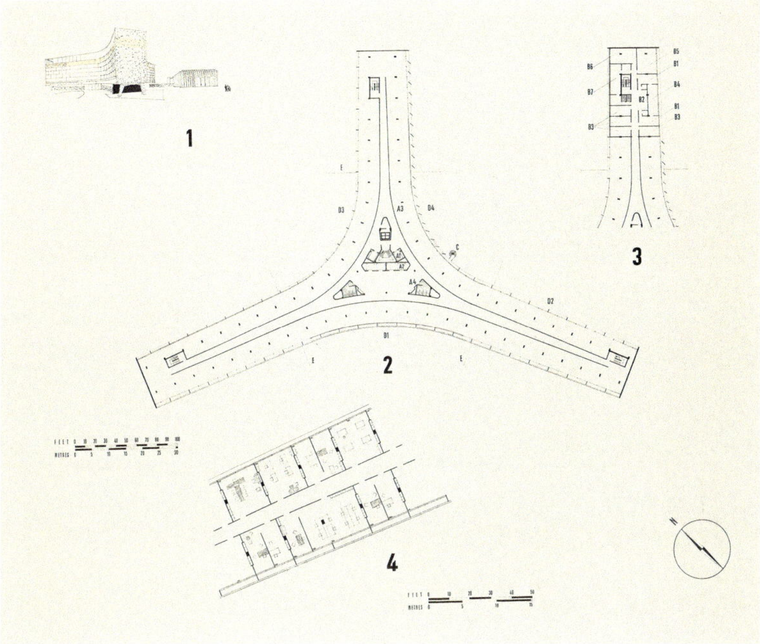

6

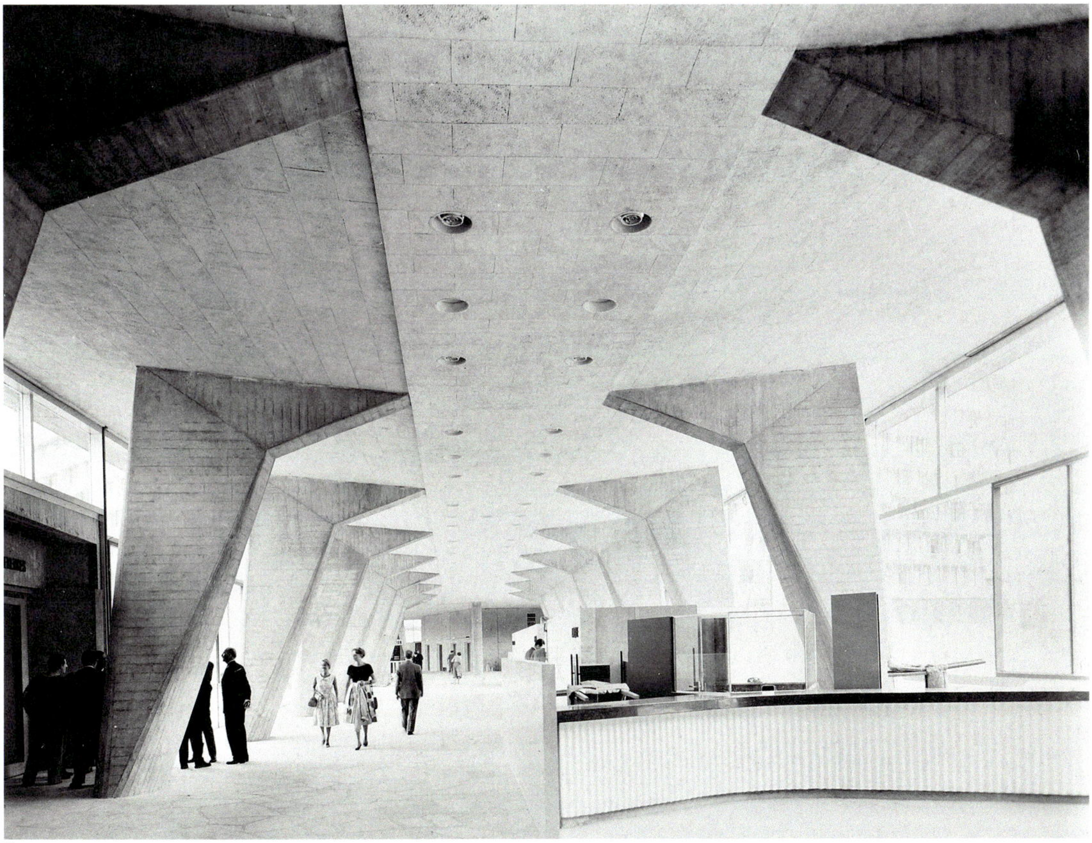

7

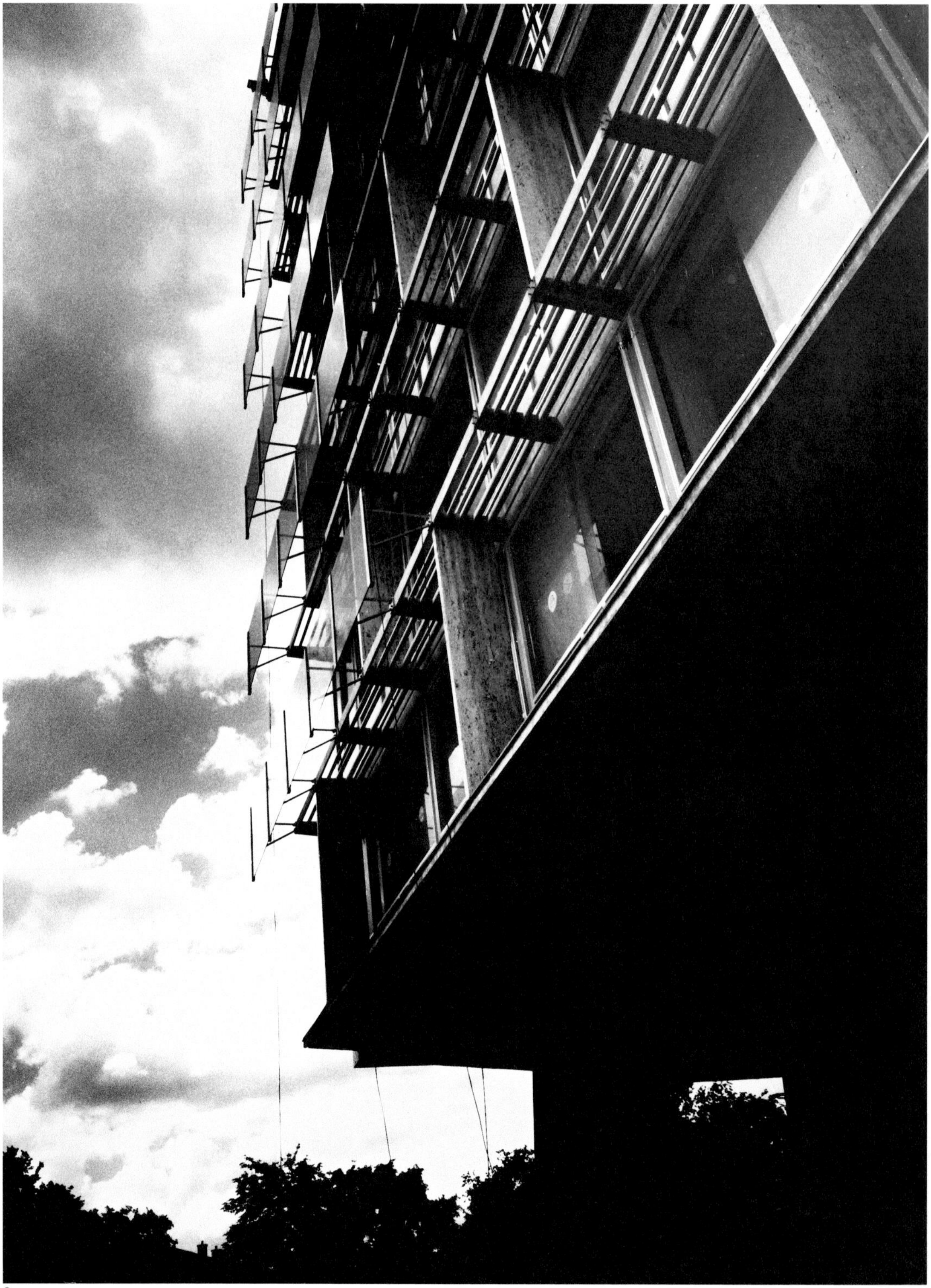

8

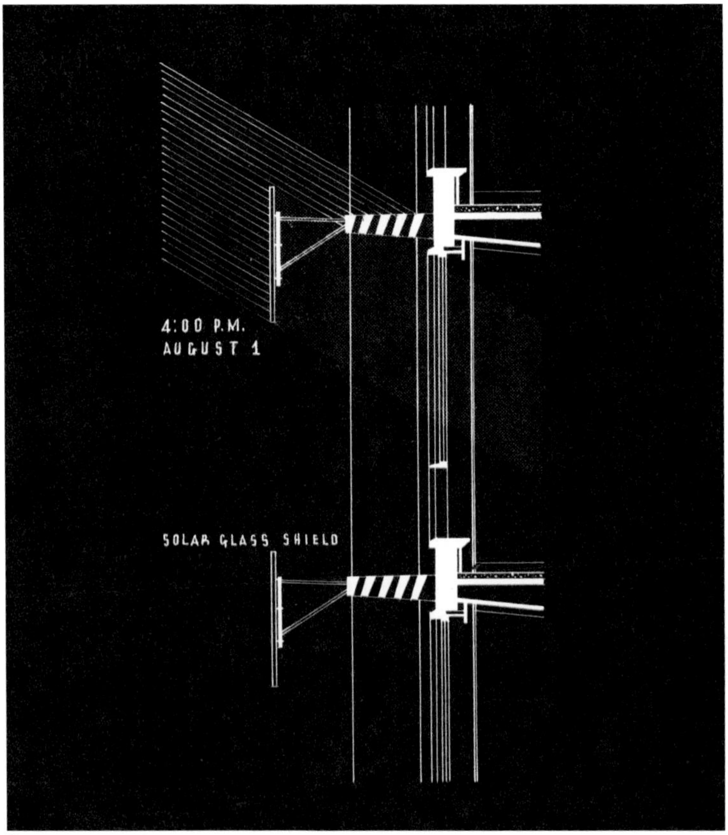

9

10

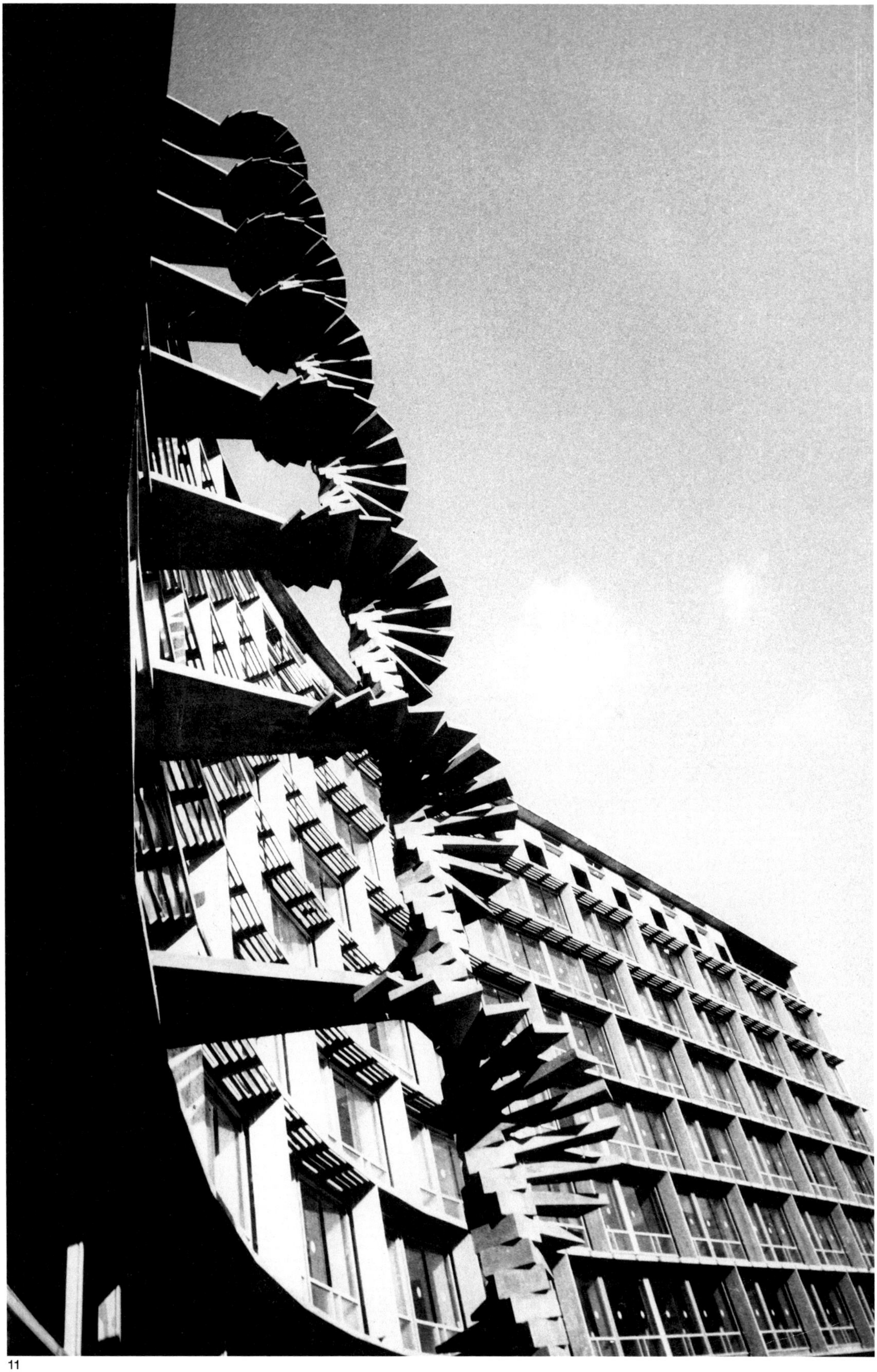

74 II UNESCO

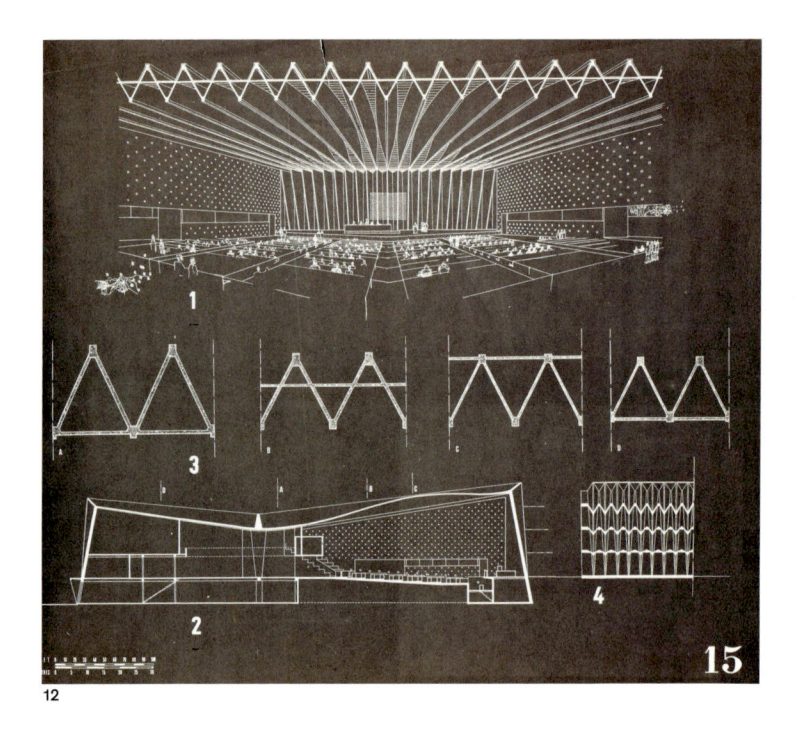

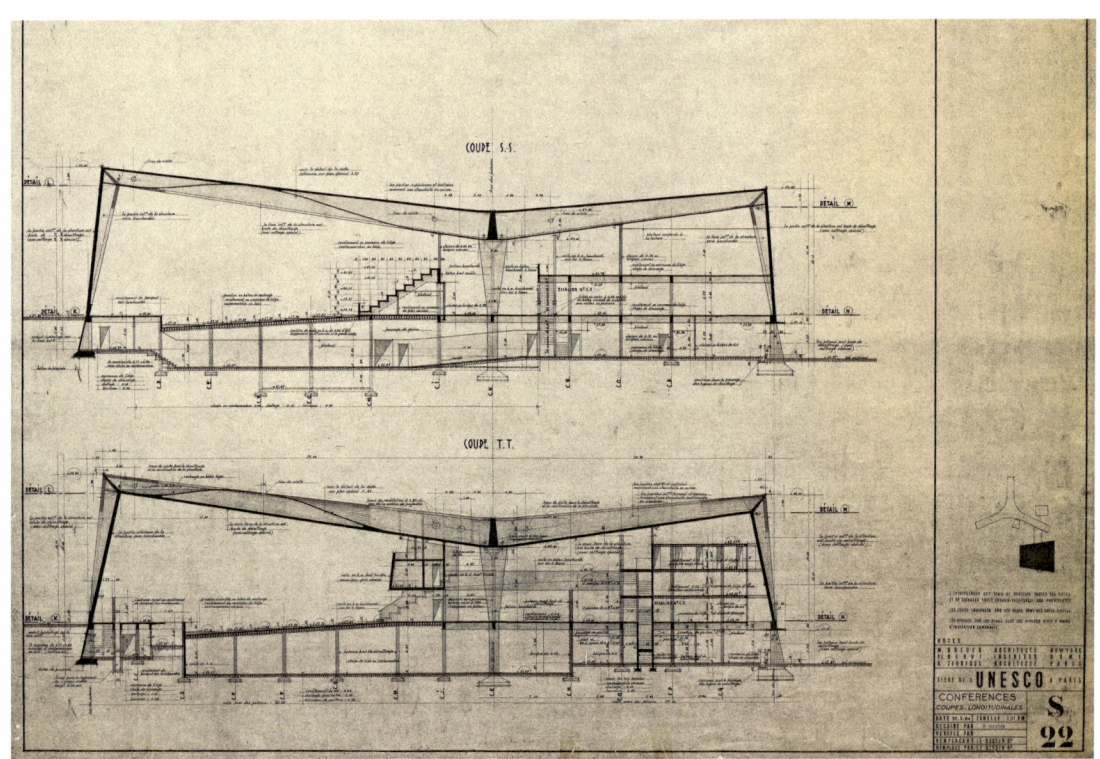

12

13

14

15

II UNESCO

16

17

18

19

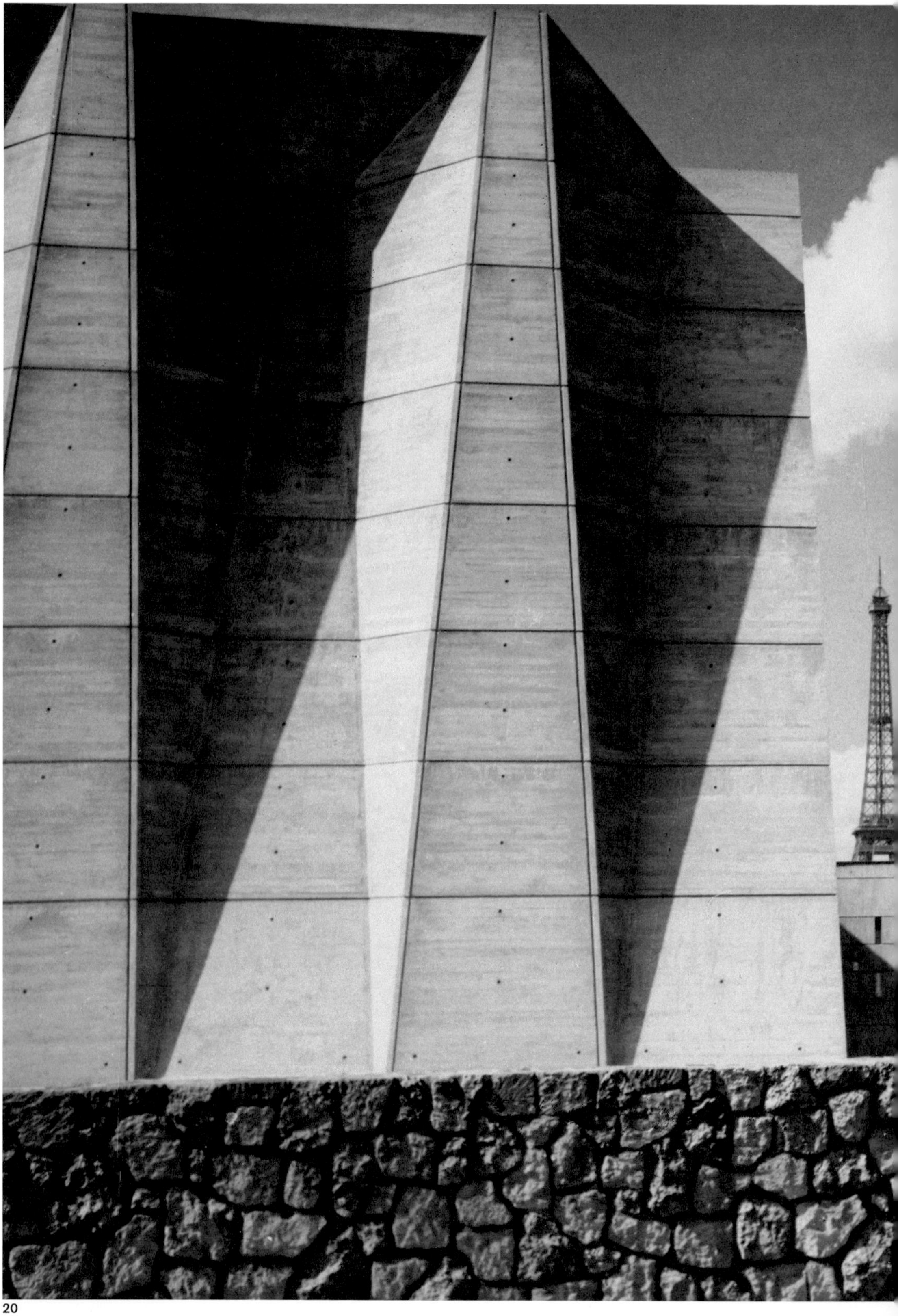

20

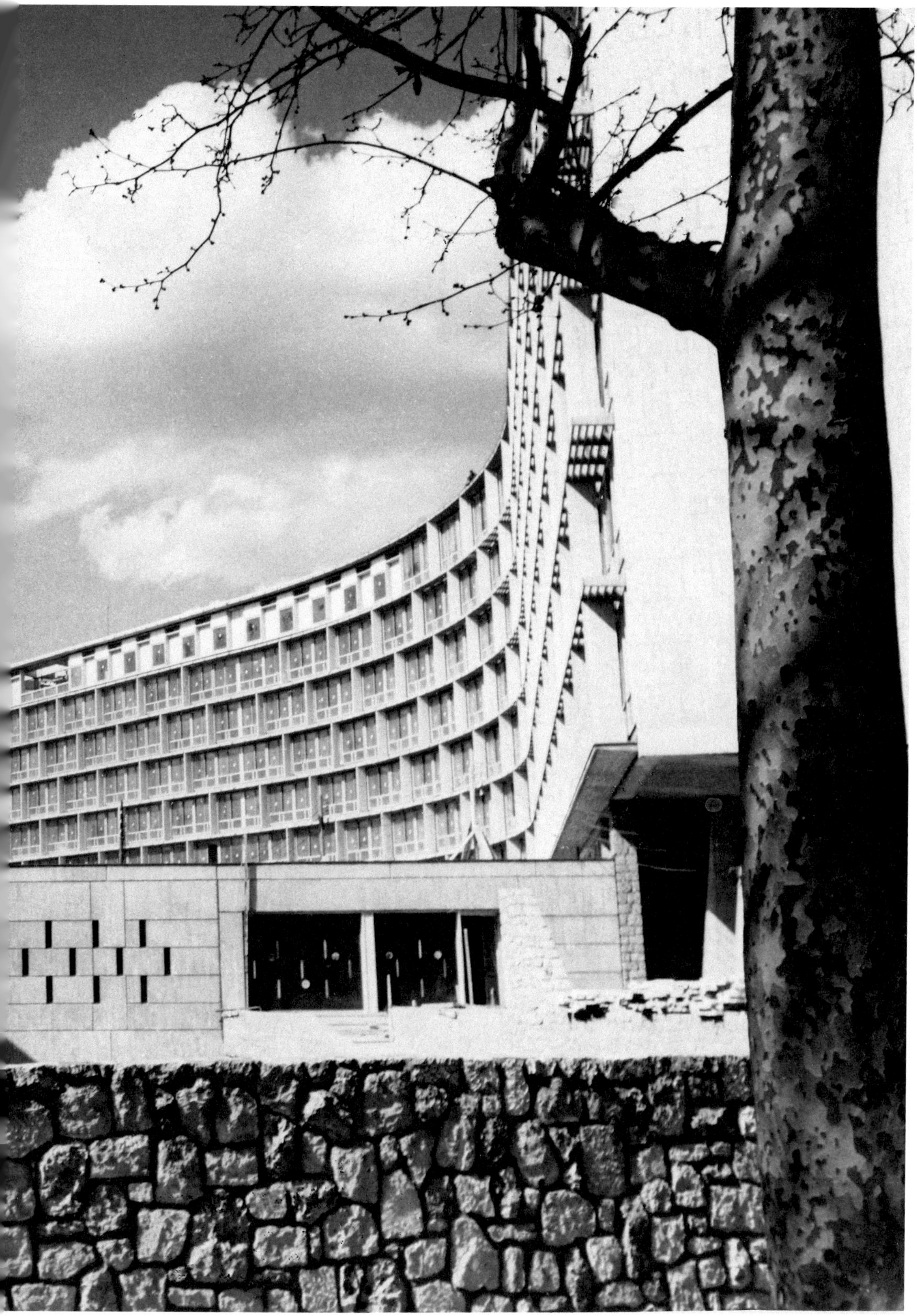

1 *Let's Visit UNESCO House!* Paris, 1948

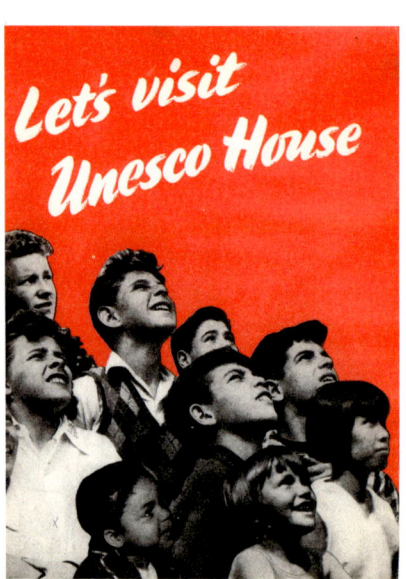

Architecture and Mediocracy at UNESCO House

Lucia Allais

When the Italian architect Ernesto Rogers recalled his role in the design of the Paris headquarters for the United Nations Educational, Scientific, and Cultural Organization (UNESCO) in a special issue of *Casabella* published in April 1959, he offered a cautionary tale about collaboration. "The tragedy of the UNESCO Palace," he wrote, "is to a large extent the tragedy of democracy."[1] The commission had involved three schemes, two sites, and no fewer than ten architects, including some of the most illustrious figures of the modern movement: from founding fathers Walter Gropius and Le Corbusier, to mid-career practitioners Marcel Breuer, Eero Saarinen, Lúcio Costa, and Josep Lluís Sert, the engineer Pier Luigi Nervi, and Rogers himself. Yet, despite this remarkable concentration of talent, as Rogers recounted, a protracted design process had yielded compromise after compromise, and ultimately "mediocracy" had prevailed. With this term, Rogers not only called the building mediocre (an assessment supported by many others) but laid the blame squarely on the process.[2] In this he added UNESCO's headquarters to the list of buildings that apparently manifested the growing pains of modern architecture at mid-century. Since the early 1940s, internationalist architectural circles had been abuzz with discussions of how modern architects would fare under pressure to take on ever larger and ever faster building commissions, through collective, cooperative, corporate, or bureaucratic design methods. In 1947, Henry-Russell Hitchcock had even bemoaned that the corporate reorganization of design processes had split modernism into two, "the architecture of bureaucracy and the architecture of genius," each demanding its own mode of interpretation.[3] Work produced under individual direction was fundamentally different from work produced by a group, Hitchcock argued, and should be judged according to different criteria.

Rogers tacitly agreed in his article on UNESCO. He avoided attributing any aspect of the scheme to anyone on the team, asked each collaborator to write a testimonial, and, as if to preempt critiques, took readers on a tour of the site, where he invited them to see the failure of "democracy" in the architecture itself. The Secretariat made a "noble gesture" in the city, but its interior space "failed to elevate." The fact that the complex dwarfed the human scale with its large and far-apart volumes showed a "sacrifice [of] individuality to the consortium of humanity." So, rather than being a "Monument to World Culture," the UNESCO House was merely the result of "a competent application of a common language," devoid of "accents and inflections."[4]

Other critiques soon followed suit. In August 1959, the Italian critic Bruno Zevi called the UNESCO complex hopelessly episodic, "not a masterpiece but a work in pieces." Zevi annotated the plan of the complex with question marks to indicate where the architects had committed grammatical errors and concluded that the "UNESCO Building strikes, but doesn't convince."[5] If Rogers compared architecture to a spoken tongue, Zevi focused on syntax and the written word. A year later, the American critic Lewis Mumford turned his attention to the lifespan of language, writing in a scathing *New Yorker* review that the complex was a collection of modernist "clichés." Mumford saw only trite architectural phrases and blamed the client again: a "caricature of the bureaucratic process" had provoked a building of "elephantine mediocrity."[6]

Thus, as soon as it was built, UNESCO's headquarters entered the history of modernism as a symbol of failed collaboration, bringing along three analogies between architecture and internationalism: modernism could be an international tongue, but UNESCO's complex spoke only a bland Esperanto; modern architecture could be monumental, but UNESCO's architects had only enlarged hackneyed forms; and design could offer lessons in diplomacy, but here collaboration had produced only mediocrity.

To an extent, all architectural histories of the United Nations and the League of Nations have been driven by the desire to make an analogy between design and diplomacy.[7] But UNESCO was not just another international commission. As the UN's cultural arm, it was intended to be the keeper of collective values in all cultural production and to foster a global distribution of creative power, both historically and currently. Even the building's naming conveyed this desire to coalesce a mass public. Initially a reference to other "famous houses of the world," including those of the old diplomacy such as the White House, the moniker "UNESCO House" also recalled the socialist building programs of the early twentieth century such as the *maisons du peuple*.[8]

In light of this collective charge, we should not be too quick to let the original architectural team—Rogers and company—set the terms by which we interpret how architecture and international politics intersected at UNESCO House. Rogers's own editorial effort to gather his collaborators in one master narrative in *Casabella* seems especially suspicious in light of the absence from this feature of the one architect who directed the building's development and execution and who is often credited as its lead designer—Marcel Breuer.

The UNESCO complex leads a double life in architectural literature: as a Breuer work and as a collective one. Any new analysis therefore pushes us to get past the critical polarity between architectural genius and bureaucracy that was invented in the 1940s and directs us instead to changes the modern notion of authorship has undergone in cultural production at large. As Michel Foucault pointedly wrote in 1969, although the idea that an author controls his or her works had come under relentless attack by modern writers and artists since at least the turn of the twentieth century, with the "author" being finally declared "dead" around 1967, in fact institutional and commercial forces have continued to validate the notion that creative works originate from an individuated author and have sustained the social and economic "functioning" of this author in culture at large. "It is not enough," Foucault cautioned, "to repeat the empty affirmation that the author has disappeared.… Instead, we must locate the space left empty by the author's disappearance, follow the distribution of gaps and breaches, and watch for the openings this disappearance uncovers."[9] If the death of the author announced the triumph of the reader, Foucault recommended paying close attention to the institutions, such as copyright, where the "author function" had been shaped in the eighteenth century and continued to be tightly controlled, even if under the name of freedom of interpretation.

Taking a cue from Foucault's critique, this chapter revisits the design of UNESCO House as an event in both architectural and international history. The design process unfolded in two phases: a schematic phase full of false starts, and a development phase in which tasks were clearly assigned. Modern architects, I argue, were expected to act as "geniuses" in the first phase and as "bureaucrats" in the second, and Breuer was the critical figure in this pivot. Two photographs aptly illustrate the shift: one shows all the designers loosely sitting and standing, in 1952, around a conference table littered with

2 UNESCO design team at work on the Porte Maillot scheme. Left to right: Saarinen, Nervi, Rogers, Gropius, Le Corbusier, Zehrfuss (standing), Breuer (standing), Markelius

sketches [2]. The second finds Breuer and collaborators hunched over a drafting table in 1954, in a temporary Paris office, with an oversize plan hovering on the wall above them.

p. 65/1

Rather than anchor this episode in Breuer's career, I propose to situate it in UNESCO's evolving mode of cultural governance, during a shift toward "technique" in international politics. Different strands of thought about architecture as an instrument of international politics converged under UNESCO's umbrella in the early 1950s. Some saw buildings as communication devices, while others saw them as manifestos, and many also expected UNESCO to provide international architectural standards. All expected that collective creation would facilitate collective reception. When it came time to design the headquarters, Breuer was the genius-bureaucrat, so to speak, who came to occupy the breach in authorship opened up by this uncertainty.

Architects and/as Consultants

The modern architects who designed UNESCO House were doubly delegated. On the one hand, they were chosen by UNESCO's Headquarters Committee. On the other, they were delegates of the CIAM (Congrès International d'Architecture Moderne), an international group that was created in 1928 as a "congress" of European architectural avant-gardes and that has since been credited with no less than the "invention of the modern movement."[10] CIAM had always modeled itself frankly, if antagonistically, on the "new diplomacy" that had been established at the League of Nations in 1919.[11] The end of World War II brought to the world stage a whole new cast of internationalists, many of whom, including UNESCO's first director general, Julian Huxley, were friendly to architectural modernism. CIAM leaders therefore had good reason to hope that they could associate themselves with UNESCO officially, and they repeatedly tried to establish a formal relationship.[12] But it soon became clear that the goals and methods of the two organizations were not entirely aligned. After all, UNESCO required its affiliates to have open memberships, whereas CIAM was, in the words of one perceptive bureaucrat, "a completely independent vanguard organization."[13] Once CIAM architects shifted their focus to obtaining the headquarters commission, this vanguardism proved decisive.

The first official action taken by UNESCO's Headquarters Committee was to establish a distinction between two kinds of architects: designers on the one hand, and consultants on the other. In this manner, the committee could recruit its design team from both the CIAM and the Union Internationale des Architectes (UIA), a comparatively conservative organization also affiliated with UNESCO.[14] The designing architect would be chosen from the UIA, and the CIAM would act in an "advisory" capacity. Then, having established this division, the Headquarters Committee immediately decided to name Le Corbusier one of the consultants. This was in fact a way to exclude him—a demand of the British and American delegations, who invoked the acrimonious experience of his participation in the design of the UN building in New York as a rationale.[15] More to the point, the exclusion was done by "including" him, but in a group that could not claim authorship. Having been designated as an advisor, Le Corbusier was disqualified from being appointed as architect.[16] In other words, UNESCO used the distinction between architect and consultant strategically to police the author function for its headquarters building, treating only one group of architects as authors.

After this division between architect and consultant had been established, the UNESCO House project was designed three times, on two sites. The first site, on the Place de Fontenoy, was protected by strict design regulations: at the edge of the Haussmanian city fabric, it was on axis with the Eiffel Tower and shared a roundabout with Ange-Jacques Gabriel's eighteenth-century École Militaire. In November 1951, the French architect Eugène Beaudoin, whom UNESCO had chosen from a UIA-provided list, designed a half-curved, half-bar building that followed the geometry of the roundabout [3]. Gropius, who had joined Le Corbusier in the team of consultants now known as "the Five," called this scheme "half Beaux-Arts, half Modern" and led the effort to have Beaudoin's scheme rejected.[17] Under Gropius's leadership, a new team of three architects—Breuer, Nervi, and Bernard Zehrfuss—was appointed to replace him, and they were henceforth called "the Three."[18] This turn of events was hailed as a "victory for modern architecture," because it distributed CIAM members on either side of the architect/consultant divide. The building was designed a second time by the entire team, beginning in 1952, on a new site at the city's periphery, near the Porte Maillot. A frankly modernist glass slab, fronted by a parabolic entrance canopy, the Secretariat sat on a plaza atop an underground mat of public

3 Eugène Beaudoin, UNESCO Headquarters, first Place de Fontenoy scheme, 1951

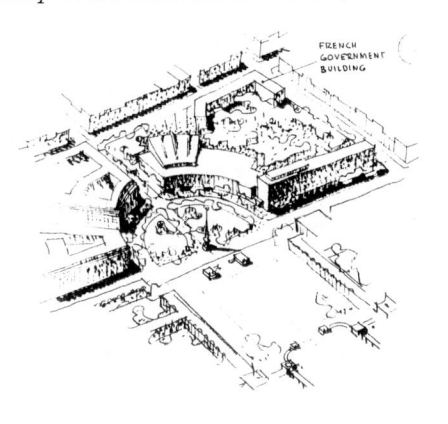

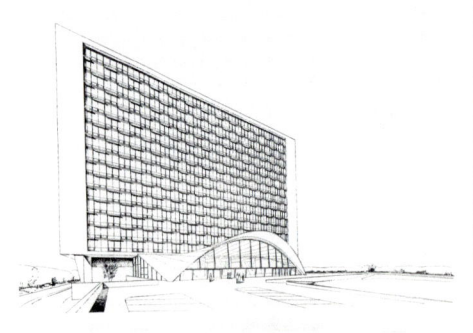

4 Breuer-Nervi-Zehrfuss, UNESCO Headquarters, Porte Maillot scheme, 1952
5 Breuer-Nervi-Zehrfuss, perspective view of final scheme. From: UNESCO, Avant-Projet Place de Fontenoy. Paris, April 3, 1953

spaces [4]. This scheme was made public, but Le Corbusier, who continued to push to be allowed into the Three, called it "faux-CIAM."[19] By contrast, the French press found the scheme *too* modern (calling it a "Notre Dame of Radiators") and pressured Parisian authorities to withdraw the site in protest.[20] Finally, the entire project was relocated to the original Fontenoy site, now with most design guidelines lifted, except for height restrictions. The final scheme was produced by the same group, with the Three now known as BNZ. They retained the division of the program into three volumes, reshaping each: the office building became a Y, the Conference Building a trapezoid, and the intermediate spaces a low and linear band traversing a garden-like site [5].

This intricate history has been recounted multiple times, as a latter-day battle of the ancients and moderns that unfolded on an evolving front.[21] But little has been made of the fact that, despite complex machinations, the distinction between two kinds of authors held fast. For example, both sets of "schematic designs" published in 1952 and 1953 opened with a dedication page that featured the hand-signatures of "the 3 executive architects," whereas "the 5 architects of international repute" were mentioned in a typographic list.[22]

The design process did, furthermore, expose CIAM as bureaucracy without a design method. Indeed, the congress offered no particular recommendation for how its members should collaborate on the design of a single project from scratch.[23] No less than three different modes of co-authorship can be detected among the nine architects on the UNESCO team who were also CIAM members. One faction, which we could call the *new monumentalists*, was led by Le Corbusier, forcefully seconded by Sert and Sigfried Giedion. They saw the UNESCO commission as "CIAM's first team job" and an opportunity to validate their ongoing manifesto about the "synthesis of the arts."[24] The second group could be designated *corporate builders*. Led by Eero Saarinen and quietly supported by Wallace Harrison, its attitude was pithily summarized by the remark, "Let us at least end up with a building."[25] Most powerful was a third group we could call *total designers*, consisting of Gropius and Breuer, who were appointed leaders of the Five and the Three, respectively. Once Bauhaus masters, later partners in London in the 1940s, and now informed by Gropius's membership in the most experimental of all the American-style architectural "corporations," The Architects' Collaborative (TAC), they thought it was best for CIAM to "avoid acting as a body."[26]

This contest of collaborative methods within CIAM, combined with the architect/consultant technicalities within UNESCO, had the potential to turn the entire UNESCO commission into a public relations disaster for internationalists on both sides. But the controversy over authorship was entirely eclipsed by the triumphant reception that was given to the final schematic design of UNESCO House when it was made public in May 1953. One component of the scheme in particular, the Secretariat building, was dramatically presented as a new international architectural standard—a "three-pointed star" according to the client, a "Y-plan" according to the architects.[27]

The designation of the Y as a new international "standard" originated with Marcel Breuer, who used it to resolve the conflicting expectations of contextualism and universalism that had been set in the design. In a press release written by his office, he preemptively answered the questions of whether the Secretariat had been "designed to have an 'international' or a 'Parisian' character" by calling it "the result of a continuous design investigation which started 20 years ago and represents a standard solution for an efficient 'continental' type of office building with direct daylight, view and natural ventilation for all offices."[28] The neutral tone of this description might seem anticlimactic in light of the project's heated history. But Breuer deployed the tempered language of technocratic innovation knowingly. He knew the logic and public appeal of standardization well. He had been the youngest of the Bauhaus masters and the only one among them to produce a line of mass-produced furniture, founding a separate company called Standard Möbel.[29] Since leaving the Bauhaus, he had gone on to a prolific career as the author of serialized designs—of chairs and of houses, in collaboration with a number of colleagues and companies.[30]

Breuer did not claim to have standardized the Y alone. Many other modern architects across Europe had sought to furnish, or equip, the functional city with Y-shaped buildings since the late

6 Backström & Reinius Gröndal, 1944–46; Le Corbusier, three-pointed skyscraper for Algiers, 1937
7 Stuyvesant Six redevelopment proposal (unexecuted), New York City, USA, 1944
8 Jean Tschumi, Nestlé Headquarters, Vevey, Switzerland, 1959. Photograph by Pierre Izard, 1960. Published in Jacques Gubler, ed., *Jean Tschumi: Architecture at Full Scale,* Milan, 2008, p. 212.
9 BNZ, proposal for UNESCO Building 4, 1960

1930s: Le Corbusier had designed a three-pointed Algiers skyscraper, and Backström & Reinius had proliferated Y-shapes in a housing complex near Stockholm [6]. Unlike at UNESCO, those Ys were volumetrically subsumed by other features of the massing, such as the height of the skyscraper or the pitched roofline of the housing project. A history of Y-plans can also be traced in Breuer's career leading up to this moment: a double-pronged plan for the 1936 Civic Center of the Future, then one as an object in the 1943 Stuyvesant Six housing development in New York, and another in a South Boston development [7].[31] The UNESCO House marks a clear departure: a freestanding object, as was the Boston project, it combines the curved convex corners of the Civic Center of the Future with the isometric proportions of Stuyvesant Six. But at UNESCO the "standard solution" stood by itself, curvature exaggerated, arms elongated, anchored in a single center.[32] The Y had been bent to blend into what Breuer called "continental" urbanity—characteristics of cities like Paris, where the urban fabric can be modern but not tall. On the one hand, it acknowledged street geometry, while, on the other, the building was an object. And on the inside, the building's gentle bend allowed the circulation to morph from a minimally dimensioned corridor at the ends into a wider and inhabitable public space at the center, without any sharp angles.

The shape of the Secretariat had an extremely productive afterlife. Before the building was even completed, copies began to appear. In 1959, the Swiss architect Jean Tschumi designed a headquarters for Nestlé whose shape was so frankly derivative of its UNESCO antecedent that Bruno Zevi praised it as a point-by-point improvement [8].[33] For Tschumi, the UNESCO team had proposed a new typology, which other architects were invited to improve upon.[34] By 1960, when UNESCO needed an addition to accommodate the growing number of member-states and BNZ was reconvened to design various options, they proposed one scheme that would have *repeated* a smaller copy of the Y on the corner of the site, as if the large Y had spawned an offspring [9]. Much later, buildings such as Erling Viksjø's ministry building in Oslo continued the variations on the bureaucratic theme. As late as 2003, OMA (Office for Metropolitan Architecture) submitted a competition entry for the NATO headquarters featuring a UNESCO Y as part of a larger, tentacular office complex. But if it started as a scalable and repeatable type, the Y also demonstrated an uncanny ability to mutate. Breuer used double Ys for IBM and for the Housing and Urban Development headquarters. Other architects for international agencies borrowed the device of a bendable, double-loaded corridor that curves around office cores: Eero Saarinen's World Health Organization building in Geneva inverted the tapering, and the Berlaymont building for the European Commission in Brussels made the Y into an X.

The mutability of this new "standard" shows that the UNESCO Secretariat building was in some ways already more than a Y; instead its success derived from the flexibility it offered in form and image.[35] Despite Breuer's insistence that the Y was a product of a "continuous" process, its design clearly received a jolt through the UNESCO collaboration, which pushed it from being a Y to no longer being one. How, then, did an invention that was latent on the international architectural scene for decades suddenly materialize, not only as a new standard but a new *kind* of standard? This jolt, in fact, can be located precisely during a meeting that took place in February 1953 over the course of three days.

Three February Days in Paris
The UNESCO House's plan was generated during a three-day meeting in Paris in February 1953. This meeting was chronicled after the fact by Breuer in a lengthy and confidential "Office Memo," a document remarkable because Breuer formatted the discussion by giving each architect a first-person voice as if he were a character in a play, describing design moves as declarative statements.[36] A narrative of the design process can therefore be reconstructed by correlating this document with the voluminous number of sketches and drawings that were produced and promptly archived by the various protagonists.

Breuer had made sketches before arriving in Paris, arranging various volumes diagonally across the diamond-shaped site [10.1]. A Y-plan already appears in these sketches: first, spanning the entire site, and then as one of several volumes, including an "egg" [10.2–4]. Once Breuer arrived in Paris, he, Nervi, and Zehrfuss composed a set of alternatives, either by adding an additional low building to span the space between the Y and the egg [10.5–6] or by reshaping the whole toward one corner [10.7–8]. Once the Five arrived, Breuer presented, as the most current solution [10.9], a scheme with the Y-plan at the center and an egg-shaped conference building toward the roundabout. Breuer's memo begins at this point, and I recount its story below, adopting the present tense to evoke its theatrical quality.

The next three days unfold in a steady cycle of morning critiques and afternoon design sessions. The first morning session is taken up entirely by Le Corbusier, who critiques each part of the scheme [10.10]. "The office building is impeccable," he declares, but "the connection is not a connection" and the "conference building should be dispersed" because "round forms are not architectural." Breuer points out that the egg is organized around a large, open-air central garden [10.11]. But Le Corbusier scribbles aggressively over it, insisting it is too crowded [10.12]. After the group breaks for lunch, Breuer returns to the studio to find Saarinen, who has just flown in. Saarinen suggests a rotation [10.13], first with the egg toward the back, then the south [10.14]. They should "reorient the main approach towards the Place de Fontenoy," he argues. Breuer agrees, and he shows an earlier sketch [10.15] but explains that he has encountered "strong resistance" to this idea. He explains others' preference for a wide palatial forecourt facing the avenue by saying they have a more "Latin" sensibility [10.16].

The next day, a revised egg scheme is presented [10.17]. Le Corbusier still wants to disperse the assembly building, this time asserting that it "should be more like the diagram"—a diagram on the wall that arranges the program in a double-star formation and that would eventually be redrawn and published as a bubble diagram with the final scheme, to explain how the program is distributed across the site. Le Corbusier also begins to sketch the urban axes that traverse the site [10.18] in order to argue that the entrance should be from the back, an option he also sketches [10.19]. At lunchtime, Gropius privately tells Breuer he thinks the approach should be from the Place de Fontenoy, and Breuer again makes his comment about Latin "resistance." In the afternoon, while the others visit the site, Breuer, Saarinen, and Zehrfuss [10.20] move the Y closer to the north but maintain the approach from the south.

The following morning, Gropius opens the meeting with the surprising but welcome proposition that the building "cannot turn its back to the roundabout" after all. In a shocking development, Le Corbusier agrees, but goes further: the building should "follow the curve" of the roundabout, as "a gesture to the Parisian authorities." To this Breuer responds with the most important statement about collective authorship in the entire episode: "I would not like to be responsible for that quarter curve. Not only the Paris authorities should act as our critics but also our friends and our students, other architects, ourselves."

At this moment, when the language of moral responsibility threatens to creep into the discussion, Lúcio Costa suggests a "change of shape" and proposes an asymmetrical Y that more or

92

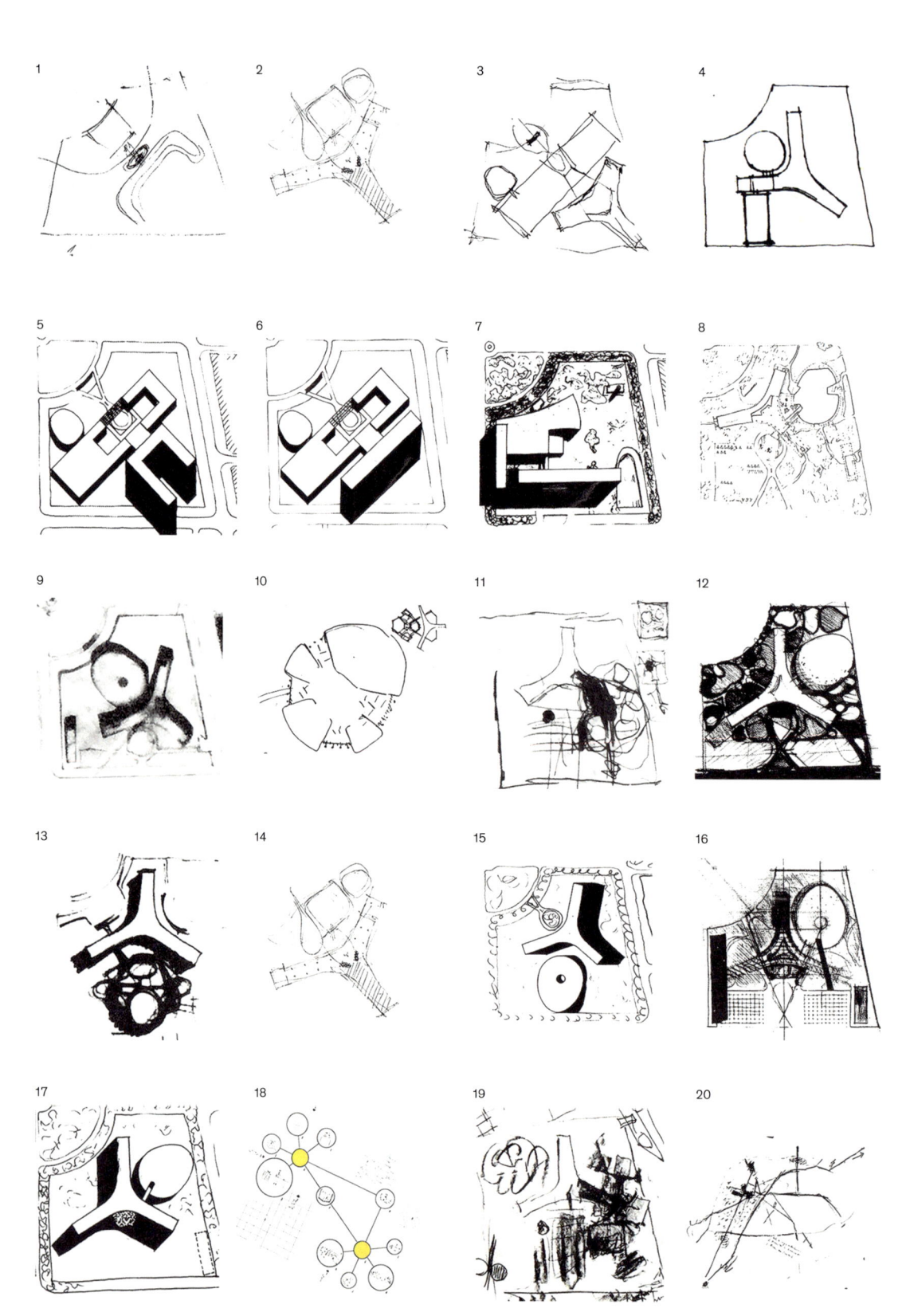

Architecture and Mediocracy at UNESCO House

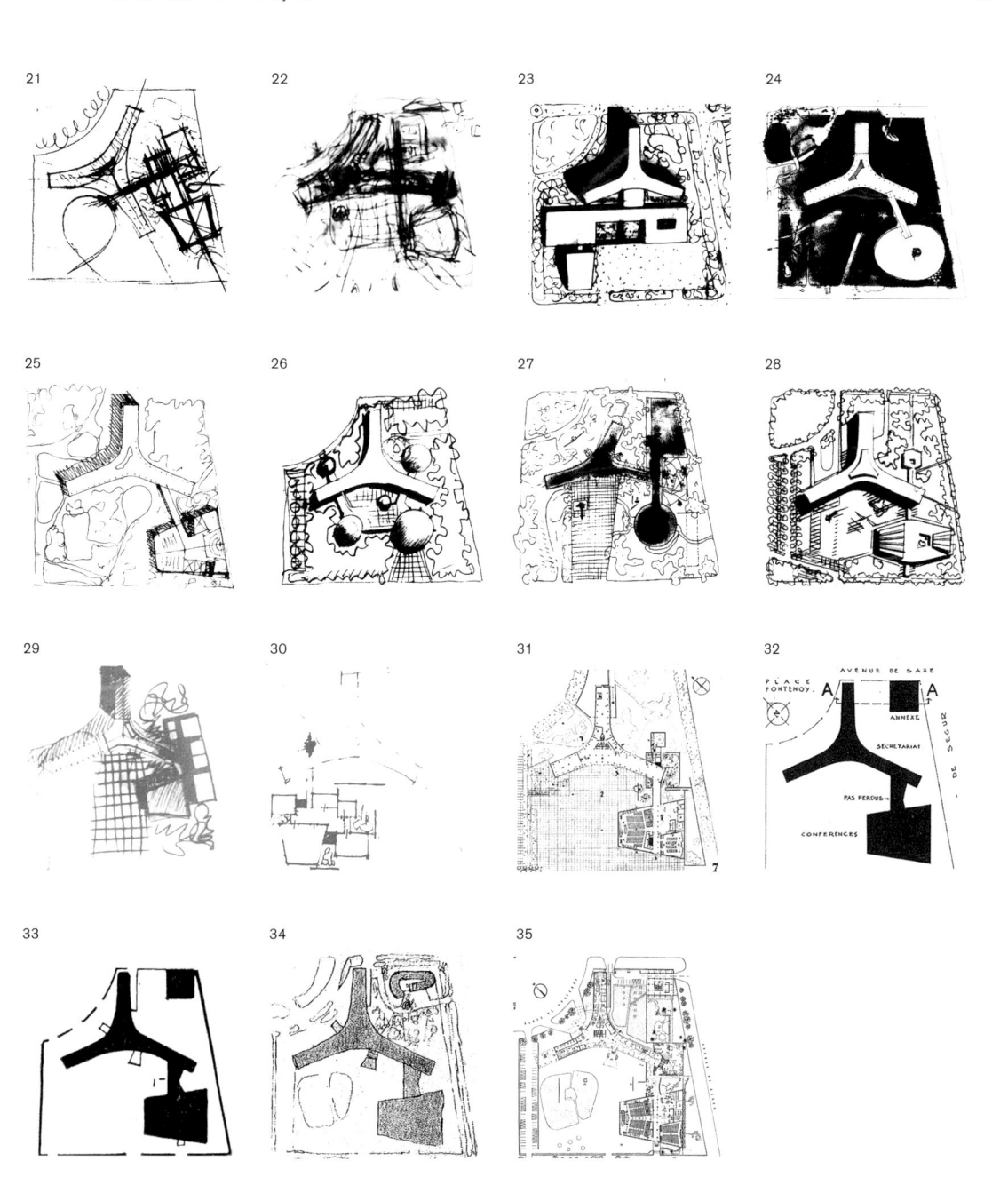

10.1–35 Sequence of sketches made by "the Three" and "the Five" during the three-day working session in Paris in February 1953

less follows the curve *but also* addresses the south [10.21]. He suggests relocating the Conference Building to the southernmost corner, concentrating the rest of the mass in a barbell scheme to the north. Le Corbusier is elated—"Costa found the solution"—but Breuer protests that he has already tried something similar and that the corridors are too long and the site plan inefficient [10.22]. Still, over his objections the group endorses the plan and assigns Zehrfuss the task of drafting it, with help from Nervi, before adjourning for a visit to Le Corbusier's studio. "It ruins the office building," Breuer confesses in private. Saarinen agrees: the Costa scheme is "hopeless," but "one thing [is] good in it: Couldn't we put the Egg in the south section?"

That evening, three parallel design efforts are set in motion [10.23]. Breuer works on relocating the Conference Building to the south corner: first as an egg, then as a trapezoid [10.24-25]. Meanwhile, Saarinen sketches a scheme in which some of the bulk of the assembly building is taken out to an annex building that "balances the composition" [10.26]. All the while, Nervi and Zehrfuss continue to formalize the Costa solution, which is then presented first thing the next day [10.27].

Everyone agrees that the result is completely unworkable. Costa complains that his scheme is "unrecognizable." The office building, Breuer concludes, "is bastardized." Once attention is turned to Breuer's sketches [10.28], everyone agrees the new assembly building location is good, although Le Corbusier finds it too big and asks that it be "exploded" once more. The rest of the afternoon is spent watching Le Corbusier draw this explosion [10.29]. Breuer helps, offering a patio-like garden turned toward the Suffren avenue side [10.30]. But in the evening, after Le Corbusier has gone, a smaller group resolves to make a proposal to UNESCO, using a combination of Corbusier's "exploded composition" and Breuer's trapezoidal assembly building [10.31]. The next day the proposal is presented to the Parisian authorities, then to the UNESCO planning committee, and it is accepted by both.

In the immediate aftermath of this design meeting, the tenuous agreement is maintained just long enough for the Three and the Five to produce a final report for the General Assembly. The basic site plan changes little. To address what Gropius called the "paralyzing space-effect," dramatic concrete canopies are added at the entrances [10.32].[37] To address Le Corbusier's concern about the connection between the volumes, the lobby is reshaped and set against a small garden, and the annex is moved to the north corner of the site [10.33]. Le Corbusier makes a last attempt to shape this annex into a spiraling lobe but fails [10.34]. At this point, the scheme is made public [10.35].

The point of recalling the design process in this manner is not to detect individual authorship for each specific design move; on the contrary, it is to witness a gradual *de-authoring* of form. Given the strong personalities involved and the strident opinions voiced, this de-authoring is not immediately obvious. Breuer's memo seems to introduce a battle of wills about the meaning of curvature. At first glance there appear to be only two positions available: contextualist ("the curvature ... pays deference to the past") and typological ("the curved negative corners were *not* designed [to] complete the semi-circle").[38] But by looking more closely at these drawings we find a multivocal and multilayered conversation. In the margins of the plan sketches, various hands have quickly drawn elevations in a graphic conversation between formal signatures: Breuer's filleted corners, Le Corbusier's spiral, Costa's shallow arcs, Saarinen's spheres, Zehrfuss's parabolas. In a sense the curves drawn by each hand articulate an individual position and can even be connected to other buildings in each architect's oeuvre. An exchange at the opening of the meeting confirms that the very use of the pen was perceived as permission to have a literal hand in the design: Le Corbusier asked if he was "authorized to use a pencil and paper as a means of discussion" and Breuer acquiesced: "We, the team, want to have an exchange of opinions. I don't see why not with pencil on paper."[39] This transnational battle of personal design signature also echoed a stylistic debate that was occurring across the world, especially in Latin America, about the increasing use of undulating and curvilinear modernism made possible by reinforced concrete.[40] But not all curves in these drawings belong in this gestural register. There are also conventional curves: the building is sometimes shaped into a human isotype with raised arms; Costa's massing echoes the shape of the Eiffel Tower. And a curved line that resembles an unfinished infinity sign, representing a car drop-off, pushes the building into its curvature from the south, where no such line exists in the urban fabric itself.

The graphic negotiation on the page, in other words, concerns not only *what* to design but also *how*. The site begins as a broad swath traversed by cardinal points, then becomes a restricted field of action, bounded by toxic adjacencies. The form shrinks to the center, and only then do adjustments begin. What begins as a problem of geometry morphs into a problem of typology, and it eventually becomes a question of figuring, of bending a thickened mass and its various appendages. In what follows, I suggest that the design process was a debate about literal and figural bending: what to bend, how, and how far.

Bending
Bending is a useful term for explaining the schematic phase of the UNESCO design because it operates on multiple registers. Its first valence is of course formal. In plan, the Y-building is bent, one of the walls of the lobby is bent, and in section the butterfly roof of the Conference Building repeats this bending horizontally. These formal bends also produce a perceptual bending. Across the site the visitor's visual horizon is caught and bent along the edges of the form, alternatively enclosing the view or chasing the eye: toward the Eiffel Tower, around the winged concrete canopies, down the tapered pillars, and up the spiraling staircase.

p. 72/10, 11

There is also a moral dimension to bending, which emerges from the intense discussions surrounding the commission: the combined language of moral rectitude, formal rigidity, and ethical responsibility, all married to a sense of historical weight—for example, Giedion's sense that the UNESCO commission was a "test of moral strength" and "inner integrity" for the modern movement itself.[41] Bending is a way to talk about how these external pressures were internalized by architects, especially Breuer, whether or not they used the term specifically in their contentious exchanges.[42] Recall how Breuer reported his reply to Le Corbusier's contextualist concessions. He used a language of culpability (asking not to be held "responsible for that quarter curve") but also denied caving in to an opposing force ("the Parisian authorities"). Instead he invoked an internal integrity motivated by an accumulated and collective architectural superego ("our friends, our students, other architects, ourselves"). This internalizing impulse also led Breuer to ventriloquize each of his colleagues in his peculiar memo, as if to absorb their positions before adjusting his own. Bending describes the accommodation of a person trying to retain integrity while also reacting to an external force field.

Lastly, there is also a broader political charge to the word *bending*, connected to the fact that one of UNESCO's main cultural missions in the 1950s was to humanize bureaucracy itself. As one retrospective analysis put it, UNESCO had the rare quality among all other international organizations of being *both* intellectually flexible *and* politically progressive.[43] This feature reflected its weakness as a specialized UN agency, but from the outside, once this cultural flexibility was seen to inhere into its architecture, the building's bendable plan became attractive as a headquarters type for bureaucracies of all kinds, whether corporate, governmental, or nongovernmental, precisely because it could appear more malleable and less orthodox—more like UNESCO.

The manifold resonances of bending put particular pressure on Breuer's role in the collaboration. Breuer's understanding of bending as an operation that determines the authorship, ownership, and originality of a design standard was colored by his previous experience with the development of the "cantilever chair" in the 1930s, one of the most iconic design standards to have come out of mid-century European modernist circles. It was the furniture company Thonet, which specialized in bent wood, that first used the language of bending in chair design, advertising the feat of manipulating a material that did not want to bend: wood.[44] Bending was a material process, but its use in certain hands could register a particular signature—and thus make designs available to claims of authorship. Thus Thonet was one of the first companies to copyright its chair designs. In the late 1920s, this material bending became more audacious: not only wood but also steel was bent by furniture designers, and in the switch from wood to steel, bending became more than an assertion of will over material. The cantilever chair in particular appeared to let the body float in space with no support from back legs, and it did so with a single continuous bending steel pipe. As such, it exemplified the corporeal disciplining of the hand of the designer through "the line," a method that pervaded design and art education at the turn of the twentieth century. But now this personal act of internalization was also externalized, as if, by drawing a line on a piece of paper, the designer had materialized a body in space.[45]

If the form of the cantilever chair seemed to express human mastery over raw materials and human behavior, the industrial production of the chair complicated the question of how this human creative gesture should be credited. Breuer was the first to license and mass-produce a line of cantilever chairs for Thonet, but two other designers had produced a cantilever design first: Mart Stam and Mies van der Rohe. Breuer's design was the third.[46] As various companies sought to patent the design and fought various legal battles over its authorship, the "bending" method (explicitly named as such) used in each chair became a litmus test of whether design was to be considered a technology or a craft. If the chair was deemed "crafted," its form would matter to its authorship; if it was a technology, it was its resilience—its ability to bend—that would

11 Two sides of a sketch: for Stuyvesant Six housing (L) and the profile for the "Geller chair" (R)
12 Sketch for Stuyvesant Six
13 Detail sketch for a bending corridor in Stuyvesant Six

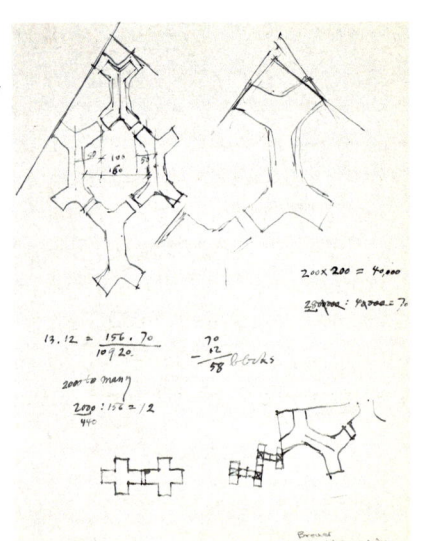

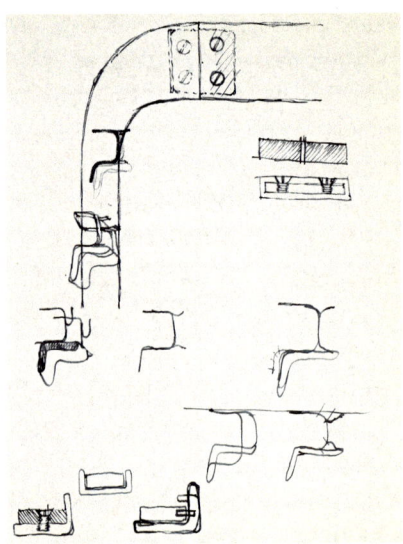

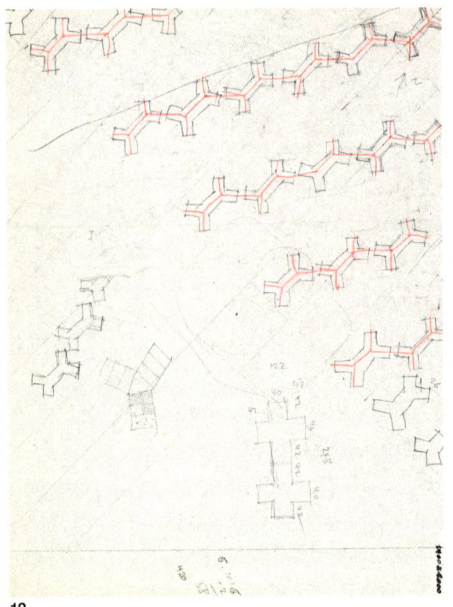

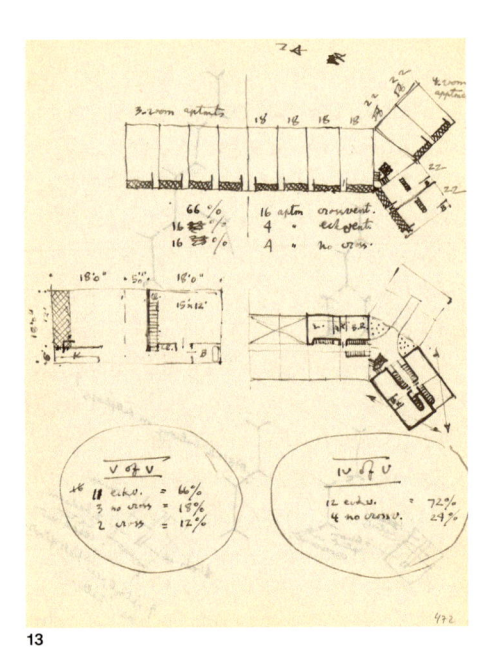

determine its novelty. In neither case would the personal signature of the designer alone matter. Indeed, Thonet was able to produce a design of Breuer's because, for a period of time, it was deemed to be the same as the one designed by Stam, which, by visual standards alone, was recognizably different.[47] The cantilever chair, in other words, helped give birth to a new kind of design-author.

The significance of this precedent for UNESCO House can be grasped very quickly from one sheet of sketches from 1944, where Breuer connected the bending of a chair to the bending of a Y-shaped building [11]. On one side, the sheet contains plan sketches for Stuyvesant Six—the housing proposal with a branching pattern of Y-shaped housing towers. Although each tower is a separate object, Breuer conceived of them as traversed by a continuous line, abutting each Y to one another. By a fortuitous coincidence, a drawing has shown through from the other side of the sheet at exactly the center of one of these Stuyvesant Ys: a profile of the Geller chair, a wood variation of the bent cantilever chair Breuer was also designing. On the recto, a material is bent into a chair; on the obverse, a plan pattern is bent into a housing scheme. That this line is "bent" rather than "broken" is suggested by two accompanying sheets: one on which Breuer has drawn the corridor as a single red line, threaded continuously from Y to Y, and another, on which he has drawn an enlarged plan of a curving corridor at its core—an anticipation of the one he would eventually build at UNESCO [12,13]. In other words, Breuer had already worked out here the bending device that would make the Y an innovative space-saving plan in UNESCO House years later. At every branching off of this "red thread" in the housing, we can imagine the bending elbow of a chair and the core of a UNESCO Y.

The point is not that the Y of UNESCO House should be attributed to Breuer alone. The point is that the bending at the scale of the building was a reinvention of modernist bending at the scale of the chair and that this reinvention further distanced the idea of bending from a direct, material gesture, thus opening the way for a proliferation of experiments for indirect design control. Furniture could control a body's position, designers could control the process of material assembly, and now modern architecture could control social behaviors through the design of a housing pattern for the first "function" of the modern city according to CIAM: "living." UNESCO House, then, appears as a third step in this progression from bending a material to bending a double-loaded corridor, with the urban function being manipulated no longer "living" but "work".

14 *Pas-perdus* at the League of Nations (top L), the United Nations (bottom L), and UNESCO House (R)

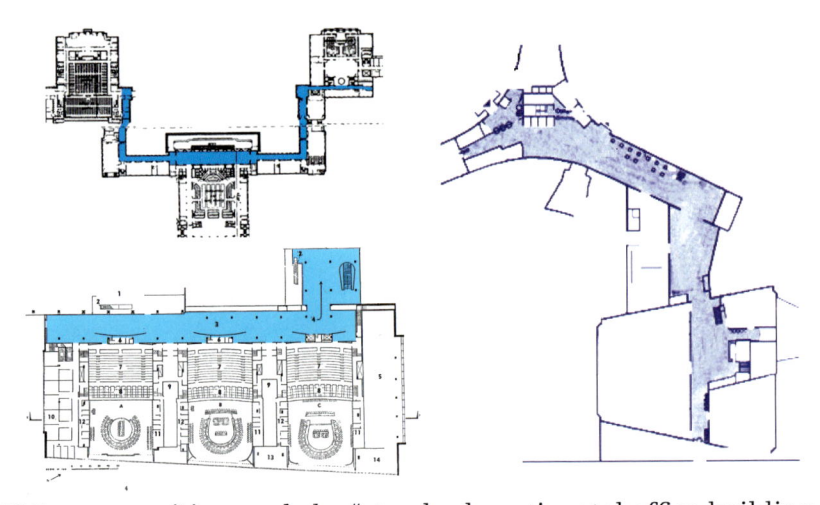

If European cities needed a "standard continental office building type" in 1953, it is because the postwar reorganization of labor mobilized increasing portions of western European society for the needs of administrative work.[48] The UNESCO corridor is loaded not with apartments but with offices, and in the schematic design set the building is even drawn as an empty tube, to be filled with a "typical" detail.[49] On the ground level, public space is conceived as a spine bent around two nodal points. This public space, named the *pas perdus* in reference to French palace architecture, had been a feature of international diplomatic institutions since the end of World War I. In the League of Nations, the corridor snaked its way at 90-degree angles; in the UN it was segmented. At UNESCO, the *pas perdus* was reinvented as a pliable spine, weaving a public promenade across the site [14].

p. 69/6

Expanding our understanding of bending as a design operation returns us to the unique features of bureaucracy as an architectural program. Building on Foucault's work, historians and theorists of bureaucracy have argued that the postwar triumph of the "bureaucratic phenomenon" was predicated on the fact that control systems were being increasingly *removed from* that which they actually control, into separate bureaucracies. Indeed, bureaucracies reward not behavior relevant to the task that has to be performed (in the case of the United Nations agencies, what Mark Mazower has called "governing the world") but behavior relevant to the control system itself.[50] In this light, the transfer of design control to Breuer as both a designer of forms and as the manager of an architectural team appears to offer exactly the kind of "link" between process and product that mid-century architectural critics were looking to identify—and it provides the seed for a theory of an "architecture of mediocracy."

Not a Formula but a Function

UNESCO House was designed and built in a period when "cooperation" in international organizations was a concept in flux. After the perceived failure of the League of Nations, the United Nations system had been designed in the 1940s to advance international cooperation through specific projects, rather than diplomacy alone.[51] Specialized agencies such as UNESCO were assigned a certain "function" because, as the political theorist David Mitrany has put it, "sovereignty cannot be transferred effectively through a formula, only through a function ... by entrusting an authority with a certain task."[52] Accordingly, the United Nations often abandoned the analogy with a parliament and adopted instead a "makerly" language, calling itself a system of "workshops for the world."[53] Already in the 1940s, one of the favorite models for the "functionalization" of world politics was the Tennessee Valley Authority. UNESCO's first director-general, Julian Huxley, even vaunted the TVA's architectural detailing as evidence that the architect was the "great humanizer" of the modern period.[54] But UNESCO's function was somewhat vague and controversial. For much of the 1940s, Huxley referred to its mission as "propaganda." In a 1947 manifesto, he recommended, with surprising candor, taking the "techniques of persuasion and propaganda" developed during the war and "bending them to the international task of peace, if necessary utilizing them, as Lenin envisaged, to overcome the resistance of millions to desirable change" [1].[55]

Architecture was incorporated into this communications paradigm from the start. In 1946, the General Assembly adopted a logo that turned the acronym UNESCO into a classical temple's colonnade. But this appeal to architectural permanence combined with electronic imagery; a 1948 illustration, for instance, turned the temple into a communications hub by presenting it as a node in a network of wired pedestals [15]. Architecture's broadcasting powers also permeated the lavish photo-essays through which UNESCO popularized its work for preserving architectural heritage in this period. A 1954 cover story of the *UNESCO Courier*, "S.O.S. from the Past: Saving Our Heritage in Stone," featured a Roman theater sending out an "SOS" and the minarets of Damascus telling "stories in stone." Those buildings were ancient monuments with deep architectural histories, but they were also early modern broadcasting stations [16].[56]

By the middle of the 1950s, the prevailing hope that wireless mass communication would create more pliable international minds had given way to a much more embodied notion of interna-

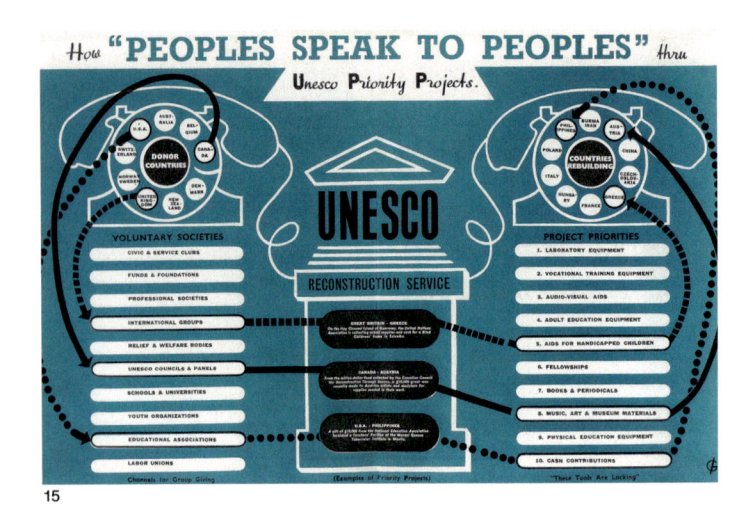

15 How "Peoples Speak to Peoples," UNESCO graphic from 1948
16 "Save Our Heritage in Stone," *UNESCO Courier* 7, no. 7, 1954
17 Diagram of specialized agencies, from *Workshops for the World,* New York, 1954. Highlighting added: "International Bodies Concerned with Technical Assistance," from Margaret Mead, ed., *Cultural Patterns and Technical Change,* Paris, 1953

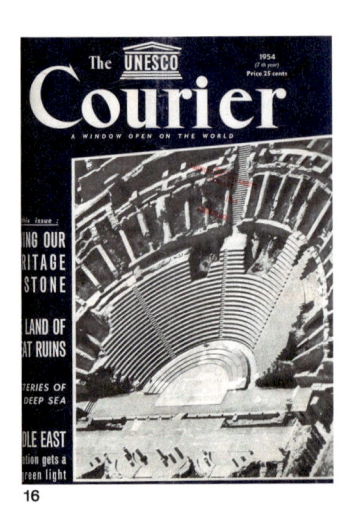

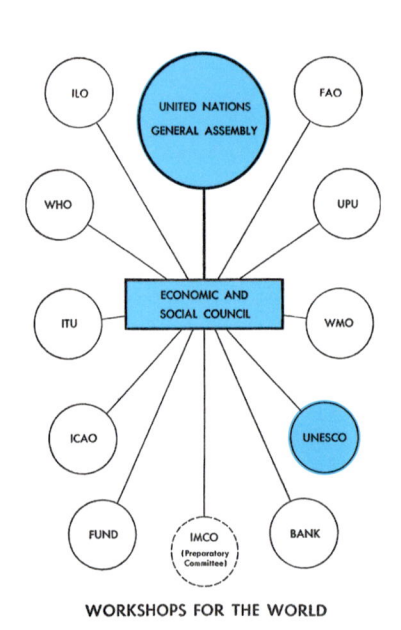

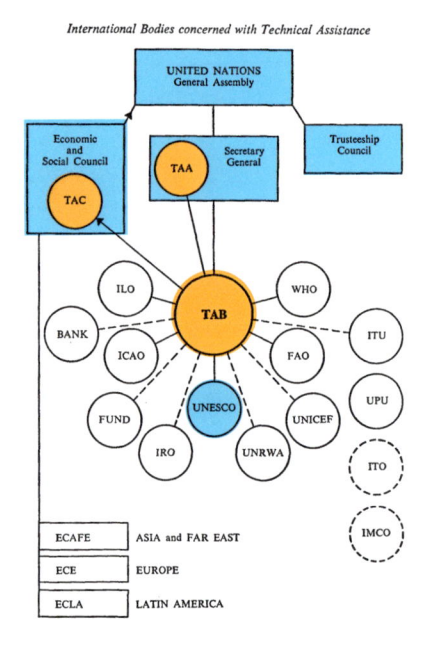

tional power. Beginning in 1954, a new focus on technique asked each UN member organization to report its financial needs to the General Assembly through a separate body, the Technical Assistance Administration (TAA). A fundamental indirectness was therefore introduced into all UN specialized agencies [17]. Technical assistance was the kind of aid that could be disbursed as technological know-how and hands-on training, and it was the main driver of the development economics that began to dominate UN cooperation during the decolonization of the Global South and that greatly accelerated after 1960.[57] But already in the 1950s, this technical turn shifted UNESCO's mission from sending messages to defining the medium of their transmission.

In its effort determine how its various programs could get more "technical," UNESCO increasingly concerned itself with studying "culture" as a means rather than an end. Social scientists were the main source of advice to internationalists who wondered how "culture" could contribute to ongoing United Nations development projects. Most famously perhaps, UNESCO's social science division enlisted the American anthropologist Margaret Mead to edit a volume, *Cultural Patterns and Technical Change*, which popularized the notion that it was possible, with the proper input from social scientists, to upgrade a country's large-scale technical systems without radical rupture or revolution, as long as one could diagnose certain cultural patterns and gradually modify them.[58] For Mead, behavior was a kind of message itself, passed down from generation to generation. Thus, in order to "shape new developments," experts required not only technical skills but also a worldview whereby "a culture is a systematic and integrated whole, … an abstraction from the body of learned behavior which a group of people … share … and transmit."[59] This discourse of technical aid adapted the earlier language of "persuasion" and "transmission," but, instead of minds, cultural action would target bodily comportment.[60] Technicality as an international program, then, spanned from the individual body to large-scale infrastructure. For example, the same issue of the *Courier* that showcased the architectural heritage of the Middle East also spotlighted technical aid in education and physical planning in the region.[61] A photographic essay showed how people there collected water from a well, and it assured readers that these methods had been studied in order to be able teach the people how to build a dam. The people were photographed ethnographically in a way that echoed Mead's attention to daily habits; the dams were photographed architecturally,

18 Representations of technical assistance in UNESCO literature. Photographs from George Fradier, "Green Light for Education," *UNESCO Courier* 7, no. 7, 1954

exuding an infrastructural mood that echoed earlier enthusiasms for the TVA [18].

The apparent gap between these two architectural modes we have seen UNESCO deploy in its technical mission so far—buildings as heritage and buildings as megastructure—was crucially bridged with appeals to architectural historicity. Consider, for instance, the recommendations that were made by the team of heritage specialists who traveled to the Middle East in 1953 to offer advice on the modernization of historic cities in Syria and Lebanon. The single most common recommendation they gave was not that monuments should be preserved one by one but that a narrative sequence should be designed to link them all together, with a highway, that paradigmatic tool of infrastructural development [19].[62] To transform the archaeological town of Baalbek, for instance, experts from UNESCO's Museums and Monuments Committee modified a Haussmannian plan, proposed by the Swiss architect Ernst Egli, that would have connected the monuments via axial perspectives and roundabouts. Instead, they worked with Lebanon's director of antiquities to propose a plan that would bend the roadways and bypass the buildings through lateral views. Similarly, in the Lebanese coastal town of Tripoli a sequence of monuments would be approachable by a highway that bent in plan *and* in section, through a tunnel piercing under and around the city's monumental core.

The architecture of UNESCO's headquarters, built only a few years later, echoes this heritage work in unexpected but important ways. Like the highways of Tripoli and Baalbek, UNESCO House was designed from the start to bend around the monumental pattern of Paris. Sketches of the city that were included in both the

19 Proposed tunnel and urban plan for the Lebanese coastal town of Tripoli. UNESCO, *Lebanon: Suggestions for the Plan of Tripoli and for the Surroundings of the Baalbek; Report of the UNESCO Mission of 1953*, Paris, 1954. Color added by the author

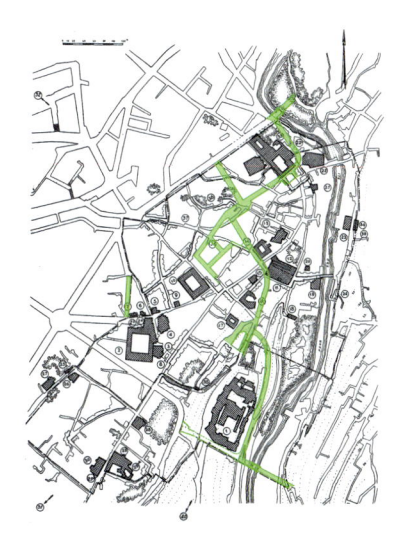

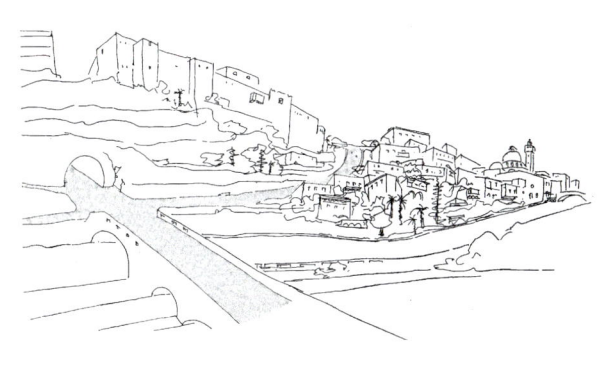

1952 and 1953 schematic sets show the city as an outline traversed by the Seine and punctuated by famous landmarks. Originally sketched by Le Corbusier during various design meetings, they belong in a lineage of Corbusian work in which he reduced the city's monumental sights to a series of "vignettes" [20].[63] But rather than rely on extensive demolition, now the UNESCO House would merely curate a sequence of sights.

p. 66/2

It may seem anathema to compare UNESCO's work for heritage preservation on the one hand with its crusade for a modernist headquarters on the other. But we should not let the apparent opposition between modernism and preservation fool us. UNESCO's heritage missions were not historicist but developmentalist—they emphasized a narrative of progress rather than a return to the past.[64] Indeed, they sought to transform historic city fabric into a series of discrete monumental nodes around which to weave a historical narrative. Similarly, the UNESCO House plan offered a sequence of historical sights. In the schematic design set, the École Militaire, which faced the Secretariat on the Place de Fontenoy, was described as "preserved and protected."[65] The roof garden of the Secretariat was designed to frame views of the Eiffel Tower and the dome of Les Invalides, becoming one of the best places from which to photograph monumental Paris.[66] Photographs of the Secretariat's construction also highlighted the infrastructural connotations of its forms, making the UNESCO building look like a dam or a highway: a piece of architectural technology delivering change. The Conference Building was also treated as a separate piece of modern architecture. Lewis Mumford was so convinced of its formal independence that he wrote a separate review of what he called a "hidden treasure." Partially tucked away, and to be discovered along the site's infrastructural spine, the Conference Building's "Egyptianizing" trapezoidal geometry seemed to make it a building designed in a former age, despite its brutalist facture.[67]

p. 77/19

Yet, unlike a highway in Lebanon, the UNESCO House was not an actual instrument of urban planning or development; it was a training ground for the cultural aspects of development economics. After all, the main audience and constituency for this alignment between the narrative of development and architectural

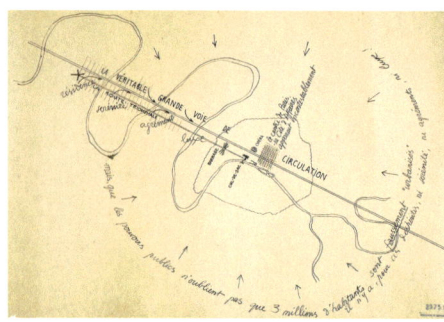

20 "Le Plan de Paris 37" (L), published in *Le Corbusier à Paris: Essai sur une esthétique de l'architecture*, Lyon, 1987, p. 125, labeled FLC 29751, and (R) "Ça c'est Paris!" in *Précisions*, Paris, 1930

historicity was not a tourist but the UNESCO bureaucrat. What, then, of the UNESCO House as a workplace? How was it experienced as daily destination by the office worker, as conference location for the visiting consultant, and occasional ceremonial site for invited heads of state? If their collective goal was to make "rules for the world," how did modern architecture contribute to their task?[68] An investigation of the last phase of the headquarters' design offers the beginning of an answer, highlighting a "technical turn" of a different kind that was produced by the design team during the final detailing of the building complex itself.

The View from Everywhere
The technical turn that I have been describing began to pervade international institutions at the same moment as the UNESCO House design was passed into the hands of a new team—Nervi, Zehrfuss, and Breuer, or BNZ—a team that was, unlike the ad hoc committee of the first phase, fashioned explicitly as a technocratic alliance. BNZ was an architectural bureaucracy in the strict sense Hitchcock intended, with members offering different strengths: Breuer as architect, Nervi as engineer, and Zehrfuss as project manager. When BNZ officially took over the commission, they immediately set to fleshing out the project that the "Five" had helped them work out in only the broadest terms. All of their detailing efforts were geared toward resolving the experience of the building from up close and from afar. Breuer, especially, developed a discourse about the role of the technical detail in design thinking that echoes Mead's ideas about cultural integration in development—namely, that small-scale patterns and details are bearers of large-scale historical change.

Breuer wrote about architecture as channeling long-term forces; he insisted on granting cultural importance to apparently purely technological or tectonic achievement. The ambition of all design, he wrote in *Sun and Shadow*, should not be "passing success" but "historic achievement … long-range improvement, and long-range progress."[69] To that end, he declared himself to be on a search for "demonstrative architectural form" on a par with the classical orders. Inventions such as the solar "glass" that he would use on the south façade of the UNESCO building were to be "guarded as the new great achievement of an open architecture." Of the sun-shade he developed for the complex, he confidently predicted it would become "as characteristic a form as the Doric column." And yet despite this search for new cultural form, what Breuer thought should be displayed was technicality itself (as a means), rather than structural achievement (as an end in itself). "Everybody is interested in seeing what makes a thing work," he wrote, but there was such as thing as "excessive structural exhibitionism."[70] The Secretariat's façades, then, offered Breuer the chance to demonstrate the cultural importance of technical control and calibration at both scales.

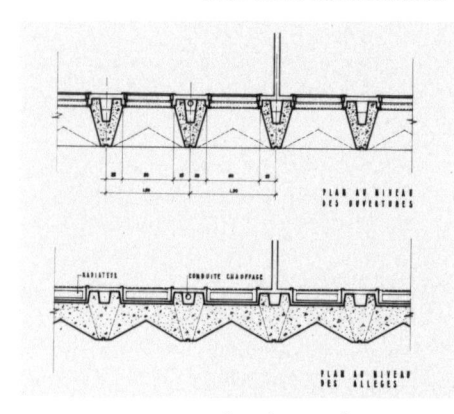

The question of how to provide equal space and a clear view to all offices on three façades with three curving exposures occupied Breuer for the better part of a year, and it led him to design three different details. On the north-facing side, a tapered concrete mullion expressed the compression of the bending concrete façade [21]. On the other two façades, a much more intricate contraption (a "sun control device") was required. It consisted of two parts— a horizontal concrete brise-soleil built above the window to break the incoming sunlight, and a vertical panel of solar glass hung out in front of the façade to cool the rays before they hit the building. Breuer called them the *eyelid* and the *sunglasses*, to convey that they were not adornments but prostheses: integrated into the structure and, in turn, necessary to integrate the façade into the context by reflecting the "grey panorama of Paris".[71] As a technical creation to be looked *at* and *through*, the sun control device performed an architectural demonstration of the kind of technical task that UNESCO's employees were asked to perform: accommodation, variation, and, ultimately, behavior modification.

21 Northern façade mullion detail

p. 71/9

p. 70/8

Breuer also used the language of accommodation to talk about the integrity of the designer and especially to applaud Nervi's pliability as a collaborator. "Nervi showed unusual elasticity in our contact," he said in 1959, "far from the passive elasticity of those structural consultants who put a beam under wherever a load appears."[72] Nervi's "genius," according to Breuer, was the ability to "participate in the continuous search for a system." And indeed, Nervi fashioned himself in the tradition of the much-admired anonymous TVA designers. For example, describing in a lecture a drawing of all the different faceted *pilotis* he had designed in various buildings, including UNESCO's, he wrote that leaving "ridges" in the formwork allowed him to visualize aesthetic variation within technical constraints. Such ridges, he wrote, expressed both "the laws of structure" and an engineer's "personal choice" [22].[73] He also drew a scale figure among all these columns,

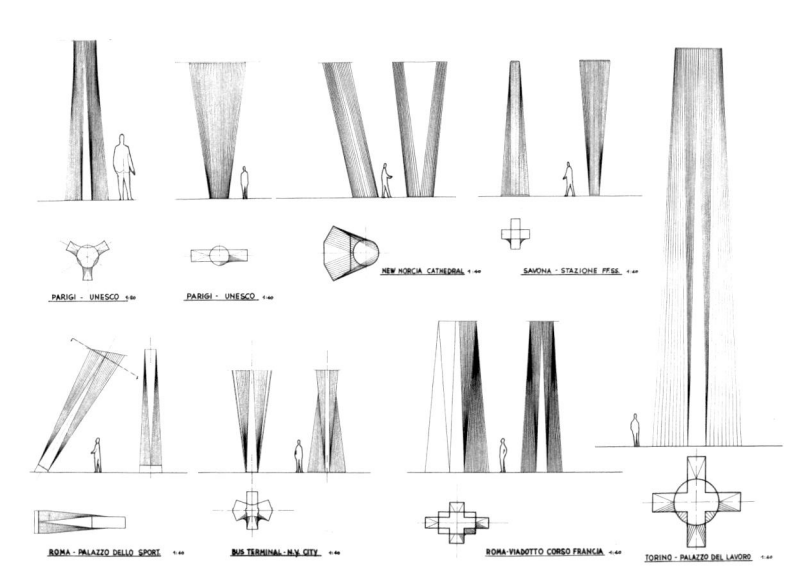

22 Pier Luigi Nervi, column details, featuring UNESCO Headquarters columns

as if to show that the architectural public was supposed to learn from this self-control by looking directly at the architecture.

Breuer's control devices and Nervi's humanizing details were clearly complementary, and detecting how these two intermingled throughout the complex provides an apt conclusion to our investigation of how the UNESCO House helped to produce a new, composite, "author function" in mid-century architecture. The entire building can be seen as a study in the contrasts and affinities between bending (a long-standing Breuer concern) and folding (usually attributed to Nervi).[74] At the scale of the entire building complex, bending and folding interact most importantly in the relation between the Conference Building and the Secretariat, which, as we have seen, is similar to that between a highway and a landmark viewed in passing along that highway. At the scale of the Conference Building itself, folding gives a plane stability and bending tests this rigidity. In the famous sectional perspective of the main auditorium space, one cut shows a corrugated folded ceiling hovering over the delegates, while the transverse cut reveals each corrugation to be a broad curve that directs their eyes toward the stage.[75]

The division of labor between bending and folding speaks to the two kinds of efficacies that architecture was expected to perform in the mid-century, demonstrating an "operationality" both discreet and far-reaching, authored yet bureaucratic. A folded plane is segmented whereas a bent surface is potentially smooth; it does not always reveal what technique has been used in its making. In other words, unlike folding, bending is a formal effect whose source, or origin point, or *author*, can be remote and invisible. Thus, a bureaucrat sitting in an office along a bent façade could look out the window and imagine controlling something far, far away. In this sense the façade offered the bureaucrat what Perrin Selcer has called "the view from everywhere"—UNESCO's unique brand of social-scientific objectivity.[76] Folding, on the contrary, is visible; indeed, Bernhard Siegert has argued that a fold is always *of* the visual field, as if a folded surface always evoked the hinge of a door to be opened.[77] The same bureaucrat, then, looking at a concrete ridge or a sun-control shade, would also see an architectural version of the role that person must perform as part of the job: to operate within a limited, technically determined range of action. The result of this combination was an architecture that visualizes anchored variation, establishing rules and giving them limited flexibility. To users and visitors alike, UNESCO House gave the impression that small, authored, local changes would have large, and de-authored, collective effects.

Conclusion: Abstracting

UNESCO House was designed at a critical moment in architectural history, when anxieties about modernism had come to an irrevocable head and bureaucratic rule-making had begun to preside over the creation of architectural forms. Its bending and folding architecture hit a note that resonated on multiple levels: with the historical self-consciousness of architects; with narratives of economic development; with the formal capacities of reinforced concrete; with the contextualist pressures put on modernism; and with the bureaucratic phenomenon as a whole, which plied people into routine behaviors and provoked imperceptibly gradual historical change.

But the final design, as this chapter has shown, was also highly original and novel in many aspects. Why, then, was it received as a disappointment? Largely because it was expected to be original, *like a work of art, or literature*. Even UNESCO vaunted the star power of its architectural team, in a commemorative special issue of the *Courier* that presented the group as an exceptional assortment of creative individuals under the label "UNESCO House Is Their Handiwork!"[78] Yet, if UNESCO championed individual creativity in other ways, for example, by promoting international laws to protect the copyrights of artists and authors, as we have seen in the case of its headquarters, the rhetoric of genius was just that—rhetoric.

I want to conclude, then, by revisiting the critical reception of the building complex in light of the discourse on the death of the author. What if the succession of critics who rushed to dismiss the project's middling mediocrity had fundamentally misunderstood the power that UNESCO invested in architecture? Take the analogy between architecture and language. In most of its activities UNESCO emphasizes not the substance of a message but the means of its conveyance.[79] The same issue of the *Courier* vaunted the modern art strewn about the site as speaking "the language of abstract art."[80] But closer scrutiny of the organization's work in the social and library sciences reveals it more commonly defined abstraction not as an aesthetic movement but as a stage in information processing.[81] For example, the institution led the charge in standardizing various processes—such as "abstracting" and "indexing"—through which scientific information can be reduced and disseminated globally.[82] These activities point us to a different valence of the word *mediocracy*: not "rule by the mediocre" but ruling through media, medium, or mediation.

By paying attention to the visual material produced for the inauguration of UNESCO House, we find innumerable instantiations of architecture as a communication device. A commemorative postcard depicts the complex as a piece of architectural circuitry laid upon the earth, with the Secretariat delaminating like a wire across the globe toward the Eiffel Tower [23]. The temple-front logo appears, but its classical symbolism pales in comparison with the operational power of this mediatic architecture. Similarly, the commemorative stamp on this postcard shows a bird's-eye view of the complex, with the Secretariat and Conference Building cartooned as prismatic objects, whose separation in space only facilitated their mechanical reproducibility, their miniaturization. Here, the much-critiqued site plan of UNESCO House becomes a graphic "abstract" of the city of Paris, which reduces certain formal and monumental features of the city and reproduces their essential core. In this media-informed sense, the architectural elements that stood separately from one another at the Fontenoy site were not fragments of a badly constructed sentence; they were packets of content waiting to be transmitted. Thus, Bruno Zevi's judgment that the building "strikes, but does not convince," is rendered moot: this architecture was not really supposed to "speak" to visitors, not even to translate among them—architecture here was not conceived as a language at all.[83]

23 Commemorative postcard for UNESCO House's dedication, November 1, 1958

The legacy of UNESCO House is not to have dealt a death blow to the modern architect as an author but to have offered architects an opportunity to occupy the breach opened up by this death.[84] The solution designed by Breuer and his collaborators emphasized process over any result. That is to say, UNESCO House was not a new creative expression of the kind an author protects with copyright, but rather an idea or a process of the kind patented by an inventor.[85] Like many other inventions, it was a deeply flawed prototype. But it has turned out to be remarkably productive of architectural dividends in the career of its authors and indeed of innumerable other architects and institutions since.

1 Ernesto N. Rogers, "Il dramma del palazzo dell'UNESCO," *Casabella Continuità* (April 1959): 2.
2 The *Oxford English Dictionary Online* (accessed September 2015) defines mediocracy as "government by the mediocre." Le Corbusier complained that UNESCO House demonstrated the "weakness and mediocrity" of all "globalizing enterprises." Quoted in Barbara Shapiro, *"Tout ça est foutaise, foutaise et demi!* Le Corbusier and UNESCO," *RACAR: Revue d'art canadienne / Canadian Art Review* 16, no. 2 (1989): 171–79, 298–307. Costa also claimed the design would "free UNESCO from the one-way street towards mediocrity." Lúcio Costa, "L'idea della curva," in "Testimonianze dei protagonisti," *Casabella Continuità* (April 1959): 6.
3 Henry-Russell Hitchcock, "The Architecture of Bureaucracy and the Architecture of Genius," *Architectural Review* (January 1947): 3–7.
4 Rogers, "Il dramma del palazzo dell'UNESCO," 4, 5.
5 Bruno Zevi, "I sei difetti del Palazzo dell' UNESCO a Parigi," *L'Architettura* 45, no. 3 (July 1959): 150–51.
6 Lewis Mumford, "UNESCO House: Out, Damned Cliché!" *New Yorker*, November 12, 1960, 113, 115, 119.
7 See Henri Stierlin, "Les organisations internationales et l'architecture: Un grand espoir," in *Werk*, no. 7 (1974): 821–67. On the League of Nations, see Stanislaus van Moos, "Kasino der Nationen," in *Werk-Archithese*, no. 23–24 (1978): 32–36. On the United Nations, see George Dudley, *A Workshop for Peace* (Cambridge, MA: MIT Press, 1994), and Victoria Newhouse, "The Battle of Designs," *Wallace K. Harrison, Architect* (New York: Rizzoli, 1989).
8 *Let's Visit UNESCO House!* (Paris: UNESCO, 1948). The various temporary locations to which the General Assembly traveled to hold its yearly conference, in Mexico City, Beirut, and Florence, each bore the name UNESCO Palace.
9 Michel Foucault, "What Is an Author?" (1969), trans. José Harari, in *Aesthetic, Method, Epistemology*, vol. 2, ed. James D. Faubion (New York: New Press, 1998), 209. See also Roland Barthes, "The Death of the Author" (1967), in *Image-Music-Text*, trans. Stephen Heath (New York: Hill & Wang, 1978), 143–48.
10 Giorgio Ciucci, "The Invention of the Modern Movement," *Oppositions* (April 1981): 68–91.

11 See Eric Mumford, *The CIAM Discourse on Urbanism* (Cambridge, MA: MIT Press, 2000), 12–13; and Joseph Vago, "Études pour la Société des Nations," *L'Architecture d'Aujourd'hui*, no. 8 (November 1931): 63–71.
12 Anne van der Goot, from UNESCO, attended the CIAM meeting in London in 1947, reporting that "CIAM will continue to be a body of a limited number of specialists, who will continue to be chosen on a selective basis." Van der Goot to CIAM, September 9, 1947, UNESCO/ 72 A 01 ICMA (henceforth UNESCO ICMA), UNESCO Archives. André Wogensky attended UNESCO's General Assembly as CIAM delegate in 1952. Giedion to Torres Bodet, November 13, 1952, E031, Josep Lluís Sert Collection, Harvard University Graduate School of Design Special Collections (henceforth, Sert GSD). Berto Lardera from the Arts and Letters section attended a special meeting of CIAM's executive committee. Berto Lardera to Carno, June 5, 1952, UNESCO ICMA.
13 Edward J. Carter to Giedion, November 20, 1946, UNESCO ICMA.
14 In 1950, UNESCO accredited both the CIAM and the UIA, arguing that CIAM would retain its "consultative status" and autonomy from the "somewhat bureaucratic and conservative opinions of national institutes of architecture." Torres Bodet to Sert, September 26, 1950, Sert Correspondence, Sert GSD.
15 As a member of UIA and CIAM, Gropius negotiated Le Corbusier's continued role. See Gropius to Sert, "Le Corbusier must [be] irrevocably excluded" (in deference to UNESCO's British national commission), November 9, 1952, CIAM Collection, Sert GSD. Le Corbusier continued to try to get the commission after the schematic design was approved. On July 25, 1953, he orchestrated a letter on CIAM stationery and signed by Gropius, Rogers, Sert, Pierre Emery, Wells Coates, and Sigfried Giedion, chiding Breuer, Zehrfuss, and Nervi for not attending the CIAM congress and reminding them that they "owed a moral obligation to the CIAM." E032, E005, CIAM Collection, Sert GSD.
16 Jaime Torres Bodet to Sert, December 10, 1951 (asking CIAM to suggest "four other consultant architects"), CIAM Collection, Sert GSD.
17 Le Corbusier to Howard Robertson, cited in Shapiro, *"Tout ça est foutaise,"* 175n22.

18 Gropius was the first to propose Breuer by way of a choice between Breuer and Sert. Gropius to Sert, November 9, 1952, CIAM Collection, Sert GSD.
19 Le Corbusier to Sert, October 27, 1952, Le Corbusier Research Collection, Sert GSD.
20 Emmanuel Devouge-Lamielle, "Ville et culture: Analyse du discours suscité par la création du siège de l'UNESCO à Paris" (master's thesis, Sorbonne, 1975), UNESCO Archives.
21 For comprehensive histories of the process, see Christopher Pearson, *Designing UNESCO* (London: Ashgate, 2010); Christine Desmoulins, *Le siège de l'UNESCO* (Paris: Éditions du patrimoine, 2016); Katrin Schwarz, *Bauen für die Weltgemeinschaft—Die CIAM und das UNESCO-Gebäude in Paris* (Berlin: De Gruyter, 2016); G. D. Growe, "The Paris UNESCO Complex," in *Marcel Breuer: Design and Architecture*, ed. Alexander von Vegesack and Mathias Remmele (Weil am Rhein: Vitra, 2002), 334; Barry Bergdoll, "Into the Fold: Breuer, Nervi and an Architecture for Assembly," in *Pier Luigi Nervi: Architecture as Challenge*, ed. Carlo Olmo and Cristiana Chiorino (Milan: Silvana, 2010), 87–115.
22 UNESCO, *Avant-Projet* (Paris, September 15, 1952): IId; UNESCO, *Avant-Projet Place de Fontenoy* (Paris, April 3, 1953) (henceforth, *Avant-Projet* 1953).
23 CIAM had grown from a small, prewar avant-garde to a larger, semiprofessional organization in the postwar period by abiding strictly to a system of regular critiques and using a "grid" of functions as graphic, conceptual, and organizational filter. On the grid, see Kees Somer, *The Functional City: The CIAM and Cornelis van Eesteren, 1928–1960* (Rotterdam: NAi, 2007); and Andreas Kalpakci, "Making CIAM: The Organizational Techniques of the Moderns" (PhD diss., ETH Zurich, 2017). Its membership had diversified and begun to fracture under the weight of a massive generational shift. On the generational split, see Marilena Kourniati, "L'autodissolution des CIAM," in *La Modernité critique*, ed. Jean-Lucien Bonillo, Claude Massu, and Daniel Pinson (Marseille: Éditions Imbernon, 2006), 62–75. Barry Bergdoll has also pointed to the generational dynamics of "the Three" in his essay "Into the Fold."
24 "[UNESCO] gave CIAM the first test to do *a real team job*, which is the way CIAM should work." Sert to Corbusier, November 5, 1952, CIAM Collection, Sert GSD (original emphasis). I borrow the "new monumentality" designation from Sigfried Giedion, Josep Lluís Sert, and Fernand Léger, "Nine Points on Monumentality" (1943), reprinted in Sigfried Giedion, *Architecture, You and Me* (Cambridge, MA: Harvard University Press, 1958).
25 These words were reported by Saarinen, who had consulted with Harrison on how to deal with "these complicated international jobs." Harrison, who led the design of the UN, replied that "the first goal to achieve is a building for UNESCO. The second goal is the finest possible piece of architecture." Saarinen to Howard Robertson, November 3, 1952, Marcel Breuer Papers, Archives of American Art, Smithsonian Institution (henceforth, Breuer Papers, AAA).
26 Gropius to Sert, November 9, 1952, CIAM Collection, Sert GSD. On TAC, see Michael Kubo, "The Concept of the Architectural Corporation," in *OfficeUS Atlas* (New York: Lars Müller, 2016), 37–45.
27 "Three Pointed Star Rises in Paris," *UNESCO Courier* (November 1958): 4. See also "From Slab to Y," *Time*, May 25, 1953, in which the director of the Detroit public library was said to have felt compelled to write Marcel Breuer to say he was "intrigued with the shape" and to ask if it could be called "trilobular."
28 Marcel Breuer, "To Articles, Jones," 5724, Breuer Papers, AAA.
29 On the Bauhaus workshops, see Barry Bergdoll and Leah Dickerman, eds., *Bauhaus, 1919–1933: Workshops for Modernity* (New York: MoMA, 2010).
30 See Magdalena Droste, "Marcel Breuer's Furniture," in *Marcel Breuer, Design*, ed. Magdalena Droste, Manfred Ludewig, Bauhaus-Archiv (Cologne: Benedikt Taschen, 1992), 7–35; and Isabelle Hyman, *Marcel Breuer: The Career and the Buildings* (New York: Abrams, 2001).
31 Marcel Breuer, "Stuyvesant Six: A Redevelopment Study," *Pencil Points* (June 1944): 66–70.
32 Giulio Carlo Argan noted this centrifugal anchoring and compared UNESCO's Y-plan to an industrial propeller, to give credit to Breuer alone by arguing he furnished the city as he would furnish a room. Giulio Carlo Argan, *Marcel Breuer: Disegno industriale e architettura* (Milan: Görlich, 1975), 72.
33 Jacques Gubler, *Jean Tschumi: Architecture at Full Scale* (Milan: Skira, 2008), 144–73; Nicole Staehli-Canetta and François Jolliet, "Jean Tschumi: Nestlé à Vevey," *AMC* 101 (October 1999): 68–73; Bruno Zevi, "Lo svizzero Jean Tschumi," *L'Espresso*, no. 61 (November 1960): 482–84.
34 Zevi, "Lo svizzero Jean Tschumi," 483–84.
35 "NATO Headquarters," *El Croquis* 131–32, OMA 1996–2006, 313–20.
36 Breuer noted it was "definitely not an exact quotation of what has been said by each participant but my interpretation as to the contents of the discussion." Marcel Breuer, "Place de Fontenoy Project: Discussions," February 9–13, 1953, including document labeled "Office Memo – Confidential," 5722, Breuer Papers, AAA. It should be noted that the drawings and sketches have been conserved apart from the memorandum, so the narrative offered here is necessarily provisional. (Unless otherwise indicated, all quotations pertaining to this project come from this document by Breuer.)
37 Gropius to BNZ, August 24, 1953, Breuer Papers, AAA.
38 Walter Gropius wrote, "The curvature of one of its fronts, pay[s] deference to the past. But the present (and the future) lie on the other side." This version is from "Annex III: Report of the International Panel of Five Architects to the Director-General concerning the Permanent Headquarters of UNESCO in Paris," 2 XC/ 3 Annex III, March 23, 1953, Breuer Papers, AAA. This division of front/back and past/future was suggested by Le Corbusier on March 23, 1953: "Rapport de Le Corbusier établi à la demande du 'Comité des 5' pour être soumis à l'Assemblée Générale par les soins du Président Walter Gropius, chargé de la rédaction décisive," 261932, Breuer Papers, AAA. Breuer

preferred a story of happy coincidence. "The curved negative corners," he wrote, were "not designed ... [to] complete the semi-circle of the place de Fontenoy," but the architects "were happy to discover that the form of the building could be used" for that purpose. Undated text in a folder labeled "To Articles, Jones," 5724, Breuer Papers, AAA.

39 Breuer, "Office Memo," 2.

40 See Barry Bergdoll, "Learning from Latin America," in *Latin America in Construction: Architecture, 1955–1980*, ed. Barry Bergdoll et al. (New York: MoMA, 2015), 23. The tendency to attribute the Y to Costa alone can be traced in part to this association of curves with Latin American modernism, though Costa himself took credit for "the curve." Costa, "L'idea della curva," 8.

41 Giedion to Rogers, June 17, 1953, CIAM Collection, Sert GSD.

42 One of the lessons of Foucault is surely that scholars need to heed words that remain unspoken in any discourse analysis. In his own words, "Historians have constantly impressed upon us that speech is no mere verbalization of conflicts and systems of domination; it is the very object of man's conflicts." Michel Foucault, "The Discourse on Language," appendix to *The Archaeology of Knowledge*, trans. A. M. Sheridan Smith (New York: Pantheon, 1972), 216.

43 Paul Graham Taylor and A. J. R. Groom, eds., *International Organization: A Conceptual Approach* (London: F. Pinter, 1978).

44 Alexander von Vegesack, *Thonet: Classic Furniture in Bent Wood and Tubular Steel* (London: Hazar, 1996). See also "Tubular Steel Furniture: Antecedents and Early History," *Journal of Design History* 3, nos. 2–3 (1990): 166–70; and Ariane Lourie Harrison, "Le Corbusier: Architect, Agent de Propaganda," *Perspecta* 45 (2012): 194–202.

45 Nicola Suthor, "Discipline as Emotion," in *The Power of Line*, ed. Gerhard Wolf and Marzia Faietti (Chicago: Hirmer, 2016), 54–71.

46 See Droste, "Marcel Breuer's Furniture"; Frederic J. Schwartz, "Marcel Breuer Club Chair," in *Bauhaus, 1919–1933: Workshops for Modernity*, ed. Bergdoll and Dickerman, 228–31. Giedion argued that these three chairs showed how a "standard form" had been dialectically "synthesized" in Sigfried Giedion, *Mechanization Takes Command: A Contribution to Anonymous History* (1948; New York: Norton, 1975), 479–508.

47 See Otakar Macel, "Avant-Garde Design and the Law: Litigation over the Cantilever Chair," *Journal of Design History* 3, nos. 2–3 (1990): 125–43; and Frederick Schwartz, "Utopia for Sale: The Bauhaus and Weimar Germany's Consumer Culture," in *Bauhaus Culture: From Weimar to the Cold War*, ed. Kathleen James-Chakraborty (Minneapolis: University of Minnesota Press, 2006), 126.

48 Michel Crozier, *The Bureaucratic Phenomenon* (Chicago: University of Chicago Press, 1964).

49 Le Corbusier, *The Athens Charter*, trans. Anthony Eardley (1943; New York: Grossman, 1973).

50 See Crozier, *Bureaucratic Phenomenon*; and Richard Edwards, *Contested Terrain: The Transformation of the Workplace in the Twentieth Century* (New York: Basic Books, 1979), 148, where Edwards states, "What distinguishes bureaucratic control from other control systems is that they contain incentives aimed at evoking the behavior necessary to make bureaucratic control succeed. It is this *indirect* path to the intensification of work, through the mechanism of rewarding behavior relevant to the control system, rather than simply to the work itself, that imposes the new behavior requirements on workers." A theoretical perspective is John O'Neill, "The Disciplinary Society from Weber to Foucault," *British Journal of Sociology* 37, no. 1 (March 1986): 42–60. See also Mark Mazower, *Governing the World: The History of an Idea* (New York: Penguin, 2012).

51 Recent histories of the League of Nations have distinguished its political "failure" to prevent war from its more lasting "technical" successes. Susan Pedersen, *The Guardians: The League of Nations and the Crisis of Empire* (Oxford: Oxford University Press, 2015); and Pederson, "Back to the League of Nations," *American Historical Review* 112, no. 4 (October 2007): 1091–117; Mark Mazower, *No Enchanted Palace: The End of Empire and the Ideological Origins of the United Nations* (Princeton: Princeton University Press, 2009); Peter Malanczuk, "Failure of the League System," *Akehurst's Modern Introduction to International Law*, 7th ed. (London: Routledge, 1997), 25.

52 David Mitrany, "A Working Peace System" (1943), in *Functional Theory of Politics*, (New York: St. Martin's Press, 1975), 118. See also Cornelia Navari, "Functional Internationalism," in *Thinkers of the Twenty Years' Crisis: Inter-War Idealism Reassessed*, ed. David Long and Peter Wilson (Oxford: Clarendon Press, 1995), 214–46.

53 Graham Beckel, *Workshops for the World: The United Nations Family of Agencies* (New York: Abelard-Schuman, 1954).

54 Julian Huxley, *TVA: Adventure in Planning* (London: Architectural Press, 1946), 94.

55 Julian Huxley, *UNESCO: Its Purpose and Philosophy* (Washington, DC: Public Affairs Press, 1948), 60.

56 "S.O.S. from the Past: Saving Our Heritage in Stone" and "Minarets of Damascus: Story in Stone," *UNESCO Courier* 7, no. 7 (1954): 4–19.

57 Technical assistance became a standard part of UNESCO's regular budget in 1954. On development, see Frederick Cooper and Randall Packard, eds., *International Development and the Social Sciences: Essays on the History and Politics of Knowledge* (Berkeley: University of California Press, 1997). See also Colin Leys, "The Rise and Fall of Development Theory," *The Anthropology of Development and Globalization: From Classical Political Economy to Contemporary Neoliberalism*, ed. Marc Edelman and Angelique Haugerud (Malden, MA: Blackwell, 2005), 109–25.

58 Margaret Mead, ed., *Cultural Patterns and Technical Change* (Paris: UNESCO, 1953).

59 For Mead, most "cultural forms" were not "flexible enough" to "protect and express all of the individual personalities." Mead, *Cultural Patterns and Technical Change*, 9.

60 For Mead's work on the body, see, for example, Sally Ann Ness, "Bali, the Camera, and Dance: Performance Studies and the Lost Legacy of the Mead/Bateson Collaboration," *Journal of Asian Studies* 67, no. 4 (November 2008): 1251–76.

61 Georges Fradier, "Green Light for Education," *UNESCO Courier* 7, no. 7 (1954): 29–32.

62 UNESCO, *Lebanon: Suggestions for the Plan of Tripoli and for the Surroundings of the Baalbek Acropolis; Report of the UNESCO Mission of 1953* (Paris: UNESCO, 1954); UNESCO, *Syria: Problems of Preservation and Presentation of Sites and Monuments; Report of the UNESCO Mission of 1953* (Paris: UNESCO, 1954).

63 See "La ville rationnelle," in *Le Corbusier à Paris: Essai sur une esthétique de l'architecture*, ed. Pierre Joly (Paris: Délégation à l'action artistique de la Ville de Paris; Lyon: La Manufacture, 1987), 111–64. On the Plan Voisin, see Thordis Arrenius, *The Fragile Monument: On Conservation and Modernity* (London: Artifice, 2012), 112–37. See also Rosemary Wakeman, *The Heroic City: Paris, 1945–1958* (Chicago: University of Chicago Press, 2009).

64 On UNESCO's contribution to the "development decade," see Richard Jolly, Louis Emmerij, Dharam Ghai, and Frédéric Lapeyre, *UN Contributions to Development Thinking and Practice* (Bloomington: Indiana University Press, 2004), 203–19. On modern architecture's imbrication with development discourse, see M. Ijlal Muzaffar, "The Periphery Within" (PhD diss., MIT, 2008). See also Lucia Allais, *Designs of Destruction* (Chicago: University of Chicago Press, forthcoming), on architectural conservation projects fitting into development narratives and schemes.

65 "Preserved and protected" is from "Annex III," in UNESCO, *Avant-Projet* 1953.

66 Lucien Hervé was hired to photograph the design, construction, and finished work. See Françoise Choay, *Le Siège de l'UNESCO à Paris*, photographs by Lucien Hervé (Paris: Vincent Fréal, 1958).

67 Lewis Mumford, "UNESCO House II: The Hidden Treasure," *New Yorker*, November 19, 1960, 213–20.

68 Michael Barnett and Martha Finnemore, *Rules for the World: International Organizations in Global Politics* (Ithaca, NY: Cornell University Press, 2004).

69 Marcel Breuer, "Structures in Space," in Breuer, *Sun and Shadow: The Philosophy of an Architect*, ed. Peter Blake (New York: Dodd, Mead, 1955), 68–69.

70 Breuer, *Sun and Shadow*, 71.

71 Ibid.

72 Marcel Breuer, "Speech on the Occasion of the Exhibit of Pier Luigi Nervi's Work at the Architectural League," March 26, 1959, 5718, Breuer Papers, AAA. See also Alberto Bologna, *Pier Luigi Nervi negli Stati Uniti 1952–1979* (Florence: Firenze University Press, 2013), 57–58; and Ernesto N. Rogers, "Introduction: A Portrait of Pier Luigi Nervi," in *The Works of Pier Luigi Nervi* (New York: Praeger, 1957), ix–xi.

73 Pier Luigi Nervi, *Aesthetics and Technology in Building* (Cambridge, MA: Harvard University Press, 1965), 23. See also Carlo Olmo and Cristiana Chiorino, eds., *Pier Luigi Nervi: Architecture as Challenge* (Milan: Silvana, 2010); Pier Luigi Nervi, *La lezione di Pier Luigi Nervi*, ed. Annalisa Trentin and Tommaso Trombetti (Milan: Mondadori, 2011); and Gloria Bianchino and Carlo Costi, eds., *Cantiere Nervi: La costruzione di una identità* (Parma: Skira, 2012).

74 Gropius attributed the folding only to Nervi, calling it "too nervous, or should I say nervous?" Gropius to BNZ, August 24, 1953, Breuer Papers, AAA.

75 Nervi, *La lezione di Pier Luigi Nervi*, 145. For Nervi, the term "bending" was a technical one, referring to the actual "bending moment diagram" reproduced in a chain-like hyperbolic line. Ibid., 142.

76 Perrin Selcer, "Patterns of Science: Developing Knowledge for a World Community at UNESCO" (PhD diss., University of Pennsylvania, 2011), 15.

77 Siegert focuses on "the fold" as "architectural media that … operates the primordial difference between inside and outside." Bernhard Siegert, "Door Logic, or, the Materiality of the Symbolic," in Siegert, *Cultural Techniques: Grids, Filters, Doors, and Other Articulations of the Real*, trans. Geoffrey Winthrop-Young (New York: Fordham University Press, 2014). See also Reinhold Martin, "Unfolded, Not Opened: On Bernhard Siegert's *Cultural Techniques*," *Grey Room* 62 (Winter 2016): 102–15.

78 "UNESCO House Is Their Handiwork!," in *UNESCO Courier: Special Issue, UNESCO's New Headquarters* (November 1958): 16.

79 At the most basic level, UNESCO's mission is to promote "peace in the minds of men," but the organization structures itself not around achieving this goal but disseminating it as a message.

80 Roque Javier Laurenza, "The Language of Abstract Art," in *UNESCO Courier: Special Issue, UNESCO's New Headquarters* (November 1958): 18.

81 This bias also sometimes applied to modern art. Roger Caillois, for instance, argued in a UNESCO publication that modern art was *unlike* language because artworks required "no translation" and could be reproduced by "mechanical means" alone. Roger Caillois, "Problems of Translation," *UNESCO Chronicle* 5, nos. 1–2 (January–February 1959): 9–14.

82 UNESCO's first international conference on science abstracting was in 1949. See "Science Abstract Experts to Meet in Paris" *UNESCO Courier* 1, no. 3 (1948): 6.

83 Zevi, "I sei difetti del Palazzo dell'UNESCO a Parigi," 151.

84 See note 9.

85 On the difference between copyrightable things and noncopyrightable processes, see Pamela Samuelson, "Why Copyright Law Excludes Systems and Processes from the Scope of Its Protection," *Texas Law Review* 85, no. 1 (2007): 1–58. More generally, see Siva Vaidhyanathan, *Intellectual Property: A Very Short Introduction* (Oxford: Oxford University Press, 2017), esp. 16–66.

1 IBM Research Center, La Gaude, France, 1960–62, contact sheet of construction photographs

Marcel Breuer: Structure and Shadow

Guy Nordenson

> It is interesting that the two most important single developments that underlie our new architecture have at their base the concept of flow, of motion: the flow of space which leads to the continuity of space, and the flow of structural forces which leads to a continuous structure.
>
> —Marcel Breuer, "Structures in Space"

Cantilever and Chiaroscuro

The former Armstrong Rubber Company building in New Haven, designed by Marcel Breuer in 1967, is familiar to anyone who has driven along Interstate 95 between New York and Boston. Although it serves as real estate for IKEA banners now, the building has always stood out in its industrial urban context. The Armstrong building bears many features typical of Breuer's later career, with its heavy massing and repeating precast concrete window bays, but it is also one of his most memorable buildings. Breuer's commission for the headquarters of the company [2] came at the insistence of Richard Lee, then mayor of New Haven. Robert Gatje, who worked with Breuer for many years, explains that when Armstrong sought to purchase the land by the turnpike, Lee "insisted anything built on the site should have an architectural presence and should be designed by a master."[1] The mayor believed the building should be tall and prominent because it would be an important city marker for the turnpike and rail traffic. Armstrong itself had no need for a tall tower and was resistant to the idea, but Breuer found a way to appease both parties. Gatje further relates the story of the commission: "Lajko [Breuer] listened to all this carefully and had a solution in mind before we had started drawing ... it was to propose the office floors be put atop the two-story research and development wing at grade and then—in order to satisfy Dick Lee—that they be raised clear of the roof below and 'hung from above' leaving

2 Armstrong Rubber Company headquarters, New Haven, Connecticut, 1967–69, south elevation drawing

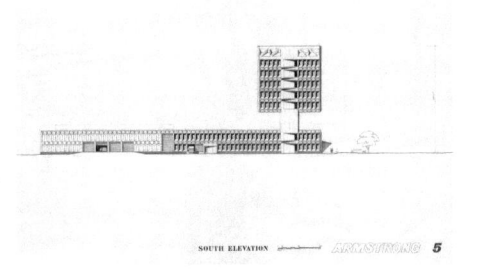

a two-story-high slot between the two building masses that could be filled with expansion space at a later time."[2] The massing of the building combines Lee's desire for height and Armstrong's programmatic and economic need for a low building by inserting "two stories of air" in the tower.[3] This meant that the office tower would hover over the lower research and development building and that the "air" between them would allow the office building to stand proud, almost like a billboard for the city.

While its prominence on the highway contributes to its memorability, Armstrong is also one of Breuer's most striking buildings because of its deeply molded precast cladding. The side elevation of the building—"one of my favorites," wrote Gatje—was shaped to express the steel structure below and to "not suggest that the concrete was doing the work."[4] Beneath the sculpted precast cladding is a steel frame with deep trusses that occupy the double-height top story and cantilever to either side of the core to support the upper floors [3]. The massive appearance of this partly suspended box is intentional and was a matter of debate between Breuer and Weidlinger Associates, the structural engineers for the project. Paul Weidlinger had been Breuer's engineer of choice since the late 1950s, when he asked them to help with problems that came up during the construction of the St. John's Abbey church and university (1953–68). A young engineer named Matthys Levy, who came to work for Weidlinger around that time, quickly became the project engineer for most of Breuer's buildings, including Armstrong Rubber. According to Gatje, Levy "fought long and hard in favor of a 'light' façade for the suspended tower. Breuer agreed with this economic logic but stubbornly insisted on the architectural unity that one material [the precast

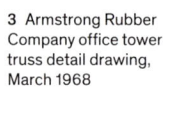

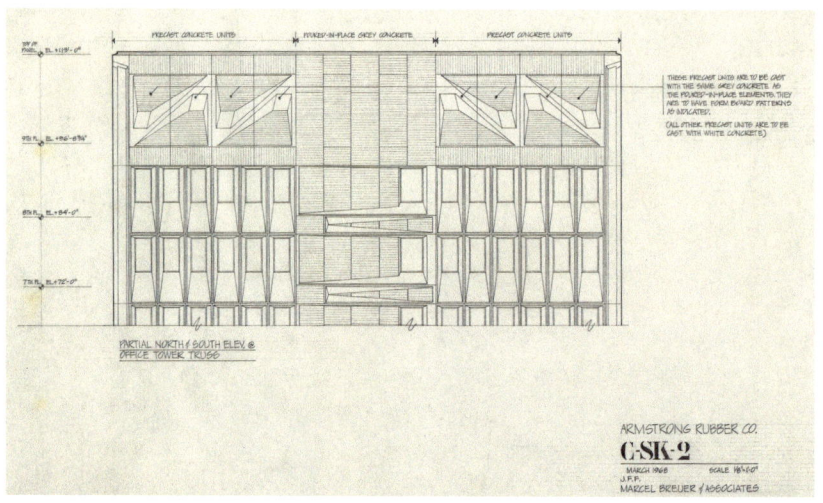

3 Armstrong Rubber Company office tower truss detail drawing, March 1968

cladding] would give its two disparate parts."[5] In effect, Breuer subsumed the actual nature of the structure into a sculpted form that expressed his idea of its effort and tectonics but did not directly reveal its material make-up. Levy has recently revisited these design discussions and recalled his objection to the misrepresentation of the structure:

> Since it's a suspended building, it seemed odd to me that that the suspended portion should have such a heavy concrete appearance. I asked why a lightweight glazed façade could not be used instead, but he [Breuer] didn't want to do that. He loved those precast concrete window panels.... The only concession he made was on the end faces of the building. There, the steel truss that holds up the floors has a concrete cover over it that mirrors the shape of the truss. We had discussed it, and he at least accepted the fact that maybe we should express the steel truss.... It's a concrete-looking building that should look more like steel.[6]

The modeling of the precast cladding on the base, truss, and wall elevations of the upper volume endow the building with a massive presence. The effect is strongest on the side elevations of the Armstrong building, where the drape-like molding of the vertical core contrasts with the tensile sinew of the truss diagonals and the serial background pattern of the deep-set precast window units. This divergent expression of structural parts—core shaft, truss, and wall cladding—contrasts with both the sculptural molding of the exposed cast-in-place concrete core shaft and the recessed precast panels covering the walls. Breuer shaped these elements for their play with light and shadow, not for their structural expression. In fact, the detailing of the precast panels covering the steel truss is especially confounding because the panel joints cut

p. 141/2 straight across the apparent lines of tension within the truss. In this sense the project produces considerable ambiguity by its different uses of concrete—cast-in-place and precast—to project a muscular plasticity, as well as to play with light, but also to confuse the expression of the underlying structure.

The distinctive use of deeply sculpted precast cladding at Armstrong Rubber is characteristic of Breuer's buildings in the 1960s and 1970s, including the unbuilt New England Merchants Bank competition for Boston, Massachusetts (1964), and IBM La Gaude in the Alpes Maritimes in France (1960–62 [1]) and in Boca Raton, Florida (1968–72), among many others. In most of these projects the precast unit is modular and repeated over the façade. *Pilotis* lift the buildings to open the ground level and also to emphasize the clarity of their boxy forms wrapped in precast cladding. In his book *Sun and Shadow,* Breuer had already expressed his ideas about some of these aesthetic tendencies: "A building is a man-made work, a crystallic [sic] constructed thing. It should not imitate nature—it should be in contrast to nature. A building has straight, geometric lines, it should be always clear that they are built—that they did not just grow."[7] Perhaps it is this desire for architecture to *look* "built" and geometric that sometimes results in Breuer's overemphasis or misplaced emphasis on the appearance of structural flows in buildings like Armstrong, St. John's Abbey, the Whitney, and Grand Coulee Dam, to name a few.

This impulse to amplify the plastic properties of concrete enabled Breuer to establish a coherent vocabulary of architectural effects. By mixing cast-in-place concrete, shaped to express the flow of forces, with nonstructural precast wall panels that retain the sinewy effect of cast-in-place, Breuer combines effects of mass and light that are unexpectedly reminiscent of baroque architecture. In a 1973 interview with the concrete company Schokbeton, he articulates this proclivity in explicit terms. Breuer explains, "Concrete allows the architect three dimensions; he can design elevations moving in and out, he can create depth in a façade, he can become a master in a new baroque."[8] I would like to argue in this essay that this "new baroque" refers to what I interpret as Breuer's clear interest in the emotional effect of structure expressed in concrete. In reading the correspondence between Breuer and his engineers and in studying the evolution of his buildings, I believe it is clear that Breuer was far more invested in the display of structural effects than he was in the literal transcription of structural forces.

The emotional effects of structure are something Heinrich Wölfflin first explored and identified with the baroque in his 1888 book *Renaissance and Baroque.* Using the book and the baroque as a way to exercise his theories about empathy, Wölfflin noted how in Michelangelo's work "form struggles with mass" and how in the relationship between a column and a wall in the vestibule of the Laurenziana there is "an unending process of impassioned agitation and furious struggle between form and mass" where columns are recessed or pressed into, not separated, from the mass of walls.[9] This for Wölfflin is the "painterly style" he sees as defining the architectural baroque: "The freedom of line and the interplay of light and shade are satisfying to the painterly taste in direct proportion to the degree to which they transgress the rules of architecture. If the beauty of a building is judged by the enticing effects of moving masses, the restless, jumping forms or violently swaying ones which seem constantly on the point of change, and not by balance and solidity of structure, then the strictly architectonic conception of architecture is depreciated."[10] The "architectonic" logic Wölfflin refers to here is what Gatje called the "economic logic" of the Armstrong Rubber building. Breuer rejected the rules that Levy had "fought long and hard in favor of" in exchange for the *chiaroscuro* of mass and form. The deep relief of the cast-in-place core and the precast cladding elements that cover Armstrong's steel structure imply the effort of the structure and the mass it sustains in addition to casting deep shadows.

Wölfflin also draws attention to the ways extreme contrast between light and dark can make a figure appear to "jump right out of the picture plane."[11] He refers to the frescoes that Raphael created in the Vatican Stanze, where such contrast gives the strong illusion of movement. The guards leaning on the left side of the *Deliverance of Saint Peter* (1514), in one of the Stanze Wölfflin mentions, are distant antecedents of the same alignment of structure and shadow that seems to fascinate Breuer. In his pursuit of the new baroque, Breuer developed a *chiaroscuro* of structure all his own. The resulting tension between the pragmatic realities of the underlying structure and its expression, sublimation, or suppression is perhaps paradoxically what makes Breuer's relationship to the structure of his architecture most interesting. This essay traces this development in Breuer's work alongside the shifts in his relationships with structural engineers, most notably Pier Luigi Nervi and Paul Weidlinger, in an effort to draw out the important but elusive role that structure plays in his architecture.

Fold and Figure

> In *drapery* painting, which needs every care, the *nude* body beneath maintains visibility, or should so: confusion of *folds* thus beware.
> —Francesco Lancilotti, *Treatise of Painting*

Collaborating with Nervi on the UNESCO headquarters in Paris (1955–58) transformed Breuer's architecture. His buildings before that, both with Walter Gropius and on his own, consisted largely of private residences. Breuer had evolved a palette of stone site and base walls under hovering and often cantilevering white stucco or cypress board–clad volumes, starting with the John

Hagerty House (1938), the Lincoln, Massachusetts, Gropius (1938) and Breuer (1939) homes, continuing with his New Canaan home (1948), and the wonderful Sidney Wolfson House in Salt Point, New York (1949). In these houses he articulates and contrasts the rustic stone walls with light, wood-framed superstructures. The superstructures of these houses are sometimes lifted above stone walls on *pilotis* to clear the landscape or water, or, in other houses, parts cantilever off and away from the stone walls. The clear distinction between infrastructure and superstructure forms a dialectic between permanent ground form and a more ephemeral vernacular as well as the tectonics of anchorage versus span or cantilever, a dynamic that continues to give these houses a lasting appeal. After some difficulties with a sagging cable-stayed porch at his first house in New Canaan, Breuer worked consistently with a Hungarian American engineer named Nicholas Farkas of the firm Farkas & Barron.[12]

The UNESCO project was the first time Breuer had worked with an engineer of such renown and international stature as Nervi. UNESCO, after all, was a whole complex of buildings, and the project catapulted his career into a new arena. Suddenly he gained commissions for all kinds of institutional work, and he took only very few residential projects. The collaboration between Breuer, Nervi, and the French architect Bernard Zehrfuss (or BNZ, as Breuer coined the trio) on UNESCO produced an icon of modern architecture. Its authorship—as Lucia Allais discusses elsewhere in this volume—remains enigmatic and interlaced and is complicated, in a positive sense, by the decadal separation in age and the different experience and disciplinary practice of the BNZ trio.[13] The integration of the flow and form of the spaces, inside and in between the structures, and the play of light on and in the Secretariat and Conference Building testifies to their excellent col-

4 Pier Luigi Nervi, Exhibition Building, Turin, Italy, 1948–49, longitudinal and detail section drawings
5 View of exhibition hall

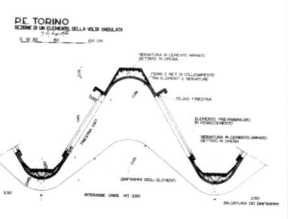

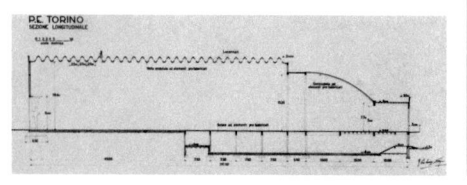

laboration. Sun and shadow were key to the planning of the buildings, including the Y-shaped plan of the Secretariat. Although the actual thermal performance of the Secretariat was poor in some orientations, the 1948–49 plan shows how the combination of flat and folded surfaces, cutouts, solids, and voids creates sharp, vivid contrasts with the raking afternoon light and shadows.

Before designing the Conference Building, Nervi had made use of a folded reinforced concrete structure for the ninety-five-meter, clear-span main hall of the Exhibition Building in Turin (1947–49, Palazzo per esposizioni) [4,5]. That exhibition hall is open at one end and capped by a semi-cupola held together by Nervi's characteristic reflected arc ribs. Both the main hall and end semi-cupola clearly exhibit the flow of structural forces, articulated in the larger space by the precast *ferro-cemento* roof units and the singular cast-in-place raked columns. The perforated units of the main hall roof form a soaring and airy Gothic design that "emphasizes the framing members [and] has firm structural supports, lightly filled in."[14]

The folded wall and roof structure of the UNESCO Conference Building [6], while similar to the Turin Exhibition Hall, is decidedly different in several key respects. While the precast *ferro-cemento* arc ribs at Turin are unitized and articulated by the skylights spread all across the roof, the Conference Building at UNESCO is made of monolithic cast-in-place concrete ribs with the only natural light coming in on either side of the space, creating a strongly contrasting *chiaroscuro* effect. The continuous walls and the overall form that presses down on the center column line also have spatial consequences that are very different from the airiness at the Turin Exhibition Hall—or any other Nervi structure for that matter. The spatial effects of UNESCO more closely resemble Breuer's later St. John's Abbey and its university church (1953–68), both in the side lighting and in the massive pleated structure pressing down overhead. This same *chiaroscuro* and raking light is present in Bernard Zehrfuss's partly buried 1975 Gallo-Roman museum in Lyon-Fourvière of two decades later. The St. John's Abbey church and the Gallo-Roman museum are structured in ribbed, exposed concrete, in both cases clearly claiming the architectonic vocabulary of the UNESCO hall. This *chiaroscuro* of pleated structural form sparsely lit from the sides clearly had a strong appeal and

6 UNESCO Headquarters, interior of main conference hall

7 Sydney Opera House, Sydney, Australia, 1958–73, lower concourse

reach at the time, as is evident in the fact that it even found its way to Sydney, Australia, in the structurally expressive and dimly lit form of the Opera House concourse designed by Ove Arup with the architect [7].[15]

The axis formed by the side entrance to the UNESCO Conference Building anchors the structure and links the building to the Secretariat by a connecting passage (the Salle des Pas-perdus and Salles Miró). This axis sets off the principal line of rounded trapezoidal columns from which the structure and space rise up on either side like wings from the core. From the outside, the roof form appears to be a continuous folded surface swooping down and up from the end walls, concealing the presence of the column supports at the center. Nervi's subtle structural design registers the columns' function in the swoop of the roof surface as it shifts up and down relative to the V-shaped and variable folds of the ribs, following the moment diagram variation from end to end [8–10]. This complex and nuanced interplay of structural logic, circulation, space, and light makes the Conference Building the *danseur noble* of the UNESCO site. While the Conference Building design is often attributed to Nervi, it is arguably the most synthetic, even symphonic work on the site, combining so completely the sensibilities and inclinations of BNZ in an original and pathbreaking work. After all, which of Nervi's later Conference Building works this well with light, form, space, and structure? The closest comparable structure is the 1971 Paul VI Vatican Audience Hall, but that, like the Turin space, is a more singular, evenly lit volume both inside and out, without any of the spatial compression and release, contrast, and *chiaroscuro* of the UNESCO center.

The joint authorship of the Secretariat building at UNESCO is easier to deconstruct. The Y-plan form, the siting, sun-shading façade, circulation, and program planning seem to come from Breuer. To this architecture Nervi incorporated an elegant structure made up of transverse bents or moment frames and splayed cantilevers spaced at 6-meter intervals along the length of each branch of the Y and merging at the center core. The framing plan is Gothic in the clear distinction of frame and infill and in the elegant sweep as it turns the curve where the three wings meet at the core [11–13]. In section, both the *pilotis* and the floor framing vary in width and depth in line with the bending moments [14]. The longitudinal floor framing, supported by the frame girder,

Marcel Breuer: Structure and Shadow

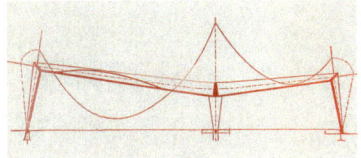

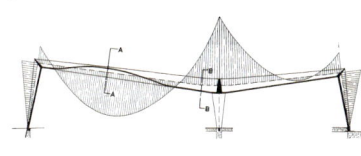

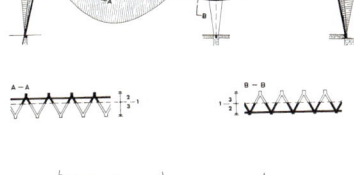

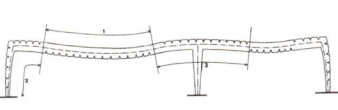

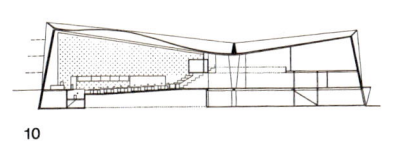

8 Construction view of Sydney Opera House lower concourse
9 Structural diagram of UNESCO Conference Building
10 Structural diagrams of bending moment and corresponding variation in rib cross section and slab position, UNESCO Conference Building
11 Automobile entrance to UNESCO Secretariat, structural design drawing
12 Construction view of lower level, UNESCO Secretariat
13 Sixth floor structural plan drawing, UNESCO Secretariat
14 Column and slab detail drawings, UNESCO Secretariat

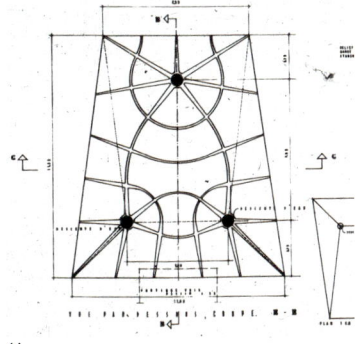

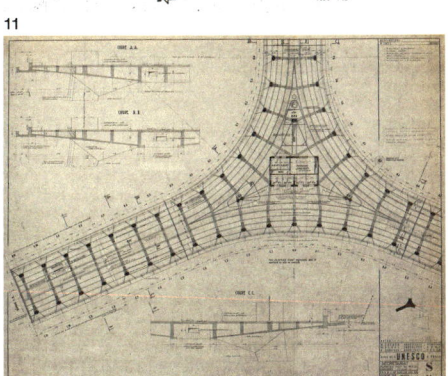

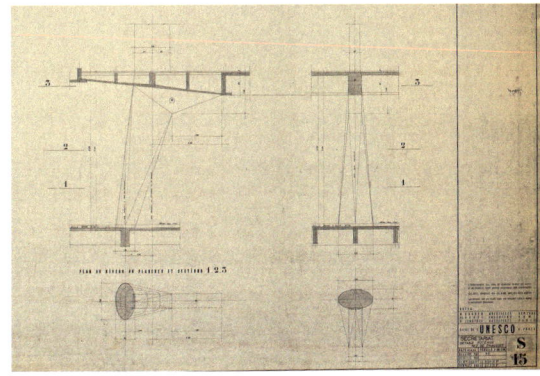

15 Transverse section drawings with structural details, UNESCO Secretariat

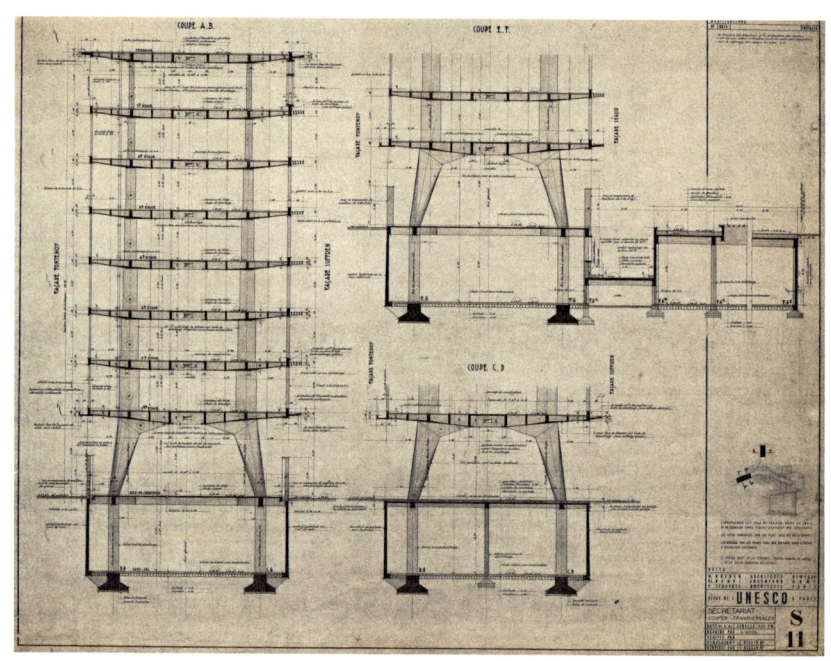

consists of concrete infill beams spaced 1.5 meters apart. The structural concrete slab is located at the bottom, at the edge of the tapered cantilevers, and extends into the central frame girder, then flips on top in the center corridor line, matching the moment diagram [14,15] that comes from the cantilever. The resulting cavity is accessible from above at the edges and from below at the center, a kind of raised floor *avant la lettre*. This "flip" of the slab is positioned so that it can serve as a flange to resist the compression side of the cantilever and mid-span bending moments—the same logic that directs the shifts of the roof slab position on the Conference Building.

The end elevation of each wing of the Secretariat is a blank wall raised on splayed columns. The columns vary in cross section in keeping with the variation in stress that changes with the bending moment along the span and also with Nervi's own sculptural development since the raked buttress columns of his aircraft hangars and stadia early in his career. In some ways these columns also anticipate the vertical tapering found in the section of raised tower of the Armstrong Rubber building (1968–70). At UNESCO, the building elevation is figural and representative of both the massiveness of the building and the strength and suppleness of the column forms that support it. The role of *pilotis* in integrating site, landscape, and building is not new to UNESCO, but the close correlation of figural form and structural logic in Nervi's design of the columns is original.

p. 78/20

"The broad forms of the baroque style are part of a totally new conception of *matter*," writes Wölfflin, "that is of the ideal aspect of matter which gives expression to the inner vitality and behavior of the members."[16] According to Wölfflin, these forms lead to a baroque style where "as matter becomes soft and masses fluid, structural cohesion is dissolved; the massiveness of the style, already expressed in the broad and heavy forms, is now manifest in inadequate articulation and lack of precise forms."[17] The UNESCO buildings do not go so far. The façades of the Secretariat have a lightness and articulation that seem almost vernacular in their adaptation to solar orientation, and their structural cohesion is taut, not entropic. What does emerge with both the UNESCO Secretariat and Conference Building buildings are the parallel strategies of using folded structures to catch stark contrasting light and shadow—both body and drapery fused as one—and of incorporating individual, serialized, figural pillars, which are both strategies that recall Wölfflin's articulation of baroque form.

The folded or pressed surface and sculpted pillar forms, adapted from Nervi's language, became key figures in Breuer's later work, including the pleated structures of the St. John's Abbey church (1953–68) and Grand Coulee Dam (1972–78) and the sculpted *pilotis* at buildings such as the HUD headquarters in Washington, DC (1965–68).[18] But when, after UNESCO, Breuer's uses of folded plates and sculpted *pilotis* were designed independent of Nervi, without his oversight, there were cracks that emerged due to Breuer and his engineer's misunderstanding of these new forms.

Breuer consulted with Nervi on the design of the church at St. John's Abbey while in Europe in the fall of 1953, and Nervi produced a sketch of the folded-plate structure [16] and a cross section. Breuer sent Gatje an annotated plan in November 1953 that relays Breuer's conversation with Nervi and the resulting modifications to the design.[19] But Nervi did not oversee the engineering, which in the end passed through several hands. During construction in the summer of 1960 the folded-plate roof structure at St. John's Abbey was found to have developed several alarming cracks. Nervi was briefly consulted.[20] Ultimately, however, it fell to Weidlinger and Levy to diagnose the cause and devise a repair.[21] Breuer had appropriated the folded form for all its spatial effects and *chiaroscuro*, but he did not fully understand the folded structure's mechanics. Folded or curved plates function

16 St. John's Abbey Church, section drawings of folded plate roof

as overscale beams, gaining their strength and stiffness by virtue of the vertical depth of the folds or curves despite the fact that they are formed of thin slabs or sheets. As beams, they are subject to bending stresses and shears in the plane of the slab, which requires steel reinforcement. If that reinforcement is missing, perhaps because the plates are mistaken for simple slabs, the concrete will crack as it did in this case.

For the complex of buildings designed from 1953 to 1967 for St. John's Abbey and its university, Breuer and his eventual partners Gatje and Hamilton Smith consulted a series of different structural engineers, including Farkas & Barron, James L. Leon of Wiesenfeld, Hayward and Leon in New York, and even the Johnston-Sahlman Company in Minneapolis, none of whom had experience with folded plates. Breuer must not have fully realized or considered this. There is a series of letters that trace this arc, starting with one dated July 22, 1957, in which Breuer fires Farkas & Barron after three years of working on the project.[22] The cause for the parting of ways was their inaccurate and incomplete construction documents. On July 23 comes Leon's proposal and subsequent engagement as engineer.[23] That was followed by his account of the cracks on April 25, 1960, where he mistakenly refers to the folded plate as "roof trusses."[24] On December 1, 1960, Weidlinger submits a rather scathing report on the cause of the cracks and the inadequacy of the original analysis and design, which, as he writes, "does not conform to current engineering practice and methods proposed in the literature regarding the design of folded plates."[25]

Breuer appropriated the folded plate form without fully understanding how it worked and thus took a risk. It is probably fortunate that it only led to cracks. While the incident prompted Breuer's consultation with Weidlinger, who did have the necessary expertise, Breuer had worked for seven years without confirming that either Farkas or Leon had the necessary understanding of the form, and he continued to work with both for some time thereafter. Breuer did not ever truly find another engineer with both the authority and authorial will of his partner in the UNESCO project. For all the irritation and disappointment Breuer expressed to both Farkas and later Leon over their struggles on the St. John's Abbey church, it did not seem to occur to him that the mismatch between idea and practice was of his doing and that he had thrust these engineers into a situation beyond their abilities. With Weidlinger he did in the end have a very capable consultant, but not—for better or worse—another Nervi.

This asymmetry in the balance of influence continues in the projects that follow. When Weidlinger and Levy collaborated with Breuer on the Third Power Plant at Grand Coulee Dam, the folded structure was confined to buttressing the walls and supported a simple flat roof. It lacks the sweep and folded wings of the UNESCO center. While the deep folding of the buttressing wall creates a powerful presence among the huge dam structures, with strongly contrasting light and shadow and a monumental interior space, it is not of the same structural types as the earlier folded-plate spans. Here the form decides the structure—the pleated walls use a structural form that is designed to resist forces in the plane perpendicular to the folds or as part of a rigid frame, as it does at the UNESCO Conference Building. At Grand Coulee the wall folds do not resist large horizontal forces and the roof is made of simply supported precast, prestressed double-T beams [17], so they are not part of a frame either. They do stand up alone during construction, which is useful, and most of all they evoke the function of the dam itself. But here the use of a recognizable structural form is for rhetorical, not functional purposes.

17 Grand Coulee Dam, Columbia Basin Project, Washington, USA, 1972–75, construction view of forebay dam

The emphasis on the *chiaroscuro* of quasi-structural form gets more complicated as Breuer explores the use of sculpted and structural precast concrete wall panels. Levy has remarked, "He [Breuer] was always interested in the structure of the building … [and] very often he tried to adapt to new technology. For instance, precast concrete. When we started using precast for façades, he picked up on it…. We had gotten involved in the Banque Lambert in Brussels with SOM and [Gordon] Bunshaft, and on that job we used Schokbeton in Europe to build the cross-shaped precast units. We found out that Schokbeton had a US venture, so we started using them, or recommending them, for precast work as well."[26]

The Banque Lambert project dates from 1958–62, in the same period as Breuer and Gatje's IBM building in La Gaude, France [1]. The use of structural precast concrete was in the air. Louis Kahn used it for the 1957–60 Richards Medical Research Laboratories, working for the first time with the structural engineer August Komendant. But the IBM building in La Gaude, designed with Gatje and the engineers Wiesenfeld, Hayward and Leon, demonstrates a first hybrid of Breuer's deeply molded precast concrete panels and the cast-in-place floor and "tree" columns. The muscularity and *chiaroscuro* of this exposed structure bears a debt to Nervi, while it also diverges from his more attenuated and Gothic structures. Here is the "new baroque." The siting of the double-Y plan of La Gaude and the placement of the upper volume on a grounded lower mass with figural *pilotis* adapts the massing of Breuer's houses and the structural *chiaroscuro* of UNESCO into a new type that is all Breuer's. A decade later Breuer and Gatje built an IBM administrative laboratory and manufacturing facility in Boca Raton, Florida, with a similar plan, elevation, and many of the same details, this time with the engineers Severud Perrone Sturm Conlin Bandel.   p.142/3–

Breuer and Herbert Beckhard's headquarters of the US Department of Housing and Urban Development in Washington, DC (1963–69), engineered by Weidlinger and Levy, blends a cast-in-place concrete base, core, and corridor with an outer bay of precast, prestressed "double-T" beams as well as load-bearing precast concrete [18]. The choice of precast, prestressed double-T beams was clearly a pragmatic one because, as Levy explains, "they were   p.144/6– available locally, and they tended to result in a lower cost for the building."[27] Breuer's combination of precast and cast-in-place concrete in the geometrically complex part of the building and load-bearing precast wall panels for the repetitive façade is in keeping with Nervi's own frugal practices. By this time, Breuer's *pilotis* are no longer integral to the overall figure and structural flow, as had been the case in the UNESCO Secretariat. In the HUD building they act as separate sculptural objects that prop up the rest of the building mass, expressing an Atlas-like effort. Breuer further develops these massive *pilotis* throughout the 1960s and 1970s in projects like the NYU Technology Building and Yale   p.218/17–

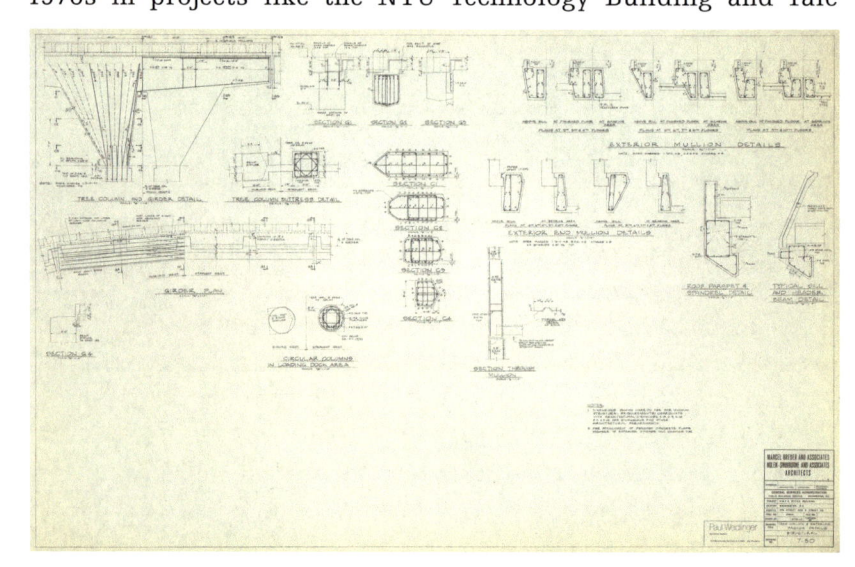

18 Department of Housing and Urban Development headquarters, Washington, DC, USA, 1965–68, column details

Engineering Building of 1967–70 and the unbuilt Bristol Center office building in Syracuse, New York, with its "bush-hammered" twin pillars. As with the folded plate and its suggestion of structural *chiaroscuro* becoming load-bearing precast wall panels, the carefully calibrated expression of structural moments and flow in Nervi's pillars evolves into the autonomous and sculptural "tree columns," which are particularly evident in the library at St. John's and at NYU Technology Building. Together these tree columns emphasize the heavy mass of the building pressing down—a stark contrast to the springy and soaring Gothic lightness that is so characteristic of Nervi's structures. In this sense, the "new baroque" separates the columns where the "form struggles with mass" from what for Wölfflin were "the effects of light: the unfathomableness of a dark depth, the magic of light streaming down from the invisible height of the dome, the transition from dark to light and lighter still."[28]

Sweep and Swerve

> A writer must be as objective as a chemist, he must lay aside his personal subjective standpoint and must understand that muck heaps play a very respectable part in a landscape.
> —Anton Chekhov to Mme. M. V. Kiselyov, January 14, 1887

Nervi was a master of thin-shell concrete structures as well as of ribbed and folded plates. The entrance canopies at either side of the UNESCO Secretariat exhibit both types: the southwest one is a hyperbolic paraboloid concrete surface, and the canopy on the north side is a flat slab on three supports with the curvilinear isostatic *nervature* that Nervi had developed with Aldo Arcangeli for the 1953 Gatti Wool Factory in Rome [11,19].[29] Breuer never actually appropriated Nervi's signature isostatic *nervature* slab for future projects, as would his student and early employee Harry Seidler, but he did enthusiastically adopt the hyperbolic paraboloid form, especially for the St. Francis de Sales church project in Muskegon, Michigan, engineered by Weidlinger. In a 1979 interview Breuer described his usage: "As you know, the hyperbolic paraboloids are used in the St Francis de Sales Church for enclosure and not for structural support. Now, this is the first time that they have been used for enclosure—they were never used in this manner before."[30] This Midwestern church has a trapezoidal-shaped

19 UNESCO Headquarters, construction photograph of automobile entrance to Secretariat

plan, similar to the St. John's Abbey church and the UNESCO Conference Building. At St. Francis the "banner" that makes up the battered front elevation of the church integrates itself into the body of the building.[31] The main structure is a continuous, straight rib wall and slab, a simplified version of the folded plates of the UNESCO Conference Building and St. John's Abbey. The ribbed walls and slab run front to back and have openings that allow narrow shafts of light into the church [20]. But it is the non-load-bearing sidewalls formed into soaring hyperbolic paraboloids that are the most striking element of the architecture. These sidewalls do not support the roof but are tied to it as they lean away into space. This adaptation of the hyperbolic paraboloid geometry for a non-load-bearing wall rather than as spanning device is not entirely new, as Félix Candela had already used hyperbolic paraboloid forms to shape the baroque space of the 1954 Iglesia de la Medalla Milagrosa in Mexico City. Nevertheless, the scale and exuberant formalism of the St. Francis de Sales walls are unique.

p. 324/7–1

20 St. Francis de Sales Church, Muskegon, Michigan, USA, 1964–66, view of chancel

With the St. Francis de Sales church project Breuer once again reinterprets the forms of Nervi while detaching them from their structural function. Weidlinger was an excellent consulting engineer, fully skilled at executing the structure of this hybrid form of ribbed wall, slab, and upright shell, but he was not Breuer's structural counterpart. He was not one to contest the distortion of structural lineage or assert his own synthesis of the hybrid form into a new type. While St. John's reuses the UNESCO Conference Building folded-plate structure, Breuer's design is also a misreading of the engineering, turning the grain of the folded plate across the flow of the space. St. Francis de Sales recombines the terms of Nervi's hyperbolic paraboloids by stripping their structural function and changing the form of the structural ribbing from a folded plate to a flatter beam-and-slab combination. These three works—the UNESCO Conference Building, St. John's, and St. Francis—share the same trapezoidal plan but otherwise restlessly recombine each other's structural forms as Breuer shapes his own new tectonic.

"The stronger the man, the larger his resentments, and the more brazen his *clinamen*," writes the American literary critic Harold Bloom. "Let us give up," he states, "the failed enterprise of seeking to 'understand' any single poem as an entity in itself. Let us pursue instead the quest of learning to read any poem as its poet's deliberate misinterpretation, *as a poet*, of a precursor poem or of poetry in general. Know each poem by its *clinamen* [or misprision or swerve] and you will 'know' that poem that will not purchase knowledge by the loss of the poem's power."[32] With this in mind, one can see that Breuer established his independent power and authority as an architect, after UNESCO, in a swerve from the influences of Gropius, Le Corbusier, and Nervi. Gropius's influence is clear in their work together and in Breuer's own residential work. Breuer's *pilotis* that lift up building forms and his interest in the plastic potentials of concrete likewise show a clear indebtedness to Le Corbusier. While the three designers are quite different from each other, Breuer combined lessons from each, especially Nervi, to create his version of the "new baroque." Breuer's work after UNESCO and after Nervi, because of its structural misreadings and the *chiaroscuro* these misreadings afford, is in a sense necessarily flawed in structural terms. Even his collaboration with Weidlinger must make way for Breuer's interpretations of Nervi's structural clarity. Again from Bloom: "A poet attempting to make this language new necessarily begins by an *arbitrary act of reading* that does not differ in kind from the act that *his* readers subsequently must perform upon him."[33] Furthermore, as Stephen Greenblatt observes of Lucretius's impact on the Renaissance in his book *The Swerve*, this *clinamen* or swerve is also a basis of free will: "The successful adaptations, like the failures, are the result of a fantastic number of combinations that are constantly being generated (and reproduced or discarded) over an unlimited expanse of time ... 'what has been created gives rise to its own function.'"[34]

The swerve of Greenblatt's account is away from religion and determinism. That Breuer's own swerve from Nervi would occur through the design of churches is also meaningful. In a 1979 interview about St. John's, Breuer proposes that "any large space which is built so that the process of construction is visible on the inside, is a religious space."[35] The St. John's abbot, Baldwin Dworschak, had asked that Breuer design "a church which will be truly an architectural monument to the service of God."[36] This is not a simple wish, given the secular roots of modern architecture. Both the secular stance that Breuer takes—"I am not a religious man"—and his misreading or displacement of structural forms that advance his "new baroque" dissociate the application of the structural form from its lineage, and one might say sensibility, gaining rhetorical force from that very sublimation.[37] Indeed the vortices of influence, religion, modernity, and sublimation represented by these churches continue to puzzle and mystify.

The breakthrough and synthesis that Breuer achieves with the St. Francis de Sales church building comes from fusing the "banner" of St. John's into the form of the building and eliminating the expressed folded plate. The resulting church building is dynamic, even if it lacks the closer alignment of structural logic and *chiaroscuro* of the earlier UNESCO Conference Building. Begrisch Hall (1959–61), part of the old NYU campus at University Heights, New York, is also evidence of this turn to a greater integration of Breuer's formal elements. The building is a center-supported monolith of carved cast-in-place concrete angled supports, structural walls, and stepped and sloping slabs subsumed in a looming integrated sculptural whole.

p. 215/15–

However, Breuer's masterpiece—the Whitney Museum of Art (1963–66)—is the most remarkable invention to emerge out of his turn from the pleated forms and those clad in deep-set precast panels. "In the quest for identity, the Whitney was designed to be instantly, almost outrageously recognizable," writes Gatje.[38] Breuer was conscious of the connotations of Madison Avenue, of advertising, and of the museum's urban context. The building would demarcate its difference and hold its own alongside commercialism and wealth. The dark granite façade was, with the exception of the contemporaneous CBS Building by Eero Saarinen (1961–65), uncommon for New York. At a time of modernist glass towers, the Whitney was a somber anomaly. And while it keeps the looming quality of Breuer's early versions of the "new baroque," the Whitney, like St. Francis and Begrisch Hall, achieves this through its overall form rather than through the surface alone.

p. 204/3

A full-height wall on both property lines to the south and east sharply brackets the Whitney site. Breuer saw this division as a means to "transform the building into a unit, an element, a nucleus."[39] Breuer described his interest in forms that are "hollow below and substantial on top—just the reverse of a pyramid ... the realization of one of [man's] oldest ambitions: the defeat of gravity."[40] At the Whitney the walls both bracket off the context and in effect hold it in place. They also appear to distort gravity by forming a kind of vertical ground plane. He had written about this idea earlier, in his 1955 *Sun and Shadow*: "You could, theoretically, pick up a continuous reinforced concrete frame and set it on an angle."[41] As with his early houses on stilts, this "gives you a sense of liberation, a certain élan, a certain daring."[42] And indeed the impression of gravity defeated was directly felt at the time of construction. For me, at the time a child recently arrived from Europe, it was as if some spacecraft had settled into the crater formed as it landed on the staid, bourgeois site.

Instead of being set up on stilts, the building mass of the Whitney appears to float in the hollowed ground, suggesting the continuation of the pyramid under street level. Altogether the massing, hollowed ground, and walls resist and even rotate the perception of gravity. This perception is emphasized as one enters the building over a bridge across the cavity below, steps across a small gap as if onto a ship, and enters a heavy concrete vestibule that is in fact suspended from the floor above. This is a different, more "crystallic" version of the "new baroque." As Wölfflin says, "the baroque required broad, heavy, massive forms.... Verticals were retained, but great projecting cornices and horizontal accents provided a strong counterweight to them."[43] What is so effective at the Whitney is this simultaneous feeling of massiveness and suspension—the subversion of the looming mass of overhead cantilevers (meaning, etymologically, to turn, from below).

This feeling of entering a ship afloat in space also adds to the experience of the building as a museum. Like the Guggenheim, the best approach to the exhibition space is from the top, accessible in the Whitney by a grand elevator. The elevator and the main stairs are contained to the south in a well delineated by a core "bar" extending the full depth of the building [21]. The galleries are themselves divided in a near golden ratio (24/60) between principal and secondary gallery, the latter in a bow to the original domestic space of the first Whitney museums on West Eighth and Fifty-Fourth Streets. Together these galleries were well proportioned for art of all kinds, including Robert Irwin's great installation *Scrim veil—Black rectangle—Natural light* of 1977 and 2013.

The Whitney also has one of the great staircases in the world— one that you could, in a Wölfflinian sense, *"salire con gravità"* [22].[44]

21 Whitney Museum of American Art, New York, 1964–66, section drawing showing stair and elevator

22 Whitney Museum of American Art, stairway

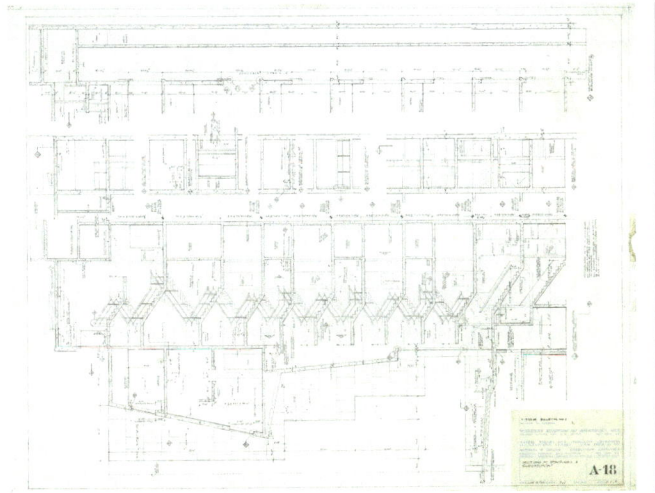

The stair combines a dynamic alternation of light and dark, compressed and open spaces, and beautiful materials—teak wood, bronze, green marble, bluestone, and *béton brut*. The concrete was bush-hammered to expose the aggregate except at the edges, which were left as cast. The sustained focus of the design and craftsmanship is unlike any other stair in New York, including the great stair at the original Museum of Modern Art, which Breuer clearly knew as its rival. The spatial delight of the main stair from the ground floor up is heightened by the true *pièce de résistance,* that is, the stair from the lobby down to the lower level. The original concept for the lobby stair was a circular one, similar in its open airiness to some of Breuer's residential stairs as well as the overlapping tread construction of the exterior UNESCO stairs. The circular stair interrupted the space of the lobby and was replaced by one alongside the south wall in the double-height exhibition space and sculpture court. It was built in the classic manner of Renaissance stairs known as "cantilever" stairs, which were popular with architects and engineers from Palladio and Inigo Jones to Joseph Freedlander (architect of the 1930 Museum of the City of New York). With the overlapping of the green marble treads, the stair can carry itself and its live loads in a cascade of shear from step to step, with the resulting torsion transmitted into the side wall. Quietly, this adds a flourish unlike any other in Breuer's, Weidlinger's, or Nervi's work, harking back to the genius of the (pre-baroque) Renaissance masons.

p. 208/7

The main structure of the museum was conceived by Breuer's "assuming it would be a completely homogeneous concrete structure." However, "Matt [Levy] pointed out that the audacious cantilevers would be severely compromised by the added dead load of their own weight and convinced Breuer that a steel and concrete composite, however impure, was the way to go."[45] In the end the

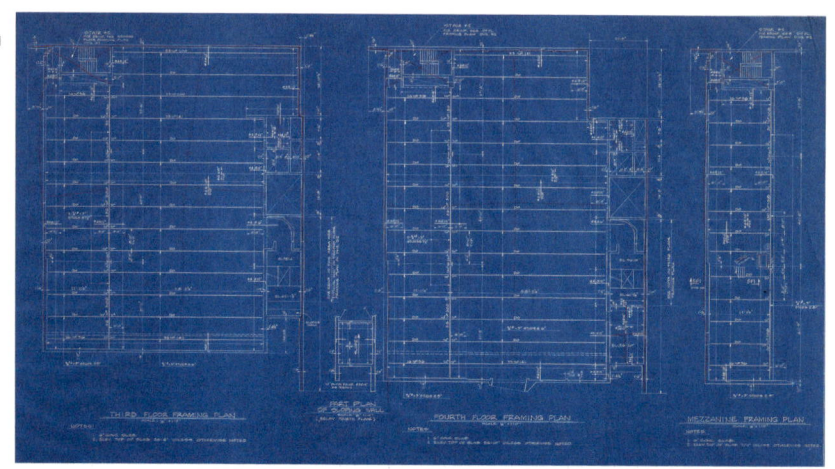

23 Whitney Museum of American Art, framing plan drawings

structure was fully concrete, including a flat plate, up to ground level, with the upper levels made of cast-in-place concrete walls and steel framing spanning twenty-four and sixty feet [23]. While the cast-in-place, board-formed concrete along the property line walls is exposed, the rest of the building façade is clad in dark granite. The ceiling is made of a heavy, precast concrete hanging grid to ensure that the steel structure is well hidden. Per the building code, the steel is also covered in fire protection. Despite the spacecraft-like autonomy of the form, the building structure is not a monolithic or homogeneous whole. Indeed, unlike many of Breuer's precast-clad buildings, the granite cladding is not load-bearing but affixed to the concrete with steel anchors.[46] In this way many of the structural details belie the Whitney's apparent monolithic character, introducing conceptual disjunctions and "impurities" in a sense, though they are largely invisible.

In a March 1959 speech on the occasion of an exhibition of Nervi's work at the Architectural League of New York, Breuer described the difference between Nervi and the American engineers he had known up to that time:

> Despite the imagination which he quietly manifested, and despite his experience and theoretical knowledge, Nervi showed an unusual elasticity in our contact. This has to be explained, because it was far from the passive elasticity of those structural consultants, who put a beam under, wherever a load appears,—move the support a bit to the right or a bit to the left, if it is in the way,—who fight stress with mass, deflection with oversized cross section. Nervi's elasticity is quite different. While he absorbs even rather basic suggestions related to the structure and accepts the requirements of the plan, his participation is a continuous search for a system: a system of geometric rhythm. Structure transcends here the bounds of sheer necessity without sacrificing any of the logic of its usefulness or even of its economy.[47]

Breuer gave this speech at the time of the construction of the St. John's Abbey church, eighteen months after he had replaced his engineer on the project and a year before he discovered problems with the folded plates and replaced the second engineer with Weidlinger. Breuer did not, as Harry Seidler was able to, continue his collaboration with Nervi. Instead he learned from his experience at UNESCO to shape his own tectonics of *chiaroscuro* and sculpted *pilotis* while relying on Weidlinger and Levy for their clearly superior understanding of construction. With Nervi, as with Gropius, Breuer had found a teacher and collaborator from whom to learn, take from, and move on. As he adapted and transformed the lessons of Nervi, misreading and swerving from that source, he did not find nor did he seek a comparable engineering partnership, and he even, with time, accepted instrumental solutions, no longer so "eager to save the structural form of the project from being completely covered by finishes and installations."[48]

The elasticity that Breuer found in Nervi is paradoxically the ability to, as Wölfflin writes, transgress "the strictly architectonic conception of architecture" while staying true to actual structural necessity and history.[49] The collaboration of Nervi and Breuer was fruitful because they could both apply and break the rules of their disciplines, testing what it was to "stay true." What is fascinating for an engineer reading his work is how Breuer both absorbed and misread the lessons of Nervi and meandered on his way to a powerful expression of the *chiaroscuro* of structure.

1 Robert Gatje, *Marcel Breuer: A Memoir* (New York: Monacelli Press, 2000), 210.
2 Ibid., 211.
3 Ibid., 211–12.
4 Ibid., 212.
5 Ibid.
6 Matthys Levy (engineer, Weidlinger Associates), telephone interview by Gina Morrow, July 2, 2014. I want to thank Gina Morrow for conducting this interview and most of all for her tireless research, for our many productive discussions over the course of 2015 and 2016, and for her careful reading and critique of this essay.
7 Marcel Breuer, *Sun and Shadow: The Philosophy of an Architect*, ed. Peter Blake (New York: Dodd, Mead, 1955), 38.
8 "Marcel Breuer," interview published in *Schokbeton* (October 1973): 4.
9 Heinrich Wölfflin, *Renaissance and Baroque*, trans. Kathrin Simon (London: Collins, 1964), 51, 52.
10 Ibid., 33.
11 Ibid., 32.
12 See Gatje, *Marcel Breuer*, 29.
13 For other essential writings on UNESCO, see Barry Bergdoll, "Into the Fold: Nervi, Breuer and a Post-war Architecture of Assembly," in *Pier Luigi Nervi: Architecture as Challenge*, ed. Carlo Maria Olmo and Cristiana Chiorino (Milan: Silvana, 2010), 87–115.
14 A. B. Halpern, D. P. Billington, and S. Adrianssens, "The Ribbed Floor Slab Systems of Pier Luigi Nervi," *Journal of the International Association for Shell and Spatial Structures* 54, nos. 2–3 (2013): 127–36.
15 Sir Jack Zunz (former chair of Ove Arup & Partners [1977–84], co-chair of the Ove Arup Partnership [1984–89], and principal structural designer of the Sydney Opera House), in communication with the author, January 2016. He says, "I took over the Sydney Opera House project in 1961. The concourse had been designed and my only contribution was during its construction. The design is essentially Ove's. He may have had some contribution from Povl Ahm and Ronald Jenkins. Ronald was certainly deeply involved in the analysis." He says further, "It is interesting to recall an incident on the site in July 1962. Utzon, Ove and I were on site looking at the progress of the construction of the concourse beams. Utzon put an arm around Ove's shoulder and said, 'Ove, these are *your* concourse beams.'" On a personal note Zunz was chairman when I was hired by Arup in 1987. He has been an inspiration for several generations of structural engineers.
16 Wölfflin, *Renaissance and Baroque*, 46.
17 Ibid.
18 Matthys Levy has said of the Department of Housing and Urban Development headquarters, "That's a job I worked on, fondly again, with Herb Beckhard. There we did a couple of things that were novel, at least in Breuer's estimation. The floor is a concrete topping poured over precast double-Ts. It is something we suggested because the precast units were available locally, and they tended to result in a lower cost for the building. Incidentally the overall cost of the building was such that it came in under the budget. Which never happens. Breuer had a fixed price contract for that job, so it didn't matter if the job came in under the budget; his fee did not change. Sometimes if you have a percentage fee and the project comes in under the budget, you lose

money; that is: you do a good job and you end up losing money. We worked on the *pilotis* with him, the large columns that are at the base of the face of the building. We helped shape them, so that they worked structurally and resulted in what he wanted to express architecturally. They were large, poured concrete *pilotis*." Levy telephone interview by Morrow.

19 Marcel Breuer noted to Robert Gatje on a plan drawing, "Dear Bob, as you probably noticed, I was not quite happy with our rectangular buttress walls. They are really not buttresses, but members continuing the sidewalls down to the foundations of course, but also to the floor slab which serves as a tension member. I wonder, whether the suggestions of the right hand border of this sheet bring something. The buttresses would have a somewhat triangular inside elevation, wide top, narrow bottom; from outside also, only more sloping; from the North and South also triangles, wide bottoms, narrow tops. Could you sketch up the variations of solutions, plans and elevations of say the East wall? Nervi is not here, this week I am in Holland for three days. But I would like to have this variation for discussion with him say around the 7th of December. In the meantime I will receive, I guess, the new plans and elevations. Please send me also a new print of the longitudinal section which I return here too. Please sketch solution II first and send it along—I think it is the better one. The buttress would still be covered with cut stone, also the top surface (the exterior sloping triangle)." Preliminary plans of church (annotated), November 1, 1953, St. John's Abbey.

20 Gatje, *Marcel Breuer*, 47.
21 Ibid., 112.
22 Marcel Breuer to Nicholas Farkas, July 19, 1957, Folder 9, Box 95, Marcel Breuer Papers, Syracuse University Libraries.
23 Wiesenfeld & Hayward send a proposal to begin work, and in August Farkas agrees to work in association with Wiesenfeld & Hayward. Wiesenfeld & Hayward to Marcel Breuer, July 26, 1957; and Nicholas Farkas to Marcel Breuer, August 14, 1957, both in Folder 9, Box 95, Marcel Breuer Papers, Syracuse University Libraries.
24 James Leon to Hamilton Smith, April 25, 1960, Folder 9, Box 95, Marcel Breuer Papers, Syracuse University Libraries.
25 Paul Weidlinger to Marcel Breuer, Confidential Memorandum, December 1, 1960, Folder 9, Box 95, Marcel Breuer Papers, Syracuse University Libraries.
26 Levy telephone interview by Morrow, in which Levy also says of the dam, "The powerhouse has a folded plate wall and a very heavy concrete ceiling to be able to support a lot of machinery. It was designed for tourists. You enter at the top of an inclined elevator on the face of the dam and you go down to a balcony inside the powerhouse and [they] take you on a tour around the powerhouse. It's such a heavy structure that it wasn't that difficult to build."
27 Levy telephone interview by Morrow.
28 Wölfflin, *Renaissance and Baroque*, 51, 64.
29 Halpern, Billington, and Adrianssens, "Ribbed Floor Slab Systems of Pier Luigi Nervi," 132.

30 Quoted in Shirley Reiff Howarth, "Marcel Breuer: On Religious Architecture," *Art Journal* 38 (Summer 1979): 257.
31 In an interview published in *Art Journal*, Breuer explains about his idea of the "banner." He says, "What I really wanted to do earlier in the St John's Abbey was to create a banner, a kind of banner which is carried in a procession, and have it develop out of the building so that this banner is not a special tower or a special structure as it is in most churches. However, I did not get the idea at that time, so I made a special structure but involved it into the functions of the church. You go through it like an arch to get into the church, and of course it carries the bells and that is an old function which is taken over there and then as a silhouette of the church, as a characteristic shape. In Muskegon, I think I went a little further with this idea of developing the banner out of the structure of the church. And that was the real idea of this entrance façade." Quoted in Howarth, "Marcel Breuer," 260.
32 Harold Bloom, *Anxiety of Influence* (Oxford: Oxford University Press, 1973), 43.
33 Harold Bloom, *A Map of Misreading* (Oxford: Oxford University Press, 1975), 69.
34 Lucretius, *On the Nature of Things*, Book IV, trans. Martin Ferguson Smith (Indianapolis: Hackett, 1969), 123, quoted in Stephen Greenblatt, *The Swerve: How the World Became Modern* (New York: Norton, 2011), 189–90.
35 Quoted in Howarth, "Marcel Breuer," 260.
36 Quoted in "Saint John's Abbey Church," *Saint John's Abbey*, http://www.saintjohnsabbey.org/your-visit/abbey-church/, accessed February 1, 2016.
37 Quoted in Howarth, "Marcel Breuer," 260.
38 Gatje, *Marcel Breuer*, 196.
39 *Breuer's Whitney: An Anniversary Exhibition, September 11–December 8, 1996* (New York: Whitney Museum of American Art, 1996).
40 Breuer, *Sun and Shadow*, 69.
41 Ibid., 69.
42 Ibid., 40.
43 Wölfflin, *Renaissance and Baroque*, 44.
44 *Salire con gravità* (ascend with gravity) are the words of Vincenzo Scamozzi, *L'idea dell'archittetura universale*, vol. 2 (Milan: Stefano Ticozzi, 1838), 679.
45 Gatje, *Marcel Breuer*, 196.
46 In 1997 the steel at the Whitney began to rust. See "Repairing the Whitney's Stone Curtain Wall," *Architecture Magazine*, September 1997. A digital version of the article may be found at http://hstrial-melkordy1.homestead.com/Articles.html.
47 Marcel Breuer, speech on the occasion of the exhibit of Pier Luigi Nervi's work at the Architectural League, March 26, 1959, Breuer Papers, Archives of American Art, Smithsonian Institution.
48 Ibid.
49 Wölfflin, *Renaissance and Baroque*, 33.

III PRECAST PANEL

In many of Breuer's most memorable buildings, repeating modular bays of reinforced concrete panels create deeply molded façades that generate striking visual effects. The technique appeared in the commission for the IBM World Trade Building near Nice, France, begun in 1960, but soon became a Breuer signature. Precast in factories for installation on the construction site, these panels were heavy and strong enough to carry their own weight, as well as in many cases the load of the floors above and adjacent. They also accommodated building services in chases—hollow channels for pipes and conduit supplying the water and power for heating and cooling the building.

By faceting the panels and combining varied panel types, Marcel Breuer & Associates developed highly sculptural façades that broke with the predominant steel-and-glass curtain wall construction. "A new depth of façade is emerging," Breuer explained in 1966, "a three-dimensionality with a resulting greatly expanded vocabulary of architectural expression. Sun and shadow."

Pioneered in buildings for IBM, the firm's panel systems addressed the technical and symbolic needs of "Big Science," the nexus of military and industrial research, particularly as it intersected with "Big Education," the expanded postwar university system. The Breuer firm deployed precast panels as a standardized solution but also customized the panels to address building functions and site conditions. In the Becton building, panels and spiky fins nod to the neo-Gothic context of Yale University, while in a new headquarters for the Department of Housing and Urban Development a more stolid configuration engages the neoclassical monumentality of Washington DC and the gridded street plan of American cities. Breuer and his associates extended this vocabulary to high-rise office buildings, including an unbuilt project for Syracuse and the firm's last completed tower, a headquarters for the Cleveland Trust Company.

1 Armstrong Rubber Company headquarters, New Haven, Connecticut, USA, 1967–69, precast concrete panel detail drawing
2 Construction view
3 IBM administrative, laboratory, and manufacturing facility, Boca Raton, Florida, USA, 1968–72, view of administration wings from laboratory wing
4 Perspective rendering of east façade
5 View of stair tower and entry between administrative wings
6 Department of Housing and Urban Development headquarters, Washington, DC, USA, 1965–68, ground floor plan drawing
7 Typical floor plan drawing
8 Perspective rendering
9 View of ground-level columns and plaza
10 University of Massachusetts, Murray Lincoln Campus Center and Garage, Amherst, Massachusetts, USA, 1965–73, terrace level plan drawing
11 Perspective rendering
12 Section drawings
13 Southeast view
14 Yale University, Becton Engineering and Applied Science Center, New Haven, Connecticut, 1964–70, elevation drawings
15 Perspective rendering
16 Precast concrete panel detail drawings
17 Partial view of rear façade
18 Cleveland Trust Company headquarters, Cleveland, Ohio, USA, 1967–71, partial façade study drawing
19 Perspective rendering
20 Bristol Center office building (unexecuted), Syracuse, New York, USA, 1968–71, precast concrete panel study drawings
21 Elevation drawings
22 Department of Health, Education, and Welfare headquarters, Washington, DC, USA, 1960–77, typical office floor plan drawing
23 Perspective rendering
24 View of southeast corner with US Capitol

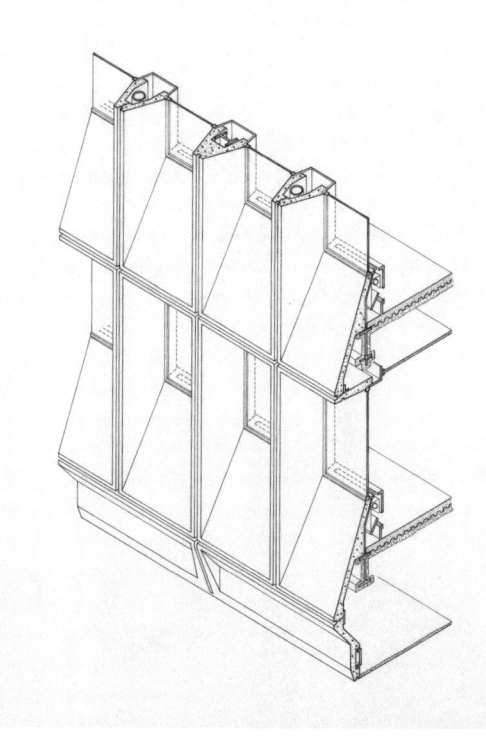

1

2

142   III   PRECAST PANEL

3

4

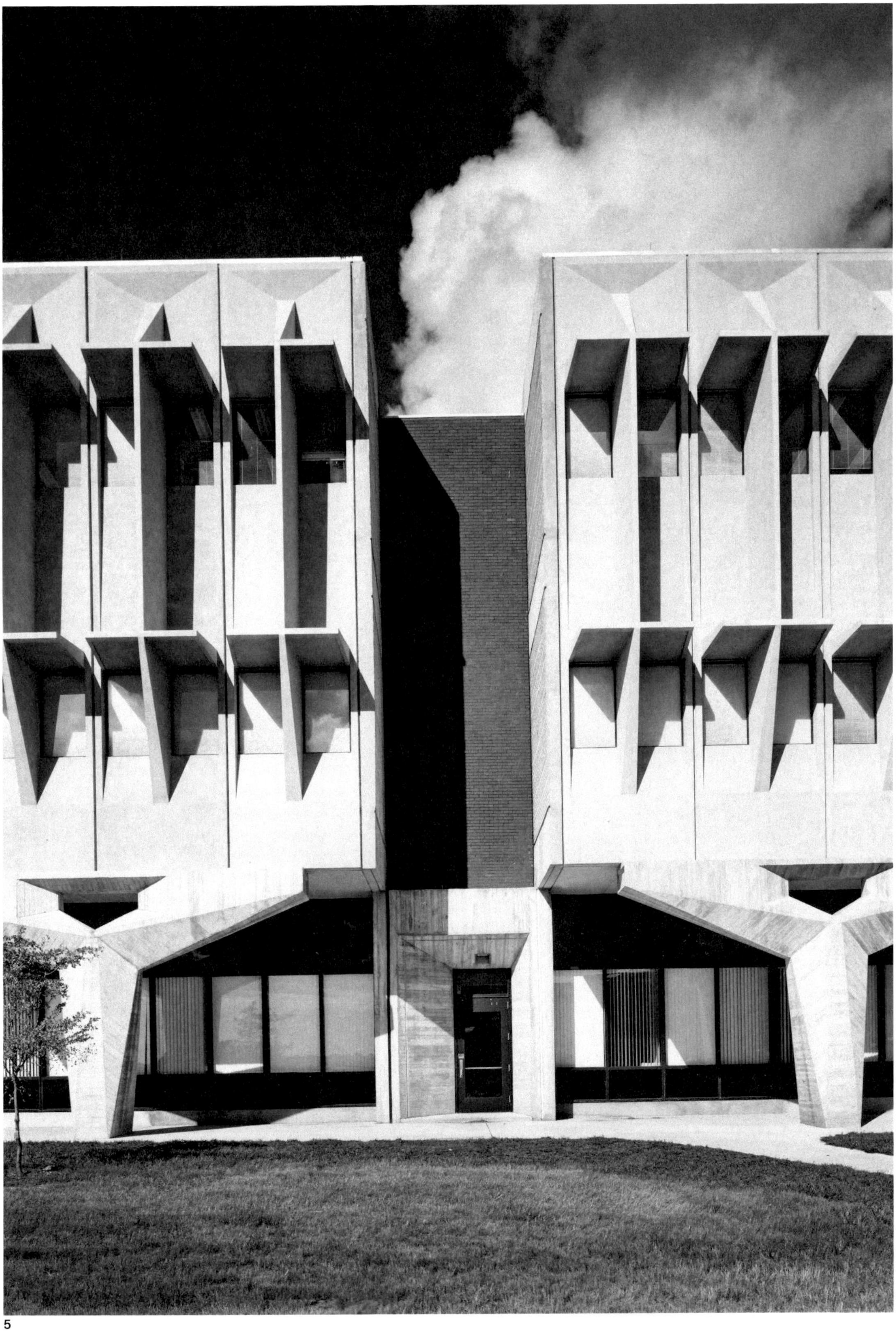

5

III PRECAST PANEL

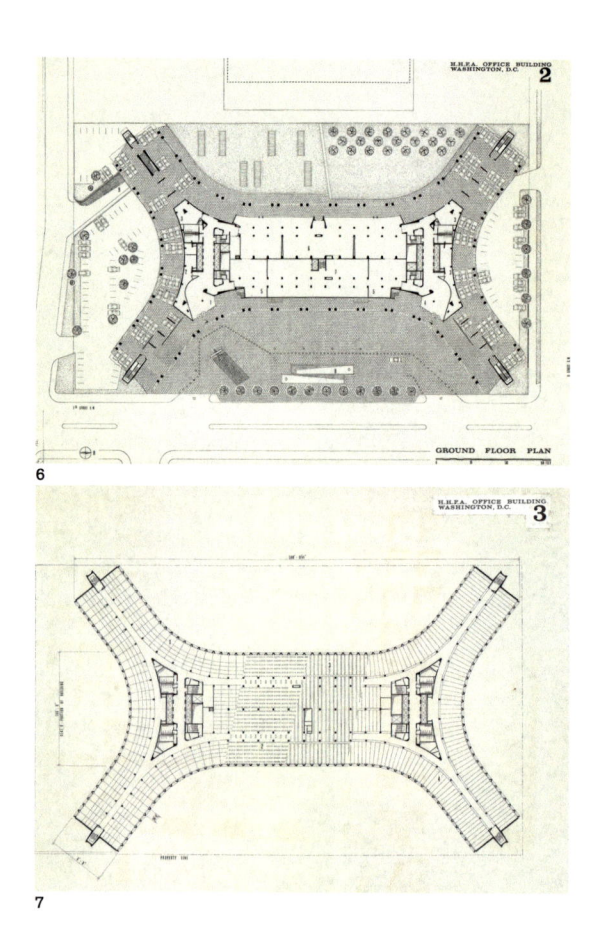

6

7

8

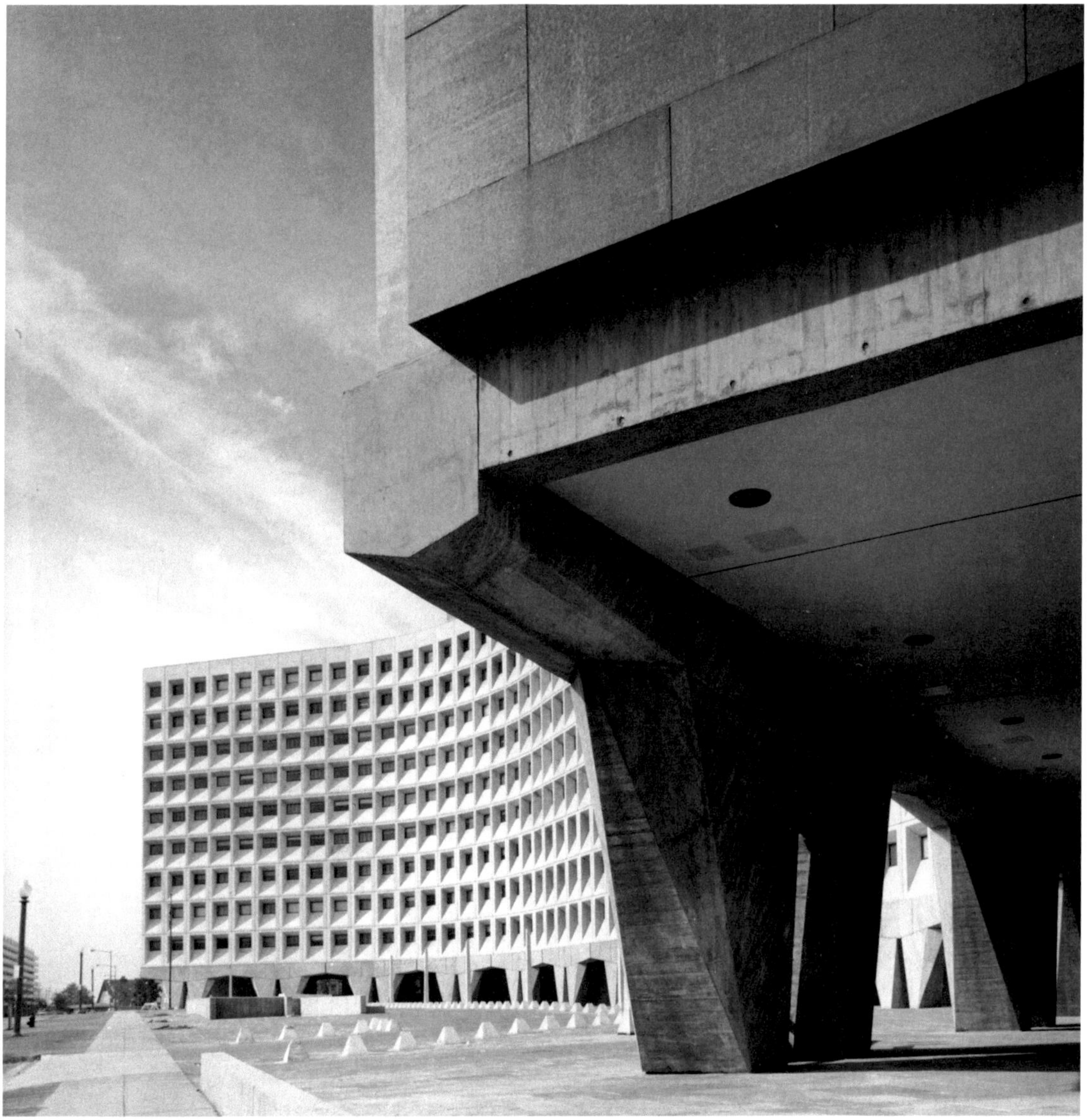

9

146   III   PRECAST PANEL

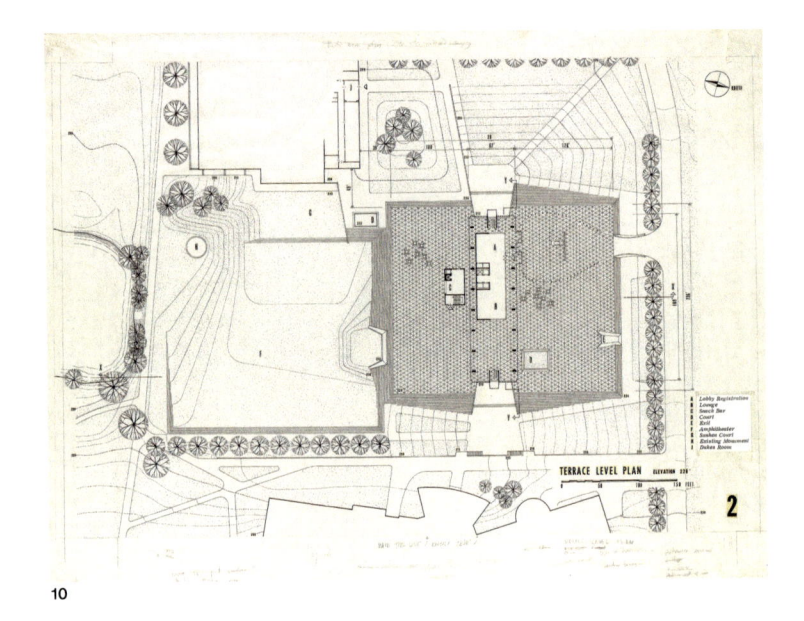

10

11

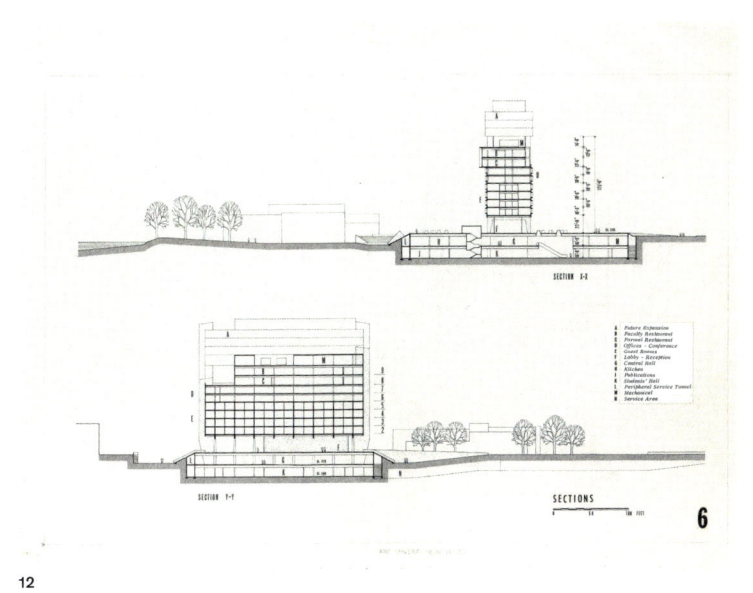

12

13

III PRECAST PANEL

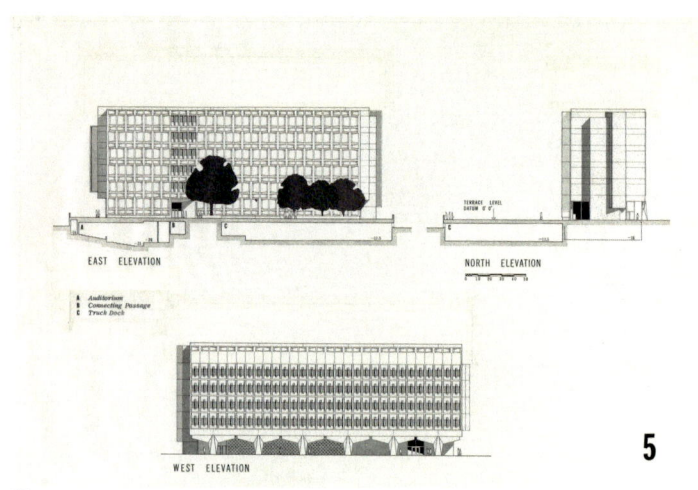

EAST ELEVATION

NORTH ELEVATION

A Auditorium
B Connecting Passage
C Truck Dock

WEST ELEVATION

14

5

15

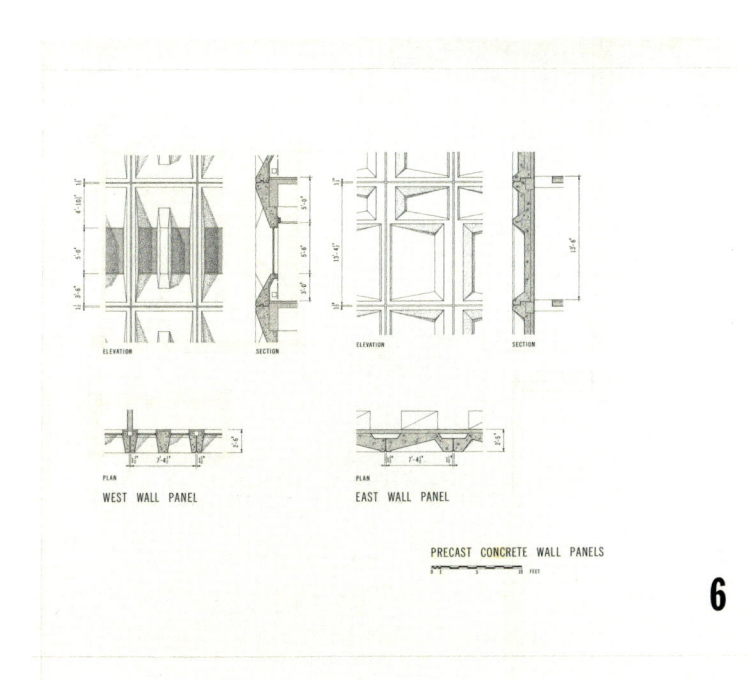

ELEVATION   SECTION   ELEVATION   SECTION

WEST WALL PANEL   EAST WALL PANEL

PRECAST CONCRETE WALL PANELS

6

16

17

III PRECAST PANEL

18

19

20

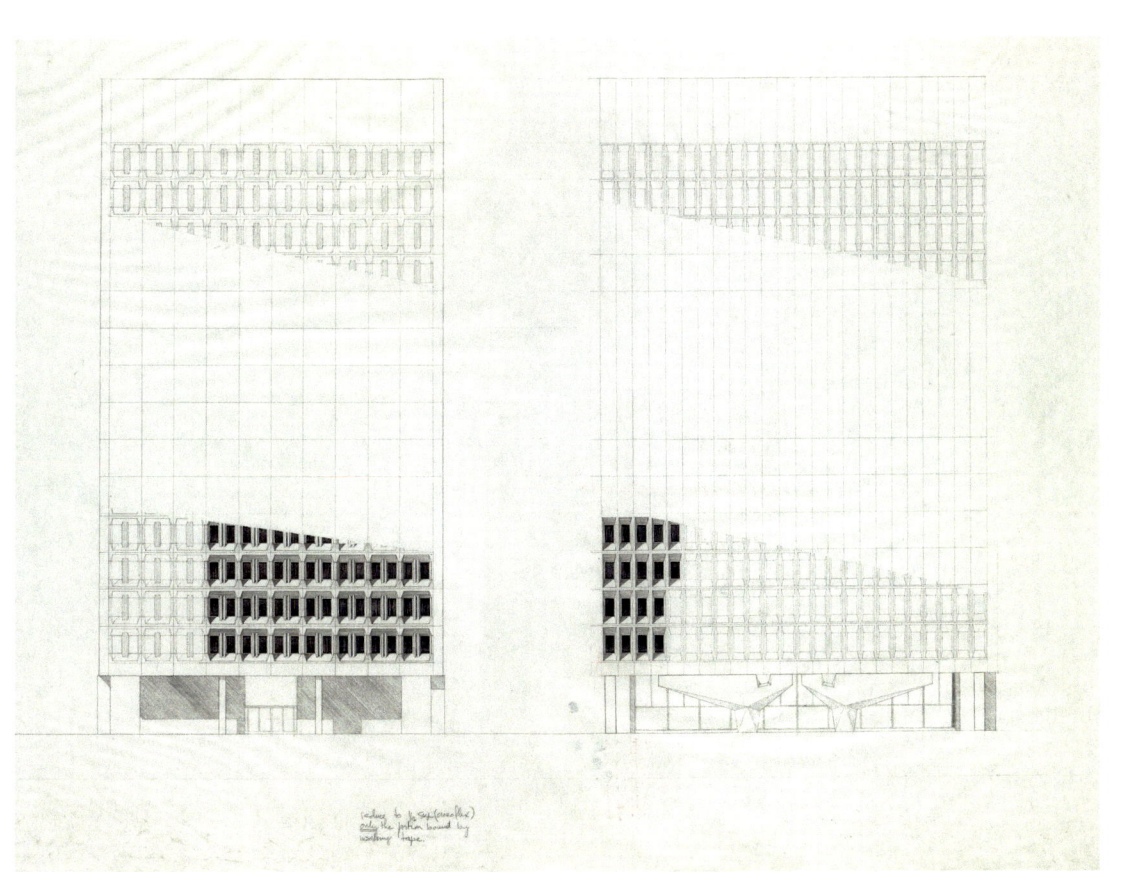

21

152   III   PRECAST PANEL

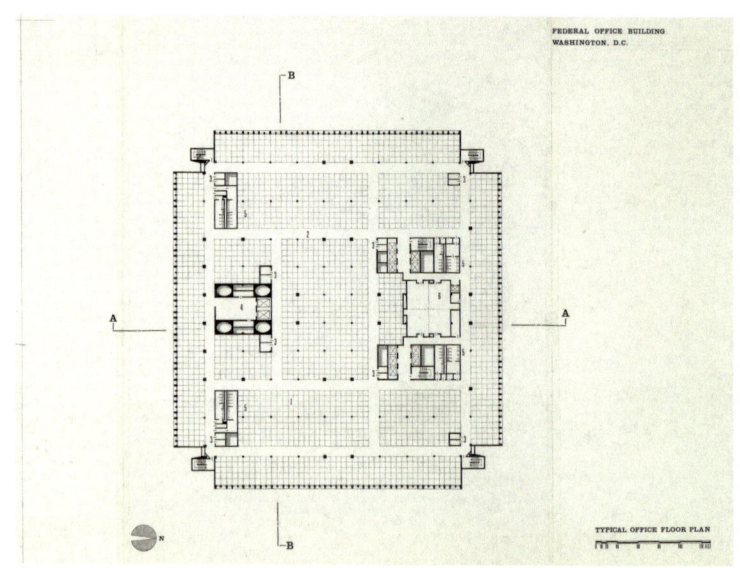

22

23

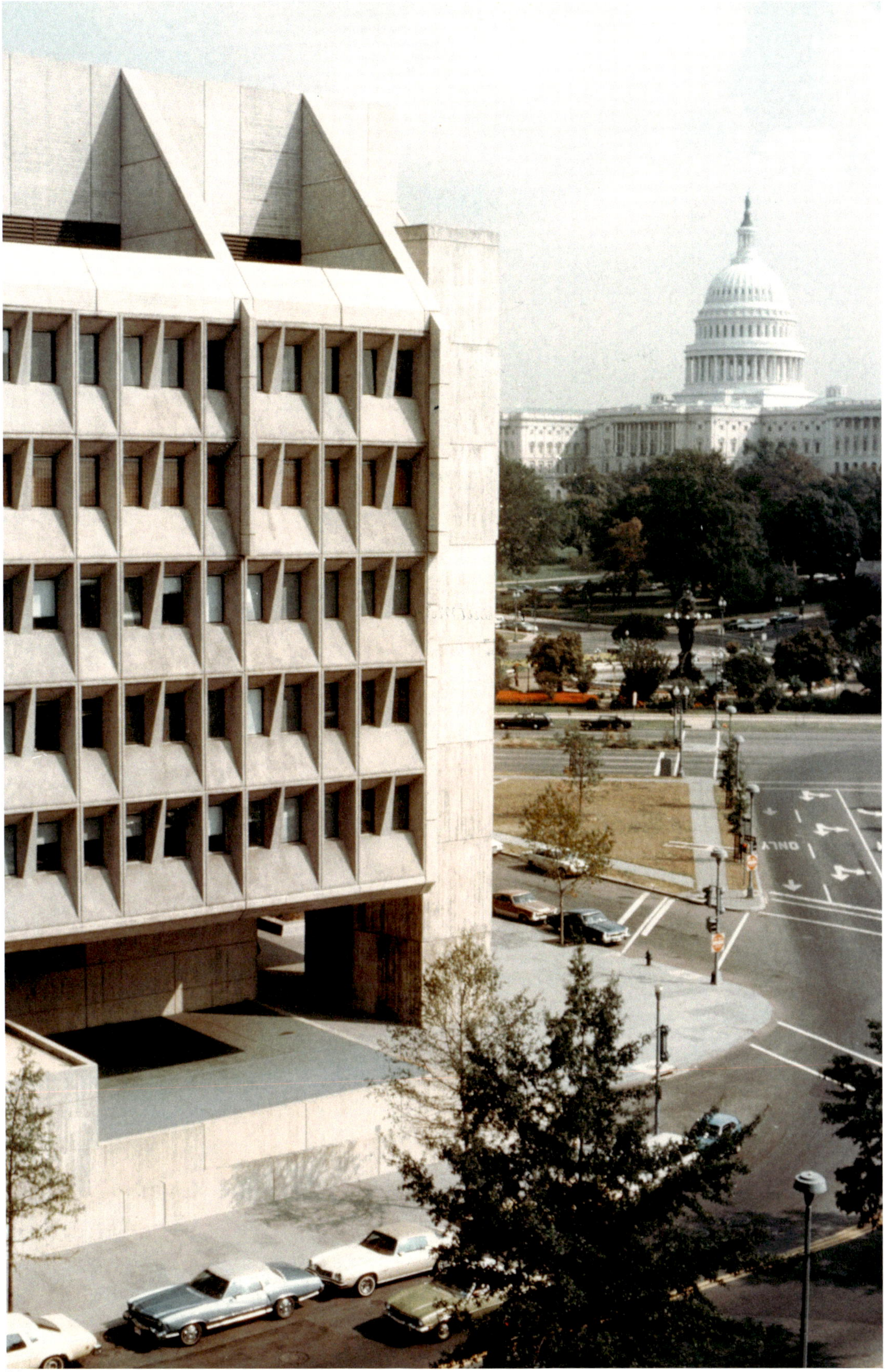

1 Garden City of the Future model, 1936, shopping center and recreational quarter

From Garden City to Concrete City: Breuer and Yorke's Garden City of the Future

Teresa Harris

In 1936, the Cement and Concrete Association, a trade organization of British cement and concrete producers, commissioned Marcel Breuer and F. R. S. Yorke to design a model comprising the center of "an entirely new and therefore 'ideal' town."[1] Breuer and Yorke exhibited the commission, known as the Garden City of the Future, twice that year—at the *Ideal Home Exhibition* in March and the *Building Trades Exhibition* held in the same space six months later—exposing the project to general consumers and those involved in the building trades. The project presented the young architects with an exciting opportunity to explore concepts of large-scale city planning. Its primary significance for Breuer, however, was that it represented his first in-depth engagement with the particularities of concrete construction, allowing him to indulge his "preoccupation with structure and its implications on form." In 1961, having had time to ponder the influence of this project on his career, he identified the model as the "turning point" where his architecture "in connection with concrete develops toward more plastic form."[2]

The Cement and Concrete Association requested "drawings for a model of a modern city, on a flat unobstructed site, with a river or sea to the south."[3] The model was to measure nine and a half by five and a half feet at a scale of one-twentieth of an inch to one foot, representing an area approximately half a mile long by a quarter mile wide. The size constraints of the commission account for some of the oddities in planning, as Breuer and Yorke only had space to provide a schematic representation of a city center rather than a complete urban plan [2]. However, because the association did not stipulate an exact location for the design, the architects did not have to contend with the idiosyncrasies of a specific site. Breuer and Yorke's original concept for the Garden City called for a residential center, consisting of flats, a school, and some small, embedded

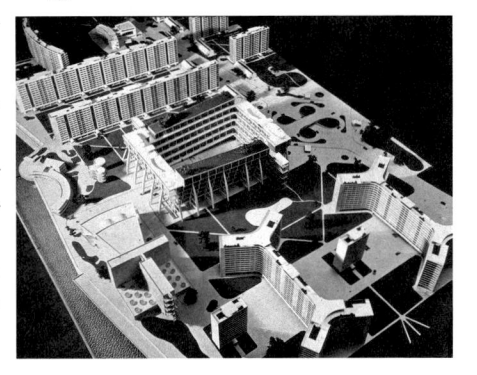

2 Garden City of the Future model

shops on the western side of the model. In the center of the scheme, a traffic exchange in the shape of a cloverleaf connected a shopping center to the major thoroughfare, below which cafés and a theater nestled in gardens lining the waterfront. Office buildings for commercial or governmental workers occupied the eastern portion of the city center. In the *Architects' Journal*, Breuer and Yorke also described planning elements omitted due to space constraints. Docks, factories, and other industrial buildings would have extended to the east, while the residential quarter would extend farther westward and the recreation center would spread "fan-wise" to the north of the cloverleaf traffic intersection. Museums, a technical center, and the requisite aerodrome were less precisely located, although the architects noted that "non-stop underground trains" would connect the town to the airfield.[4]

The client's intent and rationale for choosing Breuer and Yorke can only be surmised, as no correspondence survives. However, the trade publications of the Cement and Concrete Association reveal their interest in promoting the suitability of concrete for a wide range of building types. (Pamphlets detailing the use of concrete in nonindustrial structures, such as houses and churches, gradually appear by the late 1930s.) Breuer and Yorke offered distinct but complementary areas of expertise that made them an inspired choice for the client. On the one hand, having studied and taught at the Bauhaus, Breuer had impeccable modernist credentials and could boast of success in domesticating an industrial material; his tubular steel furniture sold well enough to support him through the lean years of the worldwide economic depression. Yorke, on the other hand, played a pivotal role in educating British audiences about modernism and new materials. He was the first secretary of MARS (Modern Architectural Research) Group, founded in 1932, and his book, *The Modern House*, celebrated continental modernists already using concrete for domestic architecture.[5] He also possessed technical expertise and a long-standing interest in modern building materials and prefabrication showcased in his weekly "Trade Notes" column in the *Architects' Journal*.[6]

Although each partner's individual contribution to the design of the Garden City of the Future is difficult to discern, their partnership agreement specified that only one of the partners would take the lead on any given project and make a final decision if the two disagreed on a strategy or approach.[7] Breuer appears to have taken the lead on the Garden City of the Future model. He claimed as much in a 1942 letter to Marion Becker, director of the Cincinnati Modern Art Society, who hoped to include Breuer's work in an exhibition on demountable architecture called *Shelter in Transit and Transition*. Breuer wondered if she would also "be interested in a photograph of a large scale model which I designed during my partnership with R.F.S. [sic] Yorke in London."[8] But we do not have to take Breuer's word for it. The prevalence of building types developed by Breuer in earlier projects points to his authorship, as does the assertion of Randall Evans, an employee in Breuer and Yorke's office at the time, that the Garden City of the Future was "90 per cent Breuer."[9] Jeremy Melvin also notes that it was Breuer who accepted invitations to lecture on the project despite his difficulties with English.[10]

Breuer conceived the model as a "utopian and schematic suggestion for the rebuilding of a city center."[11] With no actual location, he and Yorke had near complete freedom, which they used to create a textbook example of functional planning as promulgated by the Congrès internationaux d'architecture moderne (CIAM) of which Breuer was a founding member.[12] In a lecture on the Garden City of the Future given at the Polytechnic School of Architecture at the University of Westminster in 1936, Breuer spoke of his interest in CIAM's efforts to formulate guiding principles for urban design based on thorough research into the "social, hygienic, technical and legal conditions in the larger cities of the different countries of the world."[13] Each zone within the model clearly illustrates one of the "four functional categories of 'dwelling, work, transportation, and recreation,' the basic components of the CIAM 'Functional City.'"[14]

Concrete as Building Material in the Garden City of the Future
First and foremost, the Garden City of the Future was an advertisement for concrete as a universal material. The model offered Breuer a chance for aesthetic experimentation driven by the need to provide his client with a wide range of forms that could be produced using concrete. As many observers have noted, starting with architectural historian Henry-Russell Hitchcock in his 1938 catalog accompanying an exhibit of Breuer's work at Harvard University, Breuer borrowed from earlier projects and included them with slight modifications in his Garden City of the Future model. The site's theater is a "suaver and more graceful version" of Breuer's entry for the Ukrainian State Theater competition in Kharkov [3], the apartment buildings

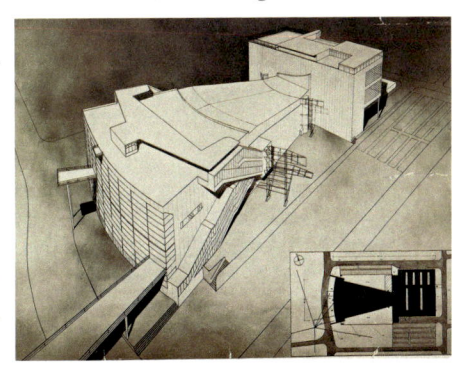

3 Ukrainian State Theater (unexecuted), competition, 1931, aerial perspective rendering

bear a striking resemblance to various concrete-slab flats Breuer designed in the 1920s, and the cloverleaf traffic pattern was first developed for a competition to redesign Potsdamer Platz.[15] However, the project also served as an incubator for the modular structures that would dominate Breuer's later career, many of which are analyzed by others in this volume.

Material and architectural style were inextricably linked in the Garden City of the Future. Only modern technologies such as steel and reinforced concrete allowed architects to erect buildings tall enough to achieve high densities with relatively small footprints, freeing up space for parks and plazas.[16] Breuer embraced the possibilities inherent in these new materials but was also careful not to equate their use with modernism, stating that "the basis of modern architecture … is not the new materials, nor even the new form, but the new mentality … the manner in which we judge our needs."[17] Architects could build a modernist structure in wood and stone or a traditional building in steel and glass depending on the way they approached the problem to be solved. That being said, Breuer acknowledged that "reinforced concrete often leads to characteristic new forms."[18]

Breuer's architecture prior to his work with Yorke in London had been largely rectilinear, and the increased reliance on curves in the Garden City of the Future was a response to reinforced concrete's unique structural characteristics. Later in his career, Breuer would talk of reinforced concrete as a "completely plastic medium" that allowed "continuous, fluent tension-structures."[19] But in 1936 Breuer did not yet understand how to fully exploit this unique quality of reinforced concrete, and so the most sculptural elements of many buildings appear in peripheral places like staircases, canopies, and buttresses. These plastic elements enabled Breuer to experiment with smaller details before taking risks with the structure of larger buildings. It is perhaps not surprising that the smallest building—the cloverleaf-shaped café located near the shopping center—is also the most experimental in form [1].

4 Model of slab apartment building (Apartmenthaus, Modell), 1923–24

Like many other modernist architects of the time, Breuer created building types for each function within the Garden City of the Future. The residential buildings represent an evolution of the various concrete-slab apartment buildings Breuer designed in the 1920s, beginning with a model that Breuer entered into a competition sponsored by *Bauwelt* [4] and continuing through to the compe-

5 Großsiedlung Siemensstadt, Apartment House Complex (unexecuted), competition, Spandau-Haselhorst, Berlin, Germany, 1928, aerial view drawing and perspective rendering

tition design for Großsiedlung Siemensstadt in the Spandau-Haselhorst area of Berlin [5].[20] The model for *Bauwelt*, dating to 1923–24, reveals Breuer grappling with the idea of a mid-rise apartment complex of seven stories and incorporating ideas from many other sources, including Le Corbusier's proposal the previous year for six-story housing complexes containing duplex apartments and hanging gardens in the Ville Contemporaine. But the debate over low-rise versus high-rise housing had already been going on for years. A decade earlier, German garden city advocates argued against multistory apartment buildings upon hygienic and moral grounds. According to common theories of disease at the time, bad air moved upward and no amount of cross-ventilation could retard that movement. Therefore, multiple families stacked one above the other necessarily resulted in a less hygienic situation than single-family homes. These housing reformers believed that the attached gardens and outdoor work and recreation spaces of row houses afforded health benefits that multistory apartment buildings could provide their residents only at great additional expense due to the high cost of land in most urban areas. In addition, for many of these reformers, the family represented the fundamental unit of society and required its own private space.[21]

Unsurprisingly, Walter Gropius and many other members of CIAM would come down on the other side of the debate, jettisoning what they perceived as outdated moral ideals and emphasizing the economy of high-rise building, particularly if surrounding land was given over to shared green space.[22] Many CIAM proponents, especially the Soviet members, substituted a collective ideal for that of the private family home, with the aim being that communal facilities and spaces accompanying high-rise buildings would fundamentally transform societal norms, ushering in a "socially superior mode of life."[23] Breuer's 1924 slab apartment design, from a decade before the Garden City of the Future, incorporated elements from both sides of the debate [4]. Like the low-rise row houses favored by the garden city movement, his apartment building was only two rooms wide so that all rooms would have access to natural light and ventilation.[24] Similar to modern Soviet collective housing, his design incorporated balconies that ran the entire length of the building, thus providing access to individual duplex apartments. Staircases placed at either end provided access to the long balconies in turn.

Breuer further developed the concept of the slab apartment in a series of unbuilt designs prepared in the late 1920s with the assistance of Gustav Hassenpflug, his former student at the Bauhaus. The drawings for the 1928 competition entry for Großsiedlung Siemensstadt [5] show three long, thin rows of apartments eighteen stories high with two-story row houses for single families tucked between the imposing lines of the high-rises. Breuer emphasized the horizontality of the taller buildings and the standardization of construction, which was devoid of decoration aside from the visual rhythm provided by stairwell towers. The towers protruding from the building's surface found a faint echo in the punctuation of vertical supports subordinated to the balconies running the length of the building. Despite the fact that the design called for only three rows of high-rise housing, the project clearly could be expanded ad infinitum, hinting at a type of urban planning that relied upon the undifferentiated repetition of standardized forms like that found in Ludwig Hilberseimer's *Großstadtarchitektur*, published the year before, in 1927.

This early inclination toward standardization makes Breuer's approach to the apartment buildings of the Garden City of the Future all the more surprising in that he took great pains to differentiate the façades through rhythmic patterns of fenestration and balconies. The crescent-shaped apartment complex of the Garden City of the Future [6,7]—despite its distinctive form, which bends around the central axis of the protruding stair tower— is closest in taxonomy to the design for a slab apartment building that Breuer produced while at the Bauhaus. Here, however, Breuer seems to have settled on a mid-rise height of twelve stories in order to comply with "calculations [that] have shown that this height provides the most rational utilization of site area."[25] The twelve-story plan was also the most cost-effective construction in terms of foundations, structural framework, elevators, and other mechanical equipment.[26] In line with his earlier work, galleries run the entire length of the concave façade of the Garden City apartment complex, offering access to the apartments. Unlike most of his previous housing designs, however, this one had a repeated pattern of openings in the façade to offset the monotony of standardized elements. Gardens on every other floor extend through the full width of the building and alternate with groupings of two horizontal windows, creating a rhythmic pattern most noticeable on the convex side of the building. The diagonals created by the balustrades of the switchback staircases at either end protrude from the façade, visually capping the predominantly horizontal structure. Breuer also encased the central staircase in glass, through which one could see the uninterrupted flights of concrete treads. Thus, the staircases become sculptural statements—continuous forms that take advantage of concrete's structural possibilities.

The apartment complex's crescent shape complemented the smaller, concave façade of the school placed opposite, but the introduction of curved shapes into his Garden City design was not simply a formal move on Breuer's part or an attempt to emphasize concrete's material properties. Bending the complex's form compensates for its north-south orientation in that angling the ends toward the east-west sun allows some daylight to be captured. Crucially, the curve also represents Breuer's attempt to reference British tradition, particularly the Royal Crescent in Bath designed by John Wood the Younger and built between 1767 and 1775. Hitchcock made this connection in his essay, "Marcel Breuer and the American Tradition in Architecture," stating that the curved form "suggests a reference to the admirable crescents of the English housing tradition of the eighteenth and early nineteenth centuries."[27] Breuer was certainly aware of this tradition and cited the Royal Crescent as a good example of modern planning because the street of approximately one hundred houses was "so constructed that they seem almost like one building" and appeared "strongly standardized."[28] These ideas may also have been a legacy of Breuer's partnership with Yorke, as Yorke and the English architectural critic P. Morton Shand were among the first to articulate a relationship between Regency architecture and modernism.[29] Like German modern architects who located the last period of honest architectural design in the Biedermeier period, Yorke and his peers found that English architecture had developed in a truthful and logical way up until the Regency. Both groups abhorred the stylistic eclecticism prevalent in Europe during the nineteenth century but found hope for a new epoch in the turn toward engineering and the machine, promoted most famously by Le Corbusier. Breuer and Yorke clearly believed their designs moved that agenda forward.

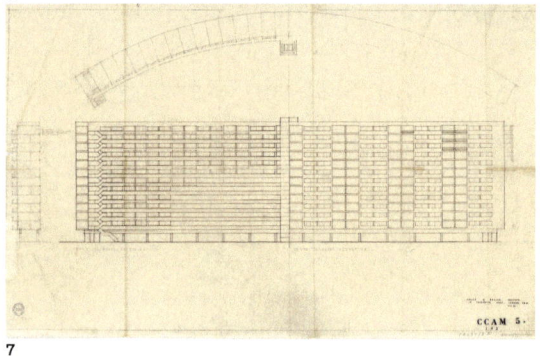

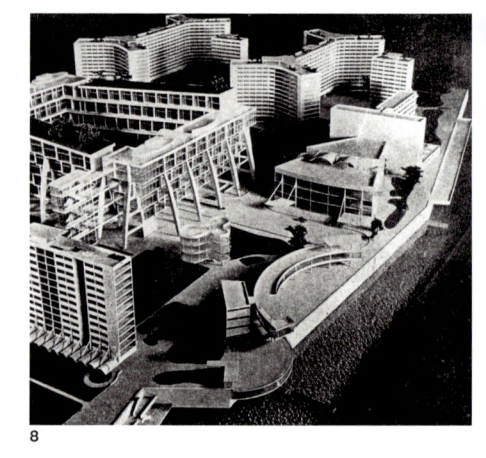

6 Residential buildings, Garden City of the Future model
7 Crescent apartment building, Garden City of the Future model, elevation and plan
8 Garden City of the Future model, shopping center and recreational quarter
9 Garden City of the Future, theater elevation and roof plan drawings
10 Garden City of the Future, east elevation drawing of shopping center

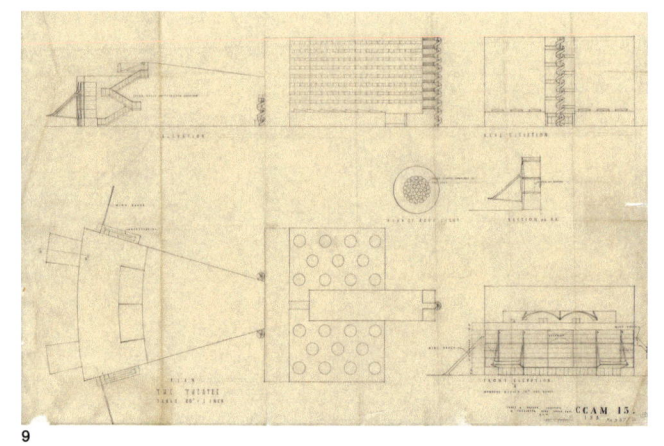

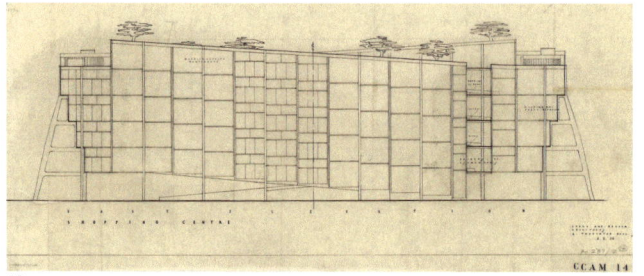

The crescent-shaped apartment building was the exception within the Garden City of the Future, as the vast majority of the apartment buildings follow the *Zeilenbau* model advocated by German and Dutch reformers, in which parallel rows of long, thin slabs are oriented in a north-south direction to maximize sun exposure. Rather than utilize a continuous, outdoor access corridor for these flats, as he had at Siemensstadt, Breuer punctuated the façade with recessed staircases that bookend repeated compositions of balconies flanked by paired horizontal windows [6]. He further accentuated the staircases by marking their entrance with semicircular cantilevered canopies at ground level on the eastern façade. On the opposite side, an uninterrupted line of longer canopies ran the length of the building, protecting inhabitants from the noise and dirt of the car traffic passing beneath the building. Each canopy was suspended by thin ribs of concrete that mimic the rods or chains holding cast-iron canopies in place on older buildings [8]. This formal gesture was likely not a requirement of the barrel-vault concrete form and belies an unwillingness to trust the structural properties of the material.

The curved forms of canopies are the most noticeable plastic element of these apartment buildings. Similar plastic elements enlivened other buildings in the Garden City of the Future. The theater [9], for example, boasted a switchback staircase on its southern elevation, although it was pressed against the solid wall surface, reducing its sculptural impact. A spiral staircase, similar to that found later on the UNESCO Secretariat, formed the spine of the theater's rear façade, while smaller spiral staircases bracketed the volume housing the auditorium. The theater also featured two different styles of canopies. Curved canopies—similar to those found on the apartment buildings but slightly wider and shallower—protected the auditorium's roof access, while flat canopies suspended from a glass façade marked the entrance to the building on the ground floor. Lastly, the original drawing for the building incorporated flaring wind braces to the side of the entrance. Breuer eliminated these braces in the model, though it is unclear whether that was an aesthetic or structural decision.

While Breuer's attempts to articulate the façades of his residential buildings reveal him grappling with the aesthetic of standardized construction, the basic spatial layout of the housing did not significantly deviate from examples of housing designed by architects such as Gropius or Bruno Taut. Breuer pursued more innovative forms in building types other than housing, particularly the shopping center at the heart of the plan [8, 10]. Contemporary viewers responded to this innovation, and the shopping center dominated the imagery of the March 1936 article on the model that appeared in the *Architects' Journal.* It was also featured prominently on the cover of the as above September 23, 1936 issue of the British Broadcasting Corporation's weekly publication, the *Listener.*[30] Indeed, Hitchcock considered the shopping center the most "ambitious" and "revolutionary" structure contained in the Garden City of the Future [8, 10], noting in particular the diagonal movement of the floors and the "half-biological, half-mechanical" braces supporting the building.[31]

Breuer conceived of this shopping center as a squared-off spiral of covered terraces along which shoppers could stroll free from the menace of car traffic. In fact, incoming traffic from the cloverleaf junction passed directly under the building to park in the spaces provided beneath it. Pedestrians could enter the shopping center at various points, including the banks of escalators found in service volumes on either side of the building. For Breuer, the spiral arrangement of the shopping center offered multiple benefits. All stores had access to natural light, and shoppers could survey the entirety of the shopping center from any vantage point along the ramp. Unlike a large department store but similar to the shopping district of a small town, the shopping center would offer consumers a variety of independent shops with dissimilar wares in close proximity. The inverted ziggurat form, combined with the tilted floors of the ramp, also injected a certain amount of dynamism to the design. Most importantly, however, it created a civic space, the equivalent of a large public square with the surrounding "streets" stacked vertically. This allowed him to counter the arguments of critics of modernist planning who lamented the loss of social interaction that routinely occurred in traditional streets. Breuer had found an ingenious way of maintaining the open planning espoused by CIAM while transplanting those lost social interactions into contained spaces, protected from weather and traffic.

In his 1936 lecture at the Polytechnic School of Architecture, Breuer acknowledged that the shopping center utilized a "very similar construction" to that of a hospital with eleven hundred beds he had designed for Elberfeld, Germany, as a competition entry in 1929 [11].[32] p.36/4 Both featured a stepped, inverted form, with each floor extending beyond the limits of the floor below. The hospital also incorporated braces to help support the upper floors, although the braces were perfectly

11 Hospital for eleven hundred beds (unexecuted), competition, Elberfeld, Germany, 1929, perspective rendering

rectilinear and reduced to the thinnest possible diameter—as opposed to the thicker, subtly swelling members supporting the shopping center. The difference in shape stemmed from the different materials to be used; the hospital building was to be executed in steel, while the shopping center utilized reinforced concrete. Thus, the shopping center embodied what Breuer would later call "the 'new structure' in its most expressive form ... hollow below and substantial on top," but it did so without fully exploiting concrete's ability to create seemingly unsupported cantilevers.[33] From this perspective, the shopping center exemplifies Breuer's somewhat conservative use of concrete throughout the model and affirms Ada Louise Huxtable's 1960 observation in a monograph on the engineer Pier Luigi Nervi that because it is "the nature of man—and of the architect—to cling to accustomed patterns, there has always been a tendency to use new materials in old ways."[34] Ultimately, Breuer would learn to use concrete's "unique monolithic nature" to create "huge open spans, thin-shelled vaults, startling cantilevers and free-curving shapes," but he would do so by partnering with engineers like Nervi who more fully understood the capabilities of the material.[35]

Perhaps the most fruitful experiment in the Garden City of the Future was the office building with forked ends [2, 8]. Unlike many of the other buildings, it had no precedent in Breuer's work, but he would return repeatedly to this form later in his career, especially when he began to produce large-scale office and commercial buildings. This early prototype of the office building featured more conventional glazing, as Breuer had not yet discovered the endlessly modifiable technique of creating modular façades out of concrete precast panels (see Precast Panel Portfolio). Of course, the glazing was only conventional by later standards. As even Lewis Mumford conceded in a negative review of Breuer's Secretariat building at the UNESCO complex (1955–58)—which borrowed heavily from the office buildings of the Garden City of the Future—glass curtain walls were still fairly innovative in 1936. The experimental nature of the Garden City office buildings was further emphasized by the three styles of glazing incorporated into the building. Breuer's intention might have been purely aesthetic, but the type of glazing appears to be determined by each façade's orientation to the sun.

These office buildings did not feature the sculptural elements that graced the other buildings of the Garden City of the Future, but the very form of the buildings reveals Breuer's interest in activating the plastic possibilities of the edifice as a whole. There

12 Hans Poelzig & Erich Zimmermann, competition for a high-rise near the Friedrichstraße train station, Berlin (Hochhaus am Bahnhof Friedrichstraße, Berlin), 1921, perspective rendering
13 Le Corbusier, Macia Plan, Barcelona, Spain, 1935, site plan drawing
14 Garden City of the Future, plan drawing
15 Le Corbusier, plan drawing of Ville contemporaine de trois millions d'habitants, 1922
16 Karl Ludwig Hilberseimer, Hochhausstadt, east-west street, 1924

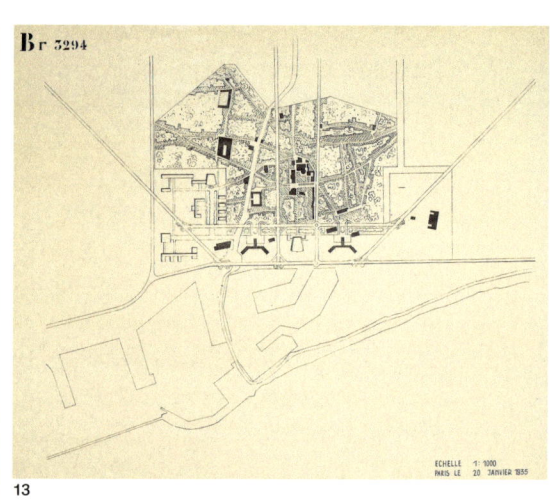

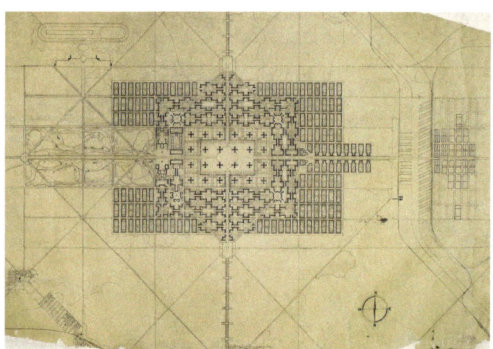

are a number of possible inspirations for Breuer's formal innovation here. Isabelle Hyman notes that the forked design is similar to Hans Poelzig's 1921 plan for a skyscraper near the train station on Friedrichstraße in Berlin [12].[36] It also seems likely that Breuer was aware of the Y-shaped buildings in Le Corbusier's Ville radieuse (1930) or in his waterfront design for Plan Macia, a 1933 urban renewal project for Barcelona [13]. However, if Breuer did make reference to Poelzig or Le Corbusier, he did not blindly copy them; rather, he modified and built upon these precedents, doubling the Y-shaped forms and connecting them with a long horizontal bar. Various economic rationales support Breuer's design. Adding the forked ends to a slab structure increases the amount of office space available without significantly increasing the land necessary for its execution. In contrast to a traditional office building, which might fill its entire parcel, no room in this design would ever be far from a window. Instead, these forked structures offered all offices access to natural light. Lastly, the plan allowed the efficient placement of elevators so that two mechanical cores could service the entire building. One need look no further than Breuer's double-Y shaped designs for the Van Leer office building in Amstelveen, Netherlands (1957–58); IBM Research Center in La Gaude, France (1960–62); or the Department of Housing and Urban Development in Washington, DC (1965–68) to see the importance of the Garden City of the Future within Breuer's oeuvre.

Breuer's Contribution to Modernist City Planning
The Garden City of the Future [14] offered an early and compelling formal alternative to the influential urban visions of the 1920s that had helped shape CIAM principles of urban planning such as Le Corbusier's Ville contemporaine (1922) or Hilberseimer's Hochhausstadt (1927), an extreme example of the *Zeilenbau* model [15, 16]. Breuer accomplished this feat not by overthrowing CIAM principles but by creating space for playful experimentation within the rigid framework of the four functions. In fact, Breuer's approach to planning echoed his approach to architecture: curves and sculptural groupings of buildings provided a counterpoint to the plan's underlying rectilinear grid, just as sculptural elements relieved the visual sameness of standardized construction.

While the details varied, modernist circulation strategies relied heavily on a hierarchy of streets based on traffic flow. Highways moved people and goods efficiently between quarters of the city, avoiding secondary streets serving local through-traffic. Pedestrian paths were ideally separated from vehicular traffic entirely. In many urban plans, the grid of streets defined the fabric of the city, especially in residential neighborhoods. This was as true in Le Corbusier's *maisons à redents* and block housing in the Ville contemporaine as it was for the *Zeilenbau* model in which rows of parallel housing are contained by perimeter streets, even if the buildings do not engage the street in a traditional manner. Breuer still organized the Garden City of the Future using a grid framework, but the grid does not reveal itself as a network of streets. Instead, the primary orthogonal grid is visible largely in the placement of the buildings themselves, which are oriented to the cardinal directions. The second grid appears in the diagonal network of pedestrian paths that is overlaid upon the first at a forty-five-degree angle. In other words, Breuer suppresses the secondary streets visually; the highway and pedestrian paths are clearly visible, but local traffic is hidden underneath the buildings. The highway delivers drivers directly to their homes, shopping, or work, where they can park in underground parking garages or at ground level beneath apartment and office buildings raised on *pilotis*. Much of the travel within a neighborhood was then conducted on foot. The architects made walking easy for inhabitants, with minimal distances between residences and schools and with stores selling basic amenities interspersed within the residential areas. Leaving each quarter was equally effortless due to the location of a major subway stop beneath the central cloverleaf, easily accessible from any of the three zones shown on the plan. The subway entrances also allow foot traffic to cross the highway safely underground.

Breuer achieved two interrelated ends by suppressing the secondary streets. First, he achieved a "simplification of traffic conditions" created by "fewer house doors, fewer streets, and above all, fewer street intersections."[37] In fact, the only visible intersection in the entire plan is the prominent cloverleaf junction, which Breuer held up as "a new solution of an urgent traffic problem."[38] The cloverleaf, which he had first proposed between 1928 and 1929 to alleviate traffic problems at Potsdamer Platz in Berlin, prevented the stoppage of traffic at street intersections through the use of an "over bridge" in one direction and an "under bridge" in the other.[39] In the Garden City of the Future model, the cloverleaf connected the east-west highway to one running north-south. Here, Breuer distilled the cloverleaf to its purest form. Unconstrained by surrounding buildings, it served as a rational roadway system designed to move cars quickly and efficiently rather than as a solution to the historical tangle of streets that converged at

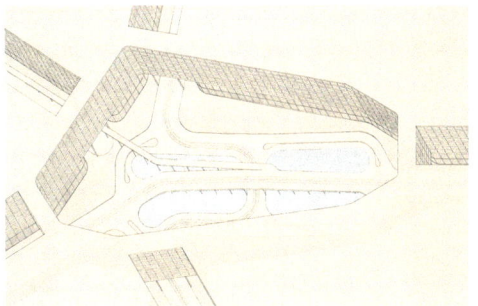

17 Garden City of the Future, cloverleaf detail drawing from 1936 article in the *Architects' Journal*
18 Potsdamer Platz project (unexecuted), Berlin, Germany, 1929, axonometric drawing

Potsdamer Platz [17, 18]. Of course, the curves of the cloverleaf also represented another structure that could be constructed out of concrete, recalling the primary purpose of the model.

Secondly, the suppression of secondary streets allowed for a rich interplay of architectural forms within the urban plan as the groupings of buildings did not have to take streets into account. Individually, Breuer's buildings followed the logic of standardization—with construction that took advantage of the repetition of forms and the industrial production of windows and fixtures—but this logic of standardization did not extend to the city as a whole. Buildings were seen in relation to each other, not simply as repeatable components of the plan. Breuer injected life into his composition through the sculptural grouping of buildings and the judicious use of curves and diagonals, recognizing a human need for variety and contrast often lost in the modernist drive toward standardization. For example, the small and large curves of the school and the crescent-shaped apartment building faced off across a sports field, creating an area of visual focus within the residential quarter. Similarly, the double-Y-shaped office buildings alternated with smaller, perfectly rectangular edifices, forming an arresting composition at the eastern edge of the plan. Curves also dotted the plan in the form of individual buildings—most strikingly the freeform, cloverleaf café that prefigured the Ariston Club in Argentina (1947–48)—and landscape features, such as ponds and manicured areas of grass. Creating buildings that required curved floor plates would certainly have increased the cost of construction, potentially undermining arguments about cost efficiency put forth by proponents of modernist city planning and housing proposals. However, those extra costs could be minimized if the school design were repeated in neighborhoods throughout the city.

Of course, it must be remembered that the Garden City of the Future was not a true urban planning manifesto but rather a showcase of concrete structures embedded in a schematic and rather small city center. The schematic nature of the Garden City of the Future becomes very clear if one tries to imagine the outlines of Breuer's entire city, particularly the circulation scheme. How large an interval would exist between cloverleaf exchanges? How would the street network be defined away from the city center? Breuer talked about extending the residential quarter toward "open country, where there would be a group of lower flat buildings, and some individual houses" but left the particulars of their extent and arrangement somewhat vague.[40] He also stated that the roads serving these private houses "could, if necessary, be adapted to the street plan of the central area."[41] This implies that another unspecified street plan might be implemented.

Another consequence of the schematic nature of the design is that some elements function better as aesthetic objects than infrastructure. Most strikingly, the highway that slashed through the city at an oblique angle signaled the importance of automobile transportation but marked a fault line in the plan. This was most obvious in the staggering of the *Zeilenbau* so that the residential buildings opposed green spaces on either side of the highway rather than lining up with similar buildings, as would occur in a more straightforward use of the grid. The networks of diagonal footpaths surrounding the *Zeilenbau* were also staggered on either side of the highway. While it provided great visual interest, this staggering undermined the logic of circulation as motorized traffic could not easily pass from north to south unless it used the cloverleaf junction. In addition, changing direction on the highway could only be accomplished by virtue of the same cloverleaf or one of the subterranean crossings provided at intervals between main traffic crossings. What is clear is that while Breuer valued the clarity and economic advantages of functional principles of planning, he was occasionally willing to sacrifice pure rationality for grand aesthetic gestures.

The Reception of the Garden City of the Future

Modernist buildings and plans were still a novelty to most English visitors to the Ideal Home Exhibition, where the model was first exhibited in March at Olympia, an exhibition space in West Kensington, London.[42] The Ideal Home Exhibition started as a publicity venture of the *Daily Mail*, which presented the exhibition annually, beginning in 1908, but it morphed into one of the largest venues for the display and sale of domestic wares in England.[43] The show presented visitors, especially women, with a vision of the future centered on a modern domesticity that embraced labor-saving machines. Modern architecture, however, was presented as one stylistic possibility among many and certainly not the most desirable one [19]. The Building Trades Exhibition, held in the same venue six months later, was a similarly commercial venture. Although its exhibitors were more willing to experiment with modern design for the stalls, an equally eclectic range of styles was represented, with pavilions advertising traditional materials immediately adjacent to stands promoting the merits of concrete or bent plywood.[44]

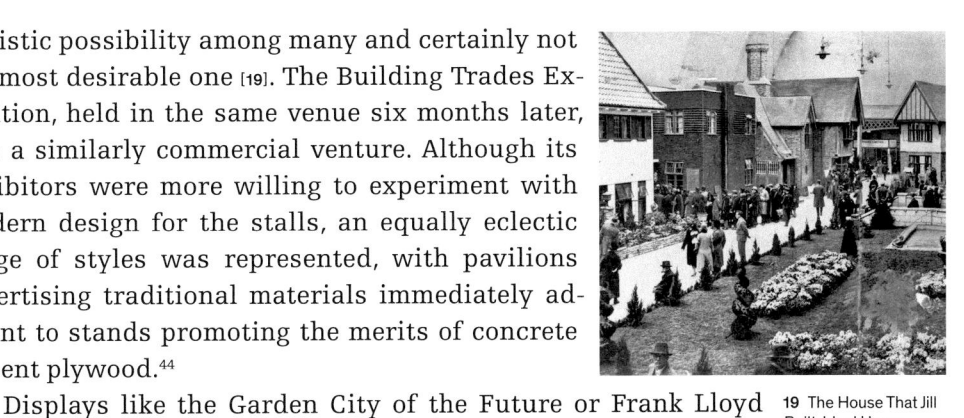

19 The House That Jill Built, Ideal Home Exhibition, London, 1930

Displays like the Garden City of the Future or Frank Lloyd Wright's nearly contemporaneous Broadacre City were part of a larger fascination with possible futures presented at exhibitions such as these, and one can view the model as an attempt to familiarize the public with modernist architecture and planning without scaring them off entirely. The title given to the project connects Breuer's radical vision for a city to a type of planning that would have been familiar and even beloved in England, where Ebenezer Howard first proposed the garden city in 1898 as an antidote to the rampant speculation and crowding in industrial cities. Even more importantly, the garden city movement remained not only familiar but the "dominant school of thought on the future city in pre-1950 Britain."[45] From contemporary publicity surrounding the exhibits and subsequent attempts to explain the model to audiences in the United States, it is clear that the actual relationship to the garden city movement was tangential, filtered through the lens of municipal housing projects that Breuer would have been familiar with from his time in Germany and through the lens of CIAM debates, which borrowed much from garden city ideology without acknowledging the source.[46] Howard never specified a style of architecture to go along with his scheme for new cities of thirty thousand people, although he and many of his followers preferred the enclosed street described by Camillo Sitte. Unlike the Nazis, who would appropriate the quaint, nostalgic aesthetic and back-to-the-land ideology mistakenly equated with the garden city movement, Breuer and his colleagues in CIAM adopted the underlying ideals of functional planning and separation of traffic along with an understanding that communal good should supersede individual profit-seeking.[47] CIAM and its unacknowledged predecessors focused on reform of land policy as an instrument for achieving their goals, allowing planners to gather large tracts of land, which were necessary for building high-density housing, and rethink the street grid.[48] Breuer alluded to some of these arguments in a 1939 article on the Garden City of the Future in the *Boston Herald* in which he stated that private enterprise was not equal to the creation of the city of the future: "Such developments go so deep into property legislation that reforms in land ownership would probably be a primary requirement when it came time to make major changes in the layout of an old city. By reforms, I mean, in principle, a greater consideration on the part of the landowner for general needs."[49] This statement was consistent with the CIAM line advocating the communal good, but it stopped short of the collective ownership of land endorsed by Howard as a central tenet of the garden city or the public expropriation of land championed by anti-capitalist urban theorists such as Hilberseimer.

Whether Breuer was successful in softening the unfamiliar qualities of his project for its original British audience is debatable. The *Architects' Journal* succinctly captured the ambivalence of the British public toward modern design in general and toward the Garden City of the Future in particular, reporting that "though it is a city in miniature it is nonetheless enough to stimulate or horrify quite profoundly according to the spectator's convictions."[50] Not surprisingly, the Modern Architectural Research (MARS) Group enthusiastically embraced Breuer and Yorke's vision of the future city. Yorke was a founding member of the group, which was the official British chapter of CIAM, and its ranks were filled with Breuer's circle in London, including Shand and Coates. The MARS Group featured the model prominently in the entrance hall of their *New Architecture* exhibition, held in January 1938 at the New Burlington Galleries in London.[51] Unlike the popular exhibitions at which the model had previously been displayed, the MARS Group devised the *New Architecture* exhibition specifically to further the cause of architectural modernism. The MARS Group exhibited the model unchanged but jettisoned all references to garden cities, which they viewed as suburban rather than urban, calling it the "Concrete City" instead.[52] This change in nomenclature accomplished two things. First, it shifted the focus away from the future orientation implied in the original name, indicating that the solution to urban ills offered by the model was possible with existing technology and need not wait for some unspecified moment to come. Second, it brought the materiality of the scheme to the forefront.

The Garden City of the Future would have an impact far beyond the local scene of London modernists. While the fate of the original model is unknown, photographs of the project had spread across the globe by the end of the decade. The editors of *Byggmästaren*, a journal of Swedish building, were aware of the model, as were representatives of Kaigai Bunka Tyuo Kyoku (Central Bureau for Foreign Cultures) in Japan.[53] Photographs of the model appeared in a four-volume Japanese publication devoted to the modern house between 1933 and 1940, published by the Society of International Architecture.[54] They also appeared in the catalog for the Museum of Modern Art exhibition *Bauhaus 1919–1928*, in a section exploring the activities of Bauhaus members after the close of the school. Students discovered the project through photographs included in a 1938 exhibition of Breuer's work mounted at Harvard University after he had immigrated to the United States and through José Luis Sert's book *Can Our Cities Survive?*, which elaborated upon CIAM's urbanistic principles. Photographic images were also included in a number of museum contexts, including the *Space for Living* show at the San Francisco Museum of Art mounted by the Telesis environmental research group in 1940 and an exhibition on demountable architecture called *Shelter in Transit and Transition*, organized by the Cincinnati Modern Art Society in 1942.[55] In addition, professors such as Justus Bier, a German-born art historian at the University of Louisville in Kentucky, wrote to Breuer in 1938 requesting slides of the Garden City of the Future, revealing that knowledge of the model had made its way to the heartland of America less than two years after it was first displayed in London.[56]

The burst of attention that accompanied the initial display of the model had fallen away by the mid-1940s as the war and the need to rebuild destroyed housing occupied many architects. However, writers such as Peter Blake (and Breuer himself) would continue to point to the importance of the model in the trajectory of the architect's career. Breuer's next attempts at urban schemes would be unthinkable without the Garden City of the Future.

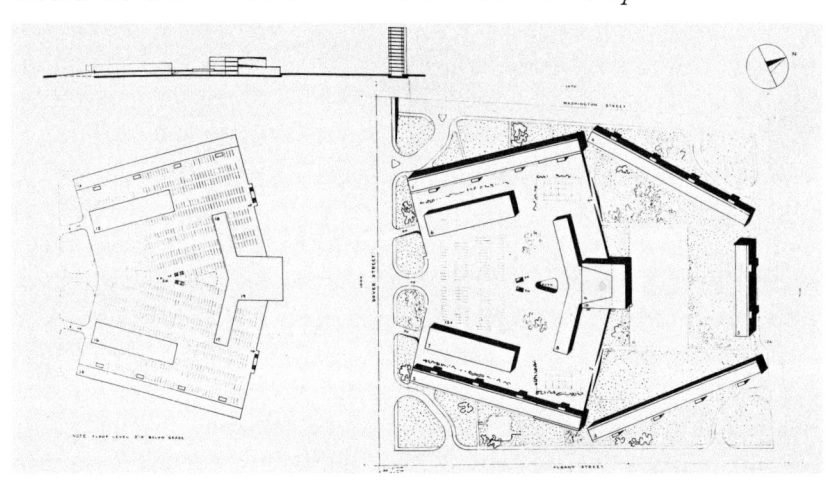

20 South Boston redevelopment plan (unexecuted), Boston, Massachusetts, USA, 1943, plan drawings

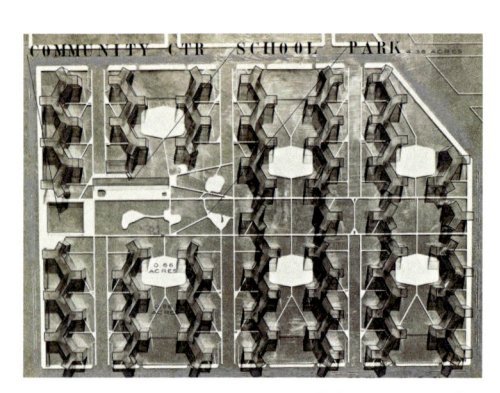

21 Stuyvesant Six redevelopment proposal, aerial view of model

The unbuilt South Boston Redevelopment Plan [20], designed in 1943, illustrates the elaboration of ideas initially developed in the Garden City, specifically the rhythmic elaboration of the façades and the use of sculptural groupings of buildings. In it, repeatable, horseshoe-shaped assemblies of buildings with differentiated façades surround a park containing a low-rise school building and shops. A year later, in a competition entry for Stuyvesant Town called Stuyvesant Six [21], Breuer would turn the *Zeilenbau* of the Garden City into chains of linked double-Y apartment buildings organized around community facilities. Even the ZUP de Bayonne, built decades later, starting in the mid-1960s, and discussed in this volume by Kenny Cupers, reveals that Breuer's basic strategies had not changed. In fact, the tendency toward sculptural groupings of buildings present in the Garden City of the Future had become even more pronounced; the sinuous line of apartment buildings lining the crest of the hill at the ZUP de Bayonne set off the symmetrical composition of the city center in which community structures were surrounded by six U-shaped residential complexes.

p. 265/18

Breuer's later urban schemes reflected contemporary architectural debates regarding the importance of the city center. A final attempt to reposition the Garden City of the Future in reference to those debates came in 1955. In his overview of Breuer's career in *Sun and Shadow*, Blake rebranded Breuer and Yorke's model as the "Civic Center of the Future."[57] It is unclear whether the impetus for this name change came from Blake or Breuer, but Breuer continued to refer to the project by its original name, the Garden City of the Future, throughout the 1940s, even as Sert and Sigfried Giedion issued a call for modern civic centers rooted in a "new monumentality." According to Eric Mumford, these two men would eventually conceive of the civic center as a "fifth function" of CIAM's Functional City, and Blake's renaming of the design reflected his attempt to link Breuer's model to discussions that would gain enough importance to provide the theme of the eighth CIAM conference on the "heart of the city" in 1951.[58] Breuer would eventually adopt this nomenclature too, as evidenced by a 1961 letter to Cranston Jones.[59] The label would stick and the project was exhibited as the Civic Center of the Future in the 1972 retrospective exhibition of Breuer's architecture at the Metropolitan Museum of Art in New York.

Sert and Giedion numbered among the most ardent early advocates of CIAM's urban vision, and they devoted equal energy to addressing the criticisms of the Functional City that arose as the basic concept reached beyond the circle of devoted modernists. In 1940, Lewis Mumford declined to write an introduction for Sert's book *Can Our Cities Survive?*, citing fundamental doubts as to the comprehensiveness of CIAM's four functions. In a private letter to Sert, Mumford protested, "The four functions of the city do not seem to me to adequately cover the ground of city planning: dwelling, work, recreation, and transportation are all important. But what of the political, educational, and cultural functions of the city[?] … The organs of political and cultural association, are, from my standpoint, the *distinguishing* marks of the city: without them, there is only an urban mass."[60] Mumford's refusal forced Sert to explore the importance of the civic center. By 1951, in his essay in the publication proceeding from CIAM 8 titled "Centres of Community Life," Sert expressed a viewpoint closer to Mumford's and called for an urban and architectural frame that would facilitate social and intellectual contact among the inhabitants of a city.[61] The civic center of the 1940s was now called the city core, but the principle behind it remained the same. The core was modeled on the idea of the public square that had been central to Western ideas of planning since the Greeks but was now overlaid with the open planning principles espoused by CIAM. Sert went so far as to advocate multiple cores: one for each sector of the city in addition to a larger, central core that would serve the city as a whole.[62]

In describing the type of architecture associated with the core, Sert described steps toward a "greater freedom of plasticity," but a plasticity still beholden to function and eschewing historical styles.[63] This phrasing certainly echoed Giedion's call for a "new monumentality" in a pathbreaking and aptly named 1944 essay that drew on a similar criticism of CIAM planning principles as expressed in Mumford's earlier letter to Sert. Though long a champion of modern architecture, Giedion was skeptical when it was "entrusted with monumental tasks involving more than functional problems." He reflected on people's need for a monumental architecture that could symbolize the social and ceremonial life of a community. This monumental architecture was part and parcel of the civic centers that contemporary cities were lacking and that would arise only when planners viewed cities as not "mere agglomerations of jobs and traffic lights" but as expressions of the emotional life of the community. For Giedion, only true artists were capable of producing these monumental buildings by creating a transcendent simplicity that did not rely on historical stylistic trappings or literal symbolic gestures.[64]

Sert inserted Breuer's Garden City of the Future into this debate about the civic center by using an unattributed photograph of the model in his book *Can Our Cities Survive?* to show one possibility for laying out the "central area of a modern borough unit."[65] He praised the grouping of community functions and the pedestrian scale of the endeavor. Seen in this light, the sculptural groupings of buildings Breuer included in the Garden City of the Future—in particular the crescent-shaped apartment building and school—reflect a prescient attempt to embed centers of civic focus and engagement within the individual residential quarters of the city. What Sert seemed to be focusing upon, however, was Breuer's grouping of the shopping and recreational elements at the center of the model. Lewis Mumford (and perhaps Giedion) would have been ideologically opposed to the view of community put forth here. Breuer's theater represents the only nod to culture, and instead of cultivating artistic, political, or cultural life, the gigantic shopping center places consumerism at the center of the scheme. While marketplaces have long been crucial communal gathering spaces in European cities, they were usually balanced by other plazas representing the political or religious ideals of the society. Moreover, in the design for the Garden City of the Future, the functions of government are shunted into the Y-shaped office buildings to the east. These buildings, which could just as easily house commercial interests, betray a very different view of government than those put forth by earlier planning movements like the City Beautiful.

In Breuer's defense, CIAM's emphasis on a technocratic meritocracy did not require the symbolic civic buildings for which Mumford yearned; competent bureaucrats acting in the background quietly took care of governing without the need for grand rhetorical gestures meant to inspire citizens to participate in democracy. Breuer, like Le Corbusier and many other members of CIAM, was not particularly political or religious, and saw little reason to supplement CIAM's four functions, although Le Corbusier did include a separate area for public services in his scheme for the Ville contemporaine. Breuer maintained this apolitical stance for much of his career. In *Sun and Shadow*, he took architects to task for talking about "subjects like politics, economics and sociology in which they were not particularly expert" rather than focusing on "the potential contributions of architecture."[66]

It is also true, however, that the version of a civic center found in the Garden City of the Future lacked the clear organization of later examples, such as Le Corbusier's civic center at Saint-Dié (1945) or that of Sert and P. L. Wiener's Civic and Commercial Center for the city of Cali in Colombia (1950) [22]. Likewise, the individual buildings of Breuer's civic center did not attain the monumentality advocated by Sert and Giedion, in part because these buildings were not expressions of higher cultural or social goals.

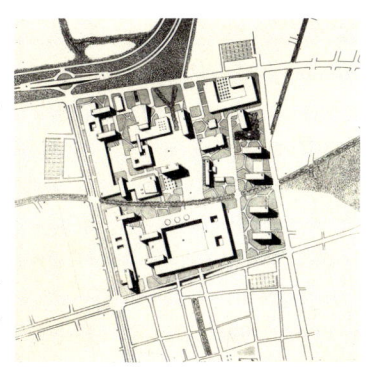

22 Joseph Luis Sert and P. L. Wiener, Civic and Commercial Center, Cali, Colombia, 1950, site plan drawing

In the end, despite the versatility of the model—which easily carried the diverse meanings ascribed to it by its various names—and contemporary fascination with the project, the Garden City of the Future did not achieve the influence of Le Corbusier's plans for the Ville contemporaine or Hilberseimer's Hochhausstadt. Part of this can be attributed to the fact that Breuer's project did not fit neatly into teleological narratives of the development of modernism; the Garden City of the Future lacked the graphic simplicity of Le Corbusier's and Hilberseimer's plans, as well as the novelty that attached to them as some of the earliest representations of modernist planning ideals. Breuer also lacked Le Corbusier's prolific writing skills and talent for self-promotion, focusing instead on the daily challenges of running a successful international practice. In addition, Breuer's project fell victim to larger societal trends such as the postwar move toward suburbanization, especially in the United States, along with the backlash against CIAM principles represented by advocates such as Jane Jacobs, who saw the "tower in a park" model ripping apart vibrant urban communities in the service of a formal ideal. Even within CIAM, the soulless urban agglomerations resulting from strict adherence to functional planning were challenged in the 1950s by Alison and Peter Smithson and Team 10, who hoped to "construct a hierarchy of human associations which should replace the functional hierarchy of the Charte d'Athènes."[67] All of these trends meant that schemes like the Garden City of the Future which were based on that functional hierarchy fell out of favor. What is difficult to measure and often left out of the historiography of this pivotal and instructive work is the possible influence that Breuer's model had on students of modernism who were exposed to it in any of its various iterations between 1937 and 1945. Breuer provided an alternative formal interpretation of CIAM's principles rather than a theoretical overthrow, allowing curves and an appreciation for the aesthetic grouping of buildings based on human communal needs to reenter the modernist planning lexicon. It is therefore not hard to imagine that Breuer's plastic concrete forms, along with those of Le Corbusier at places like Chandigarh, influenced the design of a wide range of twentieth-century city plans, from British New Towns to urban renewal projects like Albany's Empire State Plaza and the monuments of Brasilia.

1 Marcel Breuer, "Garden City of the Future," draft of lecture, F. R. S. Yorke Papers (YoF/2/2), Royal Institute of British Architects (RIBA).
2 Marcel Breuer to Cranston Jones, January 13, 1961, Marcel Breuer Papers, 1920–86, Archives of American Art (AAA), Smithsonian Institution.
3 "A Garden City of the Future," *Architects' Journal*, March 26, 1936, 477.
4 Ibid., 479, 482.
5 Jeremy Melvin, *FRS Yorke and the Evolution of English Modernism*, with a memoir by David Allford (Chichester, UK: Wiley-Academy, 2003), 26, 28.
6 Ibid., 22, 25. Yorke's first column appeared on March 22, 1933.
7 Marcel Breuer, draft of partnership contract with F. R. S. Yorke (1935), Marcel Breuer Papers, Special Collections Research Center (SCRC), Syracuse University Libraries.
8 Marcel Breuer to Marion Becker, October 8, 1942, Marcel Breuer Papers, SCRC, Syracuse University Libraries.
9 Alan Powers, *In the Line of Development: FRS Yorke, E Rosenberg and CS Mardell to YRM, 1930–1992* (London: RIBA Heinz Gallery, 1992), 18.
10 Melvin, *FRS Yorke and the Evolution of English Modernism*, 89n12. The Cement and Concrete Association paid P. Morton Shand to translate Breuer's lecture into English. The F. R. S. Yorke Papers at the Royal Institute of British Architects include a copy of the lecture, with notes in Breuer's hand indicating phonetic pronunciations of vowels and difficult words. See documents in the F. R. S. Yorke Papers (YoF/2/2), RIBA.
11 Breuer to Becker, October 8, 1942.
12 In 1928 Breuer was appointed to the original Comité international pour la résolution des problèmes de l'architecture contemporaine (CIRPAC), the central committee governing CIAM, as a representative of Hungary. He was also among those who helped to organize the Fourth CIAM Congress, although he did not attend it. Eric Mumford, *The CIAM Discourse on Urbanism, 1928–1960* (Cambridge, MA: MIT Press, 2000), 26, 76–77.
13 Breuer, "Garden City of the Future," draft of lecture, 3.
14 Mumford, *CIAM Discourse on Urbanism*, 5.
15 Henry Russell-Hitchcock, "Marcel Breuer and the American Tradition in Architecture" (1938), 14, Marcel Breuer Papers, SCRC, Syracuse University Libraries.

16 John R. Gold, *The Experience of Modernism: Modern Architects and the Future City, 1928–1953* (London: E & FN Spon, 1997), 69.
17 Breuer, "Architecture and Material," in *Circle: International Survey of Constructive Art*, ed. Leslie Martin, Ben Nicholson, and Naum Gabo (London: Faber and Faber, 1937), 194.
18 Ibid., 202.
19 Marcel Breuer, "Structures in Space," in Marcel Breuer, *Sun and Shadow: The Philosophy of an Architect*, ed. Peter Blake (New York: Dodd, Mead, 1955), 68, 71.
20 Isabelle Hyman, *Marcel Breuer, Architect: The Career and the Buildings* (New York: H. N. Abrams, 2001), 303.
21 Bernhard Kampffmeyer, "Das Ideal der Kleinwohnung," *Gartenstadt* 6, no. 2 (February 1912): 18–19.
22 In 1929, Gropius gave a lecture entitled "Low-, Mid-, or High-Rise Building?" at the second CIAM conference in Frankfurt. Mumford, *CIAM Discourse on Urbanism*, 38–39.
23 Moisei Ginzburg quoted in Mumford, *CIAM Discourse on Urbanism*, 38.
24 Hyman, *Marcel Breuer, Architect*, 303.
25 Description of the Garden City of the Future in Martin et al., *Circle*, 182.
26 Breuer, "Garden City of the Future," F. R. S. Yorke Papers (YoF/2/2), RIBA.
27 Hitchcock, "Marcel Breuer and the American Tradition in Architecture," 14.
28 Carl Warton, "What Cities of the Future Will Look Like," *Boston Herald*, December 31, 1939, B3.
29 Melvin, *FRS Yorke and the Evolution of English Modernism*, 29, 31.
30 A short article on the exhibition of Breuer's work at Harvard appeared in the *Boston Transcript* in 1938. It also selected the shopping center for special attention out of all the buildings exhibited in the show. "Designer Here Plans Stores Like Interior of Honeycomb," *Boston Transcript*, July 19, 1938, Marcel Breuer Papers, SCRC, Syracuse University Libraries.
31 Hitchcock, "Marcel Breuer and the American Tradition in Architecture," 14.
32 Slide list, F. R. S. Yorke Papers (YoF/2/2), RIBA.
33 Breuer, *Sun and Shadow*, 69.
34 Ada Louise Huxtable, *Pier Luigi Nervi* (New York: George Braziller, 1960), 19.
35 Ibid., 14.
36 Hyman, *Marcel Breuer, Architect*, 85.
37 Description of the Garden City of the Future, in Martin et al., *Circle*, 183–84.

38 Ibid., 183. Breuer published his design for Potsdamer Platz in "Verkehrsarchitektur— ein Vorschlag zur Neuordnung des Potsdamer Platzes," *Das Neue Berlin* 7 (1929): 136–41.
39 Description of the Garden City of the Future, in Martin et al., *Circle*, 183.
40 "Garden City of the Future," *Architects' Journal*, 480.
41 Description of the Garden City of the Future, in Martin et al., *Circle*, 184.
42 Wells Coates had recently built Lawn Road Flats, one of the first modernist apartment buildings in London. As late as 1946, a vocal segment of the population had still not embraced the complex, awarding it second place in *Horizon* magazine's "Ugliest Building" competition. Jack Pritchard, *View from a Long Chair: The Memoirs of Jack Pritchard* (London: Routledge & Kegan Paul, 1984), 22.
43 Deborah S. Ryan, *The Ideal Home through the 20th Century* (London: Hazar, 1997), 9, 12, 16. "For example, between 160,000 and 200,000 visitors attended the Exhibition in 1908 during the 14 days it was open … by 1937 attendance had climbed to 620,000 and it reached an all-time high of 1,329,644 in 1957." Ibid., 17.
44 David Dean, *The Architect as Stand Designer: Building Exhibitions, 1895–1983* (London: Scholar Press, 1985), 14. In fact, stalls had been designed by such luminaries as Le Corbusier, Charlotte Perriand, and R. T. F. Skinner. Exhibition work was the one area consistently open to modern designers, who struggled to obtain commissions in the face of suspicion of their "novel ideas and untried methods." Ibid.
45 Gold, *Experience of Modernism*, 80.
46 In my dissertation "The German Garden City Movement: Architecture, Politics and Urban Transformation, 1902–1931" (Columbia University, New York, 2012), I describe the ways in which Weimar-era housing programs borrowed freely from the ideas promulgated by the Deutsche Gartenstadtgesellschaft. See also Mumford, *CIAM Discourse on Urbanism*, 3.
47 José Luis Sert, *Can Our Cities Survive? An ABC of Urban Problems, Their Analysis, Their Solutions* (Cambridge, MA: Harvard University Press, 1900), 41.
48 Gold, *Experience of Modernism*, 59.
49 Warton, "What Cities of the Future Will Look Like," B3. Breuer answered a questionnaire sent out by a "large industrial corporation" to "outstanding research men in the United States and Canada, seeking their ideas as to what sort of world we will be living in 20 or more years hence." Ibid.
50 "Homes and the Public," *Architects' Journal*, March 26, 1936, 471.
51 Eric Mumford does not list Breuer as a member of MARS in his *CIAM Discourse on Urbanism*. However, the brochure for the *New Architecture* exhibition indicates that Breuer was actively involved in the design and organization of the exhibition. Modern Architectural Research Group, *New Architecture: An Exhibition of the Elements of Modern Architecture Organized by the MARS (Modern Architectural Research) Group, New Burlington Galleries, January 11–29, 1938* (London: New Burlington Galleries, 1938), 23.
52 F. R. S. Yorke also refers to the project as Concrete City in a letter to Breuer at Harvard in which they discuss published drawings of the scheme. F. R. S. Yorke to Marcel Breuer, May 17, 1938, Marcel Breuer Papers, SCRC, Syracuse University Libraries.
53 Melvin, *FRS Yorke and the Evolution of English Modernism*, 100 and 111n51.
54 国際建築協会 [Society of International Architecture], 現代住宅 1933–40 [*Modern House 1933–40*], vol. 1 (Tokyo: Kokusai Kenchiku Kyōkai, 1941), 202–3.
55 Breuer to Becker, October 8, 1942.
56 Marcel Breuer to Justus Bier, May 12, 1938, Marcel Breuer Papers, 1920–86, AAA, Smithsonian Institution.
57 Peter Blake, "Work and Projects: 1920–1937" in Breuer, *Sun and Shadow*, 14.
58 Mumford, *CIAM Discourse on Urbanism*, 188, 202.
59 Marcel Breuer to Cranston Jones, January 13, 1961, Marcel Breuer Papers, 1920–86, AAA, Smithsonian Institution.
60 Lewis Mumford to José Luis Sert, December 28, 1940, quoted in Mumford, *CIAM Discourse on Urbanism*, 133.
61 José Luis Sert, "Centres of Community Life," in *The Heart of the City: Towards the Humanisation of Urban Life*, ed. J. Tyrwhitt, J. L. Sert, and E. N. Rogers (New York: Pelligrini and Cudahy, 1952), 6.
62 Ibid.
63 Ibid., 13.
64 Sigfried Giedion, "The Need for a New Monumentality," in *New Architecture and City Planning: A Symposium*, ed. Paul Zucker (New York: Philosophical Library, 1944), 552–56.
65 Sert, *Can Our Cities Survive?*, 71.
66 Marcel Breuer, "Thoughts on the City," in *Sun and Shadow*, 54–55.
67 "Report of the English Group," quoted in Mumford, *CIAM Discourse on Urbanism*, 237.

1 IBM Research Center, La Gaude, France, 1960–62

Atomic Bauhaus:
Marcel Breuer and Big Science

John Harwood

> Supposing I tell you that fundamental research is like rolling a billiard ball up a mountain that's shrouded in fog? You roll it up easy and it comes rolling back to you. You roll it up very hard and it does the same. Then you roll it up medium and it disappears. What happened?
> —M. Stanley Livingston, Brookhaven National Laboratory

> I know most people think the Whitney is my most successful building, but my personal favorite is La Gaude.
> —Marcel Breuer to Robert F. Gatje

Marcel Breuer's "personal favorite" project, one to which he and his associate Robert F. Gatje would return twice over a decade and a half as they designed additions, was a research laboratory. La Gaude, a village in the foothills of the Maritime Alps in southern France, was shorthand for the IBM Research and Development Laboratory, designed and built in its first version from 1961 to 1962 [2].

2 View of IBM at La Gaude from the slope below

The building was and remains crucially important, and not only to Breuer. It played a key role in defining IBM's long-term strategy for distributing itself as a multinational corporation within the frameworks of post–World War II national economies. It became the site for significant experiments in computational and satellite telecommunications as well as graphic simulation software. It also served as a multivalent monumental symbol signaling a new era of distributed, networked, and interdisciplinary knowledge administering a rapidly globalizing information economy.[1] From the perspective of the French government, the project was part of the Gaullist attempt to decentralize the national economy, and it served as a model for future policy driving the shift of multinational corporations' outposts to exurban contexts.[2] As a novel solution to the problem of designing a large, highly flexible,

3 IBM La Gaude, column detail drawings

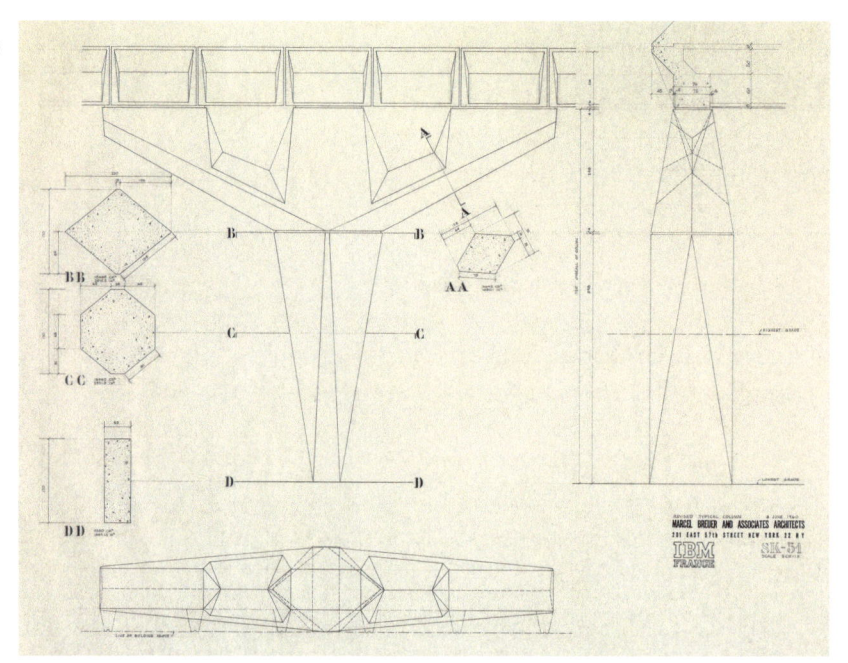

and safe laboratory building for a wide range of research and product development activities, from computation to international telecommunications, it also deserves a place among the significant innovations then unfolding in the field of post–World War II laboratory design. And, as Guy Nordenson discusses elsewhere in this volume, it marks the first time in Breuer's oeuvre that he was able to synthesize two separate structural systems—the massive cast-in-place reinforced concrete "tree column," or *piloti,* first developed for the UNESCO headquarters in Paris, and "one of his most important inventions, a deep, molded concrete façade" of precast reinforced concrete panels—into a single coherent architectural system capable of housing not only research laboratories but also corporate office buildings of all kinds [3].[3]

The origins of this synthesis are not exactly obscure. The gradual process of experimentation and development (quasi-scientific in its imitation of the very empirical research going on in the laboratories themselves) has been detailed by Gatje in his memoir of the time he spent in the Breuer office.[4] This particularly useful account of the work of synthesizing these discrete architectural elements into the IBM France building's design shows clearly how the firm developed numerous variations on the theme for subsequent designs, giving architectural historians a valuable perspective on the firm's sustained engagement with reinforced concrete as a building material from the 1950s through the 1970s. Yet Gatje's precise and provocative identification of the origins of the precast panel in an uncompleted and hitherto little-known project—the Chemistry Building (known as Building 555) at Brookhaven National Laboratory (BNL) on Long Island, New York—merits further historical examination and contextualization, for reasons both negative and positive.

On the negative side of the ledger, Gatje's explanation for the use of the panel system at La Gaude in order to accommodate the numerous electrical and mechanical services the research scientists needed is rather curious and, perhaps necessarily, rather vague owing to the air of secrecy that prevailed around nuclear research at the time. Gatje explains that Breuer, in consultation with the "chairman of the department" at Brookhaven (on whom more below), developed a scheme for Building 555 in which the obtrusive service systems supplying the labs would be relegated to a "service corridor" running alongside all of the labs, so that maintenance and changes to the services could be conducted without interfering with the delicate experiments going on inside the laboratories. This schematic design, Gatje claimed, became "one of the seminal schemes for postwar laboratory layout" and gave the firm experience that later yielded numerous commissions for laboratory designs.[5]

This explanation—the undoubtedly ingenious and insightful account of an architect, rather than a historian of architecture or science—is fine as far as it goes, but it leaves out quite a bit. How did the plumbing and ductwork intended for the service corridor at Brookhaven migrate into the concrete panels enclosing the buildings at La Gaude? Gatje neither illustrated the Brookhaven project nor explained its transformation into IBM's distributed system of integrating electrical and mechanical services into chases at IBM: vertical chases within the section of the precast concrete panel façade and horizontal chases within the floors. Furthermore, the claim that Breuer's Brookhaven design, which was unpublished, merited seminal status at the very least requires context. How were *chases*—the increasingly ubiquitous and necessary hollows and openings threaded through and around the structural frameworks and behind the surface treatments of modern architecture—reconfigured in the architecture of "Big Science" before and after World War II, and in truth how innovative or influential was Breuer's scheme?[6]

Thankfully, there are also some positive reasons to delve into such questions. The previously obscure Brookhaven project has recently resurfaced after years of being hidden away in inaccessible filing cabinets at BNL, with the only documentation of the project being black-and-white copies of Breuer and Gatje's preliminary study and some incomplete correspondence. Jack Preses, a research chemist at the laboratory, recently made many of the documents related to the design of Building 555 available to the public, and he gave me access to several memoranda that provide insight into the intricacies and difficulties of designing laboratories for nuclear research. Retelling and resituating both designs—Brookhaven and La Gaude—within this context offers a novel explanation for Breuer's satisfaction with the accomplishment that was the IBM France laboratory—one that reveals the peculiar and syncretic isomorphisms of Breuer's late designs in a new light as well. As I will show, in the Brookhaven study there are few if any of the heroic and sculptural gestures associated with Breuer's architecture of the 1950s and early 1960s. Not only did the project end at only a schematic level of development, but the project was pitilessly technical in nature. There was little if any room for extravagant symbolic gestures. Nonetheless, the project represents the first time that Breuer was able to deploy a reinforced concrete structure—possessed of a unique material quality—to house a complex mesh of services in a specially dedicated chase system—a strategy that would become a primary feature of his late architecture. He would go on to design three more laboratories following a similar scheme. At La Gaude, he and Gatje developed in the integrated precast concrete panel a lasting and broadly applicable solution to the interrelated problems of controlling the external environment via the façade. Their innovation provided dedicated space for mechanical services and produced a suitably monumental aesthetic that would capture in symbolic terms the cultural status and high stakes of scientific research in the post–World War II era.

Building 555 in Its Historical Context
Breuer's involvement in the Brookhaven project was a product of his personal connections to the far-flung and rapidly growing institutions of scientific and technical research in United States and elsewhere after World War II. Intended as an expansion of the nascent national laboratory system for nuclear research and situated at a disused World War I barracks at Camp Upton on Long Island, BNL was one part of a massive federal project to realign and coordinate the research efforts of numerous military, industrial, and academic institutions in the eastern United States that began in late July 1946. Chief among these institutions were the major research universities. Scientists from the leading universi-

ties in high-energy nuclear research in the region formed Associated Universities Incorporated (AUI), a strategic partnership of Harvard, MIT, Yale, Cornell, the University of Rochester, Columbia, the University of Pennsylvania, and Johns Hopkins (with the SUNY campuses added later).

Unlike the earlier "capitals" of the Manhattan District, such as Argonne National Laboratory near Chicago and Clinton Engineer Works (later renamed Oak Ridge National Laboratory) in Tennessee, BNL was intended from the beginning as a site for "basic" as opposed to "applied" research. Accordingly, its founders (represented by an eighteen-member board of directors drawn from the faculties of each of AUI's member institutions) sought to develop a culture of open-ended and deeply collaborative research that would escape easy control by government agencies—and potentially the all-too-rapid weaponization of techniques discovered in the course of their research. The eventual structure of the contract and campus that formed BNL was tidily summarized by Eldon Shoup, the vice president of AUI:

> The plan provides for a large, centrally located laboratory ... [whose] *financial* support will be provided by the *government*, while the resources of scientific knowledge, ideas and initiative will derive from all universities, private and public laboratories and industry. The function of *program* and *policy control* is a joint responsibility of government and the contractor. The function of *management* is entrusted to the contractor. The contractor in this case assumes the responsibilities of management, not for financial profit, nor for special benefit of any one or all nine universities, but as a trustee on behalf of all participants in nuclear research and education in this region.[7]

Although Camp Upton was not "centrally located" in the United States, the conceptual blueprint of concentrating scientific capital through a networked and layered distribution of authority that Shoup describes was the ur-structure of the 1950s military-industrial-academic complex: government-owned, contractor-operated (GOCO) contracting.[8] Profits might still be gleaned from the sale of patents to industry, and the risk of failures would be absorbed by the potentially bottomless reserve of credit and the large military budgets set by the US government during the Cold War.

The complex negotiations over this new form of sponsorship for scientific research—what would soon become known as "Big Science"—are a fascinating story in their own right. Peter

J. Westwick and Robert P. Crease, the official historian of Brookhaven National Laboratory, have historicized those dealings in impressive style.[9] There is too little room to relate this history here; what is of interest in terms of this argument regarding Breuer's architectural contributions to Big Science is how architects came to play a role in articulating and concretizing the abstractions of the new hybrid corporate-government organization. Architects such as Breuer provided pragmatic and aesthetic solutions to the numerous problems facing scientists working with radioactive materials.

BNL's first architect was a Breuer protégé, J. Georges Peter, hired by the first director of the physical plant at BNL, Philip Morse. Peter was French American and was a product of Harvard's Graduate School of Design, where he had studied under Walter Gropius and Breuer. Upon graduation, he worked for the Gropius and Breuer office during World War II, and he was involved in their Aluminum City Terrace defense housing project in New Kensington, Pennsylvania, in 1941. During World War II he was the architect for MIT's Radiation Laboratory, where he designed new buildings for radar and radio navigation research.

In search of an opportunity to "plan an entire environment" for large-scale scientific research—rather than deal with single buildings and retrofits—Peter was pleased when Morse approached him to take over the gradual transformation of Camp Upton into a laboratory. Despite the large amount of misinformation regarding nuclear physics research circulating in the mass media at the time, the *New Yorker* published a revealing and reliable article on BNL describing the severe limitations on funding for these changes.[10] Peter's quoted comments provide crucial insight into the specific design strategy the Atomic Energy Commission (AEC) and AUI employed at Brookhaven: "Morse and I want to get *the calm atmosphere of a university*. That seems to be rather important.... Mess halls into animal farms, gyms into graphite warehouses—cyclotrons, piles. I've reconverted before, but there's an odd kind of extra pressure to this job. Maybe people ought not to know when they're having a hand in something that's historic."[11]

Although he strove to design a university atmosphere, Peter was clear that BNL was distinct from a university, by virtue of both its utilitarian beginnings (a barracks could hardly attain the picturesque or Beaux-Arts character of a modern American university campus) and its novel organizational form. Peter preserved many of the buildings as they were, simply stabilizing them over the short term while working on a longer-term solution.

He convinced both Morse and the AEC—working against firm resistance—to retain the bare-bones amenities already existing on the site: a gymnasium, a theater, and a swimming pool. Following an early survey of the camp by the engineering firm Stone and Webster, from 1946, Peter set up a program of modular expansion for independent departments, segregating the physicists from the biologists, the biologists from the chemists, and so on. With this simple gesture, the spatial organization of BNL was harmonized with its emergent hybrid organizational form.

Morse and Peter's aim to create "the calm atmosphere of a university" at BNL coincided with a desire to model the organization of the labs according to the traditional divisions between disciplines in the natural sciences. Physics, chemistry, and biology would be organized as separate departments, within which further subdivisions—identified as "disciplines" in their own right—would be maintained. Although this university model had begun to erode by the late 1960s as the labs were gradually reorganized on the model of private corporate research laboratories, that model was the basic organizational feature of what became known as the "Brookhaven concept."[12]

The AEC and AUI elected to allocate the modest available resources to the two primary research reactors and other large-scale equipment, such as the Cosmotron. BNL's scientists remained crammed into the former barracks buildings. Still, Peter stayed on, perhaps in hope of further opportunities to redesign the campus. Such an opportunity eventually arrived in the person of the ambitious and celebrated isotope chemist Jacob Bigeleisen. Recruited to BNL in 1948, Bigeleisen was incensed by a 1958 report from the directorate of the lab claiming that "the Chemistry Department is well housed in good quarters and will not need additional space for ten years."[13] Bigeleisen immediately argued for creating a Chemistry Department Building Committee that would pressure the directorate to improve the quality of the department's facilities. He noted in a July 1959 report that the improvised nature of the labs, housed in several leaky and decrepit barracks buildings, had begun to "bar ... easy communication and collaboration between scientists, one of the most important ingredients of research."[14]

Bigeleisen pressed further, however, arguing forcefully that the very "way the Laboratory went about planning was a disaster." Up until 1959, BNL scientists had essentially designed their buildings—often little more than lightly renovated barracks—by committee, often in secret. They would then hand their schemes over to an outside architectural firm, selected by the Atomic Energy Commission, over which no member or deliberative body at BNL had any control. Architecture had slipped through the cracks of GOCO management.[15] Moreover, due to the highly specific programmatic demands of *nuclear* chemical research, BNL's chemists could not make do with standard-issue chemistry lab facilities: "Most laboratories were built in a stereotyped design whose shortcomings were becoming evident."[16] Instead, Bigeleisen suggested, BNL should consult with an "outside architectural firm to work with us in planning the building … before any request was made to AEC for building design."[17] Under this pressure the director of BNL, Leland Haworth, approved the formal creation of a building committee, to be chaired by Bigeleisen; this committee then proceeded to visit various laboratories (including Eero Saarinen's Bell Labs building in Holmdel, New Jersey, which Bigeleisen "did not find user friendly").[18] It also brought in an impressive list of paid and unpaid architectural consultants. Three of these consultants—Lawrence Anderson, chair of the Department of Architecture at MIT; Albert Bush-Brown, architectural historian at MIT; and Paul Rudolph, dean of the School of Architecture at Yale—were selected because they worked for two of the universities that made up AUI, the consortium that served as the contractor operating BNL for the AEC. Five leading architects were selected from firms that had experience in building facilities for large-scale institutions: Marcel Breuer, Ludwig Mies van der Rohe, I. M. Pei, Eero Saarinen, and Edward Durell Stone.

A nearly year-long period of consultation concluded with the Building Committee's decision to hire Marcel Breuer and Associates to begin planning the new building. It appears that the continued presence of J. Georges Peter—Breuer's former student and employee in the Gropius and Breuer partnership—in the laboratory's planning office may have influenced the decision to hire Breuer. Another factor in the decision may have been Bigeleisen and Dodson's extensive interviews with outside architects, during which Breuer showed considerable enthusiasm for the unusual initiative taken by the Building Committee, as well as an aptitude for understanding the unusual and rigorously technical demands that a nuclear chemistry research facility placed upon its designers. This admiration was mutual. Immediately following his visit to Brookhaven in May 1959, Breuer wrote to Bigeleisen expressing his gratitude to the chemists: "Your proposal to retain an architect as advisor during the programming stage of the new Chemistry Building, while not without precedent, is still sufficiently unique to excite the admiration of architects familiar with the difficulties which may arise later unless great care and thought are given to the program at this time."[19] Breuer went on to outline the scope of his proposal to study the program, and he then neatly summarized the aims of the project in perfect harmony with the ethos of Big Science: "Underlying all of the above will be an attempt to crystallize an architectural approach developed in co-operation with the members of the Chemistry Department, which will show the way in which the final building design can embody those qualities of informality and human scale which will tend to promote an easy and natural exchange between the people using the building."[20]

The scientists were impressed with Breuer's grasp of their problem, and "favorably impressed by similar studies" carried out by Breuer's office, in particular those done in preparation for designing the library and classroom buildings at Hunter College, in which Breuer had shown a knack for deferring to the expertise of his clients.[21] It appears that a contract was in place by early 1960, offering a maximum $12,000 fee plus reimbursements for expenses.

Breuer assigned his young associate Gatje "to study the need and working habits of each of the units of [the] Department" over the course of a full month in May and June 1960, which involved conducting interviews with members of the scientific, supporting, technical, and secretarial staffs. He visited the department an additional eleven times between June and November of that year.[22] Gatje also studied the relationships between the various chemical disciplines represented by the scientists and their technical staffs, which led him to produce a diagram [4] that coordinated disci-

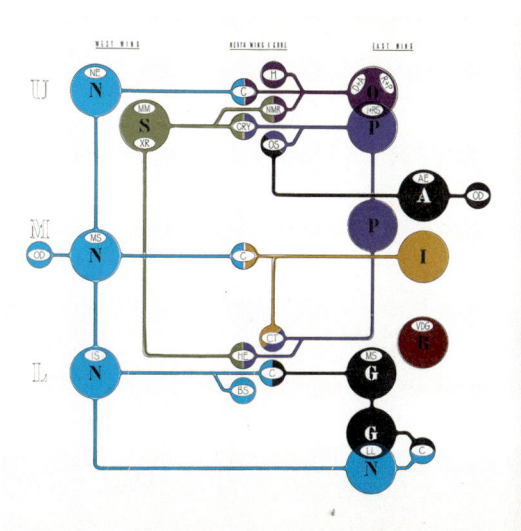

4 Brookhaven National Laboratory, Chemistry Building (Building 555, unexecuted), Long Island, New York, 1959, relationship diagram

plines, general and specialized laboratory spaces, office spaces, and the wings of the proposed building into a coherent system of interconnections. This topology of interdisciplinary scientific practice then became the key concept driving the specific configuration of "flexible" laboratory and office space in the building. The basic idea behind the diagrammatic approach was that each discipline would receive space and total autonomy in proportion to its level of anticipated research activity and staffing; then, between these autonomous areas, labs and other shared spaces would be arranged to facilitate interdisciplinary research programs. This complex arrangement could be achieved, Gatje surmised, through a roughly cruciform building, which provided ample space at both the center and edges of the building to accommodate the junctures between disciplines. By further layering the laboratories on top of one another in a three-story building, the necessary "communication and economy" that had been desirable but awkwardly realized in the Chemistry Department's makeshift quarters could be formalized through a carefully considered system of proximities (e.g., inorganic chemists and physical chemists would be located in an area that allowed their mutual use of the constant temperature room, whereas the inorganic chemists and nuclear chemists would need equal, shared, and convenient access to counting rooms used to measure radioactive isotopes).

Gatje also concluded, in keeping with standard laboratory design practice, that a rigorous modular system would improve future capability for flexible arrangement of the laboratories. However, these two organizational principles, relatively commonplace in post–World War II American research laboratory design, needed to be governed by a third principle, unique to atomic research labs, which was developed elsewhere in the landscape of the national laboratory system.

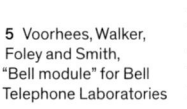

5 Voorhees, Walker, Foley and Smith, "Bell module" for Bell Telephone Laboratories

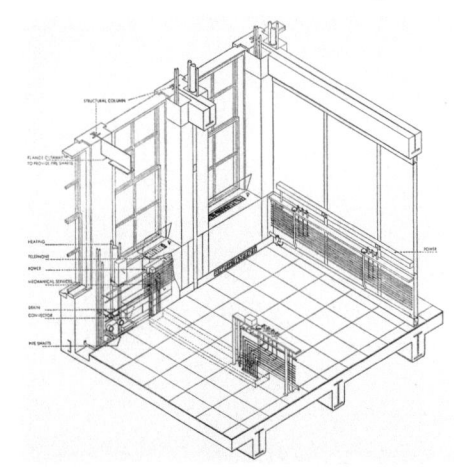

The gold standard of conventional scientific laboratory design was the so-called "Bell module," developed through close collaboration between the architect Ralph Walker of the New York–based firm of Voorhees, Walker, Foley and Smith, and the plant manager for Bell Telephone Laboratories, James G. Motley [5].[23] Their key insight was that the basic unit of the research laboratory "was not a room but a space"

or "module" that "is to be considered as a unit of work space determined by human needs. It is dimensional only through its use factors."[24] These dimensions were wholly variable, dependent upon the tasks specific to particular modes of research or administrative work. In practical terms, planning according to the flexible needs of the research laboratory required the removal of the electrical and mechanical services of the building either to vertical chases that would form shared walls between laboratories and a central corridor of the building *or*—in the case of "wet" chemistry and experimental physics conducted in specially controlled atmospheric and simulated weather conditions—a series of chases located in hollow "wet columns" that would serve a flexible arrangement of "island" or "peninsula type" work benches.

Although atomic research laboratories required much the same treatment as their conventional counterparts, the Bell module approach was at once paradigmatic and inadequate. As the first theorists of an "architecture of nuclear buildings," Elisabeth K. Thompson, the San Francisco architect and editor of *Architectural Record*, and Bernis E. Brazier, the Denver-based architect and former manager of facility development under Robert Oppenheimer at Los Alamos, explained in *Architectural Record* in June 1957, "everything … is governed in the nuclear building by imperative considerations of protection for personnel (and for building and equipment) from the invisible and insidious radioactivity of materials used in nuclear research."[25] Brazier and Thompson identified two primary "philosophies" for nuclear research laboratory design. In "DDD" or "3D" design (dilute, disperse, and decontaminate), architects laid out laboratories in a progression of rooms running from "cold" (clean) to "hot" (highly radioactive) spaces and deployed multiple means of protection, ranging from protective suits to "master-slave" controls for remote manipulation of radioactive materials to massive concrete and metal "shielding walls which enclosed large volume 'cells' or 'caves.'"[26]

The second philosophy, known as "CC" (concentrate and confine), was the brainchild of Nelson B. Garden, chief of health chemistry at UC Berkeley's Radiation Laboratory, a state-of-the-art facility designed by the leading modernist architect Erich Mendelsohn.[27] This approach required creating a "transportable plywood, plastic, or metal box" within which the experiment could be conducted. This box was essentially a miniature laboratory rendered as a piece of shielded equipment whose scale could be adjusted to the specific experiment and that would be immediately connected to a highly shielded exhaust and waste management

6 "Concentrate and confine" laboratory plan
7 "Concentrate and confine" laboratory box
8 Schematic plan drawing, Building 555

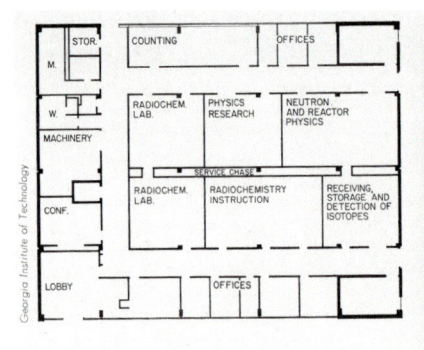

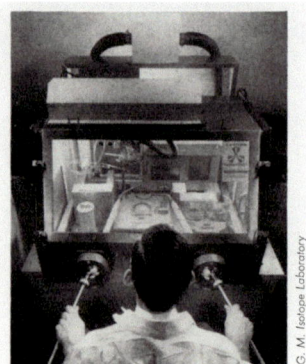

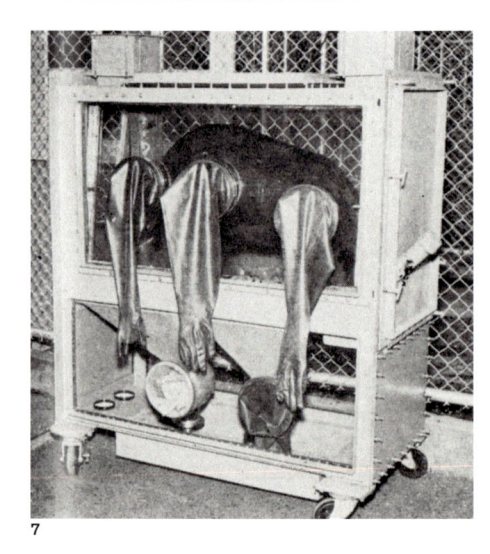

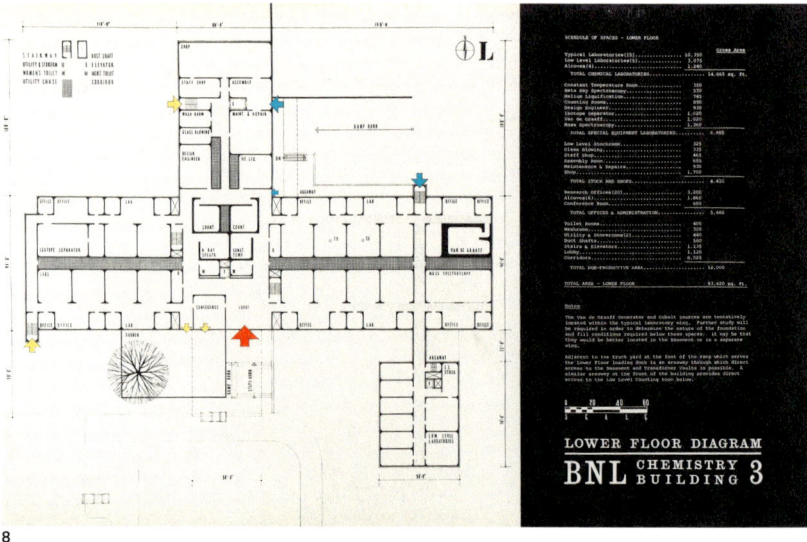

system [6]. Such an approach reenvisioned the *architecture* of the laboratory as a structural armature for housing a complex system of chases designed to protect scientists from the dangers of radiation and to isolate experiments from one another. Brazier and Thompson's article included a plan diagram of an early CC lab at Georgia Tech, and it showed how this approach led designers to replace the vertical chases of the Bell module with a single massive chase [7]. Located either at the core or the periphery of the building, this chase could service an entire building both horizontally and vertically, eliminating the need to thread the various highly insulated and potentially hazardous exhaust systems throughout the building between the floors and ceilings.

As the schematic plans and sections of Breuer and Gatje's study show [8], in keeping with a broader trend in nuclear research laboratory design, the Brookhaven chemistry lab design took the CC approach, albeit with a unique twist. As Gatje recounts in his memoir, this change was at the direct behest of Richard Dodson, who chaired the department.[28] After an intensive back-and-forth dialogue with Dodson and his colleagues, Gatje settled on a cubic module of twelve feet. Four such modules would allow for a generously proportioned, high-ceilinged standard laboratory measuring twenty-four feet square in plan and twelve feet in height, which could then be subdivided into two (twelve feet by twenty-four feet) plan labs for smaller experiments or expanded into much larger spaces intended to house instruments that required placement in the middle of the room for access from all sides. The interior walls were to be made of four-inch, non-load-bearing cement block, which could easily be removed and built elsewhere. (In the eyes of architects and chemists alike, the "industry standard" of Hauserman metal partition walls was hardly more efficient and would have added significantly to the building's cost.)[29]

The deep arrangement of two rows of laboratories laid out along the service corridor meant that offices had to be set along the periphery of the building. Taking advantage of the Chemistry Department's standing tradition of working in open areas, Breuer and Gatje proposed glazing the outward-facing wall of each laboratory to allow natural light into the building and staggering an alternating set of office and "alcove" spaces at the outer edge of the building. These alcoves eventually became offices in their own right, were usually given to doctoral students and postdocs, and served as spaces for interdisciplinary collaboration.[30]

So far, so good. Yet, one persistent problem remained. Although the "Berkeley box" approach was useful for materially and spatially isolating the scientists and their equipment from the radioactive materials on which they were working, it did not successfully isolate the sophisticated and sensitive counting apparatus necessary for measuring minor changes in levels of radioactivity. Because of the presence of two research reactors at BNL, nearly the whole campus was contaminated by unusually high levels of radioactive isotopes of argon, along with several other radioactive contaminants. Although it was believed that heavy argon would present little threat to human health, it consistently ruined the results of experiments conducted within the chemistry labs.

To shield the laboratory's interior spaces from this contamination, Breuer and Gatje revived a component of the DDD lab designs: the concrete-and-metal wall. Rather than laminate these materials, however, as previous laboratory architects had done, Breuer and Gatje proposed manufacturing a structural concrete aggregated with metal powders (e.g., lead), which would create a formidable but extremely thin and fungible protective layer inside and outside the building. As the plans show, the thickness of the metal-impregnated concrete walls erected around the counting apparatuses could be varied according to the required levels of sensitivity. And, for the most sensitive instruments, Breuer and Gatje proposed a subterranean installation for "low level labs," protected by much thicker concrete-metal walls and separated from the rest of the building by an "areaway." These walls would serve as a crucial component of the apparatus: they would be poured around recycled artillery barrels from pre–World War II warships, forged and cast before the first atomic explosions. The resulting enclosures would be among the cleanest—in radioactive terms—spaces on the planet.[31]

The novelty and technical efficacy of the BNL Chemistry Building design thus proceeded not simply from deployment of the "Berkeley box" approach but through the way it exploited this type of chase design. It effectively synthesized the two dominant spatial and technical principles of nuclear laboratory design with previous conventional laboratory design principles and then rendered the entire design workable through an inventive use of reinforced concrete as a combination of structure and shielding apparatus. The "Berkeley box" chase became a means of interconnecting and coordinating all of these elements of the design; the unique use of concrete effected a higher and more subtle level of environmental regulation over the interior of the building than anything the Breuer office had previously encountered.

Ironically, despite the elegance of the solution, government officials deemed Breuer's firm unqualified to fulfill the commission. After BNL accepted the study, the actual job of completing the design and constructing the building was awarded to Fellheimer & Wagner, a New York–based firm. After a brief misunderstanding in which Fellheimer & Wagner copied a conventional chemistry research laboratory it had designed for Union Carbide in Charleston, West Virginia, the firm's two principals, Roland A. Wank and Fred Adams, completed the building following Breuer and Gatje's specifications.[32] It opened with an official dedication ceremony as Building 555 on October 14, 1966, and years later Bigeleisen and his colleagues adjudged it to be a tremendous success.

The IBM France Research and Development Laboratory, 1960–1976
Despite the disappointment of losing the commission, Breuer had gained something very valuable from the intensive experience of designing the BNL Chemistry Building. He had realized that reinforced concrete could be applied not only to the engineering problem of enclosing vast spaces with a minimum of vertical structural components and not only to the ever-growing demand for architectural materials fungible enough to provide meaningful sculptural and symbolic forms in the face of an increasingly dehumanized technocratic society. He had also found a key to solving the problem of *environmental control.*

The commission for the IBM laboratory at La Gaude came to Breuer via Eliot Noyes, his former student and architectural collaborator, who was at the time heading up the most intensive phase of the IBM design program. The IBM consultancy, which also involved the office of Charles and Ray Eames, Edgar Kaufmann Jr., George Nelson, and Paul Rand, was charged with remaking every aspect of IBM's material apparatus to achieve an organic and managerial unity throughout the multinational corporation's far-flung operations. The central concept in this drive, as Noyes insisted repeatedly, was the rigorous management of the corporation's *environment*: "If you get to the very heart of the matter, what IBM really does is help man extend his control over his environment.... I think that's the meaning of the company."[33] It is hard to imagine a commission in which Breuer and Gatje could press further their effort to achieve environmental control through the exploitation of tectonic, electrical, and mechanical systems.

The development of the design can be tracked through an extensive series of drawings preserved in the Marcel Breuer Papers, archived at the Syracuse University Libraries. IBM's requirements for the building were detailed by IBM France Département central Immobilier, the French arm of IBM's rapidly expanding Real Estate and Construction Division (RECD). Final authority to approve designs rested with C. F. de Waldner, the president of Compagnie IBM–France. The main requirements included ample natural light throughout the building and a large, 1.2-meter module that could coordinate the building's structure with the raised flooring required for large-scale computing systems, which contained relatively large air-handling equipment to cool the machines.[34] Unlike the Brookhaven lab, there were few research activities beyond the air-conditioned and heavily wired computer labs that would have required the use of walls to control radiation or other environmental forces. IBM thus insisted upon a maximally open plan.

It is this last requirement that seems to have led Gatje to propose threading mechanical, plumbing, and electrical systems through a system of corridors running within the exterior walls of the building. Yet, it is also plain from sections of the precast panels that the dimensions of the beveled surfaces of the panels were at least in part determined by the need to accommodate the raised false floors of the computer labs and the air-conditioning units running along the wall below the windows throughout the building [9]. The top and bottom panels also included an orthogonal element whose dimensions conformed to the heights of the chases for air ducts and the concrete beams supporting the floor

p. 256/4

9 IBM La Gaude, typical wall section drawing
10 Wall section drawing showing false floors of computer rooms

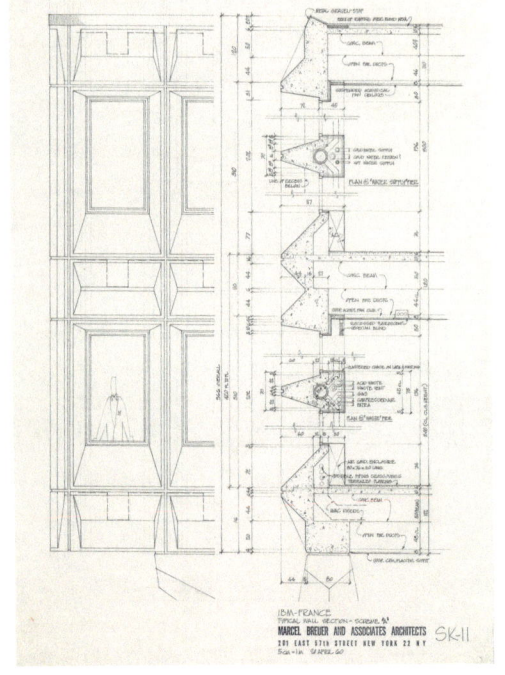

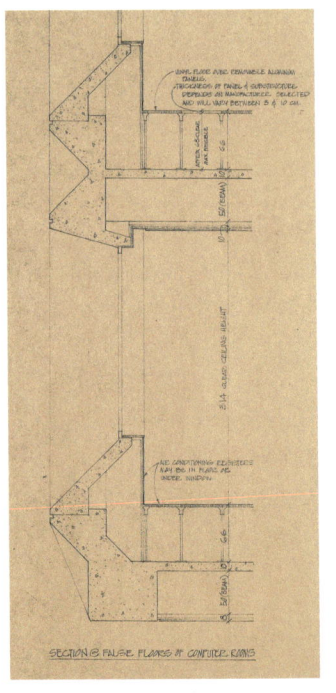

and ceiling. Since the IBM facility did not accommodate much "wet" research at the time, the wall chases, as built, only served to house electrical conduits [10]. However, in memos dating from after the completion of the first building, Gatje indicated that sufficient space was provided for "the possibility of a rack of 100% accessible process piping … 5 or 6 lines high."[35] To move these systems vertically, Breuer and Gatje provided hollows for the required systems in narrow "supply" and "waste" piers—essentially heavily modeled mullions. In the drawings, these are detailed as piping systems for "acid waste," "waste vent," "gas," "compressed air," and an "extra" small-gauge pipe.

The end result was one in which each highly sculptural "window-wall" unit provided a tectonic expression of the technical systems threaded through the building. The highly concentrated and concealed corridor at Brookhaven had become distributed throughout the building via its façades and floor systems. Breuer and Gatje's solution therefore not only expressed the presence of those systems but also made them integral parts of the enclosure separating the interior of the laboratory from the surrounding environment. The deeply molded façade did not merely serve to control "sun and shadow," as the former penetrated the building's windows in the manner of Le Corbusier's *brise soleil*; the façade also controlled the interior environment from within the wall. This was the fundamental "counter-environmental" logic of IBM's entire building program, and the La Gaude laboratory was perhaps its most monumentally imposing realization.[36]

In conclusion, Breuer's late institutional architecture was largely motivated by the desire to integrate technical systems with sculptural, architectural form, and the chase served as the crucial conceptual and organizational element in that integration.

In his only sustained piece of writing on the innovation, "The Faceted, Molded Façade: Depth, Sun and Shadow" (1966), Breuer argued that the steel-and-glass (and aluminum, and rubber, and fiberglass, etc.) curtain wall could not form an adequate "skin" for a building because it is at odds with the structural, aesthetic, and technological qualities that define the wall as the place where "climate is tamed and transformed."[37] The curtain wall can neither contain nor express in aesthetic terms the technical essence of architecture: "The glass wall—as an expression of modern technology—seems to conflict with technology itself."[38] By contrast, his precast concrete panels can be designed for a variety of technical requirements: they may be load bearing and structural; they may offer chases and hollows for pipes, ducts, and heating-cooling equipment; they may form projections for sun protection; they may be solid or may contain large openings; they may combine all of these.

What about aesthetics? A new *depth* of façade is emerging; a three-dimensionality with a resulting greatly expanded vocabulary of architectural expression. Sun and shadow.[39]

Breuer and Gatje's great achievement at Brookhaven and La Gaude was to exploit concrete in ways that no other architects had. Here were walls that could "tame and transform" the environment to provide human comfort yet also control that same environment for the benefit of the technical systems of scientific research [11].[40]

Breuer famously claimed that "the great architectural virtue of reinforced concrete is that it can be molded to express its builder's thoughts precisely."[41] In the case of large-scale, high-tech research, the "builder" is both architect and scientific institution. Since reinforced concrete architecture could be made to "reflect the stresses in the structure with photographic truthfulness," it could serve as a new universalizing and normalizing force within a society that Breuer (along with many others) saw as increasingly atomized, divided between a world of science and a world of art.[42] Even if (as Guy Nordenson shows elsewhere in this volume) Breuer sometimes deployed the surface effects of structural truth against the grain of actual structure, his optimistic vision, developed in the wake of Brookhaven and La Gaude, was that technology could serve as a common ground for reuniting those areas of human endeavor: "Technology, rather than endangering the artist, fuses him with the engineer, with the scientist."[43]

The "stresses" mediated by Breuer's and Gatje's concrete techniques were not only structural but also environmental and managerial. Developed in the crucible of the culture of public and private research and development, the precast panels could be arrayed in a curvilinear "Y"- or "H"-shaped plan suggesting both a cellular membrane or bourrelet protecting the vital exchanges occurring within the larger organism of the corporation *and* the economy of carefully mediated exchanges between that interior and the outside world.[44] Part of what made the La Gaude laboratory a vital success was that it realized this simple biological metaphor with such elegance and proof-of-concept. In addition, it

11 IBM La Gaude, view of cast-in-place concrete columns and precast concrete wall units

expressed a broader, telematic logic that was significant for the rapidly proliferating multinational corporation. Each such building was an outpost within a larger network and located in discrete spaces or territories yet linked together through electronic telecommunications networks. Thus, it is unsurprising that IBM returned to Breuer's office for construction of a variation on La Gaude in Boca Raton, Florida, built in multiple stages from 1968 to 1973, and that Gatje returned to France not once but twice to supervise the expansion of the original IBM France laboratory, each time varying the design of the panels to suit new technical demands.

Breuer's repeated use of concrete panel technology throughout much of his late work for institutions other than scientific research institutes, universities, and technology corporations turned the panel system into an architectural panacea, and this work soon fell into disrepute.[45] The structural and environmental stresses expressed in his works became evidence of a lack of "environmental control" rather than a surfeit of it. Breuer's fellow Hungarian immigrant, Dr. Hans Selye, wrote of Hippocrates's concept of *pónos* (toil), or "the fight of the body to restore itself toward normal": "The practical use of stress-producing measures of treatment had been repeatedly hailed as a panacea, each time to be rejected a few years later as superstition and charlatanism."[46] Architects working away in contemporary efforts to produce or otherwise exploit "smart" materials and walls threaded with more mechanical and electrical services than ever before may therefore find Selye's warning useful. Until we better understand the drive toward synthesis between art and science, we ought to be wary of the consequences of fixing upon a signal and single solution to all architectural problems.

1 My sincerest thanks to Jack Preses in the Chemistry Department at Brookhaven National Laboratory not only for his help in making accessible on the department's website various crucial documents on the history of Building 555 but also for making numerous additional documents available to me. My thanks, too, to colleagues who have given me valuable feedback: Barry Bergdoll, Jonathan Massey, and Romy Golan. For a short history of the La Gaude complex in the context of IBM's broader architectural program, see John Harwood, *The Interface: IBM and the Transformation of Corporate Design, 1945–1976* (Minneapolis: University of Minnesota Press, 2011), 139–48.
2 Henry Bakis, *I.B.M.: Une multinationale régionale* (Grenoble: Presses Universitaires de Grenoble, 1977).
3 Quotation from Robert F. Gatje, *Marcel Breuer: A Memoir* (New York: Monacelli Press, 2000),

101. On UNESCO, see Lucia Allais's essay in this volume.
4 Gatje, *Marcel Breuer*, 101.
5 Ibid., 93.
6 The valorization of mechanical and electrical systems in modern architecture has been a theme of architectural historical inquiry since the late 1960s. See, for example, Reyner Banham, *The Architecture of the Well-Tempered Environment*, 2nd ed. (Chicago: University of Chicago Press, 1984); and Robert Bruegmann, "Central Heating and Forced Ventilation: Origins and Effects on Architectural Design," *Journal of the Society of Architectural Historians* 37, no. 3 (October 1978): 143–66. However, such historiographical interventions—which call attention to the fact that "environmental provisions have only attracted attention when they have made some gross monumental impact on the exterior aspect

of buildings" (Banham, *Architecture of the Well-Tempered Environment*, 12)—have eschewed theorizing the very core concepts motivating the ever-increasing integration of technical systems into buildings: "environment," "management," "comfort," "survival," and so on. This essay is a small effort to build upon the major efforts of figures such as Banham and Bruegmann by paying close attention to the conditions under which a highly unusual and specified synthesis of technical systems emerged.

7 Eldon C. Shoup, memorandum to Edward Reynolds, November 10, 1947, quoted in Robert P. Crease, *Making Physics: A Biography of Brookhaven National Laboratory, 1946–1972* (Chicago: University of Chicago Press, 1999), 56 (original emphasis). The ninth university was the SUNY system.

8 On the peculiar logic of GOCO, see Seymour Melman, *Pentagon Capitalism: The Political Economy of War* (New York: McGraw-Hill, 1970).

9 See Peter J. Westwick, *The National Labs: Science in an American System, 1947–74* (Cambridge, MA: Harvard University Press, 2003); and Crease, *Making Physics*.

10 Crease makes note of several journalists, even respected science reporters, who fabricated sensational stories in order to capitalize on public fears about nuclear science. See Crease, *Making Physics*, chap. 6.

11 Daniel Lang, "A Reporter at Large: The Long Island Atoms," *New Yorker*, 20 December 1947, 38 (emphasis added).

12 The fear of overspecialization was a specter hovering over post–World War II academia and the entire national laboratory system. This fear was exacerbated by the culture of secrecy imposed by the military on any nuclear research, and it led directly to the creation of new counterinstitutions, such as the *Bulletin of the Atomic Scientists*, "founded in 1945 by Manhattan Project scientists who 'could not remain aloof to the consequences of their work.'" "Background and Mission: 1945–2017," *Bulletin of the Atomic Scientists*, www.thebulletin.org/background-and-mission, accessed September 12, 2017. This desire to desegregate the production of knowledge extended to other areas of science and the humanities; see, for example, the classic jeremiad on this dehumanization of the sciences in the postwar era, C. P. Snow's *The Two Cultures and the Scientific Revolution* (New York: Cambridge University Press, 1959). To exorcise this ghost, BNL would not only provide a place for collaboration between scientists from several different universities and disciplines but also serve as a site for international exchange of expertise and experimental data. A summer program instructed young postdoctoral fellows in nuclear science, and long-term residencies were set up to foster these connections. Peter and several BNL department heads tried to leverage the expected high demand for such international programs into a commitment from the AEC to renovate the dingy buildings at Camp Upton, but this attempt failed. Even in 1963, a chemist at BNL could still complain that "the situation at Brookhaven tends to encourage each staff member to cultivate with great thoroughness and elegance his own special garden and no general program exists which encourages breadth of scientific vision. By contrast, in a university, the teaching program keeps every staff member aware of the major aspects of his subject; while in development laboratories, continual contact with raw reality provides encouragement for the broad view." Anonymous staff member C, "Aims and Five Year Forcast [sic], Chemistry Department," November 1955, attached to R. W. Dodson to Ralph Weston, January 10, 1963, Chemistry Department Records, BNL, Upton, NY.

13 The account given here is summarized from a letter by Jacob Bigeleisen to Carol Creutz, chair of the Chemistry Department, Brookhaven National Laboratory, April 10, 1998, published on the BNL Chemistry Department website, www.bnl.gov/chemistry/History/TheChemistryBuilding.asp. Jack Preses, a BNL chemist who is responsible for collating the historical materials on the website, has edited the letter slightly, due to the fractious relationship between Bigeleisen and Tucker. Jack Preses, phone interview by author, July 17, 2012.

14 US Atomic Energy Commission, Construction Project Description FY 1961, Project 543-61: Chemistry Laboratory Brookhaven National Laboratory, Associated Universities, Inc., July 1959, 4, Chemistry Department Records, BNL.

15 Bigeleisen to Creutz, April 10, 1998.

16 Jacob Bigeleisen, Remarks at Dedication of the Brookhaven National Laboratory Chemistry Building, October 14, 1966, Chemistry Department Records, BNL, available online, www.bnl.gov/chemistry/deleted/JBRemarks.asp.

17 Bigeleisen to Creutz, April 10, 1998.

18 Ibid.

19 Marcel Breuer to Jacob Bigeleisen, May 25, 1959, 1, Chemistry Department Records, BNL.

20 Ibid., 2.

21 R. W. Dodson, memorandum to L. J. Haworth on "Study Preliminary to the Design of the Chemistry Building," September 11, 1959 (no pagination), with attached memorandum from the Building Committee to R. W. Dodson on the same subject, Chemistry Department Records, BNL. On the Hunter College project, see "Gothic Campus Gets a Contemporary Building," *Progressive Architecture* 41, no. 4 (1960): 178–88.

22 Marcel Breuer and Robert F. Gatje, "Brookhaven National Laboratory, Associated Universities Incorporated: Program for a New Chemistry Building," December 1960 (Subcontract No. S-566), 1, Frames 425–41, Reel 5732, Box OV 46, Marcel Breuer Papers, Archives of American Art, Smithsonian Institution, Washington, DC, and available online in full color at www.bnl.gov/chemistry/History/TheBreuerStudy.asp.

23 Ralph Walker, *Ralph Walker, Architect: Of Voorhees Gmelin & Walker; Voorhees Walker Foley & Smith; Voorhees Walker Smith & Smith* (New York: Henahan House, 1957), 182–83. An early capsule biography of Motley is given in *Bell Laboratories Record* 1, no. 4 (December 1925): 177. On the history of the exurban R&D laboratory in the 1930s and after, see William J. Rankin, "The

Epistemology of the Suburbs: Knowledge, Production, and Corporate Laboratory Design," *Critical Inquiry* 36 (Summer 2010): 771–806.

24 Walker, *Ralph Walker, Architect*.

25 Bernis E. Brazier and Elisabeth K. Thompson, "Laboratories for Radioactive Research," *Architectural Record* 121 (June 1957): 216–26, republished in *Buildings for Research* (New York: F. W. Dodge, 1958), 28. See also Thompson, "For an Architecture of Nuclear Buildings," *Architectural Record* 121 (March 1957), republished in: *Buildings for Research*, 62; and Carl Abbott, "Building the Atomic Cities: Richland, Los Alamos, and the American Planning Language," in *The Atomic West*, ed. Bruce Hevly and John M. Findlay (Seattle: University of Washington Press, 1998), 94.

26 Brazier and Thompson, "Laboratories for Radioactive Research," 29.

27 On this project, see the brief account given in Hans R. Morganthaler, "'It will be hard for us to find a home': Projects in the United States 1941–1953," in *Erich Mendelsohn, Architect 1887–1953*, ed. Regina Stephan, trans. Melissa Thorson Hause (New York: Monacelli Press, 1999), 259.

28 "Dick [Dodson] had the idea that all this activity could be conducted inside a 'service corridor' that would run along one side of all the laboratories. Technicians could circulate within these corridors and accomplish most of their hookups without even having to enter the labs. A second line of laboratories could be ranged along the other side of the service corridor, and a deep, efficient building plan would result." Gatje, *Marcel Breuer*, 93. See also Dodson, memorandum to Haworth on "Study Preliminary to the Design of the Chemistry Building," with attached memorandum.

29 "Brookhaven National Laboratory Chemistry Building (555)" [summary memorandum, n.d. (1960)], 2, Chemistry Department Records, BNL.

30 Jack Preses, interview by author, July 12, 2012. The best description of the culture of interdisciplinary collaboration that was so prized at Brookhaven, and in the Chemistry Department in particular, comes from Glenn T. Seaborg, the Nobel Prize–winning molecular chemist and director of the AEC from 1961 to 1971. At the dedication of the new building in 1966 he remarked, "Now, working in these so-called 'temporary' buildings was admittedly inconvenient. At the same time, however, it seems to have made for a certain informality and flexibility of attitude that is always the hallmark of an active and productive research establishment. Because of the shortages of laboratory space, many of the scientists here in the Chemistry Department had to work at their desks in what would usually have been used as corridors anywhere else.... This architectural openness served in its subtle way to promote and encourage discussion between scientists about their work as well as many other things. I am reminded somewhat of the *agora*, or market place, of the cities of ancient Greece which served as a place for both business and philosophy." Glenn T. Seaborg, speech delivered at dedication of Building 555, Brookhaven National Laboratory, October 14, 1966, Chemistry Department Records, BNL, www.bnl.gov/chemistry/history/GTSeaborg1.asp.

31 Jack Preses, interview by author, July 14, 2012.

32 Bigeleisen to Creutz, April 10, 1998. See also Jacob Bigeleisen, "Remarks at the Dedication of the Brookhaven National Laboratory Chemistry Building," October 14, 1966, Chemistry Department Records, BNL, www.bnl.gov/chemistry/deleted/JBRemarks.asp.

33 Quoted in Scott Kelly, "Curator of Corporate Character ... Eliot Noyes and Associates," *Industrial Design* 13 (June 1966): 43.

34 See the series of memoranda on the original building and its subsequent additions (designed primarily by Mario Jossa of the Breuer office) contained in Box 137, Marcel Breuer Papers, Syracuse University Libraries, Syracuse, NY.

35 Robert F. Gatje to Marcel Breuer, February 17, 1966, Folder 4, Box 137, Breuer Papers, Syracuse University Libraries.

36 See my discussion of the IBM France laboratory in Harwood, *Interface*, esp. 143–48.

37 Marcel Breuer, "The Faceted, Molded Façade: Depth, Sun and Shadow," in "The Most Recent Architecture of Marcel Breuer," *Architectural Record* 139 (April 1966): 171–86. Breuer's short essay is at the beginning of the article, on pages 171–72. The quotations are from page 172.

38 Breuer, "Faceted, Molded Façade," 171.

39 Ibid., 172.

40 Ibid.

41 Ibid., 171.

42 Ibid.

43 Marcel Breuer, "The Artist in a World of Science," lecture delivered November 4, 1967, reprinted in *Marcel Breuer, New Buildings and Projects*, ed. Tician Papachristou (New York: Praeger, 1970), 18–19. The speech is plainly marked by his optimistic reading of Snow, *Two Cultures and the Scientific Revolution*.

44 Breuer was likely aware of a popular book, D'Arcy Wentworth Thompson's *On Growth and Form* (Cambridge: Cambridge University Press, 1917), which circulated widely in avant-garde circles in the years following World War I and was popularized by Gyorgy Kepes, Breuer's friend and fellow emigré.

45 One significant critical assault on Breuer's (and others') investment in prefabrication techniques is Peter Blake, *Form Follows Fiasco: Why Modern Architecture Hasn't Worked* (Boston: Little, Brown, 1977), which strongly suggests that "brutalist" building techniques are out of step with the law, labor practices, and finance of contemporary building.

46 Hans Selye, *The Stress of Life* (New York: McGraw-Hill, 1956), 11, 32.

IV NEW YORK

New York was Breuer's home and professional base from 1946, when he left teaching at Harvard and his partnership with Gropius to set up an independent practice. The new firm established its reputation with houses—including a prominent temporary house in the Museum of Modern Art garden—but soon expanded to large-scale projects around the country and the world as it grew into a large office on several floors of a Madison Avenue office building. As with many New York practices in the boom years of Pax Americana, only a handful of commissions were in New York City itself. Manhattan has only one, but it is arguably the iconic design of Breuer's career: the inverted ziggurat of the Whitney Museum of American Art. There Breuer combined hidden trusswork with concrete and granite cladding to make a museum building in which various contradictions were held in a taut dialogue: between gallery and city, art and commerce, the heaviness of lithic mass and the lightness enabled by engineered cantilevers.

Breuer designed a number of small projects for New York area colleges, including an art center for Sarah Lawrence College as well as a library and classroom building at Hunter College incorporating terra-cotta flue tile screens and concrete column-and-shell structures inspired by Nervi, as well as by Félix Candela and other Latin American modernists. The St. John's commission opened up master-planning work, helping Breuer secure the commission to expand the Bronx campus of New York University, initially designed by McKim, Mead & White in the 1890s. Here Breuer brought the recently developed system of egg-crate structural frames developed for laboratory and office buildings to be the language for a new campus, as universalist in its assumptions as the Beaux-Arts classicism of the unfinished neoclassical master plan.

While Marcel Breuer & Associates worked globally, New York remained the primary base of the firm's practice even beyond Breuer's retirement in 1976. The architect died just weeks before a major show on his work opened at the Museum of Modern Art in the early summer of 1981. He was hailed by *Newsweek* as "the last modernist."

1 Whitney Museum of Art, New York, USA, 1964–66, perspective rendering
2 Breuer in fourth-floor gallery, 1966
3 View of Madison Avenue and East Seventy-Fifth Street corner
4 Undated sketch of façade on verso of letter from Louis I. Kahn, 1963
5 Section drawing looking southwest
6 View of Madison Avenue entry bridge
7 Stairway to lower-level galleries
8 Main lobby
9 Lower-level gallery and sculpture court
10 Corner view of the Gertrude Vanderbilt Whitney Memorial Gallery
11 Fourth-floor gallery
12 New York University, Bronx, New York, USA, 1959–70, aerial perspective rendering
13 Campus plan, 1962
14 Model of Julius Silver Residence Center, Begrisch Hall, and Gould Hall of Technology, 1959–61
15 Begrisch Hall viewed from the south
16 Begrisch Hall viewed from the west with Silver Residence Hall at left
17 Technology II, 1967–70, section looking east
18 Technology II, perspective rendering
19 Technology II, detail of south façade of laboratory-office wing
20 Technology II, view of laboratory-office and classroom wings from northeast
21 Hunter College Library, Classroom, and Administration Buildings, Bronx, New York, USA, 1957–60, undated sketches of library roof
22 Perspective rendering
23 Detail drawings of library roof
24 Interior of library

1

2

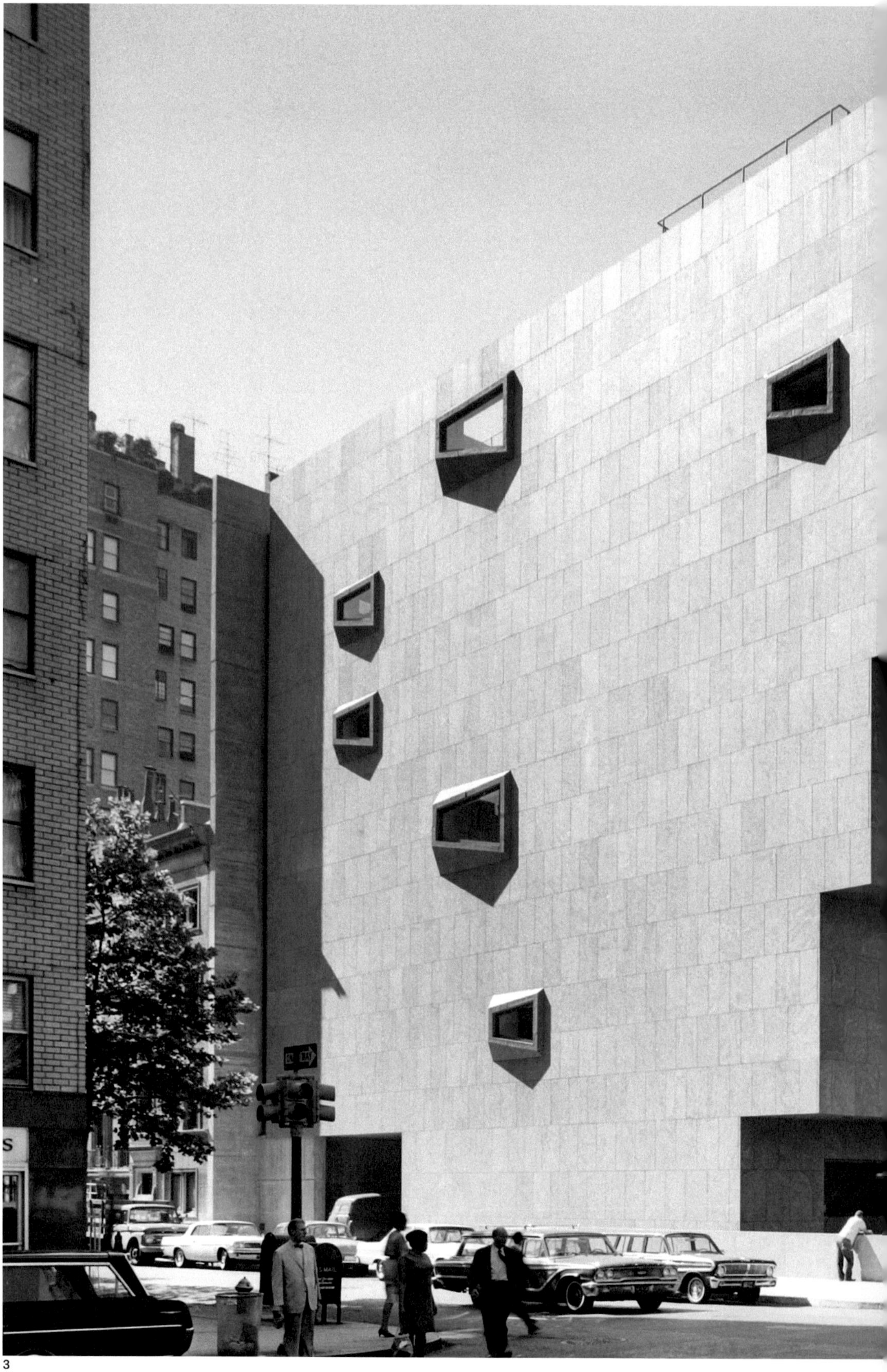

3

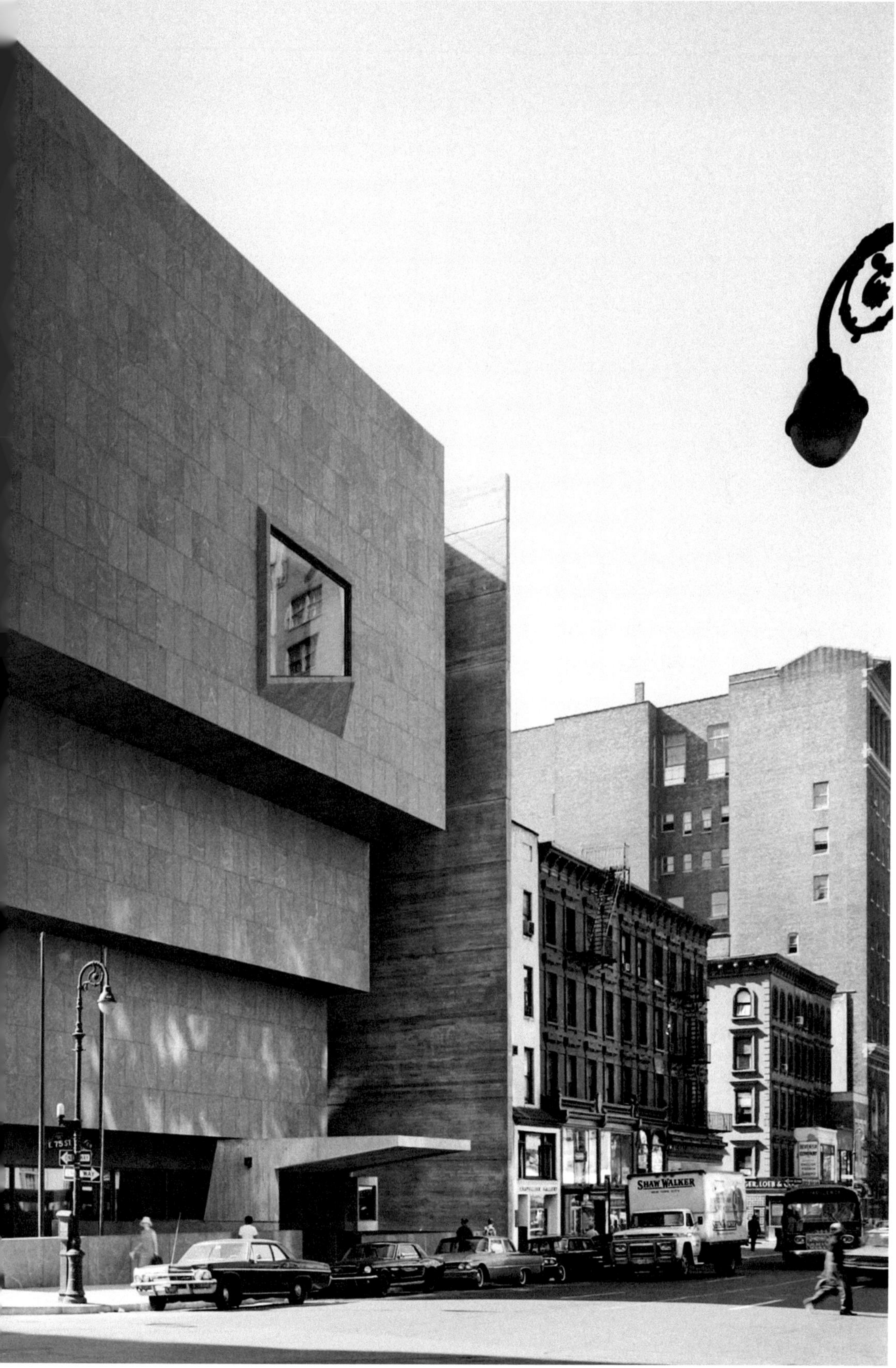
E 75 ST
SHAW WALKER

4

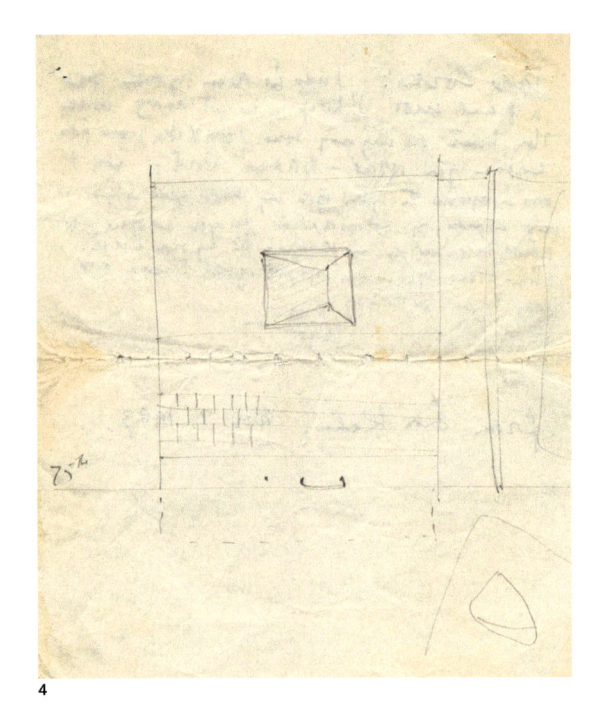

5

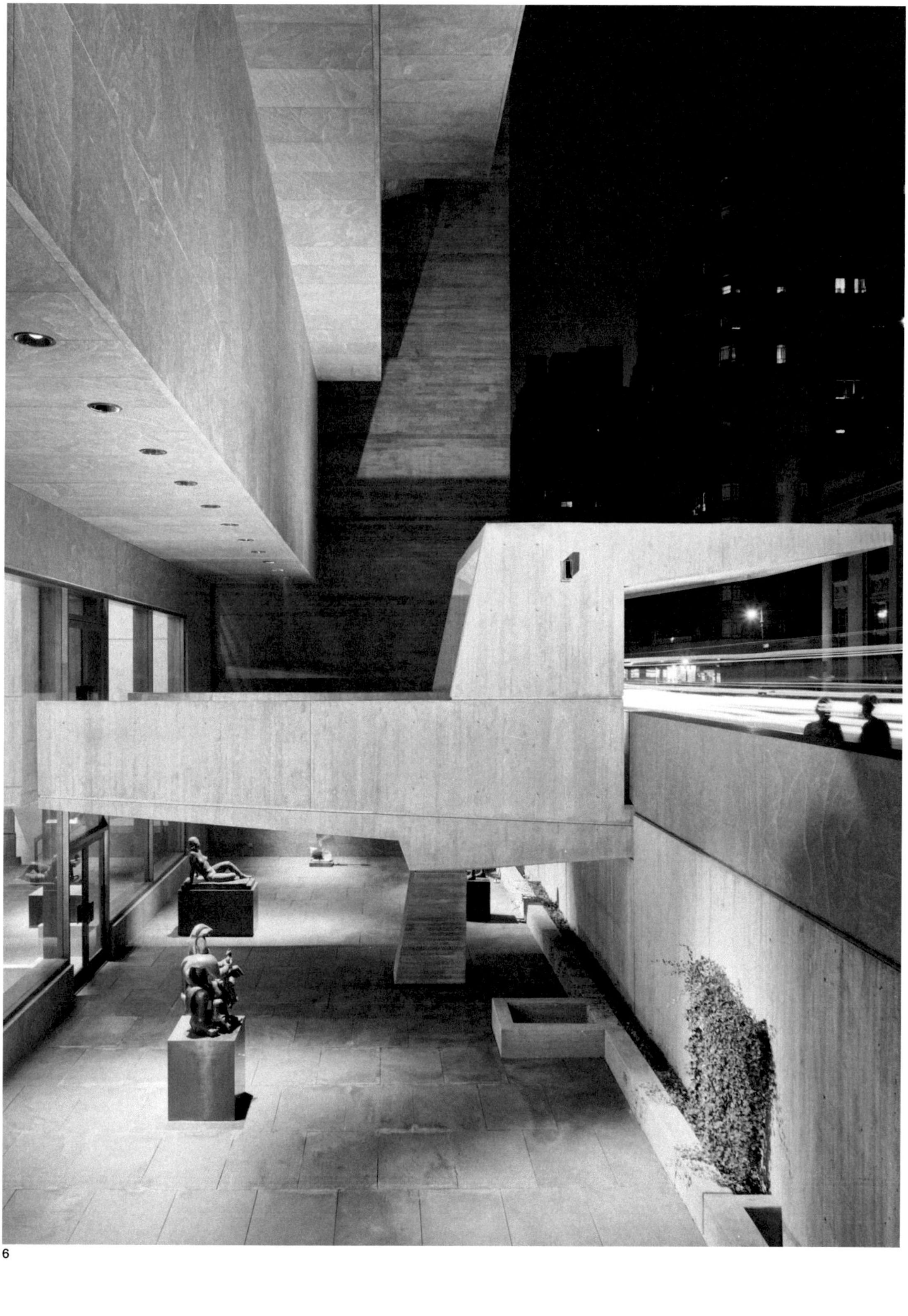

6

7

8

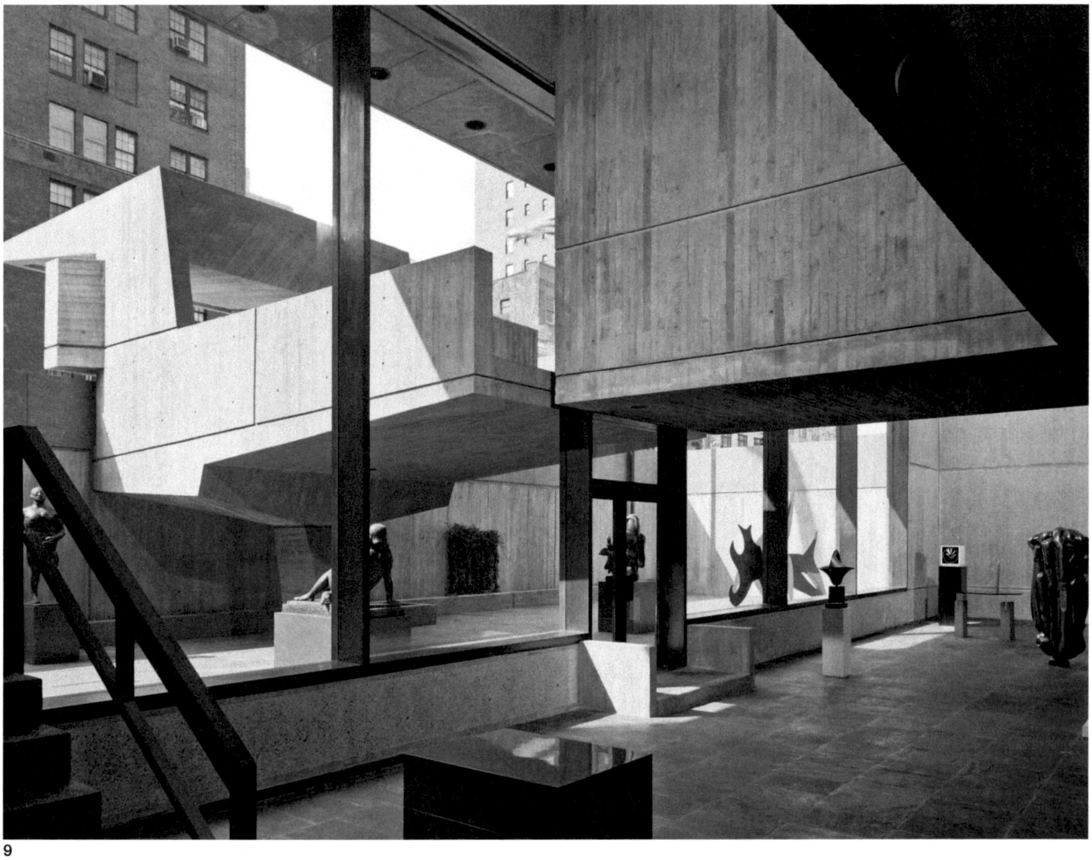

9

10

11

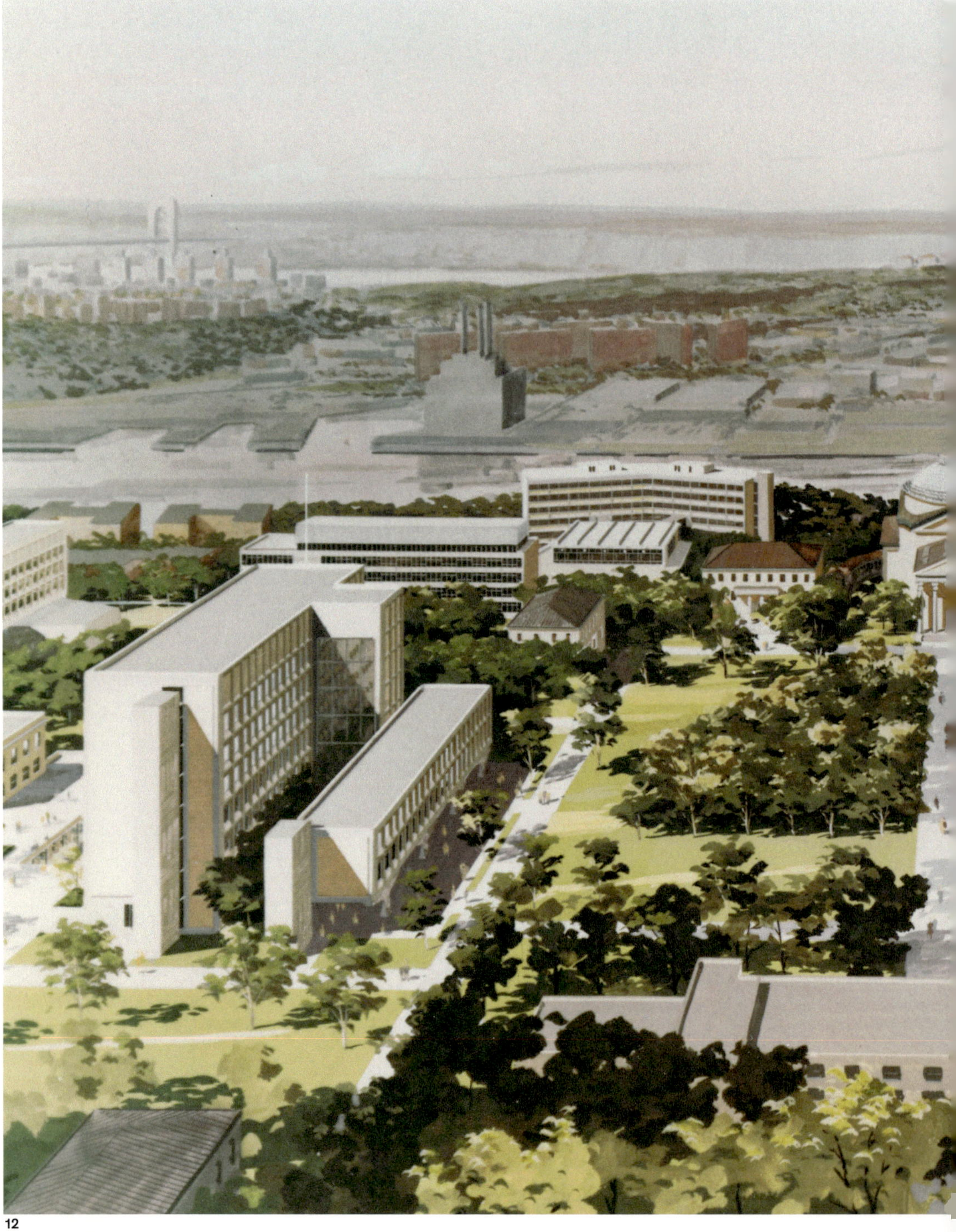

12

213

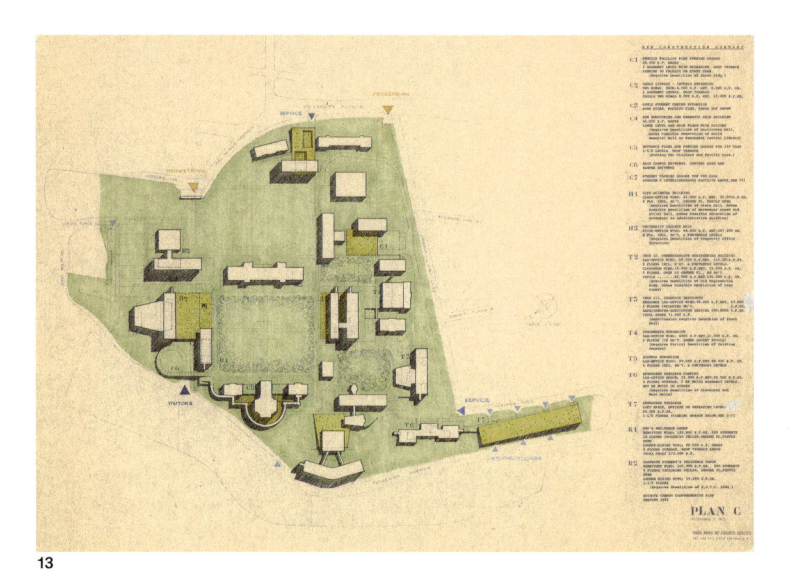

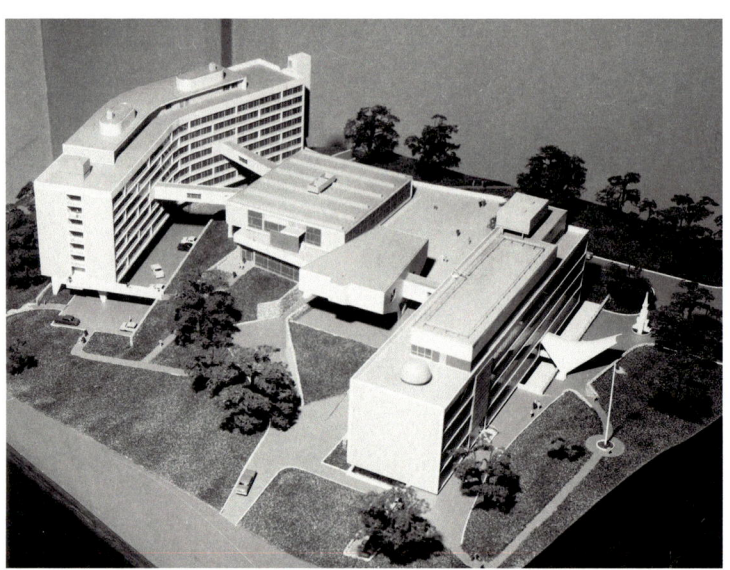

13

14

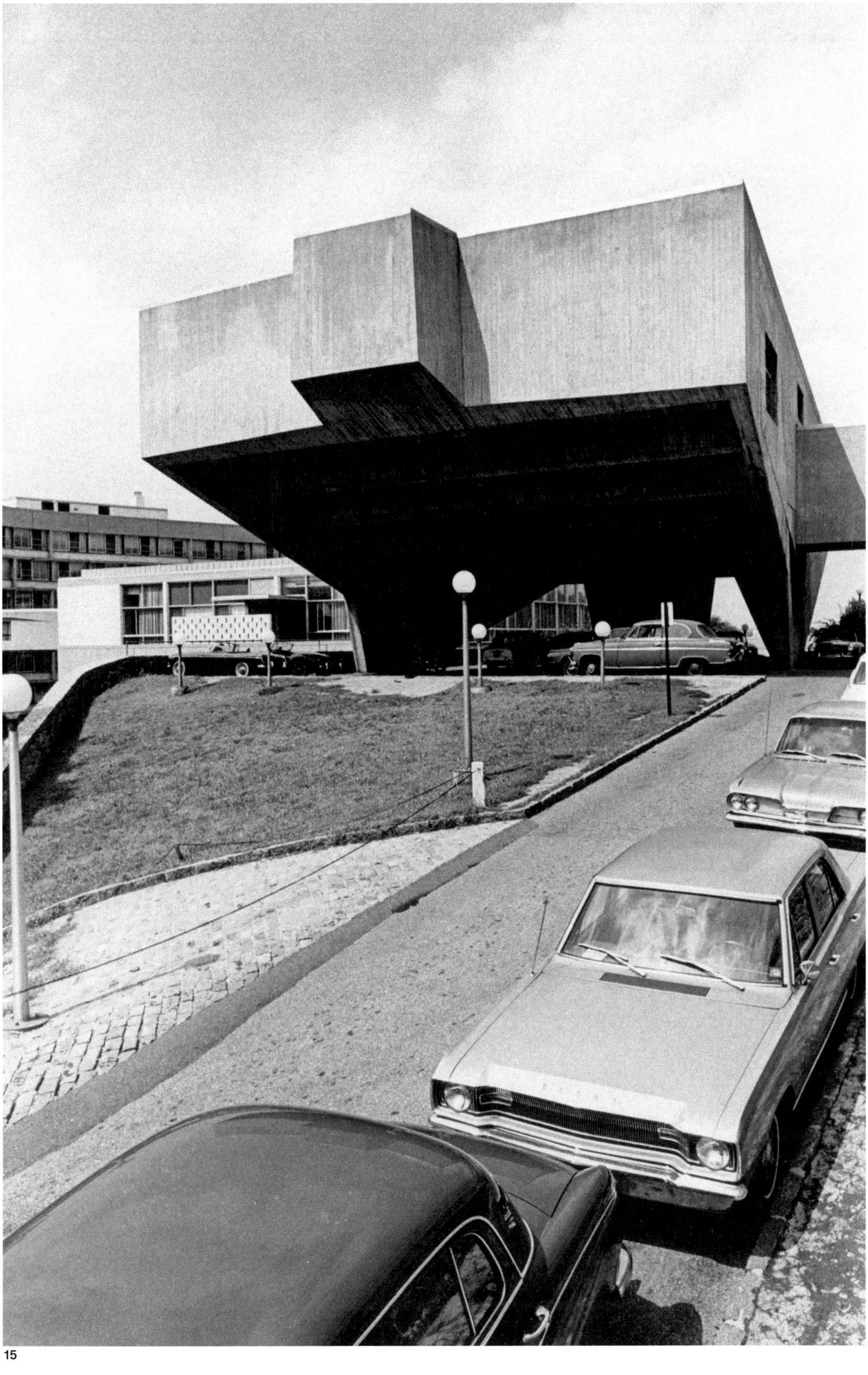

15

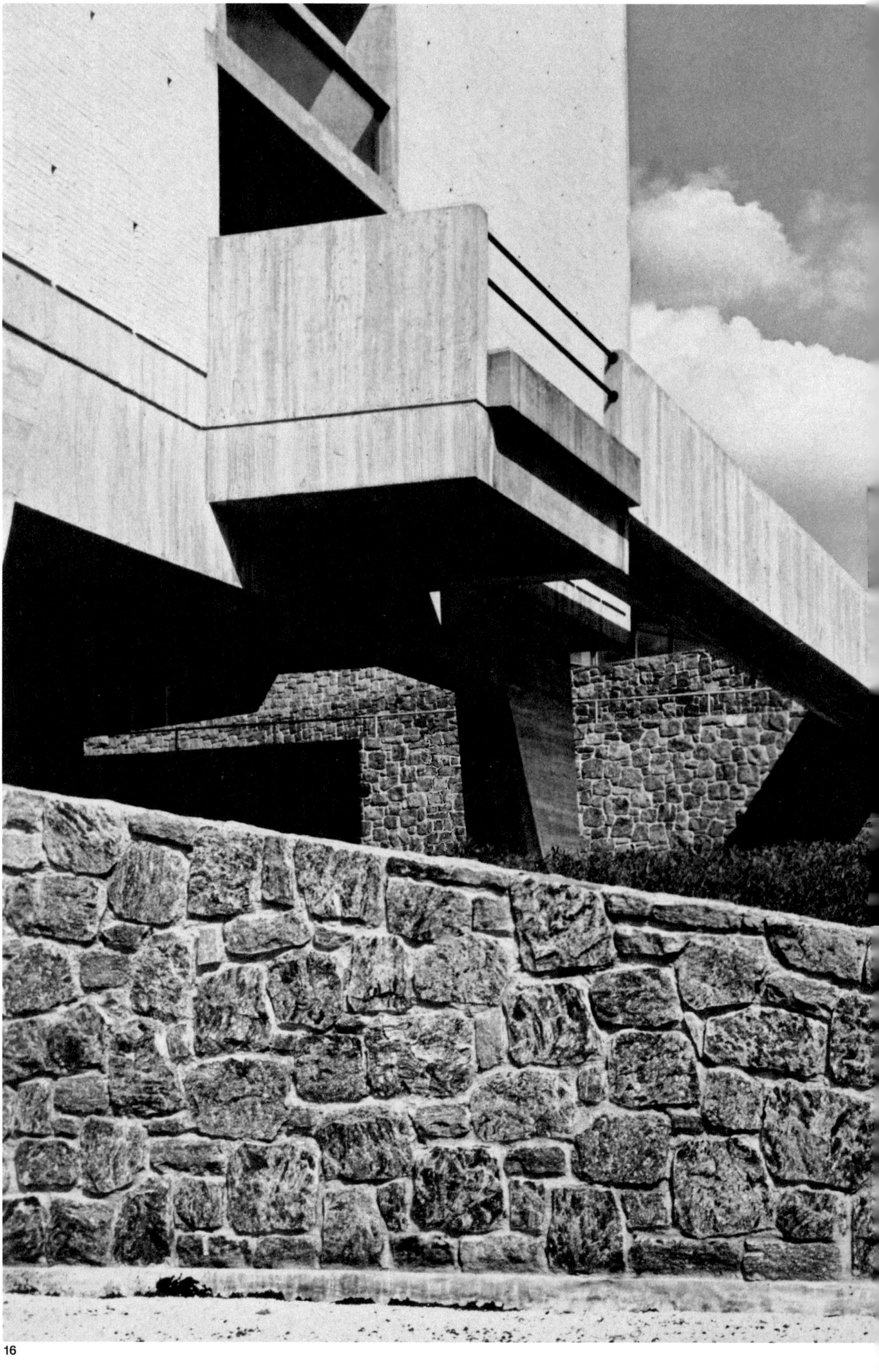

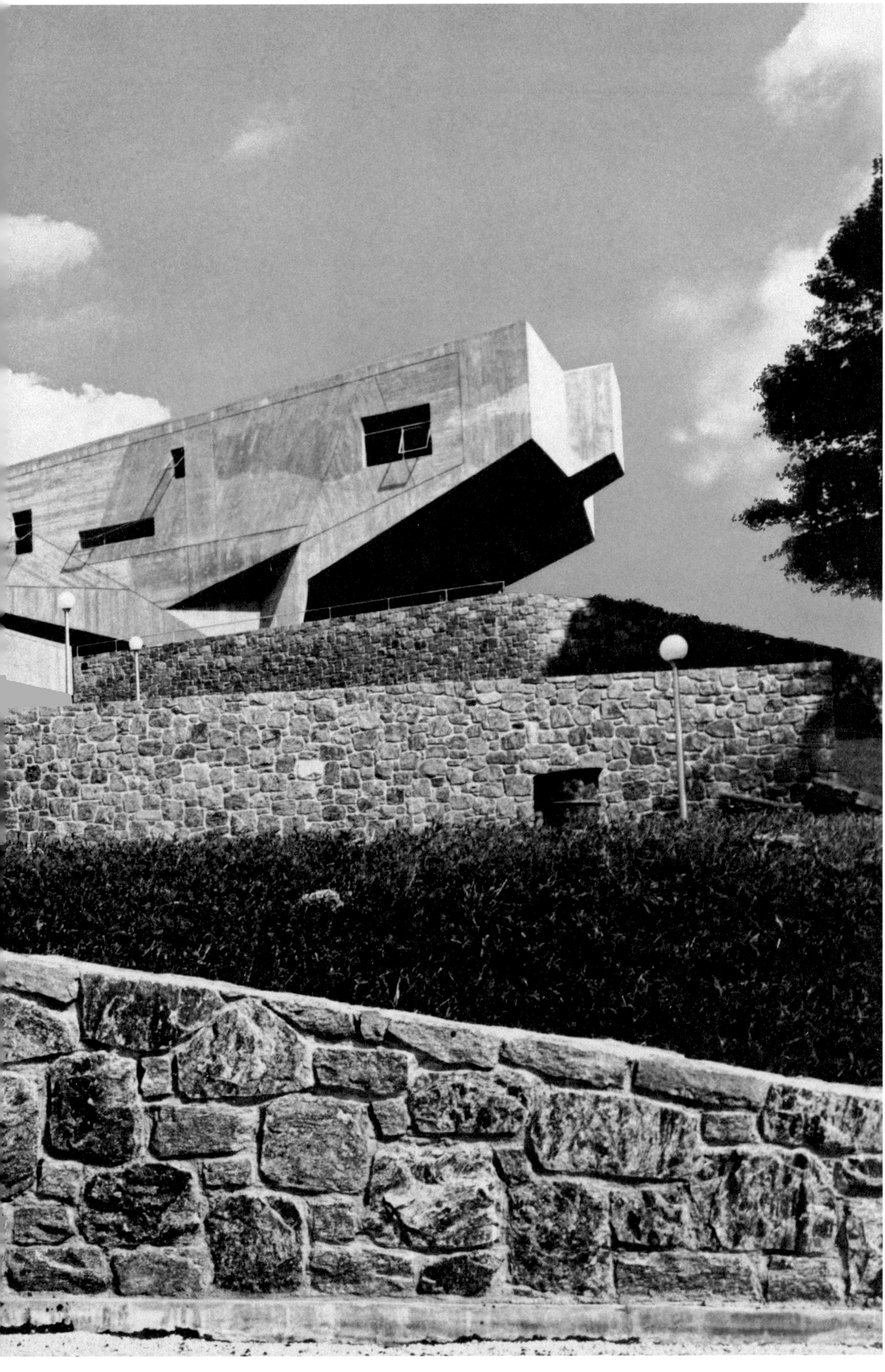

218 IV NEW YORK

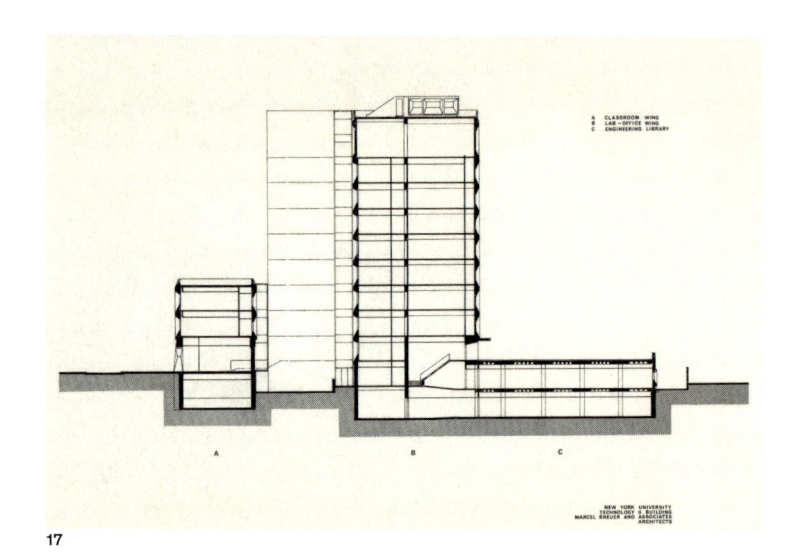

17

18

19

20

220   IV NEW YORK

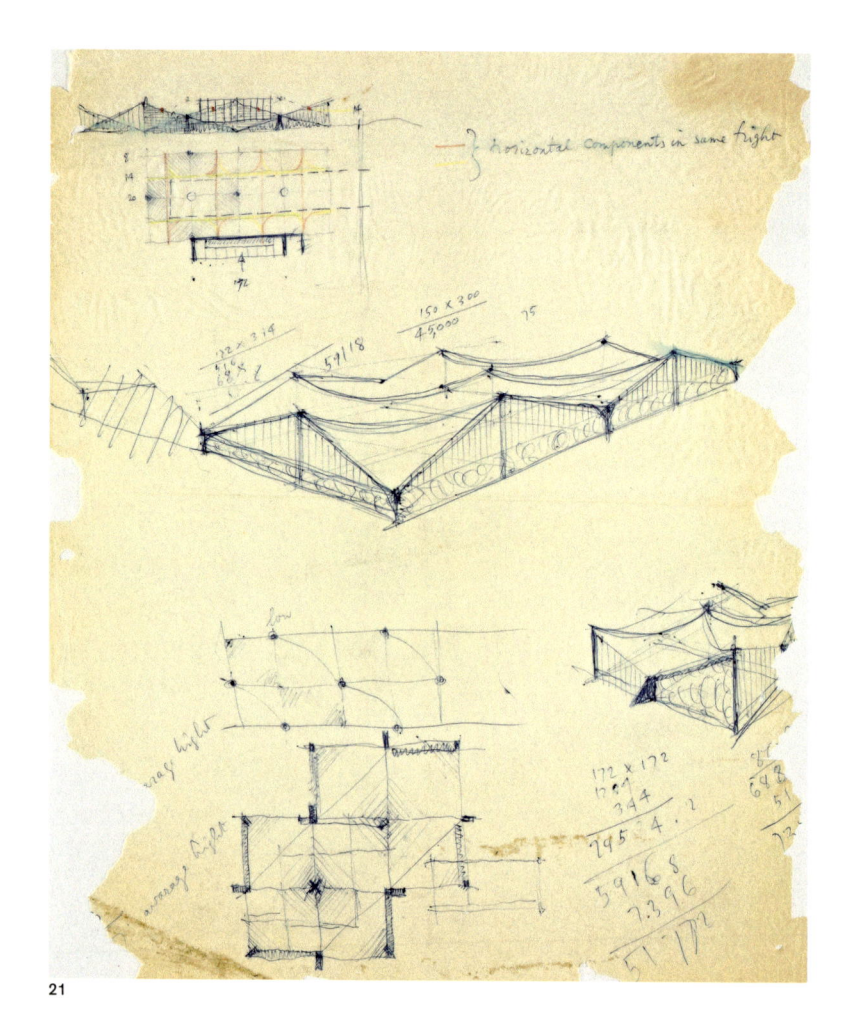

21

22

23

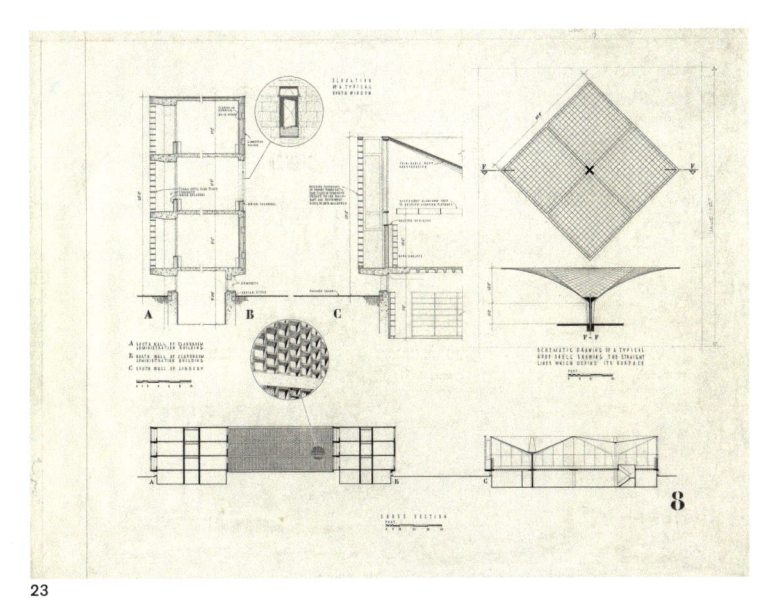

24

1 New York University, Bronx, New York, USA, 1959–61, skybridges from Residence Hall to Community Hall

Architectures of Opportunity at Breuer's Bronx Campus

Jonathan Massey

By opening campuses in Abu Dhabi and Shanghai to complement satellite centers in nearly a dozen other cities, New York University has made itself a leader in reshaping its geographic footprint to pursue academic and financial advancement. The transformation of NYU into what university president John Sexton in the early 2000s termed a "global network university" echoes prior episodes in which the institution used campus construction to restructure and reposition itself. Founded in 1831 and for most of the nineteenth century located in a growing number of buildings around Washington Square in lower Manhattan, in the 1890s the university developed an "uptown" campus in the Fordham Heights section of the Bronx, which soon came to be known as University Heights. Designed by McKim, Mead & White principal Stanford White, whose partner Charles McKim laid out Columbia University's Morningside Heights campus in the same years, the suburban University Heights campus aligned NYU with elite schools as it vied with them to attract students and faculty put off by its urban location and its history as a "university of opportunity" for immigrant and working students.[1]

This strategy worked, but not well enough for the Heights to supplant the Square as NYU's center of gravity. From 1956 to 1970, as NYU expanded into new buildings in Greenwich Village and other sites around the metropolitan area, it engaged Marcel Breuer & Associates to build out its Heights campus with new facilities for student residential life as well as for research and teaching in science and engineering in what was now a densely urbanized borough of the world's largest city. By combining muscular engineering with a humanist International style, Breuer translated the uptown campus's focus on "liberal science" so as to support the university's pursuit of applicants and research funding.

Breuer's designs won accolades from architects and critics, but they also became frameworks for contestation over campus leadership and policy, while expansion strained the university's finances. None of the new construction addressed the urban crisis engulfing the Bronx, thus setting the stage for the institution's redeployment to other zones of uneven development after NYU sold the campus to Bronx Community College in 1973. As NYU replays the University Heights game plan within new geographies of opportunity, examining Breuer's Bronx campus illuminates the strategic value of his multiple design vocabularies as well as architecture's capacities and limits in supporting institutional strategy.

Managing Enrollment

On a Wednesday afternoon in September 1963, NYU student Stephen Jasik addressed the small crowd gathered in the Bronx to dedicate the Julius Silver Residence Center. "Only four years ago the colleges at University Heights were all male," Jasik explained, "and the students came almost entirely from the metropolitan New York area. Only a decade ago the only dormitory housed 180 students. Today the colleges at University Heights are coeducational. Today students from all over the United States and from foreign countries around the world study here. Today 1,000 of our 2,300 students live on campus, 600 of them in Silver Residence Center."[2]

The residence center—more often known as Silver Hall—was a seven-story dormitory rising on piers from the base of a steep slope and linked by two lofty skybridges to a two-story "community hall" set into the brow of the hill and containing a dining hall, lounge, and other amenities [2, 3]. Picking up on Jasik's perhaps overstated rhetoric, university president James Hester, for whom NYU epitomized the "urban university" addressing the problems and promises of America's cities, celebrated the residential college as a "cosmopolitan community" of "men and women from all over the world."[3] Other speakers highlighted the opportunity that NYU afforded to Jewish students in particular. Dr. Israel Goldstein, rabbi emeritus at Congregation B'nai Jeshurun, paid

2 Plan of new MBA buildings: Silver Residence Hall, Community Hall, Begrisch Hall, and Gould Hall
3 Existing campus plan prior to MBA intervention

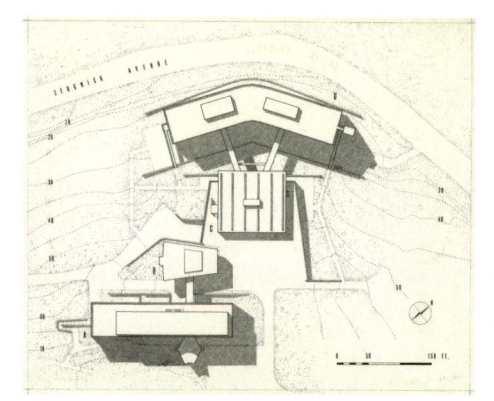

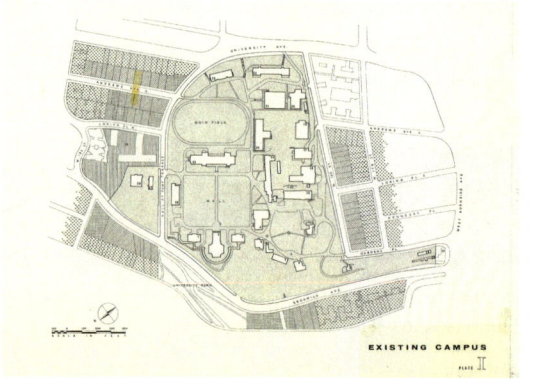

tribute to Julius Silver, the alumnus whose $4.3 million donation had paid for two of the buildings, for his work in helping to found Brandeis University and challenge quota systems restricting Jewish enrollment at American colleges and universities. University Heights was close to the Grand Concourse, the Bronx's major residential boulevard for upwardly mobile middle-class families, many of them Jewish, and since the relaxing of local exclusionary quotas in the 1920s it had attracted a large regional Jewish population.

The configuration of the new buildings signaled NYU's aim of securing its appeal to this core constituency while increasing the proportion of students coming from beyond the region and the nation. The buildings also pointed to some of the other imperatives motivating their construction. Muscular piers lifted the dormitory above parking for the cars that allowed students to cruise newly completed parkways for nights out in midtown Manhattan and weekend trips to suburban family homes. The skybridges funneled not only male but also female students from separate dorm wings into the shared social spaces of the community hall in the university's first coeducational residence. Silver Hall was an architecture of enrollment management, designed to change NYU's student population and finances.

Big Education

Complementing the Silver Center was a pair of academic buildings just to the east. Gould Hall of Technology contained fifteen research labs, fifty-five faculty offices, fifteen teaching labs, a nuclear reactor, and three seminar rooms for physics, mathematics, and electrical engineering.[4] Connected to it by a short skybridge was Begrisch Hall, a striking concrete prism of back-to-back lecture halls lofted above a plaza. The first fruit of a new master plan developed from 1956 to 1958 by the Breuer firm, this ensemble constituted something akin to the residential colleges at elite private institutions, and it signaled the university's investment in research and teaching as well as on-campus living.

This work was part of a university-wide building program initiated in 1952 by NYU's then-chancellor, Henry T. Heald. NYU was the largest private university in the country, with students enrolled in fourteen schools, colleges, and divisions at seven centers in Manhattan and the Bronx. With the Baby Boom generation beginning to graduate from high school, many colleges and universities planned for growth as they looked ahead to expanded enrollments anticipated for the mid-1960s. "Suddenly, colleges are no longer ivy-hung cloisters," observed a contributor to *Architectural Record*. "They have become Big Education—an economic entity of respectable proportions.... To meet the future demand, nearly every college has a building program."[5]

Heald had come to NYU from the Illinois Institute of Technology, where he had gained prominence in part by hiring Mies van der Rohe to head the architecture program and to design the institute's campus. At NYU, Heald and his successors, Carroll Newsom and then James Hester, hired leading architects from the generation that followed Mies, including not only Breuer but also Philip Johnson and I. M. Pei, who both completed significant projects around Washington Square during the 1960s. In 1959 alone, NYU was pursuing substantial expansion at four of its centers, with seven buildings totaling $35 million under way just that year, including $6.3 million to build the Breuer buildings at the Heights campus.[6] A self-study report issued in 1956 projected enrollment increasing from thirty-seven thousand in 1955 to fifty thousand a decade later, with the student population doubling at the Heights.[7]

At the same time, the recent integration of New York's public colleges and universities into the State University of New York system (SUNY, founded in 1948), along with expansion of the City University of New York (CUNY), was challenging NYU's draw in its immediate metropolitan area, from which some 80 percent of its students originated. The university responded by increasing its focus on specialized and advanced graduate-level professional education, enhancing its undergraduate liberal arts and science programs, and investing in substantial campus construction. At the Heights, a "physically attractive and uncrowded" campus showed poor enrollments but possessed "the atmosphere of a 'small college within a great university.'"[8] Most "Heightsmen" came from New York City or nearby suburbs, and many commuted from home, leaving the campus quiet on weekends. By recruiting more students from beyond commuting range, administrators hoped to boost the residential population and create a "seven-day campus."[9]

In combining facilities for scientific research, teaching, and residential life, the new buildings also highlighted NYU's expansion of its College of Engineering so that technological graduate programs rivaled the undergraduate offerings of University College. University leaders summed up their vision for this binuclear Heights campus with the term "liberal science," conjoining the humanistic study of liberal arts with the pursuit of engineering, physics, and other fields.[10]

Breuer and his colleagues provided NYU with an architecture for its cosmopolitan, coeducational liberal science. The focal point of the Heights campus was Gould Memorial Library (1900), a domed building modeled on the Pantheon but rendered by Stanford White at a more intimate scale and set at the crest of the hill that fell away from campus to the Harlem River [3]. A pair of academic halls flanked the library, with a grand exedral colonnade connecting the buildings and housing the busts of NYU's renowned Hall of Fame for Great Americans. To the southeast, a group of undistinguished buildings that had been added to the original ensemble provided the existing science and engineering facilities. Set between these two clusters representing the humanities and the sciences, the new, open quad rounded out the components of a residential research university. By placing the seven-story Silver Hall dormitory at the base of the hill, the Breuer team gave all four of the new buildings a scale comparable to that of the adjacent McKim, Mead & White ensemble while setting the major building entrances on a plaza level continuous with that of the mall fronting the library [4]. A shallow V-shaped bar that curved at its apex, Silver Hall lightly echoed the contour of the Hall of Fame exedra (an early version was an arc that directly quoted the colonnaded hemicycle) without challenging the dome's primacy. The concrete and buff brick of the new buildings nearly matched the materials of the older buildings, while the new rubble-faced retaining walls resembled those supporting the library rotunda. Augmented by carefully considered alignments, these affinities suggested continuity of humanistic enterprise even as modernist forms and heroic concrete structures signaled a synthesis with engineering.

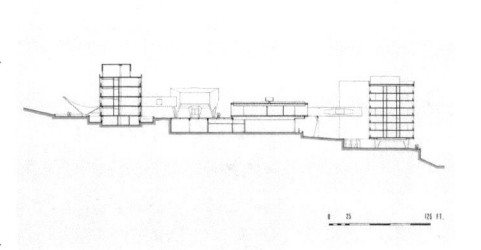

4 South-facing section through Gould Hall, the Community Hall, and Silver Residence Hall

This was consistent with the larger character of the master plan, which integrated existing buildings and lawns into a continuous landscape partially subdivided into open precincts. The first round of buildings had been completed to Stanford White's design in the early twentieth century, establishing a mall running from a residential and athletic zone on the east to an academic zone on the west dominated by the library's rotunda and colonnade. Subsequently, the campus had developed according to a new plan designed by the architect, historian, and curator Fiske Kimball, who served as NYU's chief architect from 1925 to 1955. New buildings included the Gould Student Center, a low brick-and-limestone dormitory facing the library at the east end of the mall.

Designed by Eggers & Higgins in a neoclassical modernism that they also employed in NYU buildings at Washington Square, it too reflected the Jeffersonian neoclassical sensibility that Kimball brought from a prior stint at the University of Virginia.

Finalized in 1958, the Breuer plan projected towering new academic buildings framing the mall to the northeast and southwest, with lower bar buildings mediating between the enlarged scale of these major additions and that of the original group. Additional buildings for research and instruction filled out the existing engineering-and-science zone to the south of the mall, particularly to the southwest, where new construction replaced the mansions left from the estates that had previously occupied the site. The Silver Residence Center and another proposed new dormitory bracketed the campus at its edges.

p. 212/12

Hyphens and bridges drew adjacent buildings into more tightly integrated ensembles in some places, and they recurred within the buildings as links between primary masses and discrete stair and elevator towers. Asymmetry and calibrated misalignment disrupted axiality, which remained only in local symmetries such as those aligning the Silver Hall dorm with its dining hall. Formally distinctive signature elements—mostly trapezoids or five- and six-sided polygons, often containing auditoriums—were interspersed as figures of campus community.

UNESCO on the Harlem

In the mid-1950s, NYU had sought funding to create an international education center in which American and foreign students would learn together. "What we need is a breakthrough in international relations and exchanges that will go beyond the formal language of agreements, contracts, laws and treaties," explained the university's chancellor. "To use the language of Unesco, there should be 'more peoples speaking to peoples.'"[11] While the center did not move forward, the Breuer buildings at University Heights reflected similar motivations, and its architecture telegraphed that alignment by evoking UNESCO House, the Paris campus for the United Nations Educational, Scientific, and Cultural Organization. Breuer was lead designer on this complex, which was one of the highest-profile modernist institutional buildings under way in the mid-1950s, as Lucia Allais explains elsewhere in this volume. The firm reworked the UNESCO Secretariat plan to create the Silver Residence Hall, using a design that even included sunshades like those on the Paris building, though these were not implemented. They adapted the Secretariat's hyperbolic paraboloid (hypar) entry pavilion to create a similar entry for Gould Hall. The Conference Building, a large auditorium pulled out to create a heroic object-building in folded-plate concrete, had its corollary in Begrisch Hall. These parallels reflected the aspiration for NYU's uptown buildings to have a "cosmopolitan" character that would position the university as an up-to-date coeducational school aligned with northeastern elite private colleges and global governance institutions. Within this framework, each building played a distinct role.

Coeducation Machine
Consider Silver Hall, at 612 beds the largest residence hall on the Bronx campus and the only one to house both women and men. While Silver was not dedicated until fall 1963, students had moved in two years earlier. Women had studied in some of NYU's divisions for decades, but coeducation at University College was new. The first female students in the undergraduate college had enrolled in fall 1959, after a multiyear university-wide "self-study" had concluded that the school should admit women, in part to increase tuition income.[12] In fundraising for Silver Hall, the university emphasized its role in addressing "the critical need for women's residence facilities," noting that after NYU announced its plan to admit women to University College, it had been able to admit only 128 of 350 applicants due to a lack of campus housing.[13]

Accordingly, a primary motivation for the construction of Silver Hall was to attract female applicants by cultivating a compelling coeducational campus life. Marcel Breuer & Associates (MBA) brought deep experience in generating modernist architecture for academic institutions, including some from which NYU hoped to siphon applicants. While teaching at the Bauhaus, Breuer had created furniture for the new Dessau buildings designed by his mentor Walter Gropius, and the two of them had subsequently developed an unbuilt campus plan for Black Mountain College (1939–40) among many other collaborations.[14] When NYU hired the firm in 1956, it was completing buildings at the Institute for Advanced Study in Princeton as well as at the Bronx campus of Hunter College, a CUNY school that, though based in Manhattan, had also established a second campus in the Bronx, as well as branches in the city's three other boroughs.[15] MBA was particularly well qualified to design the new residential center because Breuer had previously designed campus buildings for women's colleges. A dormitory design for Smith College (1945) and a completed residence at Vassar (Ferry House, 1949–50), just up the

5 Sarah Lawrence College, Art Center, Bronxville, New York, USA, 1951–52, upper level plan drawing
6 Silver Residence Hall and Community Hall plans
7 Silver Hall floor plans
8 Typical room layouts for women and for men

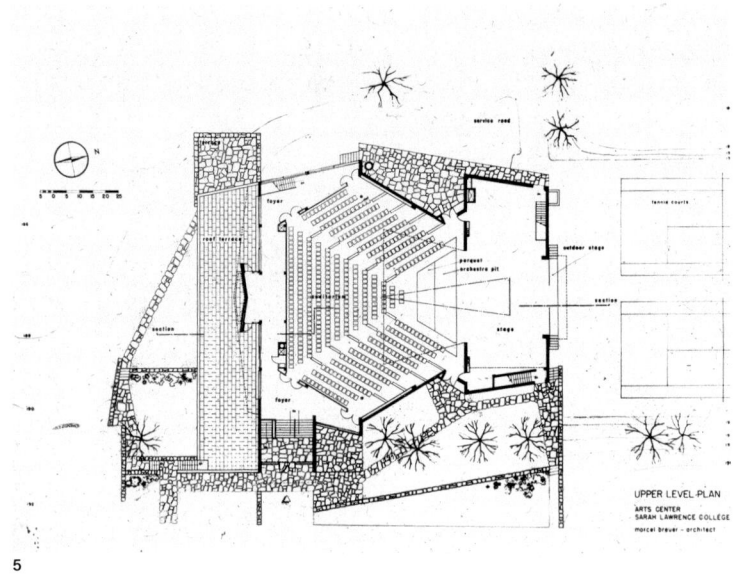

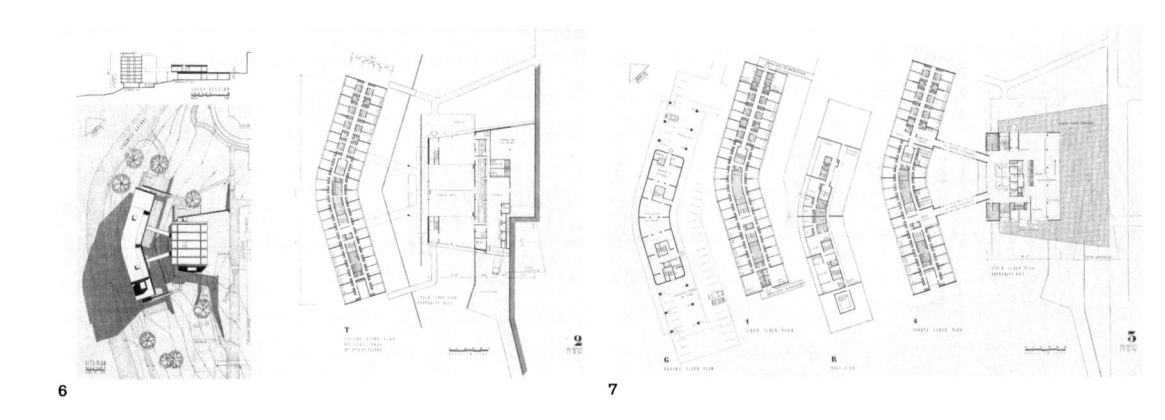

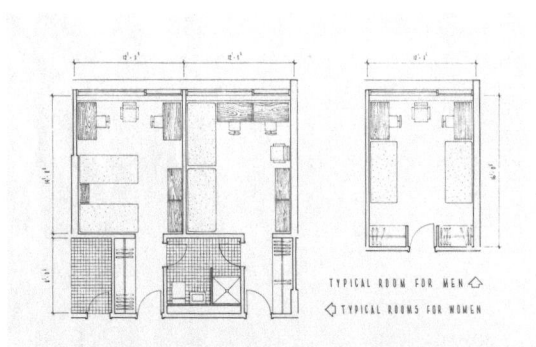

Hudson River in prime NYU recruiting territory, had given Breuer experience in designing for one of the main demographic groups NYU was aiming to attract, and he had recently completed an arts building (1951–52) [5] at nearby Sarah Lawrence, another elite private women's college.

The planning of the Silver Residence Center, with MBA partner Hamilton Smith in the lead, manifested the institution's conception of gender as a binary, symmetrical in concept but asymmetrical in fact. The building was segregated into a men's zone encompassing the southern and central portions of the building and a women's zone to the north [6]. Separate skybridges connected each of these zones to the campus. One pair of open spans was placed at level two, and a second, much grander pair of enclosed spans was above, at level four, where they connected at a security station and control desk in the upper level of the community hall [7]. Elevators and stairs integrated each of these zones vertically through the building, leading to separate sundecks on the roof.

On a typical floor, the men's zone contained rows of doubles along each side. These were served by a pair of corridors that flanked a central service zone with shared bathrooms and gang showers. In the women's zone, slightly larger rooms, with larger closets, were laid out as a series of doubles along a central corridor, with a single-occupant bathroom shared by each pair of rooms [8]. Both wings contained single-sex resident and visitor lounges, supplemented in the women's wing by ironing rooms and a communal kitchen. These differences gave the women's wing a more domestic scale than the men's, recoding assumptions about gender that were more pronounced in NYU dorms such as Judson House, a women-only residence at Washington Square that promotional brochures marketed with images of patterned wingback chairs, wallpaper, and a coffee service offered under matronly supervision.[16]

The square community hall centered on the dormitory boomerang. Its upper floor, at plaza level, contained a lounge, information office, post office, switchboard, and a residential suite for three counselors, along with the control desk. Its lower floor, half buried in the hill, contained the kitchen and service areas for its main feature: a big, high-ceilinged dining hall for six hundred people, which doubled as a social hall for dances and a large meeting room.[17]

The design of Silver Hall celebrated the gender dichotomy where it yielded certain kinds of formal elaboration such as bravura engineering—the skybridges—but masked its asymmetries.

As highly articulated as the façade is, it reveals nothing of the differences in room types and layouts in the male and female dormitory zones, and though the male wing extended through the center section, the skybridges were symmetrically placed.[18] While translating differences in program and function into compositions of disparate elements was the essence of Breuer's architectural method in this period, at the Silver Residence Center the architect suppressed differences associated with gender to present coeducation as a project of identical paths to a shared future.

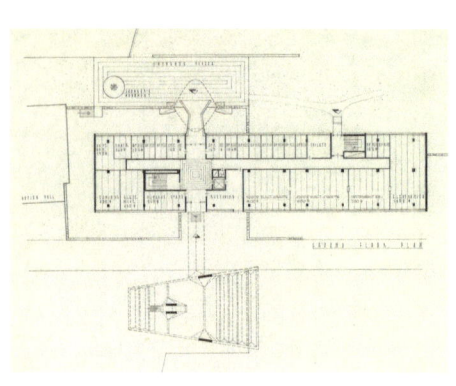

p. 214/14

Liberal Science

With Robert Gatje in the lead, the Breuer team laid out Gould Hall as a bar building on a four-foot planning module with central corridors flanked to the east by offices and to the west by labs [9]. The long east and west façades are framed by projecting slab edges and a parapet that together form a concrete frame infilled with horizontal bands of glass-aluminum-and-panel windows above brick spandrels. Subdivided into square bays by narrow brick reveals that align with window mullions, the bands alternate between two window configurations. Staggered notches in the concrete slab edges and parapet counterpoint the bay rhythm. Proportioned consonantly but metered differently, these elements stack four floors high to form an International Style layer cake. The basement, clad in fieldstone with a narrow strip of windows above, is set back from the floors above. Exposed to the south and west, where the land falls away toward the river, it sits below grade to the east and at the north end, where a moat separates it from the adjacent building and surrounding walkways. A fifth-floor penthouse, likewise set back from the main floors, is clad in corrugated metal. The north and south ends of the bar are monolithic panels of brick punctuated by staggered bands of vertical reveals similar to those that cap Silver Hall.

9 Gould Hall and Begrisch Hall ground floor plan

A counterpart to the domed library, Begrisch formed the centerpiece of the new quad. "Unconventional, canted, and cantilevered," in the words of *Architectural Record*, and "typically Breueresque," this compact but high-impact jewel foregrounded the value of teaching as a mediator between scientific research and residential community through its placement and also through its form, derived from the back-to-back conjunction of large and small stepped lecture halls.[19] Like Konstantin Melnikov's memo-

p. 215/15-1

rable constructivist landmark, the Rusakov Workers' Club (1927), Begrisch Hall deployed the cantilevered auditoriums to generate formal drama, intensified by the heavy lightness of concrete projecting above a largely open ground plane. The large lecture hall was fitted with a special projection system to support science teaching. Called the epidiascope, this unusual multimedia "blackboard" included an overhead projector sharp and bright enough that instructors could leave the room lights on as they projected models, diagrams, and photos onto a large projection screen or displayed live microscope images.[20] Press reports and university memos reported that the building was lifted above ground so that TV trucks could pull up beneath the auditorium and plug into wiring that would allow television recording and the live broadcast of lectures inside—perhaps to extend Heights teaching into NYU's "Sunrise Semester," through which the university broadcast lectures on morning television.[21]

Found Heraldry
The UNESCO buildings were complemented by artworks commissioned from modern masters: Arp, Calder, Miró, Moore, Noguchi, and Picasso. While the NYU commission afforded no comparable art program, the Breuer team co-opted installations already on site as found artworks. Gould was sited just to the northwest of Battery Hill, the small rise at the bluff edge that had been the site of a British fort. Over the years, NYU had marked the location by placing at its crest a pair of cannons aimed at the Harlem River, along with the Lipton Mast, a sailing mast installed atop the hill in the 1920s as a gift from Sir Thomas Lipton, which had become something of a flagpole for the campus as a whole. In an early design for the South Mall landscape in front of Gould, Breuer proposed to carve a plaza from the north side of Battery Hill and install existing figurative sculptures by Karl Bitter on the retaining wall. That proposal was not implemented, so instead the Breuer team tuned the design of Gould and Begrisch Hall to activate these preexisting elements as complements to the new buildings.

As they developed the southeast elevation of Gould—its primary façade, facing the main approach from other parts of campus—the Breuer team factored these preexisting monuments into the design. The stair hall that sits between offices toward the south end is functionally secondary to the main stairs adjacent to the elevator and building entries, but the firm aggrandized it to address Battery Hill. They made this stair the most elegant in the whole complex, with interlocking cantilevered treads, terrazzo floors, and railings of milled aluminum and bent wood. Where it abuts the southeast façade, they gave it an exterior wall of smooth I-shaped concrete blocks, staggered to create a field of trapezoidal lights inset with frosted glass. This became a backdrop to the Lipton Mast, with the trapezoid angles matching those of the mast rigging a few feet in front of them [10]. These trapezoidal windows echoed another South Mall installation as well: the Bent of Tau Beta Pi, the engineering honor society. Materialized on the lawn as a metal sculpture mounted on a stone base, this emblem was a watch key fused to a bent, the trapezoidal frame that supports a trestle on a railroad bridge [11].

At the northeastern end of Gould, the architects placed a swooping concrete hypar entry pavilion to mark the main entrance. Entering into dialogue with the Battery Hill cannons, this entry pavilion with its tapering canopy echoed their raised profiles and from some approaches appeared to cross them, as though to challenge eighteenth-century ballistics with the power of physics and nuclear research. University photographers captured these alignments, and some even found in the hypar's curves the figure of a ship from which the Lipton Mast sprang, as well as the negative figure of a billowing sail in the gap between the mast and the pavilion's curved prow [12].

On the other side of the entry pavilion, just a few feet distant, sat the university's most important monument: the Founders Memorial [13]. Rising in the form of a Gothic finial, the memorial had been composed of elements from the university's original building at Washington Square after it was demolished to make way for construction of a larger office-and-classroom building. Ceremoniously transported from Square to Heights in 1894 during inaugural ceremonies, the ivy-covered Founders Memorial occupied the center of a small traffic circle, now incorporated into the approach to Gould. The counterpoint between memorial and vault activated another dialogue between old and new, allegorizing liberal science in its contrast between forms of knowledge: the humanities represented by the time-worn carved stone finial evoking the scholastic origins of university education, the sciences, by the crisp new cast-concrete hypar, a physical instantiation of geometries associated with the mid-century master science of physics.[22]

Approached from the South Mall, Gould engaged in a tight formal and figural interplay of alignments and contrasts with the memorial landscape of the existing Heights campus—a set of relationships highlighted by the photographs that NYU and the

Architectures of Opportunity at Breuer's Bronx Campus

10 View of Gould Hall from southeast with Tau Beta Pi bent in foreground
11 Gould Hall east façade with Lipton Mast and Battery Hill cannons
12 Gould Hall entry pavilion with Lipton Mast
13 Perspective rendering of Gould Hall
14 Community Hall and Begrisch Hall with Lipton Mast behind
15 Sketch of pour joints for Begrisch Hall

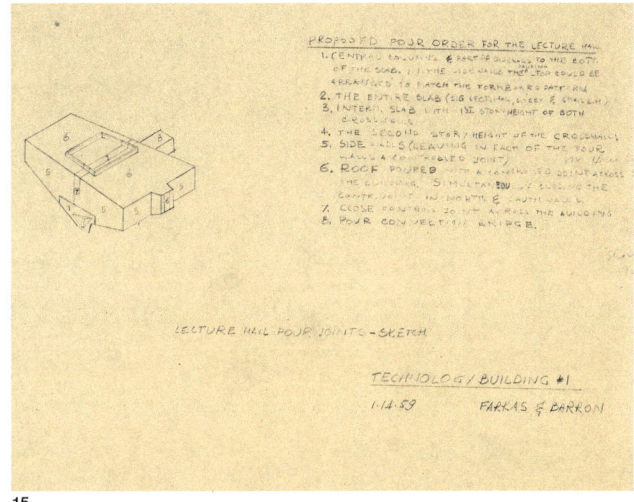

firm circulated to the press.[23] The trapezoid and hypar were among Breuer's characteristic forms, used in many settings. At Gould, the architects used them to underscore the relations between old and new, neoclassical and modernist, liberal arts and sciences, elite histories and new opportunities.

In this interplay, the Lipton Mast became a kind of ready-made banner—the term Breuer used to describe freestanding multistory sculptural elements that, in some of his religious commissions, fulfilled the role played by bell towers in church architecture. In the same period, the firm built towering "bell-banners" at St. John's Abbey (1953–68) and at the Annunciation Priory of the Sisters of St. Benedict, and the banner appeared subsequently in other projects, such as the Armstrong Rubber Company building (1966–68), as Timothy M. Rohan discusses in another chapter. Although different p.141/2 from these concrete banners in material and tectonic character, the mast, through its proximity and position, took on a similar role. So, after a fashion, did Begrisch Hall on the other side of the building. Seen from the south terrace of the Community Hall, the men's skybridge, and the upper floors of the Residence Hall, the west face of Begrisch presented itself as a banner standing before Gould and alluding to the Lipton Mast, visible above the physics building [14]. The patterned northwest façade picked up the intersecting lines of the Lipton Mast and its rigging, materializing them in shallow relief. The carefully composed formwork of the concrete façade translated crossed poles and wires into joints and reveals [15]. By varying the orientation of formwork boards, the firm made each panel a window onto a different slice of sky. At the base the architects faceted three of these panels into relief, creating a shallow tetrahedral impression that translates the geometry of rigging into a volumetric figure. Four rectangular windows of varying size and p.215/15 proportion punctuated this relief mural, each taking a different relation to its geometry, suggesting flags, perhaps, or offset bar buildings on a striated ground of lawns, walkways, and plantings. (The east face is similarly patterned, but because of its proximity to Gould and the skybridge connection, it is nowhere visible as a whole.) In this way, Begrisch gained an additional role as corollary on the west to the found heraldry of Battery Hill and the South Mall.

Neither Chaos nor Copying
As NYU began building its new Breuer ensemble in the Heights, William Wurster, dean of the architecture school at the University of California, Berkeley, argued that postwar campus planning should steer a path between "chaos and copying," and he encour-

aged architects and planners to tie new buildings to old via a "strong unifying theme."[24] Modern architecture had turned out to be as varied as eclecticism, he observed. "Much of the original social fervor has been lost in the current push for high-style abstract sculpture," he wrote. "Too often new buildings seem primarily to vie with each other for public attention, as in a gallery or a group of billboards, instead of seeking some overall unity."[25] At NYU, the Breuer firm seems to have aimed to distinguish the uptown campus through high-style abstract sculpture that was also tied into an overall unity with the sixty-year old Beaux-Arts campus. Breuer's value lay partly in the capital he had by then already accrued as a "form-giver" between the first and second generations of modernist architects. Some of it came from his track record at particular institutions with which NYU wanted to affiliate. But an essential dimension was his ability to rework and redeploy both shared and idiosyncratic forms to create complex and nuanced webs of association through material, formal, and figural play.

Funding Research

If from the grass of the South Mall near the Lipton Mast or the Bent you look to the east, your view centers on a concrete slab rising above the trees as though in a suburban corporate research park. The tall building presents the powerful visual experience of sun and shadow patterning its faceted surface. You won't see a single window.

This is Tech II, the only other building completed according to the Breuer master plan after the initial group. Led within MBA by Hamilton Smith, Tech II was easily the largest building on the campus; it added 135,000 gross square feet of offices, classrooms, and labs, along with additional square footage below grade, including a library and an auditorium [16]. Two parallel bars are linked by an elevator tower [17]. The nine-story tower-slab to the

16 Technology II, 1967–70, floor plan drawing of library level
17 Typical floor plan drawing

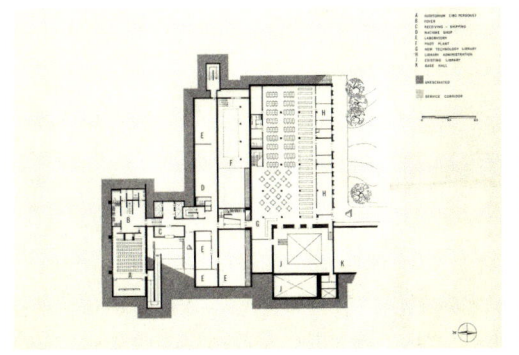

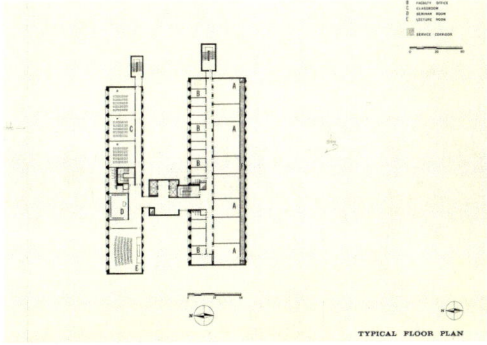

south accommodates research labs, including a high bay within the first and second floors, a tall top floor housing mechanical services, and a rooftop weather station. This research wing is laid out with offices and classrooms along the north side of a central corridor, labs along the south side being served by a shallow chase that extends the full length and height of the building. Primary entry is from the north, with the research wing forming a high backdrop for the classroom wing, which consisted of two stories of classrooms and offices lofted one floor above grade to create a covered plaza and an enclosed lobby serving as a display area and lounge [18]. Muscular piers in a flared and faceted Y shape evoke the west wall of Begrisch above paving of bluestone and Belgian block.

18 Technology II entrance elevation

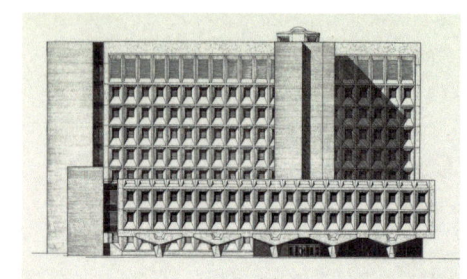

From the main doors, a corridor leads up a few steps, past the elevators, and through the research wing to a broad plaza bounded to the south by a trio of existing Eggers & Higgins buildings framing a service yard. A parallel hallway below grade connects the auditorium, buried below the lobby, to the library, set below the plaza. Relieved only by a shallow stepped well and a cluster of low shade structures and benches, the plaza does not contain a single skylight for the library below, which is granted only three windows fronting the service court. Service ramps run down from the west in the cleft between the building wings to basement and sub-basement. Each bar contains a staircase near its center, as well as a brick-clad, semidetached stair tower at its eastern end.

In early studies, the firm replicated the language of Gould Hall, envisioning bars linked by hyphens and counterpointed by a figural auditorium. As built, however, during a second construction phase in the late 1960s, the building could not be more differ-

19 Plumbing installation diagram
20 South wing service chase

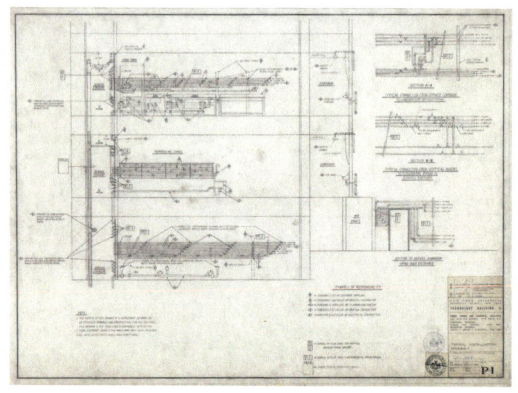

ent from its nearby precursor. Rather than appearing as a structural slab framing brick-and-glass infill, concrete predominates in the form of stacked, load-bearing precast panels. Brick provides a homogeneous cladding material with none of the formal articulation and modular metering provided by the notches in the earlier façades. Whereas the long façades of Gould illuminated and ventilated the offices, classrooms, and labs inside, while also giving them views out across campus, the big blind wall of Tech II is a giant chase, a cavity wall for the pipes, ducts, and cables that serve laboratories along the entire southwestern side of the slab [19, 20]. Approached from the existing engineering buildings to the south by way of a broad plaza, Tech II presents itself as an array of lithic masses in concrete, bluestone, granite, and rubble. Making brutalist poetry of wall panel and chase, the building monumentalizes "liberal science" by generating art from technological requirements.

Molded Façades
While in Gould the Breuer team had pulled out the lecture halls to make these most sociable of rooms a formal and expressive focus, in Tech II they suppressed the most public components—auditorium and library—below grade to showcase the repeating modular bays of panelized wall as a system that integrates structural, technical, and aesthetic considerations. The building includes six panel types in two sizes. Five of these variants are nine and a half feet wide by thirteen feet tall, weighing some eleven tons each. The most frequently used type is the blank panel with shallow indented facets; it lines most of the south-facing walls on both wings. Others are a variant with a narrow archery slot, lining part of the south-facing wall of the classroom wing; a vented panel used on the north side of the weather station; oversized nineteen-foot-tall panels on the ninth floor, inset with dark granite; and partial panels that form a parapet around the classroom wing, suggesting Gothic tracery. The northern faces of both bars are enclosed primarily by the sixth type, which contains a shallow faceted embrasure with a large window inset. Although initially designed to be permanently sealed, these windows were revised to pivot 15 percent so that outside surfaces could be cleaned from within the building.

Designed with the structural engineering firm of Farkas, Barron & Partners (frequent Breuer collaborators), the panels were manufactured by the Eastern Schokbeton Corporation of New Jersey.[26] Coverage in engineering publications reported that this was the first structural use of precast concrete panels in New York City.[27] Pipe chases were cast into the panels along with ducts for heating, ventilation, and air conditioning, so that the panels integrated the functions of structure, enclosure, and mechanical servicing. Stacked, they formed a bearing wall that partially carried the poured-in-place floor slabs. Set one row at a time atop the slab below, to which they were tied by dowels and welded steel angles before the next slab was poured atop them, the panels were finished on the interior with insulation and plaster. The lower portion of windowed panels incorporated a recess for an air-conditioning unit, to be set flush into the panel. Precast panels serve as exterior finish; poured-in-place floor slabs serve as finished ceilings.[28]

This contrast reflected an evolution in MBA's work, as Breuer increasingly channeled his creativity into exploring the permutations of precast concrete panel-walls. Breuer described the strategies his firm employed in Tech II—as well as in laboratory buildings for IBM, Yale, and other clients during these years—as examples of a new kind of "molded" façade. "The search for an exterior which would integrate the demands of an enclosure goes parallel with a new approach to the technique and esthetic of precast concrete," he explained in 1966. "A new depth of façade is emerging, a three-dimensionality with a resulting greatly expanded vocabulary of architectural expression. Sun and shadow."[29]

Funding Research
In another chapter of this volume, John Harwood anatomizes Breuer's architecture of liberal science by showing how the panelized façades of Breuer's lab buildings supported the emergence of "Big Science" at the nexus of military, industrial, and educational sectors by synthesizing the art of sun and shadow with the techniques of laboratory research and of construction in precast concrete. Guy Nordenson's chapter characterizes this aesthetic as a "new baroque" generated where art meets technique but carried forward on strictly aesthetic terms in buildings where the *chiaroscuro* of sun and shadow lacked any relationship to structural or technical necessity. As NYU officials planned Tech II, they pursued a multipronged strategy for financing the new construction. The Breuer design was a fundraising instrument. In fall 1964, MBA prepared identical document sets—one labeling the building as a graduate science facility for Big Science, the other marking it as an undergraduate facility—to support parallel grant proposals directed to different educational tiers and seek-

ing funds from state and federal sources.[30] NYU eventually secured nearly $7 million in funding from the Dormitory Authority of New York State (the state agency that financed higher education facilities), along with multiple grants from the National Science Foundation. Corporations and alumni in the engineering and chemical fields played a big part, too. Grumman Aircraft Engineering Corporation gave money to support construction and furnishing of the lounge, and the auditorium was named after William T. Schwendler. A graduate of NYU's first class of aeronautical and mechanical engineers, Schwendler was an aviation and aerospace designer who cofounded Grumman, and he became an NYU donor and trustee. Frank and Jane Begrisch funded the library, teaming up again with Schwendler, who had contributed to the funding drive that paid for Gould Hall.[31] The alignment of Tech II with the IBM La Gaude research facility (1960–62, with later expansions), the Becton Laboratory Building at Yale University (1964–70), and other leading research facilities doubtless supported the fundraising campaign.

Negotiating Governance

The Breuer buildings at NYU's Heights campus were celebrated in the architectural press and recognized with design awards from the City Club of New York, which heralded the building as "equal to the best work done by this architect and by others in this plastic medium." Peter J. Blake, the *Architectural Forum* managing editor, praised Begrisch for its "vigorous, imaginative, and highly sculptural expression of the possibilities of reinforced concrete."[32] The buildings also served their primary purposes. The Silver Residential Center attracted students. Taking up the challenge issued by the skybridges and control desk, the students played with the architectural order of gender-segregated living. When the male editors of the 1963 yearbook recalled the first day of their University College education back in September 1959, coeducation loomed large. "We were 646 on that first rainy day when the sun shined in September," they wrote, "and 77 of us had perfume in our pocketbooks, giddiness in our heads, and sex in our skirts."[33] An accompanying photo spread shows a male student using the projecting slab edge to climb across the Silver Hall façade as he crosses from the male to the female side, where two girls look on. A caption summarizes: "They came…. They saw…. They conquered."[34] A 1972 yearbook account characterized Silver as a place of dating and hookups, where a young woman wouldn't be surprised to find that her roommate's boyfriend had snuck into their room despite the curfew regulations.[35] Silver Hall was "the center of campus life" even after the university bought the nearby Fitch Memorial Hospital in 1965 and turned it into a women's dormitory.[36] "Silver Hall is where the action is," wrote the author, adding that it was where not only Tom and Jerry but also "Alice and Jane and Carol and Mary live" amid "the psychedelic lights, the sitar music and the fragrant aroma of pot."[37] A popular prank seems to have been triggering the fire alarm at night to create an opportunity for outdoor flirting in pajamas across the gender divide.[38]

Tech II similarly fulfilled its aims by attracting grant funding and supporting technological research. Its aesthetic power gave the south façade of Tech II an outsized role in the visual culture of NYU, and in the first few years after its completion it appeared regularly in *The Violet*, the University College yearbook. Breuer's track record at NYU doubtless helped him secure large commissions at the University of Massachusetts Amherst and SUNY Buffalo in the mid-1960s.

Where the buildings had shortcomings, however, these became frameworks for contestation and negotiation among NYU faculty, students, and administrators. Gould frustrated faculty members, because it lacked air conditioning, and administrators, because it lacked the flexibility needed for adaptation over time.[39] A decade after Silver Hall opened, student gripes included a poor state of repair, bad dining hall food, and resident conflicts over shared amenities.[40] More significantly, Tech II became embroiled in increasingly contentious campus politics. From the mid-1960s forward, at NYU as well as at many other universities, student objections to US involvement in the Vietnam War led to teach-ins and protests, sit-ins and walkouts. Some of these focused on the university's affiliation with companies and individuals associated with the military-industrial complex—including donors funding Tech II. In 1967 and 1968, while Tech II was still under construction, Students for a Democratic Society circulated reports on NYU's board of trustees, highlighting the alignment of board members with the defense industry. A detailed profile discussed the role of Grumman in the Vietnam War and Schwendler's lead role in designing military aircraft.[41]

From 1966 through 1969, bomb scares disrupted activity on the Heights campus, and in April 1969 arson severely damaged Gould Memorial Library. Around three o'clock one morning, three Molotov cocktails—wine bottles filled with gasoline and stopped with rags—exploded, setting fire to the building. Emergency crews found two more unexploded bottles and discovered that the fire hoses had been cut.[42] Around this time, in a separate incident, someone set fire to a file of computer cards on government research in the new School of Engineering Library beneath the Tech II plaza.[43]

Punchlisting

In November 1969, the editors of *Quadrangle*, a magazine published by undergraduates in NYU's School of Engineering and Science, issued a detailed report on the new Tech II building. Three students researched its planning, design, and construction by reviewing documents, interviewing more than a hundred people, and scrutinizing the finished structure. The authors criticized many aspects of the building's design and construction. Lab counters were made of porous soapstone, liable to staining, rather than more expensive slate. Open-pored vinyl floor tile made cleaning up spills difficult. The balcony railing in the two-story chemical engineering high bay was low and dangerously open. The exhaust system had poor fire prevention provisions. Emergency showers were too inconspicuous. Faucets placed too high above their drains splashed. Face bricks were spalling. Belgian block paving was expensive and impractical due to its irregularity. The rough aggregate finish of interior concrete walls had been poorly managed: initially produced through sandblasting, it subsequently had to be bush-hammered when the sandblasting created too much dust, raising costs by an estimated $100,000. People had "complained of scraping themselves on these walls."[44]

For the authors of these complaints, such deficiencies demonstrated poor oversight by NYU leadership. "Although many of the faults are minor, they should have been detected and corrected regardless of their magnitude.... The fact that Tech II was not a complete fiasco is a miracle." A sidebar with the heading "The NYU Run-Around" detailed evasions and redirections the reporters encountered. By publicly punchlisting the university's newest building, the engineering students detailed what they saw as a general lack of attention and achievement by administrators at both Heights and Square. A follow-up on problems with the Engineering Library bemoaned leaky ceilings and documented extensive failings in the building's ventilation and climate control system. Relaying student complaints about hot and stuffy conditions in the library, one author noted that the whole building was conditioned by a single climate control system that integrated the library along with classrooms, offices, and even labs so that "odors and impurities" from the chemical engineering labs circulated throughout the building ("totally unacceptable," according to the engineering school's associate dean). Evidently the building created a climate inhospitable to learning: in summer 1970, excessive temperatures and low oxygen levels led the school to relocate classes from Tech II to other facilities.[45]

Urban Crisis on Campus

The fires in the Engineering Library and Gould Memorial Library were major incidents for the campus, but they were small compared to those in other parts of the Bronx or even in the surrounding neighborhoods, where arsonists targeted Jewish institutions.[46] From the mid-1960s on, NYU grappled with urban decline. Always fairly self-contained—"an island in the neighborhood"— the campus became even more disconnected as its part of the Bronx, once middle class and largely Jewish and Irish, became impoverished and increasingly African American and Puerto Rican.[47] The dearth of African American students in University College, as well as limited support for those who did enroll, became ongoing subjects of student activism and negotiation.[48]

The campus racial composition had links to a broader sense that the "urban university" was disengaged from the city in crisis around it. NYU introduced new courses and programs addressing urban affairs, metropolitan leadership, and urban anthropology, as well as tutorial projects and other community partnerships. Larger initiatives such as an SDS proposal for a robust Educational Development and Community Enrollment Program failed to launch, and the SDS-proclaimed Free University of New York was short-lived.[49] Meanwhile, Joseph J. Roberto, the university

21 Joseph J. Roberto, schematic plan drawing for University Heights campus expansion

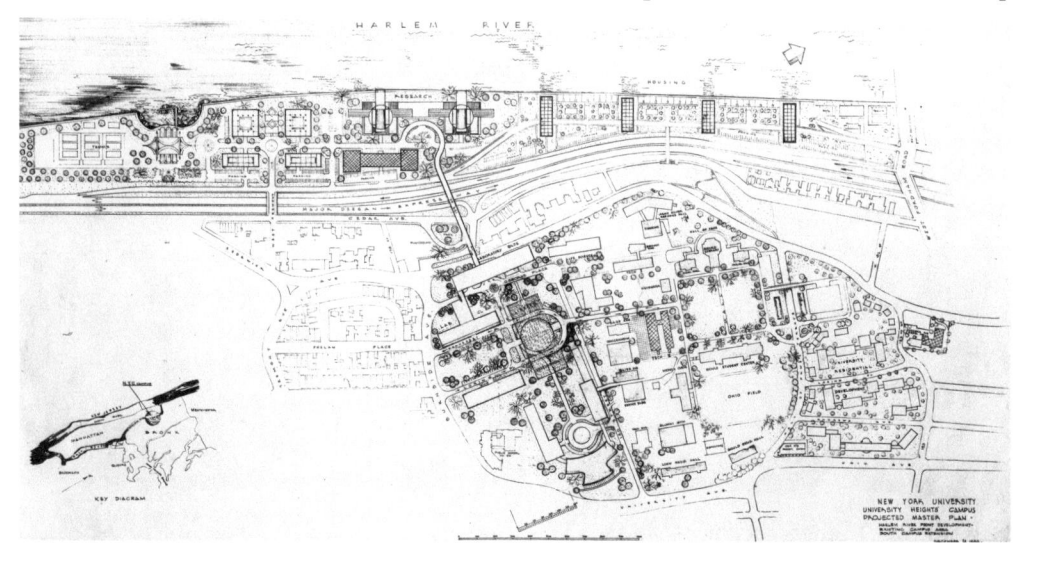

architect, reworked parts of the MBA plan as he imagined alternative designs linked to possible new funding streams. He dreamed of expanding the campus substantially and drew up schematic plans to push the bounds of the campus to the southwest between railroad and river [21].[50]

Sale

Even as the university planned its expansion in the 1950s, a topic of regular discussion was the possibility that NYU would abandon its Bronx base and consolidate operations back at Washington Square. Observing that the Square "appears firmly established as the central focus of the University," the 1956 self-study had concluded that such a consolidation was impractical due to capital investment in the Bronx location and to faculty and alumni sentiment.[51] The Breuer building program seemed to confirm commitment to the Heights.

But extensive construction across multiple campuses overextended the university's resources. By 1970, NYU's capital development debt had reached $123 million. After applications increased in the early 1960s, they dwindled: from 1969 to 1971, enrollment at the Heights dropped by half as urban crisis devastated the Bronx. A third of Silver Hall's 612 beds lay empty, despite an agreement that brought in students from nearby Fordham University. The operating deficit for 1971–72 was estimated at $10 million, nearly half due to underenrollment at the Heights campus.[52]

These woes prompted drastic action. In March 1973, NYU sold its Heights campus to the City University Construction Fund for $62 million, and it transferred the engineering faculty to the Brooklyn Polytechnic Institute. Over the following three months, the university packed up and moved out. As Themis Chronopoulos has shown, NYU's Heights campus "became dispensable due to urban decline."[53] Surveys assessed what to leave behind for the new owners and what to remove. The Lipton Mast and battery cannons remained—along with the Hall of Fame, in a joint custody agreement—but the new home of Founders Memorial was downtown, where it was installed next to Philip Johnson and Richard Foster's newly completed Elmer Holmes Bobst Library.

Completing Dr. King's Dream

Shortly after NYU left its Heights campus, Bronx Community College moved in. Founded in 1957 by Dr. Morris Meister, former head of the Bronx High School of Science, BCC was a young school on a growth trajectory. The college was based in a Tudor Revival building left vacant when Bronx Science moved into a new, purpose-built school. From 120 students and 12 faculty members at the start of classes in 1959, the college grew to 12,700 full- and part-time students in 1972, taught by 550 full-time faculty and nearly 300 adjunct instructors. As it added students, the college expanded into seven other buildings in the area, occupying 190,000 square feet of space.[54]

The Heights purchase allowed BCC to realize ambitions thwarted elsewhere. In the 1960s, the college had sought to build a new campus on a platform spanning the Jerome Avenue subway railyards less than two miles north of NYU. The design for this "Airspace Campus," by architect Aaron Cohen, at one point consisted of a large podium filled by parking for one thousand cars, carrying nine buildings flanking a central concourse running north-south one story above street level. It was to have encompassed offices and classrooms as well as a student union, a gymnasium, a swimming pool, and potentially also an art gallery, a music hall, and a large auditorium.[55] A rendering from 1966 depicts the complex in a white neoclassical modernism similar to that of Lincoln Center or SUNY Albany's Uptown Campus [22]. Later documents depict a looser arrangement of stacked slabs and platforms in a smoothed-out brutalist idiom. Initiated in 1962 with a $26 million appropriation funded jointly by city and state governments, the project was slated to begin in 1967 with a target for completion in 1973. While ground was symbolically broken in winter 1969–70, the project never moved into construction, seemingly due to poor planning and management combined with a changing political and financial context.

22 Aaron Cohen Associates, design for Bronx Community College "airspace campus" as featured in the 1966 BCC yearbook

The NYU purchase galvanized a community disappointed by the failure of its campus plans. BCC students, faculty, and staff relocated quickly in summer and early fall 1973 with high spirits. It seemed as though the move would accelerate the college's upward trajectory, and subsequent yearbooks celebrated the campus, its buildings, and the excitement of finding a way forward in the new environment. "Here my imagination can soar, playfully … seriously," hymned one caption.[56] The anticipated boost was weakened, however, by the impact of big demographic shifts. The changes to the Bronx that had made NYU's uptown gambit unviable were also changing BCC, making its population more diverse but also increasing its proportion of poor students dependent on financial aid and employment. In 1970, the CUNY system had adopted an open enrollment policy that eliminated selective admissions. While BCC had pioneered programs to help academically marginal students make the transition to college, the need to accommodate a substantial number of such students strained the college's budgets and facilities as it also shifted focus from the liberal arts curriculum geared toward preparing a student for transfer to a bachelor's degree program at a senior college to a "career curriculum" offering vocational courses leading to a terminal associate's degree.[57]

With more than thirty buildings on nearly forty acres, the Heights campus was big. But whereas its prior buildings had provided BCC with some one hundred classrooms, administrators counted only sixty-three at the Heights, so they converted research labs in the Breuer buildings for instructional use. Capital funds promised at the time of the purchase for major renovations were not allocated, so renovation and even maintenance proved challenging in subsequent years.[58] Nevertheless, the college developed a new master plan and in the 1980s began to implement it. Because most of its students were local and many studied on a part-time basis, the college had little need for dormitories. Silver Hall became an academic and administrative building, its dorm rooms and lounges reconfigured to provide offices and classrooms. Tech II was modified to accommodate science and media instruction, and it subsequently required a major overhaul of the plumbing that ran through its nine-story chase.

With its local population and large number of students holding down full-time jobs, BCC didn't need to solve the "seven-day campus" problem that had plagued NYU. Its large student population of nearly fourteen thousand in spring 1975 used the campus well into the evening, making for a lively "night scene" with its own classes, culture, and student government.[59] The Silver Residence Center dining hall and lounge continued to serve as hubs of student activity, hosting art exhibitions, dance performances, honor society inductions, and other events. The center of campus social life shifted, however, to the dining space in Gould Hall, an Eggers & Higgins building that had been the primary dorm prior to the construction of Silver. Gould came to be known as the place to party, smoke pot, snort cocaine, and play cards. Silver became the intellectual's refuge. "Those in Silver Hall are trying to learn," one student explained to an observer. "They are quiet and clean. Those in Gould cafeteria are spending their time partying, with loud music, disarray, disorder." "There's a segregation," reported another, "and those who feel they're a higher intellectual level are at Silver Hall."[60]

In a reversal of NYU's demographics, white students were "outsiders" within BCC's multicultural student population, representing 45 percent of the students enrolled in 1970 but dropping to only 5 percent over the next two decades as the population of the borough changed. Students of different racial and cultural backgrounds studied together but socialized apart, even in Gould cafeteria, which by the end of the 1970s had become a calmer place as administrators tightened regulations after closing Silver.[61] Women outnumbered men.[62]

Much as had their NYU precursors, BCC student photographers appreciated the geometry of Tech II—renamed to honor founder Morris Meister—generating abstract compositions based on the concrete panels of the building's south face and Schwendler Auditorium. The shallow plaza of Belgian block at the entrance to Meister Hall became a focal point of the campus, a prominent site for protests such as those through which BCC students in 1976 objected to proposed budget cuts and CUNY campus closures that would have further increased enrollment while cutting support [23, 24].

23, 24 Students protesting CUNY policies on the Meister Hall (Technology II) plaza in 1973–74
25 BCC students enjoying the Hall of Fame on their new campus
26 Robert A. M. Stern Architects, North Hall and Library, Bronx Community College, 2012

If the entry plaza of Meister Hall was a hub of political activity, Gould Memorial Library and its Hall of Fame terrace had a different significance. Stanford White's elegant Beaux-Arts building had a powerful collegiate iconography, and yearbooks featured students lounging on its lawns or playing amid the columns and busts of its Hall of Fame [25]. When the college built a large new library on the north side of the mall, it didn't employ the modernist language of sliding bars indicated in the Breuer plan but instead followed a postmodernist neoclassical plan completed in 2006 by Robert A. M. Stern Architects. The firm also designed the building [26], treating the new North Hall as an extension of the Stanford White ensemble that alludes to Henri Labrouste's Bibliothèque Ste.-Geneviève and McKim, Mead & White's Boston Public Library.

The architecture of Marcel Breuer & Associates, exquisitely tailored to the priorities of New York University, has proven serviceable but not especially apt for Bronx Community College. Generated by enrollment management and research funding strategies aimed at shoring up NYU's uptown long game, the Breuer buildings in the Heights served their purposes, but they were not enough to sustain the Heights gambit—a selective private institution in the Bronx—in the face of urban decline. After only a few years with NYU, however, they gained a second life in service to a different kind of "university of opportunity" within New York's public community college system. For nearly half a century now, the Heights campus has helped many thousands of students gain access to higher education, helping them (in the account of one sociologist) "to complete Dr. King's dream" of a society providing equitable opportunity for all. These factors turned the campus from an island of privilege into an "island of hope" amid a desolated South Bronx.[63]

1 The history of New York University is told in Thomas J. Frusciano and Marilyn H. Pettit, *New York University and the City: An Illustrated History* (New Brunswick, NJ: Rutgers University Press, 1997); and Joan Marans Dim and Nancy Murphy Cricco, *The Miracle on Washington Square: New York University* (Lanham, MD: Lexington Books, 2001). For its recent global reconfiguration, see John Sexton, "Global Network Reflection," December 21, 2010, https://www.nyu.edu/about/leadership-university-administration/office-of-the-president-emeritus/communications/global-network-university-reflection.html. The richest sources of documentation for the Breuer work at NYU are the Marcel Breuer Digital Archive at Syracuse University (breuer.syr.edu) and the NYU Archives, in particular the Photo Collection and the Joseph J. Roberto Collection. For assistance in researching this essay, I thank Nicolette Dobrowolski (assistant director at Syracuse University Libraries Special Collections Research Center), Janet Bunde (archivist at the NYU Archives), Cynthia Tobar (archivist at Bronx Community College Library), Robin Auchincloss (director of campus planning at Bronx Community College), and former NYU professor Jim Uleman. For editorial feedback, I thank Barry Bergdoll and Daniel M. Abramson.
2 Jasik quoted in New York University, *Proceedings of the Dedication of the Julius Silver Residence Center*, September 25, 1963, 7, Building Collection vertical files, NYU Archives.
3 Hester quoted in ibid., 13.
4 Matthew A. Postal, *Begrisch Hall at Bronx Community College, City University of New York, 2050 Sedgwick Avenue, University Heights, the Bronx: Built 1956–1961, Marcel Breuer and Associates, Architects* (New York: Landmarks Preservation Commission, 2002).

5 George Cline Smith, "The Prospect" (Building Type Study 274: College Buildings), *Architectural Record* (September 1959): 159.
6 "Nation's Largest University Constructing Seven Buildings" (Building Type Study 274: College Buildings), *Architectural Record* (September 1959): 186–90.
7 George D. Stoddard, Carter Davidson, J. A. Stratton, and the Office of Institutional Research and Educational Planning, *The New York University Self-Study Final Report* (New York: New York University Press, 1956), 20.
8 Stoddard et al., *NYU Self-Study Final Report*, 50.
9 "The Seven-Day Campus" (unsigned editorial), *Heights Daily News*, December 10, 1964, 2.
10 "Milestones in Higher Education: The Introduction of Coeducation at University Heights," undated typescript, 9 pp., ca. May 1960, Box 4, Series I, Record Group 3.0.6, NYU Archives.
11 "Proposal for the Establishment of an International Education Center at NYU" (twelve-page typescript memorandum for discussion with Ford Foundation), November 18, 1954, 2, Folder 12, Box 7, RG 3.0.6, NYU Archives.
12 Stoddard et al., *NYU Self-Study Final Report*.
13 "Milestones in Higher Education."
14 Project records for the Lake Eden campus at Black Mountain College are in the Marcel Breuer Digital Archive at breuer.syr.edu/project.php?id=250.
15 Project records for Marcel Breuer & Associates buildings at New York University, the Institute for Advanced Study, and Hunter College can be found through the project list in the Marcel Breuer Digital Archive at breuer.syr.edu.
16 New York University Residence Halls brochure, ca. 1959, Folder: Residence Halls of NYU, Box 15, Building Collection vertical files, NYU Archives. These architectural differences were paralleled by asymmetrical policies. Many of NYU's residential life regulations for the "Coeducational Living Experience" addressed protocol for single-sex spaces and spaces in which women and men mingled socially ("Dress in the Dining Hall shall be neat and proper at *all* times … sports shirts and slacks for the men and skirts and blouses or sweaters for the women"), and the university overlaid these with a second set of still more restrictive rules that applied only to female students.
17 "Milestones in Higher Education."
18 One article published two years before Silver Hall's completion reported that "rigid division and control will of course be maintained, but flexibility of division between the sexes has been achieved architecturally by the provision of readily movable partitioning in the center portion of the building on each floor." "Nation's Largest University Constructing Seven Buildings," 186–90. However, the plan as completed would not support this kind of reconfiguration.
19 "Nation's Largest University Constructing Seven Buildings," 186–90. See also "Flying Bridges Link N.Y.U. Campus Group," *Architectural Record* (April 1962): 139–43.
20 Described in newspaper reports as the first device of its kind in the United States, this multimedia "blackboard" was a gift from Ernst Leitz, Inc., American distributor of German optical equipment. "Blackboards Seen as Future Relics," *Heights Daily News*, December 12, 1962.
21 "Architects Award Begrisch Building Merit Certificate," undated newspaper clipping; and September 1962 public relations memo, 10 (box number n/a), Building Collection vertical files, Group # NYU 1, Series 10, NYU Archives. Sunrise Semester program records spanning from 1957 through 1977 are in Records of the Office of the Dean of Washington Square College, Series I: Washington Square Dean's Files, Subseries B: Subject Files: Sunrise Semester; as well as in Records of Office of Radio and Television, 1953–85, both in NYU Archives.
22 Butler Hall, another such preexisting element remaining from the mansion era, also figured into this set of relationships. But since it was slated for demolition—although one that never happened—it was omitted from models, drawings, and photographs through which the Breuer team studied the siting and design of the new complex in relation to the memorial landscape of the South Mall and Battery Hill.
23 See Sonic Boom Lab – YMCA 1927, Folders: "Gould – Construction" and "Gould – Exterior," Box 30, Photo Collection: University Heights, NYU Archives.
24 William Wilson Wurster, "Campus Planning" (Building Type Study 274: College Buildings), *Architectural Record* (September 1959): 163–64.
25 Ibid., 164.
26 Tech II is featured in the promotional brochure *Schokbeton: Integrity in Architectural Precast Concrete* (n.d.), 1–2, Image ID 39420-004, Marcel Breuer Digital Archive, Syracuse University.
27 "Precast Façade Panels Are Load Bearing," *Engineering News-Record*, August 8, 1968; Joseph P. Fried, "New Panels Are Tried at N.Y.U.," *New York Times*, September 15 [1968?].
28 "Precast Concrete Panels Serve as Load-Bearing Walls," *Contractor News* (August 1968): 28–29.
29 Marcel Breuer, Robert F. Gatje, Herbert Beckhard, and Hamilton Smith, "The Most Recent Architecture of Marcel Breuer," *Architectural Record* (April 1966): 171–86.
30 Compare MBA, *A proposal for a graduate science facilities grant in connection with the construction of Technology Building II at the University Heights Campus of New York University*, 17″ × 22″ print set, September 1, 1964, site plan 1″ = 50′, remainder 1/16th = 1′-0″; and MBA, *A proposal for an undergraduate facilities grant in connection with the construction of Technology Building II at the University Heights Campus of New York University*, September 1, 1964, site plan 1″ = 50′, remainder 1/16th = 1′–0″. Folder: Technology II Building, University Heights, Drawer 8, Map Case 2, Roberto Collection, NYU Archives.
31 Technology II (box n/a), Group # NYU 1, Series 10, Buildings Collection vertical files; Residence Halls – Technology II, Folder 22: Technology II, Box 15, Group # NYU 1, Series 10, Buildings Collection vertical files; John R. Ragazzini, Dean (School of Engineering and Science), to Chancellor

Russell D. Niles, July 2, 1964, Folder 26: University Heights – Gould Hall of Technology (Gould), 1962–66, Box 25, Series 12: Building Files: University Heights Center (Aerospace Laboratory – Gould Student Center), Records of the Office of the University Architect, Roberto Collection, all in NYU Archives.

32 Both quotations from the proclamation of the City Club of New York Award of Merit for excellence in urban architecture, 1964, Folder 5, Box 25, Series XII, Office of the University Architect, Roberto Collection, NYU Archives.

33 *The Violet* [yearbook], vol. 73, ed. Sandor Frankel and Dan Steibrocker (New York: NYU–University College, 1963), 46.

34 Ibid., 46–47.

35 "On the Girls' Side of Silver," *The Violet*, vol. 82, ed. Iris Beller, David Berkey, Kingsley Grant, and Scott Hornstein (New York: NYU–University College, 1972), 36–38.

36 Ibid., 36; "In Retrospect," *The Violet*, vol. 78, ed. Lois Herbst and Bert Spector (New York: NYU–University College, 1968), 163.

37 "On the Boys Side of Silver," *The Violet*, vol. 82, 39–41.

38 Ibid., 39.

39 See correspondence among Prof. Benjamin Bederson, Prof. Sidney Borowitz, Dean John R. Ragazzini, campus architect Martin Beck, and Chancellor Russell D. Niles, Folder 26: University Heights – Gould Hall of Technology (Gould), 1962–66, Box 25, Group # 11.4, Series 12, Office of the University Architect, Roberto Collection, NYU Archives.

40 "On the Girls' Side of Silver," 37; "On the Boys Side of Silver," 39.

41 Students for a Democratic Society, "New York University Board of Trustees," photocopied typescript, n.d., ca. February 1968; profile of Schwendler in NYU SDS, *Our Trustees*, a compilation of leaflets, written during the 1967–68 school year, that build on and incorporate the February 1968 material, all in Folder 15: Student Activities, Students for a Democratic Society, 1968, 1969, n.d., Box 16, Group No. 3.0.7, Series No. 1, Office of the President, Hester Papers, Alphabetical Series, NYU Archives.

42 Mike Bassett, "[Bomb] Attack Ravages Gould Chapel," *Heights Daily News*, April 18, 1969, Folder 1: Gould Memorial Library (Heights), Box 9, Group # NYU 1, Series 10, Buildings Collection, Gould Memorial Library – Hall of Fame, NYU Archives.

43 "Rebuilt Chapel to Have New Design," *Heights Daily News*, September 26, 1969, Folder 1: Gould Memorial Library (Heights), Box 9, Series 10, Group # NYU 1, Buildings Collection, Gould Memorial Library – Hall of Fame, NYU Archives.

44 Armin Wagman, Ruth Raubitschek, and Lenny Rosenheck, "Technology II—A Critical Evaluation," *Quadrangle* 40, no. 2 (November 1969): 14–18.

45 Joe Morris, "Engineering Library: Controversy Expands," *Quadrangle* 41, no. 3 (December 1970): 6–8.

46 Themis Chronopoulos, "Urban Decline and the Withdrawal of New York University from University Heights, The Bronx," *Bronx County Historical Society Journal* 46 (Spring–Fall 2009): 20.

47 "The Seven-Day Campus" (unsigned editorial), *Heights Daily News*, December 10, 1964, 2.

48 Under the heading "The White Violet," a fall 1965 editorial in the student newspaper called on the university to recruit more black students, who it said constituted less than one-half of 1 percent of incoming freshmen at the Heights. Administrators shared this goal, noting in internal memos that despite recruitment efforts in the most recent admissions cycle only forty African Americans had applied, yielding just six new enrollees at the Heights and nine at Washington Square. "The White Violet," *Heights Daily News*, October 11, 1965. See also memos and correspondence in Folder 7: Heights Daily News, Box 16, Group No. 3.0.7, Hester Papers, Alphabetical Series, NYU Archives.

49 Educational Development and Community Enrollment Program, typescript, 6 pp., n.d.; and other documents in Folder 15: Student Activities, Students for a Democratic Society, 1968, 1969, n.d., Box 16, Group 3.0.7, Series 1, Office of the President, Hester Papers, Alphabetical Series, NYU Archives,

50 Folder 7, Oversize Box 44, Series 16, Roberto Collection, RG 11.4, NYU Archives.

51 *NYU Self-Study Final Report*, 67.

52 Chronopoulos, "Urban Decline and the Withdrawal," 5.

53 Ibid.

54 Bronx Community College, *Self-Study Report*, March 1973, 1–2.

55 "New Campus Gets Final OK," *Genesis* [yearbook] (New York: Bronx Community College, 1966), 104–5.

56 *Genesis* (New York: Bronx Community College, 1974), 13.

57 Bronx Community College, *Self-Study Report*, March 1973, 4; Lillian Cohen Kovar, *Here to Complete Dr. King's Dream: The Triumphs and Failures of a Community College* (Lanham, MD: University Press of America, 1996), 81; Morton Rosenstock and James D. Ryan, *A Half Century in Pursuit of Excellence: Bronx Community College of the City University of New York* (New York: Bronx Community College, 2008), 10.

58 Bronx Community College, *Self-Study*, 1986, 2.

59 Dean Gloria L. Hobbs, "The Night Scene," *The Observer* [Bronx Community College faculty and staff newsletter], May 20, 1975, 1. See also Rosenstock and Ryan, *Half Century in Pursuit of Excellence*, 12–13.

60 Quoted in Kovar, *Here to Complete Dr. King's Dream*, 42.

61 Kovar, *Here to Complete Dr. King's Dream*, 43.

62 Ibid., 4.

63 Ibid., 2, 3, summing up popular perceptions.

Subsequent to the UNESCO buildings, Marcel Breuer & Associates completed several other major commissions in France, including one of its greatest concrete panel research labs, completed for IBM in the Côte d'Azur town of La Gaude. Partner Robert Gatje ran these projects out of a second office, in Paris. In 1960, as part of a French national initiative to promote alpine tourism, Breuer was commissioned by the banking heir Éric Boissonnas to plan and design the Flaine ski resort high in the French Alps. As in previous urban designs, the firm laid out hotels, apartments, shops, civic amenities, and sports facilities along the topographical lines of the steeply sloping valley. Complementing precast panels with wood and stone, the firm made memorable forms by dramatically cantilevering buildings over steep drops and making the chapel of juxtaposed irregular prisms.

Even larger was the ZUP Sainte-Croix, a housing complex built over a decade, beginning in 1963, as part of a new town on the outskirts of Bayonne in the southwestern corner of the country. The Breuer team designed stores and a supermarket as well as community amenities, including a youth club, a sociocultural center, a medical center, a library, a post office, a police station, and a church. Large housing slabs monumentalized the collective of the French welfare state. By varying unit layouts and panelized façade treatments, however, the firm accommodated a diversity of household types and gave residents a sense of individuation that has served the complex well, even as residents have rejected other *grands ensembles* housing projects. The firm also planned a resort town—never built—for the nearby Aquitaine coast and by 1971 had developed preliminary concepts for marina, hotels, and both low- and high-rise vacation housing. Alongside such grand schemes, the firm also completed a headquarters for the pharmaceutical firm Sarget-Ambrine near Bordeaux and a dramatic concrete shell house at Glanville near the Normandy coast.

1 IBM Research Center, La Gaude, France, 1960–62, cover of report to IBM stockholders, 1962
2 Aerial view of IBM Research Center
3 Site plan drawing
4 Column and precast panel detail drawings
5 Detail plan drawing at main entry
6 Floor plan drawing
7 Ski Resort, Flaine, France, 1960–79, overall site plan
8 Site elevation drawing
9 View from the north
10 Cantilevered terrace, La Flaine Hotel
11 View of the main square
12 Interior of La Flaine Hotel
13 View from a balcony at the Aldebaran apartment building
14 Undated perspective rendering, early design for Flaine Ecumenical Chapel
15 Flaine Ecumenical Chapel, as built
16 ZUP de Bayonne, Bayonne, France, 1966–73, construction photograph of high-rise housing block
17 Perspective rendering of town center
18 Site plan drawing
19 Perspective rendering of high-rise block façade
20 View of mid-rise housing
21 Detail of precast rubble stone walls
22 View of high-rise block, 2015
23 Sarget-Ambrine Headquarters and Pharmaceutical Laboratories, Mérignac, France, 1964–72, perspective rendering
24 Sayer House, Glanville, France, 1973
25 Resort development (unexecuted), Aquitaine coast, France, 1971, aerial perspective rendering of low-rise development
26 Aerial perspective rendering of marina and station
27 Perspective rendering of Hôtel Les Dunes
28 Perspective rendering of solarium and pools, Hôtel Les Dunes

1

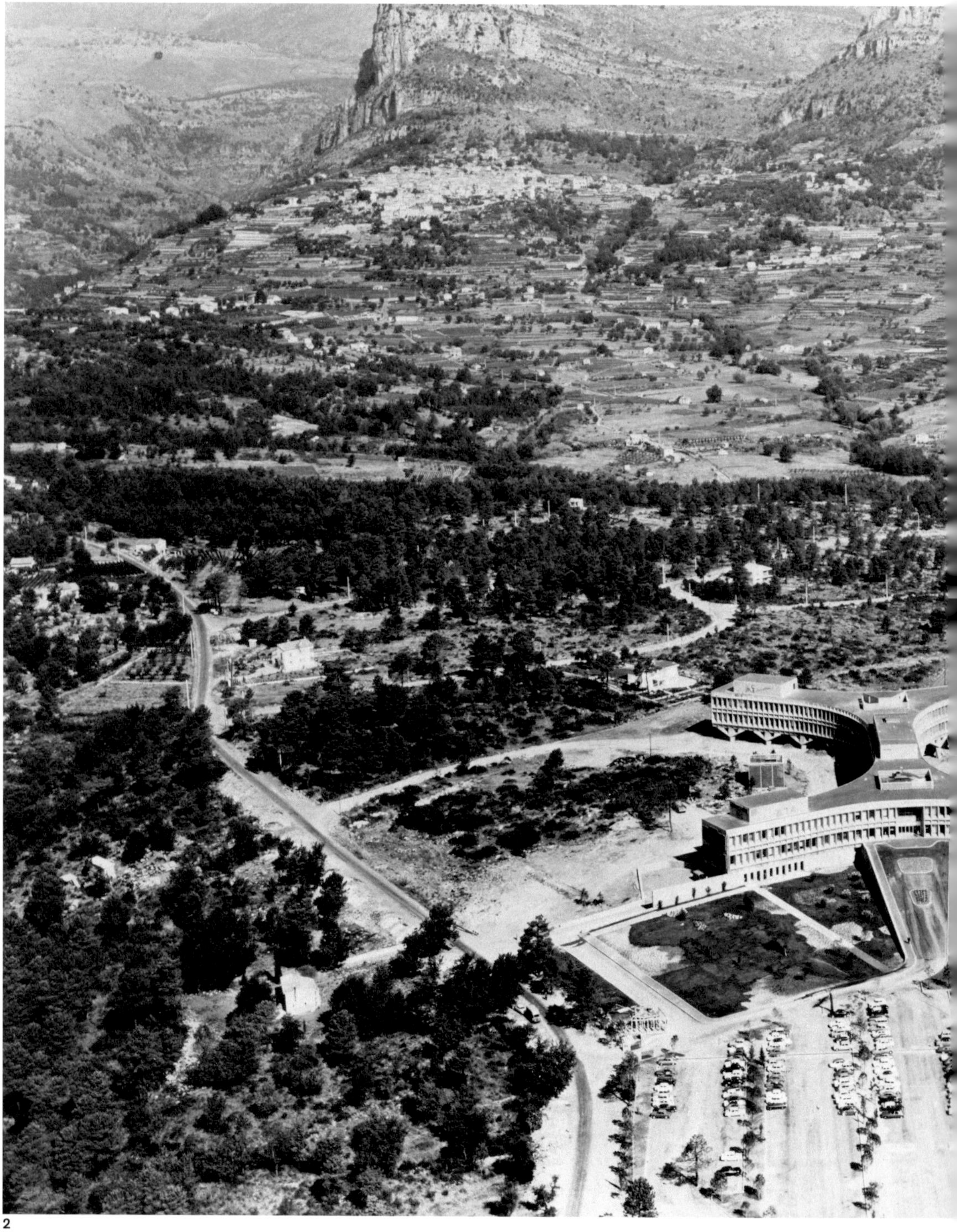

2

255

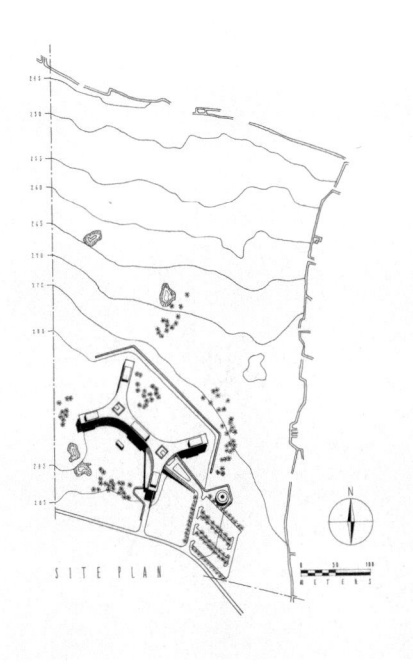

SITE PLAN

3

4

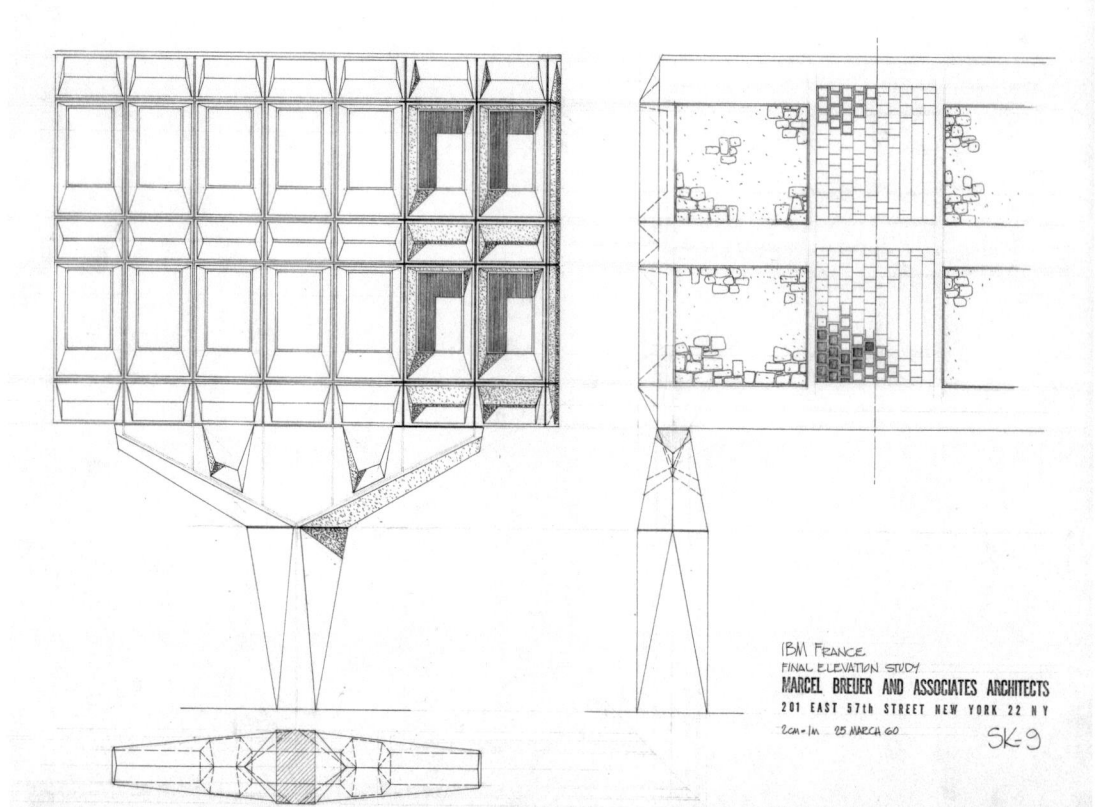

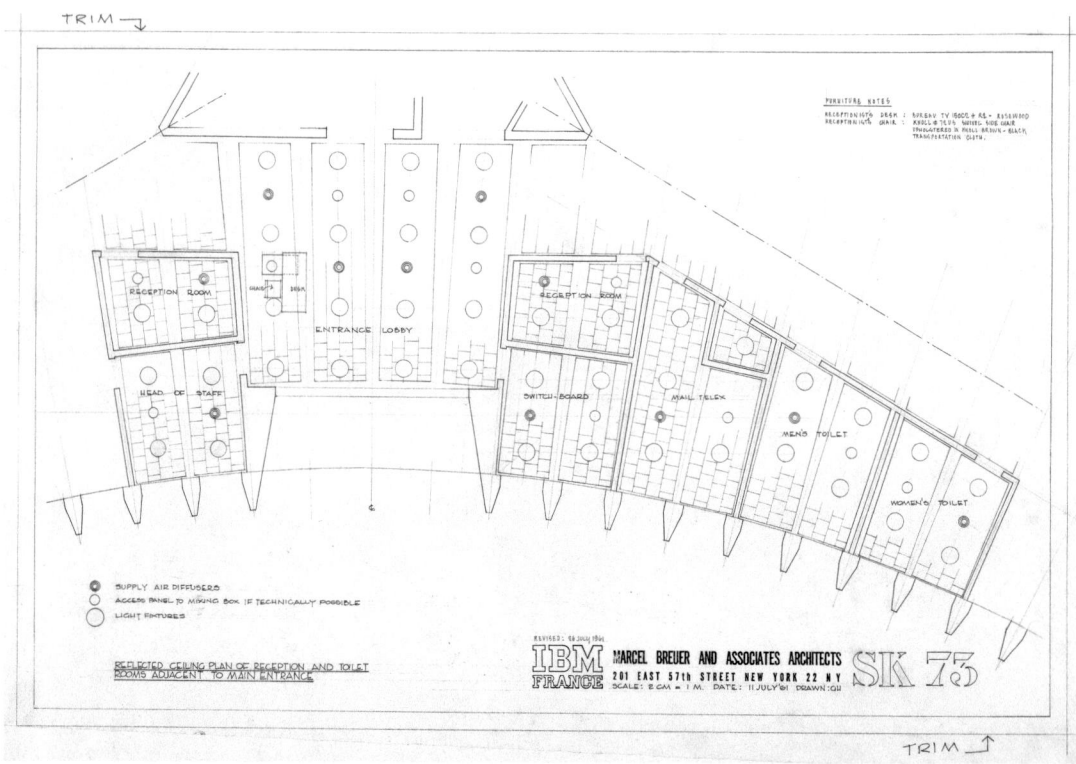

5

MAIN FLOOR PLAN

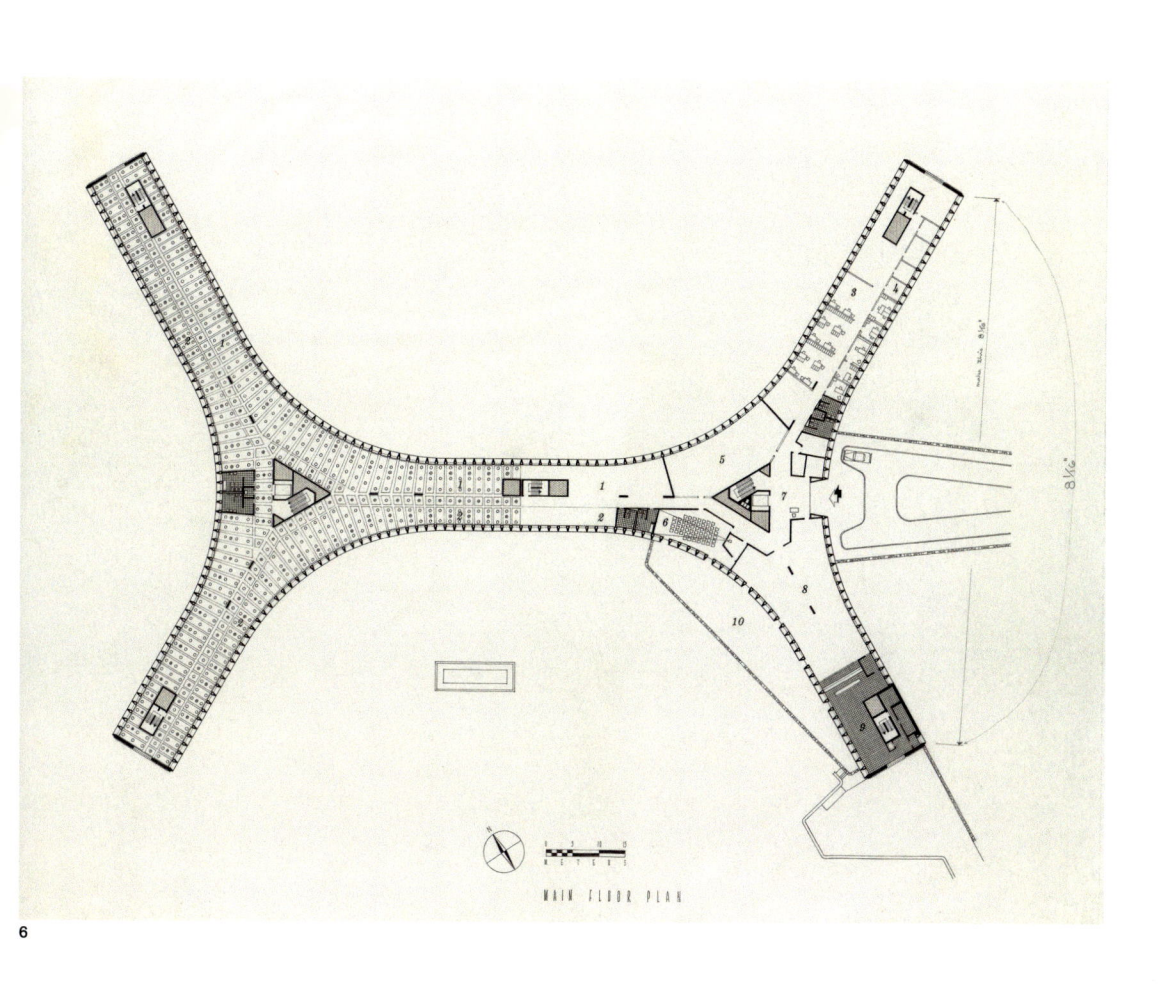

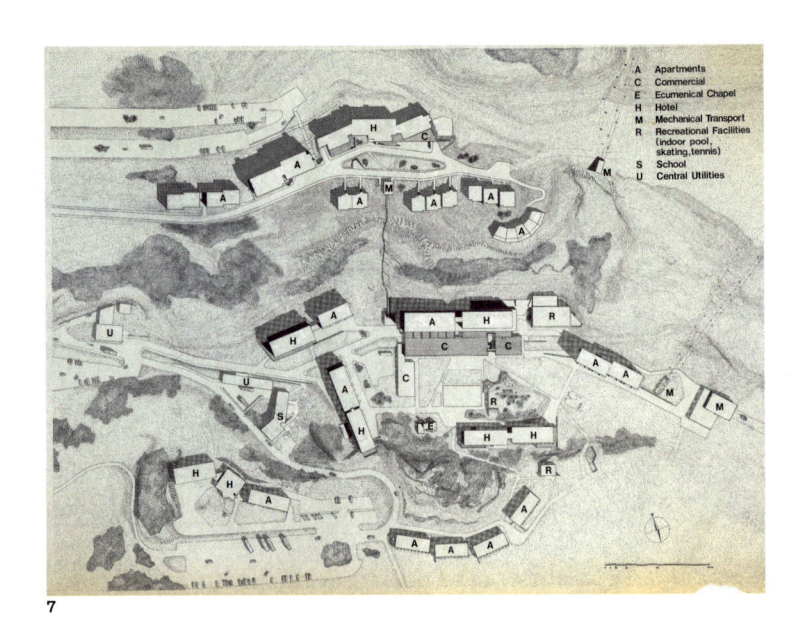

258 V FRANCE

```
A  Apartments
C  Commercial
E  Ecumenical Chapel
H  Hotel
M  Mechanical Transport
R  Recreational Facilities
   (indoor pool,
   skating, tennis)
S  School
U  Central Utilities
```

7

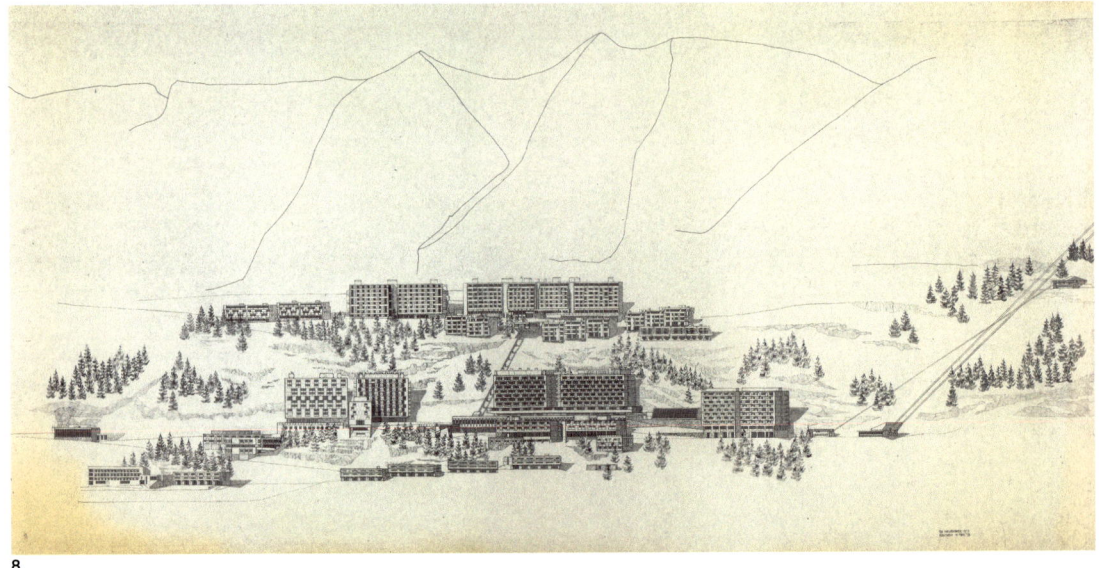

8

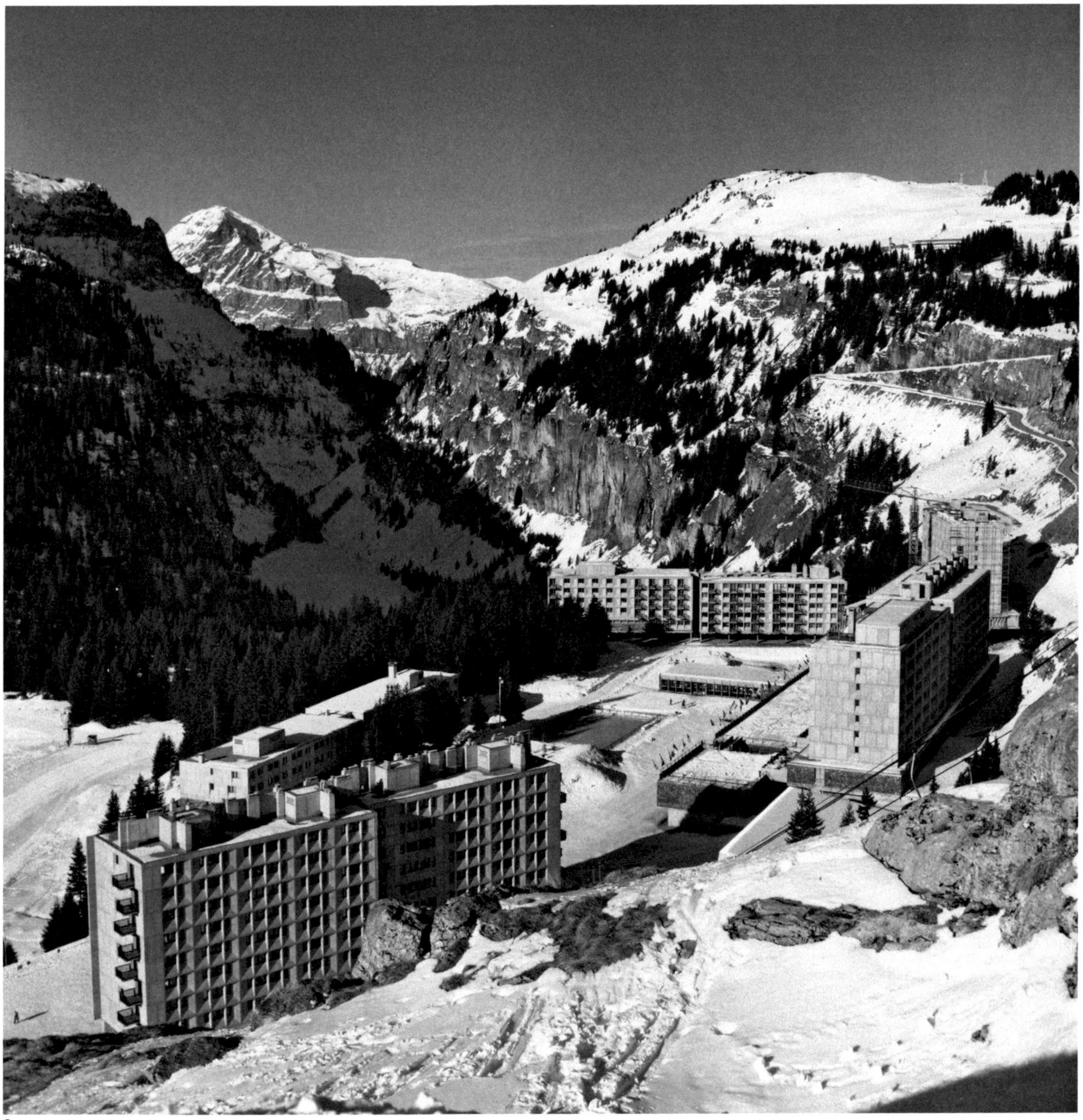

9

10

11

261

12

13

14

15

264 V FRANCE

16

17

18

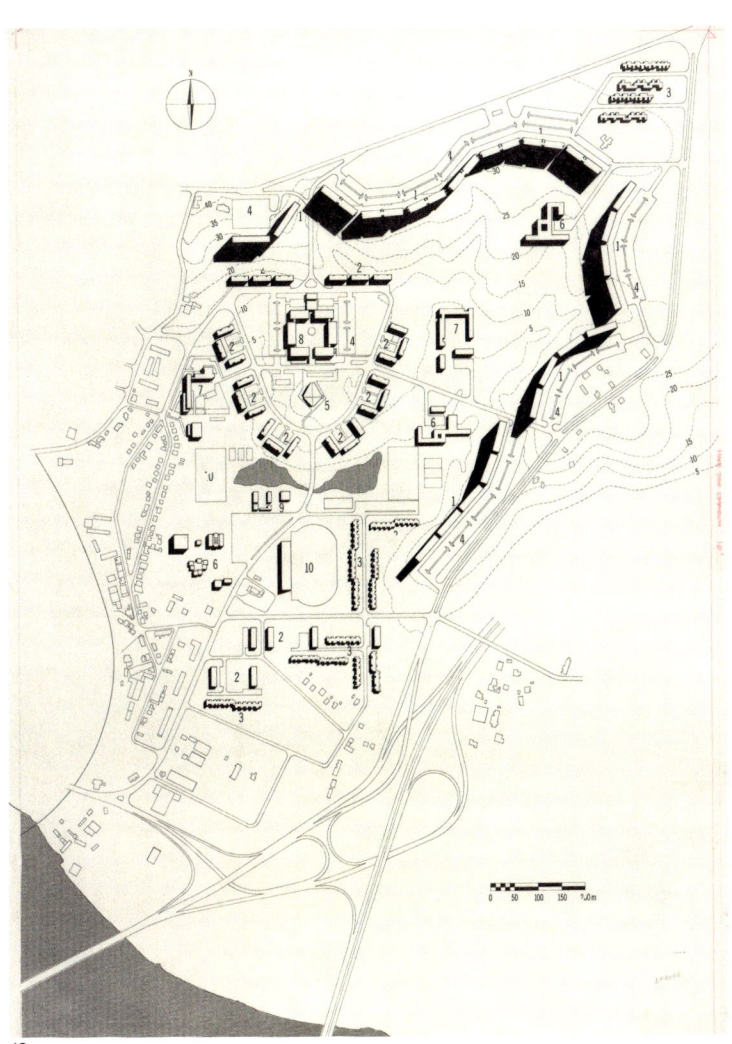

V FRANCE

19

20

21

22

V FRANCE

1'-6 3/4"

1'-0 1/2"

23

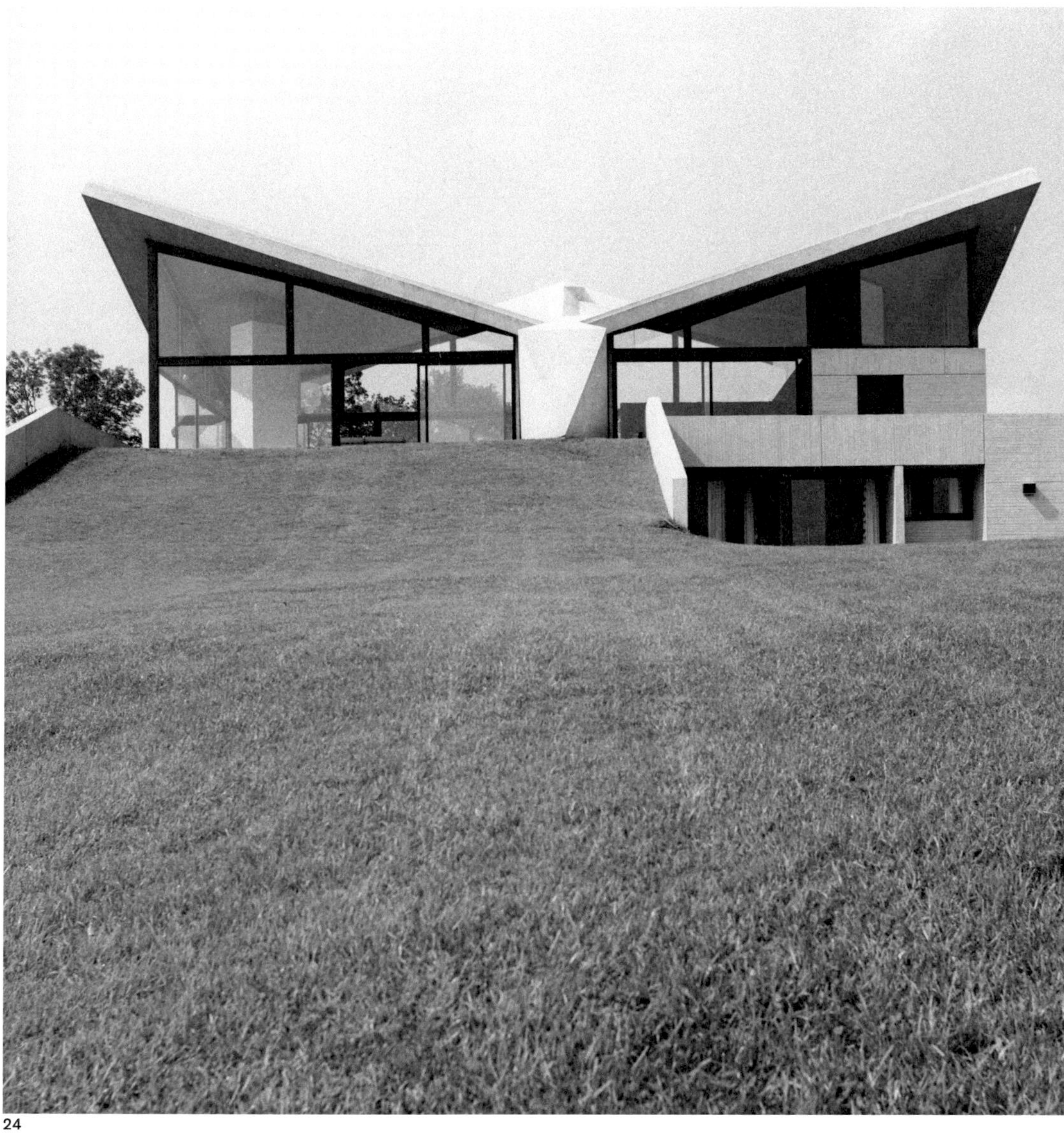

24

25

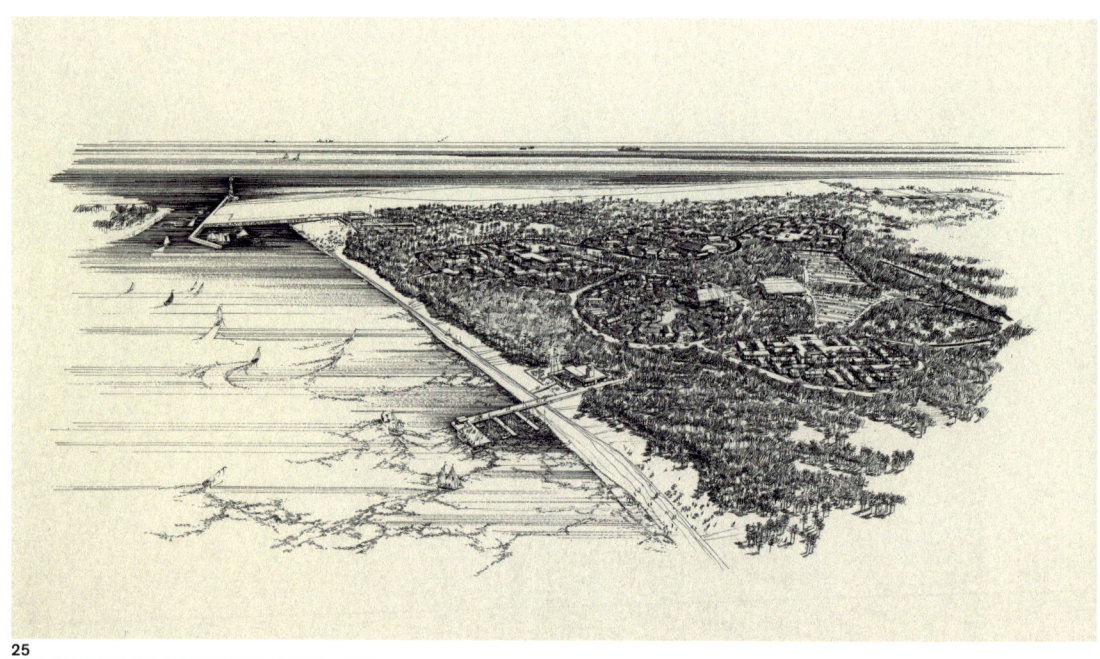

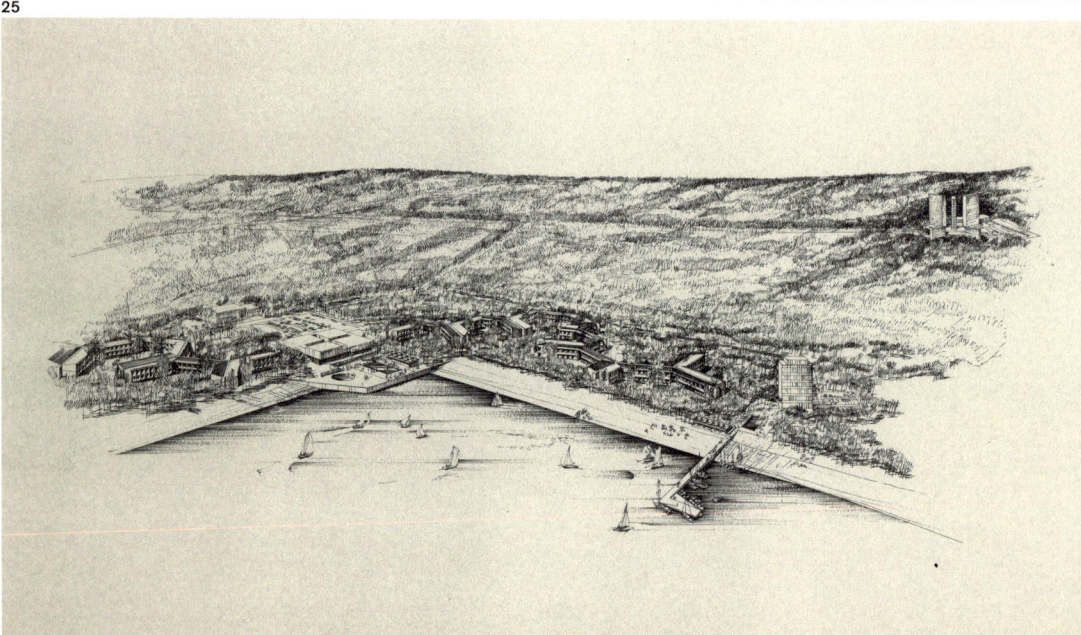

26

27

28

1 ZUP de Bayonne, Bayonne, France, 1966–73, overall view

Modernism as Accommodation

Kenny Cupers with Laura Martínez de Guereñu

Atop a hill on the outskirts of Bayonne, a port city in the French Basque country, towers a monumental chain of high-rise apartment buildings designed by Marcel Breuer. When one is traveling at high speed along the highway that connects the region with Spain, the ensemble appears glaringly out of scale. A curvilinear sculpture almost half a mile in length, it dwarfs not only the city's medieval fabric but also Vauban's sprawling fortifications and citadel of the seventeenth century [1]. The façades are made entirely from prefabricated concrete panels, evoking a seriality that reinforces the sense of alienation. Only from a closer vantage point can visitors appreciate the façades' intricate play of surface and depth and the balconies that afford majestic views of the surrounding landscape. The high-rises are part of an even larger housing project, planned in 1963 as a self-sufficient neighborhood of thirty-five hundred dwellings [2].[1] It was only partly completed over the decade that followed, but what was built still covers an area larger than the historic city of Bayonne, built over centuries.

2 Aerial perspective rendering

Even though its scale and severity astonish visitors today, the project was not unusual at its time. In the decades following World War II, France evolved from a largely rural country with an outdated housing stock into a rapidly modernized urban nation. This evolution was characterized by the massive production, at an unprecedented scale, of publicly funded housing and new towns. In suburban Paris, Lyon, and Marseille, tens of thousands of housing units rose simultaneously. Smaller provincial cities such as Bayonne witnessed an equally sweeping building boom. The Bayonne project was no different from the many other new structures, in perhaps all but one aspect: its architect. Most of the commissions for housing and new town projects went to French architects trained at the École nationale supérieure des Beaux-Arts, the country's most prestigious professional school for architecture, which had historically produced the architects of large state projects. It was not uncommon for well-established architects, some of them winners of the illustrious Prix de Rome, to be involved in mass housing projects at this time. But the choice of Breuer, a German-trained architect with an American-based office, was highly unusual. Breuer's Bayonne project in fact remained one of the very few French housing projects designed by a renowned international architect.

By the time the Bayonne project neared completion in the mid-1970s, however, France's ambitions for mass housing already seemed ill-fated. In a 1974 article, the French newspaper *Le Monde* celebrated the Bauhaus architect but concluded that "the massive ensemble of Bayonne shows that there is nothing new in collective housing blocks, for which Breuer did not find a new scheme."[2] In fact, minister of equipment, housing, and tourism Olivier Guichard had officially outlawed the construction of large-scale housing projects the year before, and the earliest projects were already being demolished in the early 1970s—relegated to the dustbin of history as failures of modernist hubris. Many of those still standing today are inhabited by the immigrant poor, and recurring suburban unrest seems to legitimize demolition rather than renovation.[3]

Caught in this downfall, Breuer's landmark ZUP Sainte-Croix in Bayonne exemplifies our still-troubled relationship with architectural modernism. Does his project illustrate modernism's self-proclaimed crisis, confounded as it was by the failure of public housing? Or does its recent renovation and proud renaming as Résidence Breuer confirm the undeniable merits of its design? Despite decades of scholarly revision, modernist assumptions about the power of architecture to shape social life continue to mar our understanding of the actual role of design in a housing system shaped by large-scale institutions and economic forces. Rather than surmise the authorial intentions of form as if it were frozen in time, we might view Breuer's ZUP as an opportunity to understand modernism as accommodation—as a process of adjustment to conflicting demands and changing circumstances. Perhaps the question then is not whether Breuer's ZUP is an ingenious tour de force, a bureaucratic compromise, the victim of a historic transition, or an unexpected success. We might ask instead how it could be any of these things at different moments in time and what this may tell us, not just about the authorship of Breuer but about the project's material and social life over time.[4]

Systemic Design

By the time Breuer was commissioned for the Bayonne high-rise in 1963, French mass housing production had become a well-oiled machine. The construction of large-scale housing was so dominant in the public mind that French administrators and architects could present these large structures as the only rational form of urban development. That did not mean they were accepted without critique. From the start, journalists spoke of the new housing as "rabbit cages," and specialists speculated about the buildings' harmful psychological effects on inhabitants. Problems with technical quality and the lack of collective amenities informed legislation and new design experiments. In 1958, the French state established the so-called ZUP, or *zones à urbaniser par priorité*, as a way to allow larger areas to be earmarked for more comprehensive urban development.[5] Tightly controlled by the centralized state, these priority urbanization zones were meant to steer urban expansion by consolidating inexpensive land parcels on the outskirts of the city. While reaffirming the desire for economies of scale through standardization and rationalization of housing construction, they were primarily meant to assure the integration of collective facilities in new projects.

It was in this context that Pierre Sudreau, the new minister of construction, and André Malraux, the first minister of culture, both attempted, on their own terms, to renew the promises of mass housing. Sudreau led a commission to improve design based on a study of everyday life in new housing areas. Malraux and his director for architecture, Max Querrien, promoted prominent modernist architects as part of their larger agenda to democratize access to high culture. Such political and architectural ambitions directly affected the planned expansion of Bayonne. Like many French cities, both large and small, Bayonne experienced significant population growth in the postwar period. National-level economic planners estimated that more than four thousand new dwellings were needed to accommodate the projected growth.[6] The majority of these were to be built in a single ZUP. Planners targeted a large swath of mainly agricultural land on the bank of the Adour River opposite the historic town [3].[7]

Two different explanations exist for how Breuer came to be involved as the architect for Bayonne's master plan. One is by way of Malraux, who seems to have recommended Breuer to the

3 Map indicating the extent of the ZUP in relation to the city of Bayonne

municipality. The culture minister was indeed acquainted with Bayonne's mayor, Henri Grenet, as a result of their work in the French Resistance.[8] The other possibility is Max Stern, founder of the Bureau d'études et de réalisations urbaines (BERU), an economic planning firm with which Breuer had already worked in connection with the Flaine ski resort project.[9] BERU was hired for Bayonne even before Breuer became its architect. Since Stern was well connected to government elites in Paris, and it is likely that he knew Malraux personally, the two explanations do not necessarily contradict each other.[10] Even though Breuer had limited experience with collective housing design, he had gained renown in France with such projects as the UNESCO building, the IBM offices, and the Flaine ski resort. Breuer was, in fact, establishing an office in Paris at this time, and Malraux seems to have personally assured his induction into the Ordre des architectes.[11] Breuer's Paris office was directed by Robert Gatje, who had moved from New York, and it included André Laurenti, a collaborator on the UNESCO project. With this new branch office and a team of collaborating local architects, among them Guillermo Carreras and Eric Cercler, Breuer seemed well equipped for the Bayonne job. Nevertheless, Malraux's choice of a Hungarian-born architect, even when he represented the prestigious international legacy of the Bauhaus, remains idiosyncratic. Apart from Breuer, the only other international architect Malraux got commissioned for a mass housing project was Oscar Niemeyer, but his design for a project in Grasse remained unbuilt.

Despite the high hopes attached to Breuer's commission, his design was framed by—and had to accommodate—the same bureaucratic planning and production system that was reshaping the country. With the help of national funds, the city bought, and in some cases expropriated, the land from private owners and then resold it to social housing organizations that would own and develop the buildings.[12] In concert with the ministry, the municipality hired BERU as consultant. By the early 1960s, an entirely new sector of such firms, private as well as publicly funded ones, had emerged in response to the postwar building boom. The design of Bayonne's ZUP was typical of this new division of labor among designers, experts, and the state administration in postwar France. BERU envisioned a range of units, depending on tenancy, funding, and form. In addition to different categories of social rental units (65 percent), there were subsidized (25 percent) as well as market-rate (10 percent) condo apartments. This housing stock was to be divided over a high-rise, a mid-rise, and a low-rise sector.[13] Breuer's design was undergirded by a regime of expertise that produced various qualities by speaking in numbers.

His master plan, first presented in February 1964, ingeniously applied BERU's programmatic parameters to the site. Topographically, the area was shaped like a bowl, sloping up from the Adour riverbank to its northern and eastern borders—an old regional road and a planned national highway. Minimizing the necessary roadwork and using the already existing green spaces, Breuer positioned fourteen-story high-rises on top of the ridge, arranging them in a series of chains that formed a gigantic crescent embracing—and towering over—the site as a whole. Each chain had its own curvature and was positioned at a distance from the next, allowing for different perspectives of monumentality and openness as one moved across the site. A second housing group consisted of mid-rise blocks, centered on the project's civic center and church. Even though all of the blocks were simple oblongs, they were positioned to suggest different group forms. U-shaped arrangements of three blocks were placed on the southeastern and southwestern ends in a parabolic shape, while the northern end terminated in two rows of oblongs. A third housing group, at the very bottom of the hill, comprised rows of single-family homes placed in a rectilinear pattern. An extensive park landscape tied the three housing groups together and was dotted with schools and sports facilities. As a whole, the layout not only suggested different scales of community formation but also served to accentuate the existing topography, with the housing groups increasing in density and scale as one went up the hill.

Even though it was inscribed in the arch-modernist concepts of green city and neighborhood unit, Breuer's master plan amounted to more than just towers in a park. It reflected, if unassumingly, a marked turn in postwar modernism toward the revaluation of traditional urbanity. For the ZUP's civic center, Breuer inverted the dominant figure-ground relationship by closely assembling six mid-rise buildings around a central square [4]. In concert with changing government expectation, Breuer was not just designing a housing estate but also the other buildings associated with a community. Even though the façades were made of the same prefabricated concrete panels found everywhere in the project, the square's ground-floor galleries recalled the prototype of a medieval market square. The

4 ZUP de Bayonne, photograph of the town center

buildings housed not only boutiques and a supermarket but also various community amenities, including a youth club, a sociocultural center, a medical center, a library, a post office, a police station, and a church. The center emulated the functional mix of traditional city centers, even if many of the amenities were new products of the welfare state rather than age-old institutions. In fact, Breuer's design typified the changing output of government-sanctioned modernism in postwar France more generally, as the state gradually shifted its goal from providing basic housing to creating lively neighborhoods.[14]

Despite the project's intricate massing, officials and citizens alike perceived Breuer's design as a bold statement about the representation of collectivity—much like other housing projects in France at this time. Placed on top of the hill, the housing slabs turned Bayonne's horizon into a monument to modernity for the citizenry as a whole—in addition to providing thousands of inhabitants with a panorama of the mountains and the historic city, with its cathedral towers and its landscape of tiled roofs. Bron-Parilly and La Duchère, two large housing projects around Lyon, also featured giant slabs, hundreds of meters long, prominently positioned on the hills. These projects were designed by French architects trained in Beaux-Arts compositional techniques, but their underlying ambition was identical. The monumentalization of collective dwelling—a Versailles for the people—recalls the utopian socialism of the early nineteenth century. It is an approach that characterizes the history of modern housing, from Victor Considerant's designs for Charles Fourier to Ricardo Bofill's postmodernist housing complexes in the French New Towns. How easily such gestures of generosity—whether in neoclassical, modernist, or postmodernist cloak—turned into vehicles of social stigmatization would become clear in the decades that followed.

A Difference in Repetition
Breuer and his team had to accommodate to stringent limitations for the housing design—both directly, through government regulation, and indirectly, through funding structures. In the decades following World War II, French welfare was administered through social abstraction and technical normalization. Families were classified according to the male breadwinner's profession and then assigned particular housing and other needs. This process of social rationalization—which was overtly classist and implicitly racist—has a much longer history, but it was especially during

the postwar period that architectural modernism began to play a particularly significant role in it. Norms for the layout and size of different categories of dwelling units were based on the sociology of household types, and they often presumed a particular architectural form—as the repetitive nature of mass housing projects across France showed. Architectural standardization made social rationalization sensible, often in the form of identical apartments with identical windows.

Breuer's design was necessarily inscribed in this rationality. That did not mean, however, that his architecture was entirely predetermined or that there was no room for invention. Even though he responded to the demand for economies of scale with a limited number of dwelling forms, Breuer introduced difference and variety where he could. For the high-rise housing, Breuer built upon Le Corbusier's influential Unité d'habitation but substantially adjusted it to suit the particular conditions and aspirations associated with the Bayonne project. Each fourteen-story slab consisted of four layers of three floors, in addition to a ground floor and mezzanine [5]. Only the middle floors of each layer were bisected by a longitudinal corridor. Three elevators, one standard and the other two skip-stop, connected the four corridors with the main entrance, which was located in the middle of the block. An additional skip-stop elevator was placed at each end of the slab. This arrangement not only minimized the circulation space but also allowed Breuer to develop a variety of dwelling types.

In the first five high-rises, each of which contained 160 units, there were fourteen different types, ranging from one-bedroom to four-bedroom apartments. The last two high-rises, built during

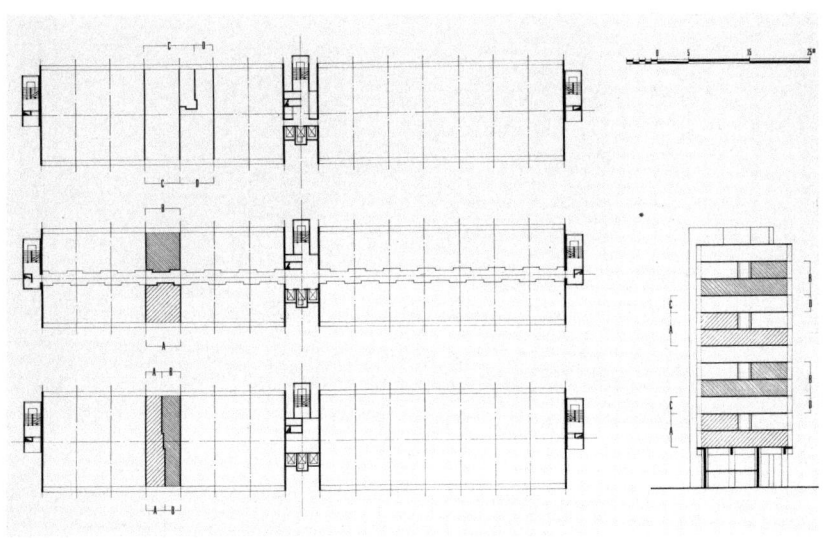

5 ZUP de Bayonne, plans and section drawing showing the organizational principle of the high-rise block

6 ZUP de Bayonne, section drawing through the high-rise block, showing the arrangement of different housing types
7 Plan drawing of the two-bedroom apartment type (F3) in the high-rise blocks
8 Plan drawing of the one-bedroom (F2) and three-bedroom (F4) apartment types in the high-rise block
9 Plan drawing of the mid-rise apartment blocks

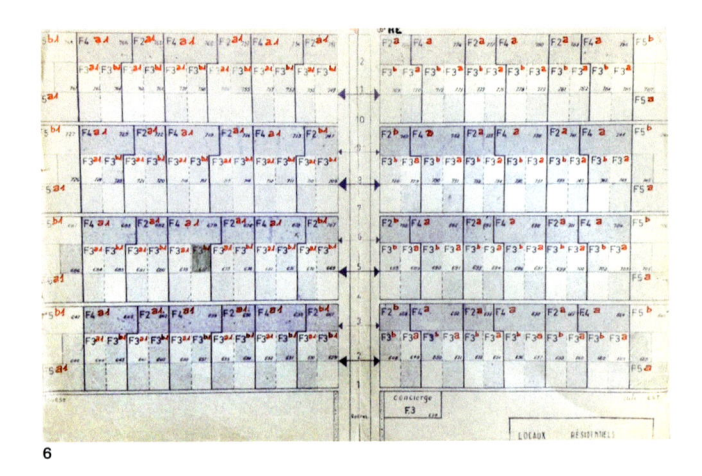

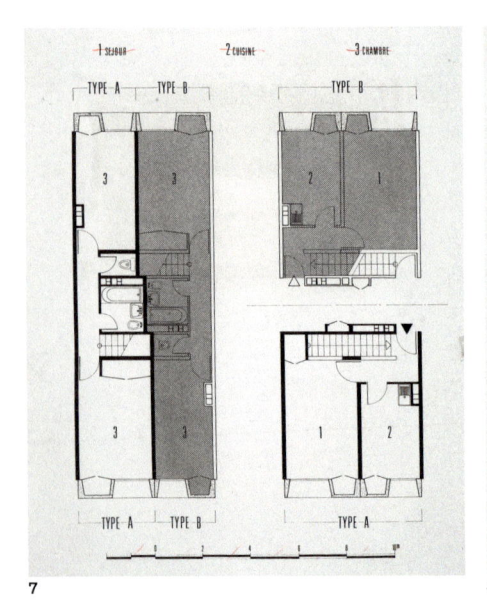

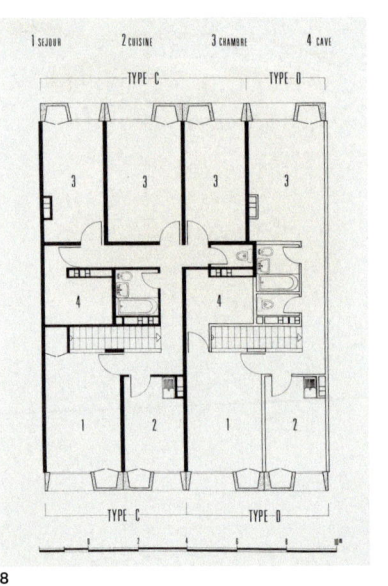

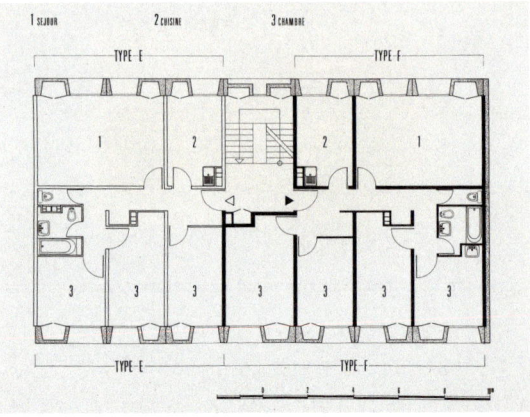

a later phase, included eight additional variants to the three-bedroom apartments—those most in demand. In addition, the last three high-rises featured balconies for the living rooms on the south façade. While this typological variety paralleled that of the Unité, the spatial organization differed significantly [6]. Only the four-bedroom apartments (termed F5s) located at the ends of the slabs were interlocked duplexes comparable to those in the Unité. The two-bedroom apartments (F3s) were simple duplexes, with living spaces on the corridor floor and bedrooms below. The remaining floors alternated one-bedroom (F2) and three-bedroom (F4) apartments. They were accessible by interior staircases from the longitudinal corridor below, unlike those adjoining the central elevators, which were meant to accommodate residents with disabilities.

What facilitated this typological diversity was a simple technical choice: a large structural bay of 5.7 meters, divided into a small bay of 2.56 meters and a larger one of 3.14 meters [7, 8]. The Unité's structural bay of 3.66 meters could either serve as a living room or be divided into two small rooms just 1.83 meters in width, whereas Breuer's asymmetrical division of a much larger bay allowed for a far more flexible organization of living spaces. This was one of his most important achievements at Bayonne. Living rooms could now be appropriately paired with kitchens, and larger bedrooms with smaller ones. In addition, the expanded structural bay allowed the interior staircases to be placed parallel to the corridor—saving space compared to the longitudinal position of the Unité's staircases—and to integrate them into the central bathroom core. Finally, with this organization Breuer managed to give each apartment, even the one-bedroom units, two exposures and thus the possibility of cross-ventilation. Nevertheless, until renovations, many applicants stated they would accept any unit in Bayonne's social housing stock "apart from the Breuer buildings!"— by which they meant the high-rise slabs.[15]

For the mid-rise housing group, Breuer designed four-story walk-ups, keeping the same system of the structural bays but alternating one large bay of 5.70 meters with two smaller ones of 2.56 meters [9]. Each block included two staircases, serving two units per floor, which amounted to sixteen units per block. Because these mid-rises were targeted not only for a higher category of social housing but also for private homeowners, they included only three- and four-bedroom units with balconies and generous living rooms occupying the full 5.7-meter bay. The promotional brochure for these units shows how the cooperative

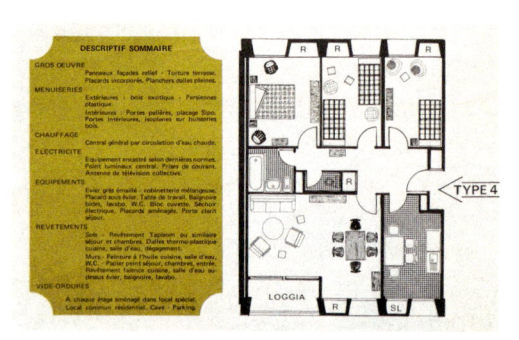

10 Marketing brochure for the ZUP mid-rise condo apartments

developer targeted a middle class intent on privacy, comfort, and amenities [10].

Unlike many French housing architects, who often adopted government-type plans with minimal variation, Breuer and his team insisted on typological diversity, even if the overall contours were already defined by BERU's programmatic parameters. The resulting housing designs celebrated a sense of the collective through repetition and monumentality, while allowing inhabitants a sense of identification with their individual dwellings. The ZUP's variety of dwelling sizes and types might well have guaranteed, or at least bolstered, the success of the project over time. It accommodated, at least in the high-rise blocks, a diversity of occupants, from younger couples and large families to the elderly. In addition, it allowed tenants to stay in the neighborhood but move to different apartments as their needs or circumstances changed.

The Thickness of a Panel

Even before Breuer was involved with Bayonne, the government had already hired a technical consultancy firm for the project's engineering. COFEBA (Compagnie Française d'Engineering Barets) was founded by Jean Barets, a man local to the Bayonne region but of national political influence.[16] Barets had given his name to a patented industrial construction method, which he had developed for the prefabrication of large concrete panels. His firm specialized in technical studies for the application of such methods in public works as well as housing projects. Barets was hardly the only one to develop concrete panel construction at this time in France. During and after World War II, the French government had prioritized large industrial firms for reconstruction and infrastructure projects, to the detriment of small-scale builders. To address the acute housing shortage, those same companies were supported by the state for the development of industrialized housing construction. The steady commissions for mass housing projects across France made new techniques of prefabrication practically free of financial risk. As a result, companies such as Camus quickly became market leaders in heavy prefabrication. Camus was a patented panel construction system by the engineer Raymond Camus, and it was exported globally after its development in the late 1940s.

Even though the resulting buildings often looked identical, Barets's system differed significantly from other factory methods, ultimately allowing Breuer to mold it in exceptional ways.[17] The differences between most concrete panel systems on the market were essentially limited to the details of their joints related to technical safety and with little consequence in outward appearance. Prefab panels were always floor-to-ceiling and in most cases included window, door, and balcony details. Barets's panels were just as heavy as Camus's, could be just as finished, and often looked indistinguishable [11]. The real difference then was in the economic logic of their production, which could occur either in a specialized factory or on-site, in a mobile workshop. Camus's factories required heavy investment, and, because of transportation costs and economies of scale, they were viable only for very large projects in large metropolitan areas. Barets's "mobile workshops" were more nimble: they could be erected on a site anywhere, even in small provincial cities such as Bayonne, and were economically viable even for "small"—as they were considered at this time—construction projects of three hundred or more housing units. By the time of the Bayonne master plan, Barets had already built more than sixteen thousand housing units with his system, from single-family homes to eighteen-story blocks, in France and abroad.

11 An apartment block constructed with Jean Barets's patented prefabrication method: "Ville verte" of Canteleu by architects Louard and Lechevallier

p. 260/11 Breuer had previously collaborated with Barets on the Flaine ski resort project, where he had gained considerable experience in building lodging for the burgeoning winter holiday market and had been able to customize the patented prefab system.[18] Breuer had beveled the concrete panels inward and given some of the windowed panels a thick, upstanding ridge. The different panels were assembled in a checkered pattern of glass and concrete, resulting in a three-dimensional façade that refracted the crisp Alpine light into a multiplicity of smoothly textured surfaces and reflections. Working from this achievement, Breuer exploited the Barets system further at Bayonne. His major innovation was in the panels' extraordinary thickness of 75 centimeters [7–9]. This extreme depth turned the panels into boxes that could be hollowed on either side. Corresponding to the asymmetrical division of the structural bays, there were two types of panels—a small one (of 2.56 meters in width) and larger one (of 3.14 meters). Breuer designed two configurations for each one, resulting in a total of four different panels to be mass-produced in Barets's mobile factory. All panels consisted of a set-back floor-to-ceiling window part and a protruding full part. The protruding full part was either flush or asymmetrically beveled inward, emphasizing the panels' ridges. This planar difference, however small, produced a different perception of the concrete depending on the angle of the sunlight falling on it. In addition, the windows could be placed to either the left or right within the panel. To ventilate the kitchens, Breuer added a protruding concrete exhaust on top of the windowsill of the kitchen panels. Once assembled, the panels produced a variegated pattern of concrete and glass, of full and hollow, and of light and shadow.   p. 266/20

The three-dimensional patterning gave the buildings both a rigorous seriality and a sense of variety. In addition to providing increased structural strength and thermal insulation, the panel system significantly enriched the interior experience of the dwelling units. By expanding the boundary between inside and outside into a usable and habitable zone, Breuer augmented the visual and physical space of the apartments. Even if the budget allowed balconies to be provided only in the later phase of the high-rise housing, his design provided a spatial generosity that was rarely seen in state-sponsored housing. The hollowed panels could be left open, but they also allowed for built-in closets, which opened up space in the rooms themselves [7–9]. The panels not only framed the panoramic views of the mountains and historic city but also protected the windows from the elements without necessitating the addition of eaves. Each window had two symmetrical shutters, which allowed inhabitants to modulate light and heat inside their apartments and created an additional layer of formal variation and movement in the façade.

12 ZUP de Bayonne, high-rise blocks as seen from the park

For the onlooker, from the outside the façade system produced changing perceptions of anonymity and individuality. Looking up from the park landscape that sloped down, the deep floor-to-ceiling windows, each with its own shutter, emphasized the dwellings as individualized spaces, private yet publicly visible [12]. For the driver on the highway and even the inhabitants of the old town, the windows of the high-rise wall suggested anonymity through ambivalence in scale, since one could either read each window as a dwelling unit or see four closely placed windows as one large opening. While the permutation of a limited number of panels conveys Breuer's sense of efficiency and control over the production process, it also signals an attempt to express, at least formally, the individuality of dwelling in a housing system that tended to produce alienating monotony.

Even more than poured-on-site concrete, heavy prefabrication entailed a reorganization of labor and expertise that many architects understood as a threat to their profession but to which Breuer seems to have responded with cunning rather than offense. Heavy prefabrication methods indeed coincided with the centralization of expertise in the construction industry. Concrete in this sense presented not only an opportunity for technical engineers, organized in corporate firms such as Barets's, but also a cause for both the de-skilling of traditional artisans and the disempowering of architects in the design process.[19] While Le Corbusier responded to this threat by inventing his own system, the Modulor—alluding to a universal humanism while aiming to reconquer dimensional normalization from the construction industry—Breuer accommodated by exploiting the potentials of system building from within.

Breuer's concrete panel aesthetic was decidedly slick compared to the artisanal *brut* use of poured concrete in Le Corbusier's Unité [13]. If concrete is not naturally or automatically a modern material, as Adrian Forty has suggested, Breuer made it modern by emphasizing the exactitude of a material that is "always at risk of slipping back into its craft and earthbound origins."[20] This engineering aesthetic was, at least in part, a product of the French prefabrication industry. Yet, despite his insistence on the industrial smoothness and luxuriousness of concrete paneling rather than the rough and irregular traces of manual labor, the aggregate panels he used to give his buildings a rusticated base suggest a more ambivalent position [14]. For these panels, Breuer valued manual labor and local stone from the quarries of La Rhune, both traditionally used in Basque house construction. This unassuming nod to regional building

13 Assembly of the aggregate panels, contact sheet

14 ZUP de Bayonne, construction of the high-rise blocks

style and the use of differently sized stones for the panels produced a variegated mediation of the building with the soil. While Le Corbusier resolutely elevated his Unité from the landscape, Breuer's attitude was multivalent. While the high-rises featured a double-height gallery on the park side, suggesting levitation, they seemed firmly rooted in the ground on the other side.

p. 267/21

With its accommodation to imposed limitations and exploitation of implicit possibilities, Breuer's design for Bayonne exemplifies an important transformation of architectural agency in the postwar period. Architecture could no longer be revolutionary, as it had been in the interwar period, or even avant-garde, in the specific sense of producing social change through design. In the postwar context of development and modernization, architecture was enmeshed in large-scale industries and bureaucracies that administered not only its production but also its consumption. Like his colleagues, Breuer accommodated to this regime, which in the case of France resulted from a close alignment between liberal capitalist production and centralized state planning. At the same time, the architect nudged some of its many restrictions, subtly turning them into architectural possibilities, by differentiating the massing, diversifying the housing types, or detailing the prefabricated panels of his ZUP.

Overhauls

By the time Bayonne's first high-rises were finished, concrete architecture was more reviled than celebrated and not just by the general public but increasingly by intellectuals as well. Jean-Luc Godard's film *Deux ou trois choses que je sais d'elle*, an iconic critique of the French postwar suburbs, identified the nefarious consequences of state-led capitalist modernization with the dreadful monotony of concrete blocks and slabs. Breuer's ZUP was being built at exactly this time of growing discontent about modern architecture, which in France had become synonymous with the alienating effects of state capitalism.[21] Breuer's high-rise housing, proudly positioned on top of the hill, was increasingly perceived as the opposite of generosity, a gratuitous attack on the landscape of Bayonne. This shift shaped the course of the project in multiple ways. The most direct impact was the gradual curbing of the project in the late 1960s and early 1970s. While the mid-rise buildings were largely realized as planned, only seven of the eighteen to twenty-two high-rises once planned were built. Single-family homes in traditional styles were later built instead, while Breuer's own proposals for low-rise units were neglected. The commercial and civic center, designed in 1965, was delayed and was finally finished only in 1975. Some amenities, such as the youth center and the hotel, were never built, while the extensive social services that were planned never materialized as anything more than some office space in a single building.

Paralleling this gradual disinvestment were crucial changes in the design process itself. Initially, Breuer was directly in charge of all design aspects, but he eventually lost control when local architects, in particular Bernard Darroquy, whom Breuer had initially hired to work with him, took over. This overhaul was only in part due to Breuer's physical distance from the site. Conflicting political interests also seemed to foster the master plan's unraveling. The design of the schools, for instance, was not in Breuer's hands because commissions were ultimately decided by the education ministry, which preferred working with a tight circle of "approved architects," apparently including Darroquy,[22] whose school designs Breuer loathed. Moreover, Darroquy changed Breuer's original design on multiple occasions without consent or even consultation. As a result, pitched tile roofs suddenly appeared on Breuer's prefabricated panel buildings surrounding the central square, despite Darroquy's earlier promise [15].[23] Breuer was dismayed by such stylistic cacophony but remained powerless. Darroquy seemed to have won

15 View of the central square, 2015

the favor of the mayor, and Breuer was gradually left out of the decision-making process. In a memorandum from 1972, Gatje reported that Breuer was concerned he was "gradually losing control of the situation, and our once proud vision is in danger of being frittered away piece by piece."[24] Breuer and Gatje even tried to have Darroquy fired.[25] Ultimately, when the municipal government engaged in an additional project for the ZUP in 1975, it hired the French architect Louis Arretche, claiming that Breuer would surely not be interested and that Arretche would be respectful of Breuer's designs. In response, Breuer officially resigned, even though he had already been effectively sidelined.[26]

Soon after the end of construction in the mid-1970s, and despite the best intentions of some planners and policy makers, the ZUP witnessed a residential mobility pattern that left much of the high-rise housing to those with no choice but to live there. In the 1980s, as inhabitants felt relegated to the high-rises, the ZUP quickly became stigmatized. That process did not occur for all housing, however. The Office Public Municipal d'HLM de Bayonne built and owned the first three high-rises and the western wing of the U-shaped mid-rises, while a second organization, the Société Anonyme d'HLM de Bayonne, was responsible for the fourth high-rise and the three western, oblong mid-rises.[27] Such internal divisions help explain the divergent social and material histories of individual buildings. The fourth high-rise stood completely empty at some point in the 1980s.[28] In 1986, more tiled roofs appeared on the U-shaped mid-rises, but only on the western ones; they were owned by the same housing company that owned the high-rises. The mid-rises on the eastern side, in private ownership, are still largely in their original condition.

By the turn of the millennium, the ZUP's decline had come to a head. The mayor's son, Jean Grenet, who became mayor himself in 1995, suggested the complete demolition of Breuer's high-rise housing.[29] When demolition of the project, so proudly commissioned by his father three decades earlier, turned out to be economically unviable, especially considering the persistent housing need in the urban region, the government slowly moved toward the idea of renovation. A complete overhaul eventually took place between 2007 and 2013, with the help of national funds. During the refurbishment, Breuer's concrete panels became a curious advantage. Their excellent thermal and sound insulation meant they did not need to be replaced or covered up, which would have dramatically altered the look of the façades—as is the case with many similar housing projects, such as the East German *Plattenbauten*. Brightly colored shutters, ranging from orange and red to purple, were added to reinforce a new image for the neighborhood, while keeping Breuer's design intact [16]. After the renovation, the high-rise complex was renamed Résidence Breuer. Its stigma seemed undone by association with the word *résidence*, which usually denotes a privately owned apartment block, and with the name Breuer. Breuer's authorship offered an opportunity to rebrand the project—to remove any negative connotations with social crisis by turning the complex into the opus of a famous Bauhaus architect. This was a self-conscious campaign to restore his professional image, as some of the planners involved in the renovation themselves confirmed.[30] The architect's iconic tubular chair proved particularly useful in this regard, even if this design was largely reduced to illustrating a desirable middle-class lifestyle [17].

16 View of the renovated façade of the ZUP high-rise block, 2015

Throughout its history, Breuer's ZUP has accommodated not only its inhabitants but also the state's conflicting demands and changing expectations, as well as the ups and downs of public perception. From a moment when the state began to question its dominant approach to housing development and design, through a period during which the ZUP was undesirable and partially

17 Marketing materials for the renovated high-rise apartments

abandoned, to a redemptive contemporary moment of celebration, Breuer's ZUP adapted ingeniously to change. At a time when the bulk of French housing built in the postwar decades is either in dire need of maintenance or slated for demolition, Bayonne's upward trajectory is telling. Even when its trajectory is not unique, it remains atypical and, as such, demonstrates how design can matter in a realm as bureaucratic as that of French housing.[31]

It remains an open question as to whether the reclamation of Breuer's ZUP foreshadows a broader nationwide shift in how the public will see and inhabit the heritage of postwar modernism. What is certain, however, is that such a revival cannot simply be reduced to the politics of public perception. When asked about the housing complex in which he has spent most of his adult life, Michel Duran, a native Bayonnais with a sense for hyperbole, is effusive about his deep respect for Breuer. Despite his limited experience with housing design, he argues, Breuer designed a housing complex "better than that of Le Corbusier." Standing on his ninth-floor balcony overlooking the park landscape and the cathedral towers of Bayonne on the horizon, he recounts his many apartment moves within the complex as his life circumstances changed, as well as the changes the complex underwent over the past decades [18].[32] Duran's personal history, so intimately interwoven with the concrete of Breuer's ZUP, as well as his extolling the joys of what he proudly calls his "Breuer balcony," throws at least one belief into question. The laments of architecture's impotence in the face of a draconian housing system suddenly appear irrelevant when standing on this balcony and grasping just how well Breuer's modernism has accommodated—and continues to accommodate—life.

18 View from Michel Duran's ninth-floor balcony at the ZUP, 2015

1 ZUP Sainte-Croix, Note de présentation, July 5, 1963, 19910710/3, Centre des archives contemporaines (hereafter, CAC followed by cataloging number).
2 "Breuer, l'architecte qui vient du Bauhaus," *Le Monde*, June 20, 1974.
3 For a general history of housing in postwar France, see Kenny Cupers, *The Social Project: Housing Postwar France* (Minneapolis: University of Minnesota Press, 2014).
4 This text has been written by Kenny Cupers based on collaborative research with Laura Martínez de Guereñu, who lived in Breuer's ZUP for one week in August 2015. She is currently working on the paper "Barcelona, Harvard, Côte Basque: A Mutual Exchange between Sert and Breuer."
5 See "Décrets relatifs aux plans d'urbanisme directeurs et de détail, aux lotissements, aux zones à urbaniser par priorité, à la rénovation urbaine, aux associations syndicales de propriétaires en vue de la réalisation d'opérations d'urbanisme," *Journal officiel de la République française*, December 31, 1958.
6 See Complement à la note de présentation, July 27, 1963, CAC 19910710/3.
7 ZUP Sainte-Croix, Note de présentation.
8 See Denis Canaux and François Xavier Leuret, "La résidence Breuer dans le quartier Sainte Croix à Bayonne: De la barre à la résidence," in "Les grands ensembles d'habitat des années 60: Un patrimoine du quotidien," *Bulletin CPAU Aquitaine* 43 (July 2008): 42; and Dominique Amouroux, *Marcel Breuer: Les réalisations françaises* (Paris: Éditions du Patrimoine; Centre des monuments nationaux, 2014), 25.
9 Robert F. Gatje, *Marcel Breuer: A Memoir* (New York: Monacelli Press, 2000), 140–41; "Two New French Towns," *Architectural Record* (August 1969): 109.
10 See Maryvonne Prévot, *Catholicisme social et urbanisme: Mauric Ducreux (1924–1985) et la fabrique de la Cité* (Rennes: Presses universitaires de Rennes, 2015), 76–80.
11 Amouroux, *Marcel Breuer*, 120.
12 See Direction de l'habitat et de la construction, CAC 19830719/14–19830719/15.
13 ZUP Sainte-Croix, Note de présentation.
14 See Cupers, *Social Project*, chap. 3.
15 Applicants' "tout le parc sauf la résidence Breuer!" request(s) quoted in Canaux and Leuret, "La résidence Breuer dans le quartier Sainte Croix à Bayonne," 43.
16 Barets sat on various government committees, including the Commission général au Plan and the Centre Scientifique et Technique du Bâtiment. See Dossier de présentation du bureau d'études techniques COFEBA, Departmental Archives of Bayonne, 12 W 24/2.
17 See Jean Barets, "Considérations pour la préfabrication lourde," *Habitation* (1965); and "Procédé Barets," excerpt from *Le Bâtiment*, special issue (1957), both in Dossier de présentation du bureau d'études techniques COFEBA.
18 Despite tensions between the two men—apparently Breuer had tried to get Barets fired from the project—Breuer was forced to work with him again at Bayonne. See Robert Gatje to Mario Jossa, memorandum of April 4, 1972, Breuer Digital Archive, Syracuse University Libraries, Syracuse, NY.
19 This goes back to the turn-of-the-twentieth-century pioneering of reinforced concrete and the establishment of technical consultancy firms such as François Hennebique's. See Adrian Forty, *Concrete and Culture: A Material History* (London: Reaktion Books, 2012), 240–41.
20 Ibid., 15.
21 At the forefront of such critiques was Henri Lefebvre. See Cupers, *Social Project*.
22 Robert Gatje to Mario Jossa, memorandum of January 12, 1972, Breuer Digital Archive.
23 Bernard Darroquy to Robert Gatje, letter of April 2, 1970; and Gatje to Darroquy, October 27, 1969, image no. 39727-001, both in Breuer Digital Archive.
24 Gatje to Jossa memorandum, January 12, 1972.
25 "If there were a way for us to supplant Bernard as architect of these two schools, it would in fact be not a bad solution. Whether this is politically or ethically possible remains to be seen." Robert Gatje to Mario Jossa, memorandum of January 25, 1972, Breuer Digital Archive.
26 Mayor of Bayonne to Marcel Breuer, letter of January 22, 1975; and Breuer's response in memorandum of January 14, 1976, both in Breuer Digital Archive.
27 Direction de l'habitat et de la construction, CAC 19830719/14–19830719/15.
28 José Luis Ecay, interview by Laura Martínez de Guereñu, Bayonne, August 2015.
29 Canaux and Leuret, "La résidence Breuer dans le quartier Sainte Croix à Bayonne," 42.
30 Ibid., 47.
31 Another example of a successful renovation is Bois-le-Prêtre, near Paris, by Frédéric Druot, Anne Lacaton, and Jean-Philippe Vassal, in 2011. See Craig Buckley, "Never Demolish: Bois-le-Prêtre Regrows in Paris," *Log* 24 (Winter–Spring 2012): 43–50.
32 Michel Duran, inhabitant of a *foyer-logement*, F2-2b, Building 7, ninth floor, apartment 95, with a balcony open to the south, in conversation with Laura Martínez de Guereñu, August 14, 2015.

1 Breuer at St. John's Abbey and University, with church and campanile in background

Breuer's Ancillary Strategy: Symbols, Signs, and Structures at the Intersection of Modernism and Postmodernism

Timothy M. Rohan

Jutting forward like the bill of a duck, the cantilevered entrance canopy at the Whitney Museum of American Art (New York, 1964–66) boldly projects out over Madison Avenue, reiterating the outline of the stepped-back, granite-clad mass rising above it. The canopy is but one example of the highly plastic, multivalent pendants Marcel Breuer often designed in order to express, symbolize, relate, or elaborate upon some aspect of the buildings he erected behind them. This approach can be called Breuer's ancillary strategy, though Breuer never called it that or indicated that he was even aware that he had developed this approach.

Breuer deployed this ancillary strategy in many different permutations during his postwar career, ranging from the enormous, billboard-like bell banner fronting the church of St. John's Abbey in rural Minnesota (Collegeville, 1953–61) to the freestanding sign-structure that told passing motorists at a major highway intersection in New Haven, Connecticut, that Armstrong Rubber occupied the remarkable, levitating concrete massing he designed for it near the road's edge (1968–70).[1]

Although the pendants themselves varied greatly, Breuer's reliance upon this strategy could quickly be dismissed as yet another example of what was pejoratively called formalism in mid-century architectural discourse. Critics employed formalism to describe a facile design approach based on a vocabulary of personal predilections used habitually to the point of being clichéd. It was one in which geometric form dominated over functional requirements, privileging the visual above all else and disregarding context, as well as one in which the design process began with a particular form or configuration chosen a priori. Most damningly, formalism ignored the social and political world or considered it secondary.

It was particularly endemic to postwar American modernism, and critics warned that the formalist approach resulted in overly abstract, self-involved, object-like buildings, isolated from their surroundings no matter what their form. In 1960, William H. Jordy inveighed against the formalist qualities of the International Style and its counterpoint, the lightweight decorative "romantic modernism" of Edward Durell Stone and Minoru Yamasaki.[2] By the late 1960s, Robert Venturi and Denise Scott Brown were decrying the "slavish formalism" of that decade's concrete monumentality, meaning the brutalism of Paul Rudolph and Marcel Breuer. In the early 1970s, Manfredo Tafuri concluded that formalism had reduced modernism to a solipsistic set of "emptied signs."[3]

In the 1970s and 1980s, such criticism of formalism helped justify postmodernism's break with modernism. Reifying this rupture, Michael Graves's infamous, unbuilt addition to the Whitney Museum (project, 1981–92) contrasted his legible assemblage of traditional forms, namely a tower, portico, and cornice or rooflike penthouse linking old and new, with Breuer's seemingly mute, hermetic, abstract geometry [2]. A complicated mediation, the Graves addition also reified how contemporary discourse had sidelined Breuer's architecture, a position from which it has not yet fully emerged.

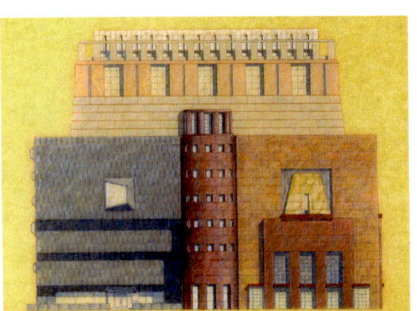

2 Michael Graves, Whitney Museum of Art addition, scheme #2, ca. 1987

But now that the polemical conflict between modernism and postmodernism is distant, one might ask a question that can aid in deciphering Breuer's abstraction and give his formalism a context that will make it less puzzling: was Breuer's ancillary strategy an intentional if not entirely conscious or articulated attempt by the architect to address some of modernism's chief problems?

The first of these problems is an internal one raised by architectural discourse itself: how to find an appropriate way to express symbolism and monumentality for institutions. Members of the modernist establishment, namely Sigfried Giedion, Josep Lluís Sert, and Fernand Léger, had called during World War II for a new, modernist monumentality to counter fascist monumentality. After fascism's defeat, Breuer and his contemporaries drew upon that discussion in order to find a monumentality appropriate for the postwar era's great new institutions, such as Breuer's UNESCO (Paris, 1953–58).

The second problem is an external one that concerned all of postwar society: mass media and popular culture. Replacing fascism as the focus of their fears (though communism of course remained a perceived threat), American cultural pundits, such as Clement Greenberg and Dwight Macdonald, warned that kitsch and the mass media would soon overwhelm established institutions, such as organized religion, art, and education.[4]

Although not given to social commentary, even Breuer decried advertising. In the first monograph about his work, *Sun and Shadow* (1956), coauthored by Peter Blake, Breuer called advertising a "specialized propaganda" that failed to tell the "whole story" of its chosen subject.[5] A supporter of Breuer, Blake offered explanations of Breuer's buildings that elaborated upon Breuer's opinions about the harmful effects of advertising.[6] Blake justified the monumentality of Breuer's Whitney Museum as an answer to the superficiality of the advertising industry and its buildings along Madison Avenue.

However, such rebukes to the mass media turned out to be untenable and conflicted. By the late 1960s, some thought architecture should learn from advertising. Blake was chagrined when Venturi, Scott Brown, and Izenour appropriated images from his 1964 diatribe against the advertising billboard, *God's Own Junkyard*, for their book *Learning from Las Vegas* (1972). Their proposal for reconciling architecture and popular culture laid the groundwork for postmodernism. Breuer himself found it impossible to ignore the omnipresence of billboard signage and corporate logos. Despite his earlier objections to advertising, by the late 1960s Breuer had turned to his ancillary strategy in order to dignify his corporate clients' signage.

Varying from the transcendent to the perplexing, Breuer's pendants encapsulate the problems of his architecture and the discipline itself in the mid-twentieth century. Breuer's ancillary strategy shows that his architecture was not simply solipsistic but shaped by external forces ranging from architectural discourse to the new highways that were spreading across postwar America.

Breuer's Formalist Poetics
Understanding Breuer's ancillary strategy entails considering how Breuer attributed powerful if cryptic poetic associations to his architectural vocabulary—the essential basis for his formalist approach to design.

To distinguish it from the established art historical formal analysis used in this chapter, the formalism practiced by architects like Breuer can be called "design formalism."[7] As was explained already, formalism foregrounded the visual, upholding geometric forms and the spaces shaped by them as architecture's primary considerations. Design formalism's postwar iteration can itself be historicized by turning to the architect and engineer Matthew Nowicki's prescient comments of 1951 about how form had come to dominate American modernism, making functional requirements secondary. Alluding to the famous dictum that "form follows function," Nowicki said that in his day "form follows *form* and not *function*" (his emphasis).[8] Rather than dismissing the formalist approach, as many critics did, Nowicki believed that a creative engagement with form would recover the aesthetic and representational aspects of architecture, among them its symbolic and phenomenological qualities. These amounted to its poetry, lost to a reductive approach to functionalism during the immediate postwar years.

Like Nowicki, Breuer believed that modern architecture was impoverished symbolically. Breuer asked in the mid-1950s, "Is there today such a thing as a demonstrative architectural form? Is there a symbol comparable with the archaic column, the gothic arch, the renaissance dome? It is, perhaps, the cantilevered slab—light and slightly resilient in the wind."[9] To invest forms with symbolism and poetry, Breuer favored those suggestive of movement and action, such as the cantilever. He preferred the oblique angles of trapezoids and rhomboids to the right angles of squares and rectangles. Employed by him so often that it alone is grounds for calling Breuer's formalism clichéd, the trapezoid could be laid flat to become a plan, flipped vertically to become an elevation, or realized three-dimensionally as a chimney.

Forerunners to the ancillary structures, Breuer's sculptural hearths brought poetry, symbolism, and drama to his houses, the building type with which he first established himself in the United States. The Gagarin House fireplace (New Canaan, CT, 1954) was the chunky, plastic cynosure of the low, dark, horizontal expanses of the living room [3]. Wider at the top than the bottom, it somewhat resembled a squat human form raising its slightly swaying arms high above a sturdy torso supported by hearth-straddling splayed legs. But if the human form is what Breuer is referencing here, it is not very legible. Such obliqueness would later incite postmodernist ire, but it was deliberate. Breuer consistently made anthropomorphic references but shied away from direct representations of the human form in compliance with modernism's prohibitions against traditional approaches to representation and figuration. Of course, others were not so circumspect. Le Corbusier had already overturned this caveat when he inscribed his Modulor Man upon the sur-

3 Gagarin House, Litchfield, Connecticut, USA, 1956–57, view of hearth

face of his apartment building, the Unité d'habitation (Marseille, France, 1946–52).

Abstract and enigmatic, Breuer's forms therefore fascinate and frustrate the viewer, inviting subjective reading confirmed only by studying Breuer's predilections. For example, Breuer's fondness for small, splay-legged African and pre-Columbian human figurines and stabiles by Alexander Calder confirms his affinity for the human form. Breuer often displayed these humanoid forms in the niches and apertures carved out of his chimney masses, thus exhibiting the inspiration and the result together. Enlarging relatively small elements into larger ones became an operation fundamental to Breuer's formalism. The vaguely anthropomorphic qualities of the Gagarin chimney are found at a vastly enlarged scale in the gigantic bell banner at St. John's Abbey (1953–61), which is contemporary to the Gagarin House (1954). Its splay-legged, paraboloid base suggests a colossus bestriding the entrance to the church [1].

Breuer's monograph of 1956, *Sun and Shadow*, showcased the poetry of his houses and suggested how these qualities could be elaborated upon in new institutional works still in gestation, such as at St. John's Abbey. The book articulated Breuer's position, but the voice was not entirely his own. Strongly opinionated, Peter Blake edited the book and wrote descriptions for each project. An architect, curator, and journalist active in postwar architectural discourse, Blake championed Breuer for many years. His writings celebrated Breuer as the heir to the Bauhaus legacy and as a poetic humanist valiantly opposed to the crassness of postwar American popular culture, though the latter characterization may have been as true of Blake, the author of the 1964 call-to-arms against roadside advertising, *God's Own Junkyard*.[10]

Taken from an old Spanish proverb, the title of Breuer's monograph, *Sun and Shadow*, captured the play of oppositions in Breuer's early postwar work out of which its poetry emerged: sun and shadow, solid and void, heavy and lightweight.[11] In the only poem he ever wrote, with words that show his formalism to be more than a simple deployment of geometry, Breuer elaborated upon how such phenomenal effects engaged with the senses to make architecture:

> Colors which you can hear with ears;
> Sounds to see with eyes;
> The void you can touch with your elbows;
> The fragrance of dimensions;
> The juice of stone.[12]

At moments such as this one, Breuer seemed to be on the brink of thinking about the possibility of engaging architecture with language. Transforming the poetry of his houses into the durable prose needed for monumental buildings became Breuer's great challenge for the 1950s.

UNESCO and the New Monumentality

The difficulties Breuer encountered in designing his first significant institutional commission, the UNESCO headquarters in central Paris (Place de Fontenoy, Paris, 1953–58), led to his ancillary strategy. Breuer collaborated on UNESCO with the French architect Bernard Zehrfuss, as well as Pier Luigi Nervi, the Italian engineer whose use of concrete to achieve expressive forms would be instructive for Breuer.

The Yale architectural historian Vincent Scully thought it problematic that Breuer based his large buildings on the small forms previously developed for his houses and furniture, a vocabulary Scully believed derived from Bauhaus graphic design. Pinpointing a symptom of Breuer's formalism, Scully wrote in 1965, "But when Breuer came into the '50s and received commissions for large projects, it seems to me that the continuation of that small-scale graphic sensibility made it impossible for him to build a monumental building—a properly scaled urban building—and has so far continued to make it impossible for him."[13]

Breuer's early difficulties with finding an appropriate monumentality were not his alone. Achieving that character had been an urgent matter since the 1940s, when modernists organized to counter the success of fascist monumentality. In their 1943 manifesto for the "New Monumentality," Sigfried Giedion, Josep Lluís Sert, and Fernand Léger advocated building large-scale, modernist civic and cultural centers to foster community and democracy. Lightweight and transparent, these structures would perpetuate modernism's established aesthetic vocabulary. To equal and surpass the classical-inspired, decorative programs of the fascists, artists would contribute abstract murals, sculptures, and even projected images. These features would also supply the decorative, symbolic, representational, and emotional qualities characteristic of traditional monumentality, which modernism had rejected after World War I as too authoritarian. After fascism had been defeated, the New Monumentality remained relevant, as architectural discourse addressed the problem of designing large-scale buildings for the post–World War II era.[14]

However, by the early 1950s, the lightweight vocabulary and transparent cladding long favored by modernism and Breuer seemed inadequate compared to the dignity Le Corbusier achieved using raw concrete in his monumental new institutional buildings, as was evident in his High Court at Chandigarh, India (1951–55). Following a direction that eventually led to the concrete brutalism of the 1960s, architects turned to heavier masonry masses, especially when designing for institutions (churches, schools, and museums) that wanted to distinguish their buildings from the spare, lightweight transparency of the International Style preferred by corporations.

Although he had leavened the lightness of his houses with masonry walls and chimneys during the 1950s, as was evident in the Gagarin House, Breuer still found it difficult to find an appropriate monumentality for UNESCO, the newly established educational affiliate of the United Nations. Achieving this character was important because critics such as Lewis Mumford had found the monumentality of the United Nations headquarters building in New York (1947–52) inadequate and its symbolism confusing.[15] The multibuilding UNESCO complex was an opportunity to correct these deficiencies.

Uneasily marrying two of the primary modernist approaches of the time, Breuer clad the UN Secretariat with a glass curtain-wall like those of International Style buildings and raised it on sturdy concrete piers resembling those of Le Corbusier's Unité d'habitation. A favorite device of Breuer's—glass sunshades—sheltered the Secretariat's curtain-wall. However, the small, delicate sunshades had little impact upon the Secretariat's glass expanses and shaded it poorly. Air-conditioning was installed soon after UNESCO's completion.

Fulfilling the New Monumentality's call for using modern art to adorn modern buildings, Breuer commissioned pieces for UNESCO by Joan Miró, Henry Moore, Alexander Calder, and others and arranged several of them in the complex's entrance plaza. Unlike how sculpture and decoration had been integrated into a building's very fabric in the past, these works stood almost entirely separate and detached from the buildings Breuer placed them before—the Secretariat and Conference Building. Thus, as freestanding elements associated with larger buildings, they anticipated the positioning of the ancillary structures and how they would bring drama to a building and help focus attention upon it. However, the spatial relationships between the sculptures and the buildings in the plaza were loose and ill-defined. Indeed, the art works' presence spoke more of UNESCO's alliance with the prestige of modern art than with an effort to achieve New Monumentality.

The most captivating piece in the plaza was in fact not a work of art. Standing unglazed and completely independent from the Secretariat, it was a remarkable concrete entrance pavilion by Nervi positioned between the inner curve of the building and the driveway, thus recalling the ceremonial qualities of the porte cocheres of the city's imposing nineteenth-century buildings [4]. The pavilion's lightness contrasted with the massiveness of Breuer's Secretariat behind it. The butterfly-shaped canopy appeared ready to fly. In a gestural fashion, it reached out toward those arriving on foot or by automobile as they entered the building. Although it did not resemble the building behind it, Nervi's dynamic entrance pavilion may have suggested to Breuer how a relatively small independent structure, well sited in relationship to a larger building, could enhance a complex, therefore making it the most obvious precedent for Breuer's ancillary strategy.

4 UNESCO Headquarters, Place de Fontenoy, Paris, France, view of Nervi's entry pavilion

Unfortunately for Breuer, the completed UNESCO complex, especially the Secretariat, disappointed most critics. Lewis Mumford said, "The Secretariat is a building almost as anomalous and transparent as a jellyfish."[16] Its main deficiency was lack of "expression"—a word whose ubiquity in the architectural discourse of the 1950s indicated how limiting and repetitive the modernist architectural vocabulary was widely felt to be. In 1954, Paul Rudolph said, "Modern architecture's range of expression is today from A to B."[17] Calling the Secretariat a palace, Ernesto Rogers wrote, "As our age lacks a religious expression of its own, the Palace is found wanting in just those ineffable mysterious forces which in the great ages of the past characterized all masterpieces, works which at once plunged their roots deeply into the soil of their particular historical moment and transcended it *sub specie aeternitatis*."[18] Rogers got to the heart of the problem: neither specific nor transcendent, mid-1950s institutional modernism was rarely satisfying or inspirational.

Developing the Ancillary Strategy: St. John's Abbey

For Breuer, the opportunity to remedy these deficiencies came in another project already under way: the church and Benedictine monastic complex for St. John's Abbey (Collegeville, Minnesota,

1953–61). Breuer's ancillary strategy developed with this project, resulting in the first of his pendants: the abbey's bold, anthropomorphic bell banner. A landmark for the laity on the prairie, the freestanding tower at St. John's was visible to Sunday mass-going drivers traveling great distances at high speeds to the monastic church on one of the highways changing the way space, time, and representation were perceived across the nation.

Breuer developed a master plan for the complex in 1953 that expanded the existing nineteenth-century monastic complex with a new church, dormitories for the monks, and facilities for the abbey's school. For inspiration, Breuer drew upon previous buildings and his favorite forms. Resembling the conference hall at UNESCO, the church's plan and front elevation were trapezoidal—Breuer's preferred quadrilateral. But other aspects were unique. The first of Breuer's ancillary structures, the 112-foot-tall concrete bell banner, consisted of an enormous trapezoid adorned with a cross and bells and raised high on a paraboloid-arched base. The anthropomorphic, colossus-like structure realized the heroic ambitions of postwar modernism as outlined by the program for the New Monumentality and advanced by evolving discussions about monumentality, symbolism, and expression. A sketch of possible configurations for the bell banner shows how the design team developed different arrangements of bells and Greek and Latin crosses and how shapes for the base and the wall were explored [5]. The chosen forms strengthened the relationship

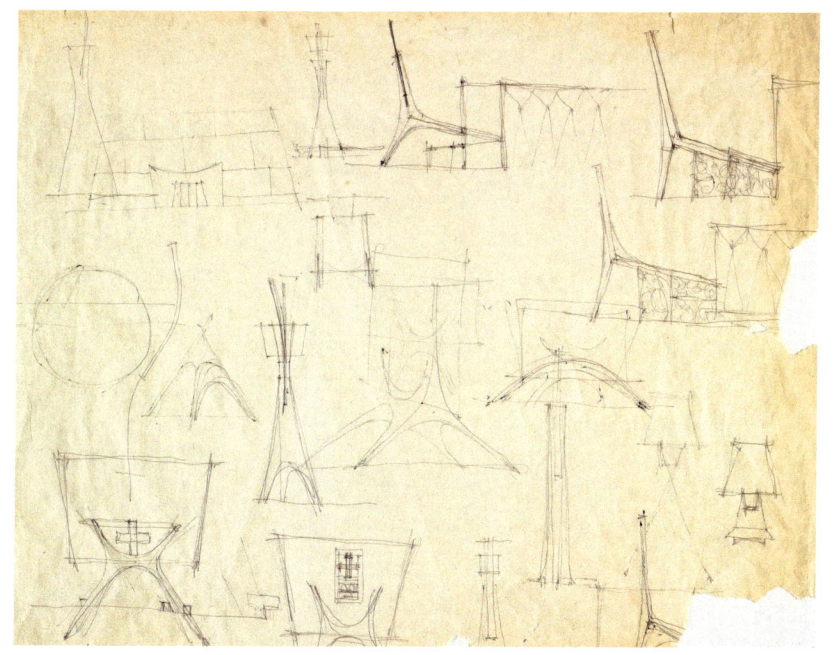

5 Sketches of bell banner for St. John's Abbey Church

between bell banner and building. The trapezoidal shape of the wall previewed the trapezoid-shaped elevation and plan of the church behind it.

Using a neologism that evoked church ritual, Breuer called the structure a "bell banner" rather than a bell tower or campanile. Established features of church processionals, textile banners decorated with Christian symbols were attached to poles and held aloft by clergy. Giving architectural form to this ritual, Breuer aligned the banner with the entrance to the church to form a processional route that Victoria Young has called the "spiritual axis." To emphasize how the chronology of the sacraments began with baptism, the banner rose above the boxlike entrance atrium housing the baptistery.[19]

Legibility of symbolism, function, and place were paramount for the monks because St. John's was the North American center of the ecclesiastical reform movement, whose mission was to clarify Catholic rituals for the laity.[20] The bells and cutout cross at the bell banner's summit were clearly recognizable symbols of Christianity. A functional necessity for the monks, the ringing of bells summoned them to masses, meals, and other communal activities. A threshold structure like many of the pendants, the bell banner mediated between the internal world of the church and its rituals and the external world of the laity, which was increasingly one of highways, consumerism, and popular culture.

Concerned about such worldly distractions, the monks raised questions about what the bell banner represented when they reviewed the project with Breuer in December 1956. Reflecting fears about advertising's growing dominance, some thought the raised concrete wall too closely resembled the billboards proliferating across America. The large flat surface inscribed with a cross could be read from a distance like an enormous sign, but one that seemed unstable to them in representational terms. One monk remembered his brothers asking if it was a "Christian symbol or a commercial symbol."[21] As experienced interpreters of symbols, they feared that Breuer's banner would discredit their church by associating it with the roadside commercial signage used to advertise stores, tourist attractions, and filling stations.

From the commerce-embracing perspective of the early twenty-first century, one might find it difficult to understand why established mid-twentieth-century nonprofit institutions considered associations with commerce harmful to their prestige, mission, and integrity. However, in the 1950s and 1960s, everyone from the establishment to the avant-garde struggled to come to terms with the acceleration of consumerism after World War II. Consumerism was blamed for alienation, loss of individuality, and the deterioration of the environment, apparent for some in the noticeable proliferation of signage along the nation's roads. Responding to alarm about the roadside billboard's proliferation, Congress restricted billboards fronting federally subsidized highways with the Bonus Act of 1958—legislation passed after years of acrimonious debates that Breuer and the monks would have been aware of as they reviewed the banner design together.[22]

After the monks questioned Breuer about his designs for the bell banner in December 1956, he reassured them that the presence of traditional forms of Christian representation upon the banner—meaning the cross and bells—would guarantee that it could not be interpreted as a commercial structure. Breuer reportedly told them, "I really don't believe that if the banner is built anyone will find the faintest comparison with commercialism."[23]

But like many in the postwar American elite, Breuer himself feared that consumerism would soon overwhelm traditional culture and institutions. In his monograph *Sun and Shadow*, Breuer denounced advertising for its reductiveness: "We are exposed everywhere to specialized propaganda—salesmanship which stresses only one aspect of a product to the exclusion of everything else. It sells automobiles, even some architecture, but it does not tell the whole story."[24] Breuer certainly echoed his era's alarmist rhetoric about advertising, but his words also demonstrated that he thought about architecture's relationship to narrative and maybe even language. In contrast to how 1950s' advertising often selected only one narrative storyline to sell a product by foregrounding a single image or slogan, Breuer thought of narrative or stories as complex and therefore closer to the loose interplay of intangible and contrasting forces that he described in his one poem about architecture's phenomenal effects upon the senses. Breuer later said of the church of St. John's Abbey, "Its story is told by the eternal laws of geometry, gravity, space."[25]

Despite his stated aversion to advertising, the omnipresent billboard was impossible for Breuer to dismiss as a model for St. John's as he contemplated ways to announce the abbey's presence to drivers on the nearby highway. Despite their aversion to commercial expression, the monks themselves had wondered about how to tell motorists about the abbey. Breuer proposed erecting a substantial sign consisting of a portion of the church's folded concrete wall near the highway exit to the monastery. Weighty and monumental, it would perform the role of a billboard

6 St. John's Abbey, perspective drawing of highway side "wall monument"

but would have none of that maligned typology's flat, lightweight qualities. Avoiding any connotations of commercialism, working drawings from 1957 call it a "permanent monument," rather than a banner or sign. Breuer attached no text identifying the abbey to the monument itself [6].[26] A part that represented the whole, or synecdoche, the structural element represented the church building itself and the institution of the abbey, thus making a satisfactory solution for the monks to the problem of roadside representation. Although never built, the permanent monument informed and shaped Breuer's ancillary strategy.

Breuer may have associated the permanent monument with developments in architectural discourse. By foregrounding a portion of the church's structure, Breuer elaborated on Nowicki's observation about how architects were beginning to use structural elements as "symbols of structure" (with "structure" meaning structural frameworks). Nowicki said, "The symbolic meaning of a support has also been rediscovered, and a steel column is used frankly as a symbol of structure even when it is not part of the structure itself."[27] Nowicki probably had in mind how Mies van der Rohe had made the steel I-beam a symbol of the structural framework of his buildings at the Illinois Institute of Technology (Chicago, 1941–58) and would do so again at the Seagram Building (New York, 1954–58).

Breuer's highway sign proposal for St. John's Abbey shows how the distinctions between symbols, structural forms, and highway signage and what they represented were softening for him even as he attempted to distinguish one from the other in his discussions with the monks.

7 University of Massachusetts, Murray Lincoln Campus Center and Garage, Amherst, Massachusetts, USA, 1967–70

Permutations of the Ancillary Strategy

In his projects of the 1960s, Breuer consistently returned to the ancillary strategy developed at St. John's, with varying degrees of success. At the Murray Lincoln Campus Center of the University of Massachusetts (Amherst, 1967–70), a freestanding, trapezoid-shaped concrete wall again demonstrated Breuer's affinity for that particular polygon, making it practically a signifier for him as architect [7]. Its purpose mysterious to the eye, the concrete trapezoid stands in solitude like an enigmatic totem before the lumbering mass of the campus center, a too literal rendition of Le Corbusier's Unité d'habitation. Is the trapezoid a sign for Breuer himself, the building, or something else? Like a piece of modernist sculpture plopped down upon the lawn with little thought for context, it has no discernible relationship to the main building and thus seems unsuccessful even as an ancillary structure. However, what it really marks is underfoot: the concrete trapezoid is in fact a chimney venting exhaust from vehicles idling in the campus center's loading dock.[28] The totem in fact responds to the needs of the internal combustion engine!

Breuer followed the St. John's bell banner with an even bolder one for another monastic community, the Annunciation Priory of the Sisters of St. Benedict (Bismarck, North Dakota, 1955–63) [8]. Breuer originally conceived of the banner as another trapezoidal wall, similar to the one at St. John's [9]. Departing from that polygonal form and the anthropomorphism of the St. John's bell banner, the Annunciation banner more closely resembled the pole-and-banner configurations found in church processionals. The pole was a pincer-like pier that held up for view across the prairie a rectangular banner pierced by a cut-out cross. The vertical rather than horizontal orientation of the rectangular wall dispelled any possible similarity to a billboard, whose rectangular form is of course usually oriented horizontally. Although the banner was separated from the church by a cloister, Breuer aligned it with the church's entrance, thus establishing another "spiritual axis" like the one at St. John's. The rectangular form of the Annunciation banner announced the rectangular plan of the church behind it, recalling Breuer's repetition of the trapezoid for banner, church elevation, and plan at St. John's Abbey.

8 Annunciation Priory of the Sisters of St. Benedict, Bismarck, North Dakota, USA, 1958–63, view of the bell tower and classroom wing
9 Study drawing for trapezoidal bell banner, Annunciation Priory

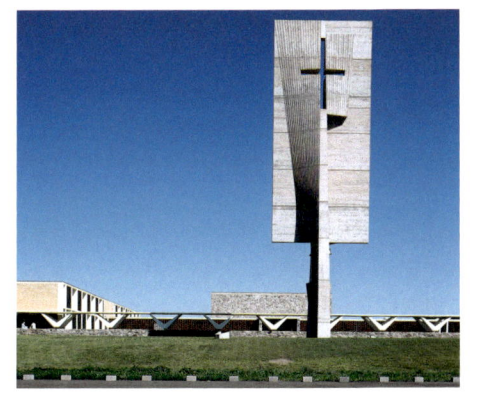

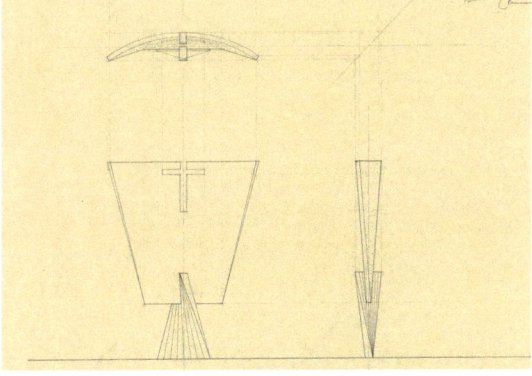

Like the St. John's colossus, the Annunciation banner also broadcast from its extensive surface area messages that invited interpretation. In addition to the symbolism of the cross, these messages concerned structure, the senses, and the environment. Breuer achieved these effects in part through his arrangement of a radiating pattern of concrete ridges that fanned out across the banner's surface, further emphasizing the perforated cross at its summit. Structurally expressive, the fanlike configuration articulated the intersection between the supporting pier and rectangular wall. It appeared to express the rising verticality of the banner as it ascended upward into the sky. Bringing to mind the line from Breuer's poem, "sounds to see with eyes," the pattern can be interpreted as giving form to the sound of pealing bells emanating upward from their housing at the banner's base. In such phenomenal ways, Breuer's best ancillary structures also moved beyond the limitations of conventional narrative and symbolism to achieve a poetry akin to the "religious expression" that Ernesto Rogers had said was missing from the UNESCO Secretariat.

Breuer turned to his ancillary strategy when he needed to make his increasingly bulky buildings seem less overwhelming. At the Whitney Museum (New York, 1964–66), the street-side entrance canopy contrasted with and yet related to the imposing dark granite structure behind it. The poured-in-place concrete canopy offered a preview of the concrete surfaces to be found inside. Intimate in scale compared to the main building, the canopy's projecting, cantilevered roof reiterated the outline of the stepped-back mass rising above it. Again recalling a nineteenth-century porte cochere, the canopy was another threshold structure mediating between the public life and commerce of the avenue and the enclosed, private, nonprofit world of high culture. The duckbill-shaped canopy jutted out over the sidewalk, inviting the visitor to embark on a processional route across a bridge and over a moatlike sculpture court recalling the entrance to a medieval castle. A cultural rather than a spiritual axis, it was a place of passage from which to observe the complex play of geometry and space that intrigued the mind and body at street level and promised greater revelations within the museum. Although Breuer tried to defuse the building's massiveness in these ways, the Whitney's air of almost fortified monumentality was still perceived as overbearing. One critic reported that it was known in New York as the "Madison Avenue Monster." Emily Genauer said, "It's one of the most aggressive, arrogant buildings in New York."[29]

p. 207/6

Breuer's longtime supporter, Peter Blake, defended the Whitney's monumentality and opacity as a symbolic reply to the other "Madison Avenue"—referring to the byword for the city's advertising firms, which were headquartered in stepped-back, glass-walled, International Style buildings along the avenue in midtown. In 1966, Blake wrote in *Art in America*, "The real reason for the Whitney's shape may be found in the language of symbolism rather than function.... The new Whitney will be art's answer to the huckster: where the ad agencies operate behind flimsy glass walls, the Whitney will be wrapped in concrete faced with granite; where the commercial ziggurats push the pedestrian off the sidewalk, the Whitney will invite him in; and where the right-side-up ziggurats down the avenue now symbolize the huckster's perversion of art, the Whitney's upside-down monolith may become a powerful symbol of art 'sailing against the currents of its time.'"[30] Blake effectively justified the Whitney's cryptic form to the magazine's readers by joining architectural discourse's internal discussions about form, symbolism, representation, and monumentality to better-known warnings about the deleterious effects of the mass media issued by critics such as Greenberg, Macdonald, or Vance Packard, who wrote best-selling books about advertising's subliminal techniques.[31]

Blake's inflated rhetoric can be discounted as more of a justification than an explanation, but Breuer himself had been adamant that the museum should not resemble an office building or venue for popular culture. At a public presentation of the design of the Whitney in 1963, Breuer said, "It should not look like a business or office building, nor should it look like a place of light entertainment."[32] To give it the dignity of the stone-surfaced museum buildings of the past, he clad the Whitney in dark granite. This choice was unusual. His preferred material at this time was unadorned concrete. The stone made an appropriate public face for the Whitney on Madison Avenue. In an anthropomorphic manner that almost gave the museum a true physiognomy, Breuer brought to mind the head of a Cyclops with its one enormous eye when he extruded a trapezoidal window from the Madison Avenue façade, as K. Michael Hays later observed in an insightful reading of the Whitney's symbolism.[33]

In a manner that Hays called "garbled," Breuer scattered trapezoid-shaped windows across the Seventy-Fifth Street elevation to enliven the surfaces and perhaps provide some type of symbolism, though this probably seemed like a worn-out and uncertain gesture even in 1966. The trapezoids corresponded to internal gallery spaces but appeared randomly applied when viewed from the exterior. Hays observed of the windows, "They look as if they are trying to be symbolic but are not quite sure what symbolic looks like."[34] The uncertainty of Breuer's symbolism is understandable when thought about in light of how immense forces such as advertising were transforming representation in the mid-1960s with graphic insignia such as logos.

Perhaps because it functioned symbolically, the increasingly ubiquitous corporate logo, such as Paul Rand's IBM logo or the work Eliot Noyes did for IBM, engaged Breuer's attention.[35] At Breuer's Torin Corporation headquarters in Connecticut (Torrington, 1966), the structure of the building inspired an ingenious sign based on the company's logo. In concept, the sign also recalled the proposed highway-side monument for St. John's Abbey. For Torin, Breuer joined two of the building's precast T-shaped concrete façade panels together to form the company logo, a giant letter T erected upon the complex's lawn at the driveway entrance to the complex. It was oriented toward the road, rather than toward other buildings or a town, like many of the new corporate campuses being built in rural and suburban areas in the United States and Europe during the 1960s, among them those Breuer designed for Torin, a multinational manufacturer of machine parts.

p. 336/32

Truly monumental, the Torin T had none of the lightweight, gimcrack, one-dimensional qualities of roadside signage and billboards for chain stores, car dealerships, or supermarkets, which Torin's administrators would have found undignified and inappropriate. Multivalent, the Torin T represented the Torin Corporation and the structural system employed in the building, again recalling Nowicki's "signs of structure."[36] But it was most fascinating as a structural form that had become a letter in the alphabet. Although Breuer may not have realized the significance of this gesture, the sign verged upon becoming language, suggestive of how the late sixties' turn toward linguistics and semiotics had begun to affect architecture.

Words: Armstrong Rubber Building
Entire words emerged in one of Breuer's most arresting later works, the Armstrong Rubber building in New Haven, Connecticut (1968–70). At this administrative headquarters and research facility, the postwar era's quest for monumentality and expression collided with its anxieties about consumerism. Fittingly enough for a collision, the building was located near the intersection of two recently completed highways, Interstates 95 and 91,

and one that was never finished, Route 34.[37] Armstrong Rubber was the client, but it was New Haven's strong-willed mayor, Richard C. Lee, who in seconds chose Breuer for Armstrong from a short list of prominent architects pulled from his desk drawer during a meeting with the company's chairperson. Lee and his planners controlled the Armstrong site and what would be built there.[38]

The project was an important part of their larger effort to revitalize this declining manufacturing city by persuading businesses and developers to hire well-known architects to design impressive new modern buildings. For this highly visible highway-side site, Lee wanted a landmark announcing the city's presence to drivers. The Armstrong edifice would be as imposing as another of the city's new modernist monuments: the nearby twenty-three story Knights of Columbus building by Roche and Dinkeloo (New Haven, 1967–69). Its four cylindrical concrete corner towers made it visible from the highway approaches to the city. Lee originally wanted Armstrong to build a similar tower, but they did not need anything so large. After being reorganized, Armstrong Rubber was most concerned about its identity. Robert Gatje, the partner in charge of the job, recalled, "The company knew that it was buying a symbolic structure that would indeed put Armstrong back into the public eye."[39]

Charged with building a symbol, Breuer accomplished this for Armstrong with a gravity-defying arrangement of rectangular masses clad in precast and poured-in-place concrete. Almost an ancillary structure itself, an administrative block topped by utilities and service equipment levitated two full floors above a low, rectangular podium base that was several times the size of the administrative block and designed to house research laboratories. Large and visible from afar, the gap between the masses was the building's unforgettable, distinguishing feature—an absence that gave the building its presence and identity. A surprisingly poetic gesture for a usually prosaic building type, it recalled the apertures found in the chimneys of Breuer's houses and in his bell banners. The open space had an ostensibly practical purpose: the gap between the upper and lower portions could be filled in with two additional floors if more office space was needed. Three squat stair and elevator towers joined and supported the two portions supplemented by piers. Viewed in section, the formation recalled Breuer's binuclear house plans of the 1950s, as Isabelle Hyman has observed. Exemplifying Breuer's formal dexterity, what was once a plan had been upended to become an elevation.[40]

10 Armstrong Rubber Company Headquarters, perspective rendering with billboard

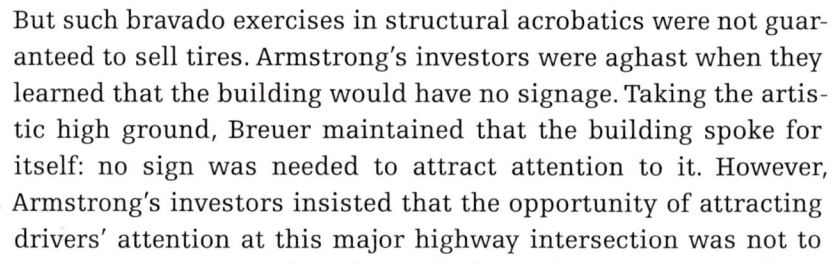

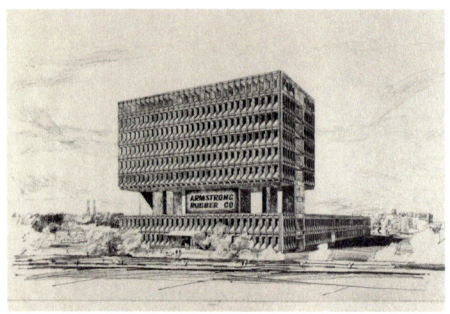

But such bravado exercises in structural acrobatics were not guaranteed to sell tires. Armstrong's investors were aghast when they learned that the building would have no signage. Taking the artistic high ground, Breuer maintained that the building spoke for itself: no sign was needed to attract attention to it. However, Armstrong's investors insisted that the opportunity of attracting drivers' attention at this major highway intersection was not to be missed. Various schemes were put forth by Breuer and his design team to announce Armstrong's presence, such as placing a sign on the building's roof or attaching one to its upper mass. The most surprising one called for inserting an actual billboard proclaiming Armstrong Rubber into the gap between the podium base and the upper floors [10].

It's a solution that raises eyebrows because it is almost an actual billboard, a form that Breuer would have not admitted to admiring in the past but whose attraction he may no longer have been able to resist, as advertising's techniques had penetrated every discipline and aspect of American life by the late 1960s. As the advertising industry knows well, the billboard is an efficient, inexpensive way to sell products. Into the gaps and voids previously kept spatially empty and powerfully abstract by Breuer strode language, expressed vehemently and in the most commercial of ways. Actual words replaced multivalent forms and symbols. This proposal could be considered a capitulation by an aging architect, or it could be the point where Breuer admitted that he liked billboards.

Of course, what it may also have been was a ruse, conceived as a commercial expression so blatant that it had Armstrong officials convinced that attaching signage to the building was inappropriate. The billboard scheme was dropped, of course, but the Armstrong leaders still demanded some form of signage. Breuer naturally returned to his ancillary strategy by proposing what Robert Gatje called a "sign-structure": a freestanding, concrete structure that would bear the Armstrong name. The sign was three stories tall in order to be seen from the highway, which was itself elevated more than a full story above the ground. However, New Haven administrators opposed it. The proposed sign-structure violated city ordinances prohibiting signs along the highway; these ordinances related to a recent expansion of the Bonus Act of 1958. In 1965, Congress passed legislation that became the Highway

Beautification Act, which further restricted signage bordering federally funded interstate highways. In 1968, New Haven officials claimed that the Armstrong sign-structure, if permitted, would encourage "every gas station and trailer park" in the vicinity to erect similarly tall signs, resulting in a Las Vegas–style strip of signs that would undermine the new array of business buildings they were planning for the frontage along I-91, a district called the Long Wharf redevelopment area.[41]

In response, Breuer and his design team proposed a solution that blurred distinctions between typologies in a fascinating way. The simple addition of a door to the sign-structure's base made it possible to categorize it as a shed or building rather than a sign. The base was large enough to house outdoor maintenance equipment, such as a tractor-sized lawnmower. The city planning officer accepted this proposal, concluding that erecting an additional building on the site to advertise Armstrong was preferable to erecting a sign.[42]

The completed sign-structure signified both building and company. The sign-structure itself resembled the building behind it [11]. The wide rectangular opening in the middle of the sign echoed the building's distinguishing gap. The combined company name and logo emblazoned upon the sign in relief lettering was the signifier for the company itself. Although impressive, the sign-structure did not strike the phenomenal notes produced by the Armstrong building itself or the earlier bell banners. Perhaps this was because after language, in the form of the Armstrong name and logo, was employed, form no longer had to be so inventive. Nor was the relationship between building and sign as strong and complex as it had been in earlier projects featuring the pendants, such as at the abbeys or at the Whitney Museum. No spiritual or cultural axis existed here. This was because in New Haven the sign's relationship to the highway intersection naturally took precedence over the relationship to the building. Not just a label for the building, the sign is oriented to the road to sell tires, like a true billboard. With the sign-structure, Breuer produced an actual advertisement for Armstrong.

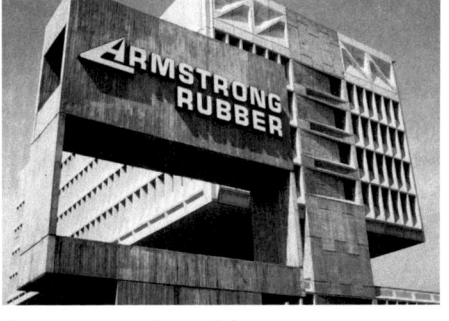

11 Original sign at Armstrong Rubber Company Headquarters

And yet despite their monumentality, the tire headquarters and its sign-structure were unable to fulfill their functions for long. In 1988, the Pirelli tire company absorbed Armstrong Rubber and put its name on the sign-structure. Pirelli, in turn,

12 IKEA, formerly Armstrong Rubber, ca. 2014

had vacated the building by 1999. In 2003, the home furnishings multinational IKEA bought the site and constructed a big-box store adjacent to Breuer's building. IKEA threatened to replace the Breuer building with a parking lot but ultimately demolished just the laboratory wing after encountering preservationist opposition. Preferring changeable rather than permanent signage, IKEA has attached to the empty building various banners advertising different promotional efforts, and it placed an LED board on the sign-structure [12]. Ironically, IKEA has in effect transformed the building into a giant billboard, a solution that might have pleased Armstrong in 1968 but that has dismayed local preservationists. One said of Breuer's building, "We didn't save it for it to become an ugly billboard."[43]

At Armstrong Rubber, the vagaries of capitalism certainly made weak and unsustainable the connection between signifier (the Armstrong sign) and signified (the Armstrong building and company), but this instability also related to a larger crisis of meaning and representation for modernism (a crisis also caused by economic change) that led to the style's perceived collapse in the early 1970s. In his 1974 analysis of late modernist architecture, Manfredo Tafuri talked of "emptied signs" or structures where the weak linkage between signifier and signified resulted in buildings without the meaning inherent in the architecture of the past. For Tafuri, this disconnect also demonstrated the inherent difficulties of delivering meaning through architectural form, especially when language was the medium—a path explored at the end of 1960s, when cultural practices took the linguistic turn mentioned previously.[44]

Modernism versus Postmodernism
Was it possible to reconnect signifier and signified, language and architecture, popular and high culture? While the Armstrong work was being planned in 1968, questions of just this kind were posed by some architects as they again considered the impact on their discipline of popular culture, a problem further complicated at the end of the 1960s by challenges to established politics, society, and culture coming from the anti-Vietnam war protesters and the feminist and civil rights movements, for example. In response to these crises, architecture in the late 1960s split into at least two camps relevant here: one that looked further inside architectural

discourse for inspiration and one that looked outside of it to find inspiration in popular culture. Breuer's work did not fit neatly into either camp, which may be another reason why the architectural discourse of the late twentieth century sidelined him.

Representing the inward-looking gaze of the first camp at the Institute for Architecture and Urban Studies in New York (founded in 1967), Peter Eisenman investigated design formalism and attempted to put it on a sounder theoretical footing in hopes of making architecture an autonomous discipline. In the 1960s, he stepped beyond the symbolism of postwar modernism to consider architecture as a system of linguistic signs—rather than commercial signs—with its own internal order and following the ideas of linguists such as Ferdinand de Saussure.[45] Breuer's formalism did not belong to this camp. Based on personal predilections practiced in a consistent but hardly systematic fashion, Breuer's approach to formalism did not have the rigor or intellectual quality of Eisenman's formalism. And yet Breuer's pendants and sign-structures approached the nebulous threshold, investigated by Eisenman, where forms became signs.

Breuer's strategies had greater affinities with those of the second camp. Robert Venturi and Denise Scott Brown looked for inspiration beyond architecture's internal vocabulary and to popular culture in the form of commercial roadside signage, resulting in the pathbreaking text *Learning from Las Vegas* (1972). In 1968, they investigated the potential of signage in studios taught at Yale University, a campus coincidentally just a mile or so from the Armstrong building in New Haven.[46] In contrast to the postwar cultural elite's ambivalent resistance to advertising, as exemplified by Breuer, Venturi and Scott Brown thought architecture should harness popular culture for its own purposes, as pop artists had already done. They criticized the postwar generation's "slavish formalism," pointing out Paul Rudolph's plastic monumentality as incoherent and impractical in *Learning from Las Vegas*, but they could easily have targeted Breuer, as Hays has suggested.[47]

One tantalizing connection between Breuer and the *Learning from Las Vegas* authors was their gentle mockery of the views of Breuer's supporter Peter Blake. Turning postwar alarm about popular culture on its head, Venturi, Scott Brown, and their coauthor Steven Izenour famously appropriated the photo of the Long Island duckling from Blake's *God's Own Junkyard* for their book. For Blake, the duckling was kitsch, exemplifying everything wrong with popular culture. In contrast, Venturi and Scott Brown were amused by the roadside stand that sold ducks and duck eggs and cleverly used it to critique postwar modernism. They called "ducks" those monumental postwar buildings whose forms symbolized their functions and related characteristics in elaborate but often unadmitted and unclear ways. Although Breuer is never mentioned in *Learning from Las Vegas*, Venturi and Scott Brown may have also been inspired by his architecture. It must be admitted that, in profile, Breuer's entrance canopy at the Whitney Museum bears an uncanny resemblance to a duck.[48]

The methods of Breuer and the *Learning from Las Vegas* authors are similar in another way as well. Venturi and Scott Brown's famous design strategy of signs and sheds resembled Breuer's ancillary strategy. Proposing an alternative to ducks, Venturi and Scott Brown suggested that independent signs like those that fronted buildings along roadside strips in Las Vegas and elsewhere should become the bearers of architectural representation. They could be erected in front of structurally simple, shedlike buildings; these signs could also be attached to sheds [13]. Venturi and Scott Brown's ancillary approach differed from Breuer's approach because it employed lightweight construction to express their anti-monumental stance. But unlike Breuer, Venturi and

13 "Duck vs Decorated Shed," sketch by Robert Venturi and Denise Scott Brown in *Learning from Las Vegas*

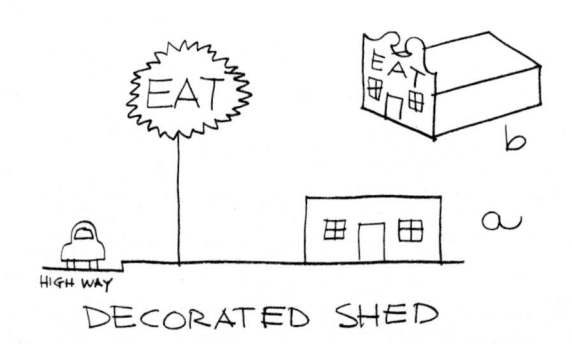

Scott Brown were conscious of their ancillary strategy and able to explain it, an ability characteristic of their highly articulate generation, which moved architectural discourse from vague poetics to defined theories.

It is unlikely that Venturi and Scott Brown consciously modeled their approach directly on Breuer's ancillary strategy. Rather than looking for direct ties between them, one might more profitably think about how the enormous social and economic forces of postwar society pushed them toward finding conceptually similar but materially, aesthetically, and ideologically different solutions. Acknowledged in different ways, the billboard and the highway affected Breuer as powerfully as they did Venturi and Scott Brown. The highway transported each of these architects to that complex intersection at the end of the 1960s where it is often thought that postmodernism accelerated past modernism for a time.

But from the vantage point of the twenty-first century, what happened at that intersection now seems more complicated. The *Learning from Las Vegas* authors did not really overtake Breuer. Performing a jujutsu move, they may instead have appropriated and transformed his methods. And Breuer may have had greater affinities with them than has been thought. Rather than simply exemplifying the duck and sheds schema defined by Venturi and Scott Brown, Breuer's ancillary structures anticipate yet complicate their concept, suggesting that despite the polemical rhetoric of the past, postmodernism from the perspective of the present resembles a dialogue, engagement, or elaboration with modernism, rather than a complete break from it. Breuer's pendants are simultaneously ducks, sheds, and signs, as is evident at Armstrong Rubber.

Formalism persisted and evolved during the postmodernist era. Venturi and Scott Brown decried postwar architecture's "slavish formalism," but adroit formal manipulations of geometric forms became their architecture's hallmark, as is evident in the marble-and-granite geometric panels that mark the entry to their Gordon Wu Hall (Princeton University, 1983). And in just as formalist a fashion, Michael Graves attempted to link postwar modernism and postmodernism together (rather than simply diagramming their rupture) when he copied and rotated the shape of the trapezoid window of Breuer's Whitney Museum for his second scheme for an addition to the museum (1986–87) [2].[49]

Formalism connotes rigidity and a closed system, but Breuer's formalism is more complex than is at first apparent. Mastering form was Breuer's way of engaging with his era's hopes for a New

Monumentality, its search for an enriched expressive vocabulary for modernism, and anxieties about mass and popular culture. With his pendants sited on the thresholds between established institutions and the larger, chaotic world beyond them, Breuer mediated between the forces that shaped his discipline internally and externally, producing an architecture that at times poetically transformed established categories.

1 My thanks to Barry Bergdoll, Jonathan Massey, and Richard S. Kaplan for their comments. My thanks also to the Newhouse Center for the Humanities at Wellesley College for its support in fall 2015.
2 William H. Jordy, "The Formal Image: USA," *Architectural Review* 127 (March 1960): 157–65.
3 Robert Venturi, Denise Scott Brown, and Steven Izenour, *Learning from Las Vegas* (Cambridge, MA: MIT Press, 1972), 138–39; Manfredo Tafuri, "L'Architecture dans le Boudoir: The Language of Criticism and the Criticism of Language," *Oppositions* 3 (1974): 37–62.
4 Clement Greenberg, "Avant-Garde and Kitsch," *Partisan Review* 6, no. 5 (1939): 34–39; Dwight Macdonald, "Masscult and Midcult," *Partisan Review* 27, no. 2 (1960): 203–33.
5 Marcel Breuer, *Sun and Shadow: The Philosophy of an Architect*, edited and with notes by Peter Blake (London: Longmans, Green, 1956), 32.
6 For Blake's work on *Sun and Shadow* and relationship with Breuer, see the memoir by Peter Blake, *No Place Like Utopia: Modern Architecture and the Company We Kept* (New York: Knopf, 1993), 138–42.
7 The formal analysis employed in this article descends from the respected method for art and architectural history of the late nineteenth and twentieth centuries developed by scholars such as Heinrich Wölfflin. Their analysis was based on descriptions of geometry, line, color, space, and other largely visual aspects, an approach subsequently elaborated upon by awareness of the many factors, from economics to gender, that shape form.
8 Matthew Nowicki, "Origins and Trends in Modern Architecture," *Magazine of Art* 44 (November 1951): 273. For new scholarship about form and formalism in postwar architecture, see Miles David Samson, *Hut, Pavilion, Shrine: Architectural Archetypes in Mid-Century Modernism* (London: Routledge, 2016). See also Cammie McAtee's dissertation on form, "The 'Search for Form' in Postwar American Architecture" (Harvard University, 2017, supervised by Neil Levine).
9 Breuer, *Sun and Shadow*, 71.
10 Peter Blake, *God's Own Junkyard: The Planned Deterioration of America's Landscape* (New York: Holt, Rinehart, and Winston, 1964).
11 Breuer, *Sun and Shadow*, 32.
12 Marcel Breuer, untitled poem, c. 1961, in *Marcel Breuer: Buildings and Projects, 1921–1961*, with captions and introduction by Cranston Jones (New York: Praeger, 1962), 11.
13 Vincent Scully, "Doldrums in the Suburbs," *Perspecta* 9–10 (1965): 286.
14 Sigfried Giedion, Josep Lluís Sert, and Fernand Léger, "Nine Points on Monumentality" (1943), reprinted in *Architecture Culture, 1943–1968: A Documentary Anthology*, comp. Joan Ockman with Edward Eigen (New York: Columbia University Graduate School of Architecture, Planning, and Preservation; Rizzoli, 1993), 27–30.
15 Lewis Mumford, "The Sky Line: United Nations Headquarters; Buildings as Symbols," *New Yorker*, November 15, 1947, 102.
16 Lewis Mumford, "The Sky Line: UNESCO House; The Hidden Treasure," *New Yorker*, November 19, 1960, 213.
17 Paul Rudolph, "The Changing Philosophy of Architecture," *Architectural Forum* 101 (July 1954): 120.
18 Ernesto Rogers, "The Drama of the UNESCO Building," *Casabella* (April 1959): viii. The Latin phrase means "under the aspect of eternity" or universally.
19 Victoria M. Young, *Saint John's Abbey Church: Marcel Breuer and the Creation of a Modern Sacred Space* (Minneapolis: University of Minnesota Press, 2014), 77–83.
20 Ibid., 17–27.
21 Hilary Thimmesh, *Marcel Breuer and a Committee of Twelve Plan a Church: A Monastic Memoir* (Collegeville, MN: Order of Saint Benedict; St. John's University Press, 2011), 19.
22 For a contemporary discussion of the Bonus Act, see Blake, *God's Own Junkyard*, 28. See also Catherine Gudis, *Buyways: Billboards, Automobiles, and the American Landscape* (New York: Routledge, 2004), 219–26.
23 Quoted in Thimmesh, *Marcel Breuer and a Committee of Twelve*, 19.
24 Breuer, *Sun and Shadow*, 32.
25 Marcel Breuer, untitled notes about the St. John's Abbey church, dated September 20, 1961, Frames 599–603, Reel 5727, Box 17, Archives of American Art, Smithsonian Institution, Washington, DC.
26 The "permanent monument" by the highway (Interstate 94, known as Route 52 in the 1950s) was never built for financial reasons. Young, *Saint John's Abbey Church*, 172n48. My thanks to Victoria Young for helping me find the set of working drawings for it: "Sample Wall to Be Erected as a Permanent Monument (nos. AA1, AA2,

A12)," dated October 4, 1957, image no. T696-014, Breuer Digital Archive, Syracuse University, Syracuse, NY. There is also correspondence, as well as a sketch about highway signage for the abbey, between Abbot Baldwin Dworschak and Hamilton Smith of Breuer's office, dated June 23, 1956, image nos. 56659-001 and 56660-001, Breuer Digital Archive, Syracuse University.
27 Nowicki, "Origins and Trends in Modern Architecture," 277, 279.
28 My thanks to Marty Smith from UMass Amherst Design and Construction Management for explaining the function of the campus center chimney vent to me.
29 Emily Genauer, "The Whitney's New Mad Scene," *New York Herald Tribune*, September 18, 1966, 33.
30 Peter Blake, "How the Museum Works," *Art in America* 54, no. 5 (1966): 27.
31 The journalist Vance Packard critiqued the methods of the advertising industry in his best-selling book *The Hidden Persuaders* (New York: David McKay, 1957).
32 Breuer said this at the presentation of the design for the Whitney Museum on November 12, 1963. See Marcel Breuer, "Architect's Statement," in *Whitney Museum of American Art*, photographs by Ezra Stoller with new photography by Jeff Goldberg, preface by Maxwell Anderson, introduction by K. Michael Hays (New York: Princeton Architectural Press, 2000), 81.
33 K. Michael Hays, introduction to *Whitney Museum of American Art*, 7.
34 Ibid., 12.
35 For Breuer's collaboration with Eliot Noyes and IBM, see John Harwood, *The Interface: IBM and the Transformation of Corporate Design, 1945–1976* (Minneapolis: University of Minnesota Press, 2011).
36 The Torin T sign proved impermanent, but adaptable. After the Torin Corporation left its building in the 1980s, the Torin T was moved to the campus of Torrington High School, where it was painted red, the school color.
37 Completed by 1965, the intersection of highways I-95, I-91, and Route 34 has a complex history. See Elizabeth Mills Brown, *New Haven: A Guide to Architecture and Urban Design* (New Haven: Yale University Press, 1976), 19–28. In 2016, the completion of a new overpass system altered the former Armstrong Rubber building's relationship to these roads.
38 Robert F. Gatje, *Marcel Breuer: A Memoir* (New York: Monacelli Press, 2000), 210.
39 Ibid., 212.
40 Isabelle Hyman, *Marcel Breuer, Architect: The Career and the Buildings* (New York: Abrams, 2001), 270.
41 Gatje, *Marcel Breuer*, 213–14. It's unclear whether New Haven planners were following their own ordinances or observing those found in the National Highway Beautification Act of 1965, which was being implemented across the nation from the mid-1960s through the early 1970s. See Gudis, *Buyways*, 219–26. For planning at Long Wharf from 1958 to 1965, see New Haven Redevelopment Agency, *Redevelopment Plan for the Long Wharf Redevelopment Area* (New Haven: City of New Haven, 1966).
42 Gatje, *Marcel Breuer*, 213–14.
43 Randall Beach, "New Haven's Loneliest Building Needs Visionary," *New Haven Register*, September 5, 2010. IKEA left the building empty for many years, but permitted a temporary art exhibition in 2017.
44 Tafuri, "L'Architecture dans le Boudoir," 42–45.
45 Eisenman explains the development of his formalism in a 2006 note to the facsimile edition of his Cambridge University doctoral thesis of 1963. Peter Eisenman, *The Formal Basis of Modern Architecture* (Baden: Lars Müller, 2006), 379–81. For a discussion of Eisenman's relationship to Saussure's linguistics, see Rosalind Krauss, "Death of a Hermeneutic Phantom: Materialization of the Sign in the Work of Peter Eisenman," in *Houses of Cards: Critical Essays by Peter Eisenman, Rosalind Krauss, and Manfredo Tafuri* (New York: Oxford University Press, 1987), 166–87.
46 Breuer was also completing a building for Yale at this time: Becton Engineering and Applied Science Center (1967–70).
47 Hays, introduction to *Whitney Museum of American Art*, 12–13.
48 Lampooning Breuer's seriousness, Venturi and Scott Brown later mounted a photo cutout figure of Hiram Powers's sculpture *Greek Slave* (1844) atop the Whitney's entrance canopy in 1976 to advertise the exhibition *200 Years of American Sculpture*. In effect, Breuer's structure became a platform for a billboard. Hays regards this act as a deliberate joke. Hays, introduction to *Whitney Museum of American Art*, 10.
49 Of course, repeating the trapezoid was Graves's attempt to answer those who thought his first proposal for the Whitney completely dismissed Breuer's building. For the history of Graves's addition to the Whitney Museum, see Robert A. M. Stern, David Fishman, and Jacob Tilove, *New York 2000: Architecture and Urbanism between the Bicentennial and the Millennium* (New York: Monacelli Press, 2000), 954–61.

In the early years of Breuer's office in Manhattan, opened in 1946, his commissions were largely for single-family houses in the fast-growing suburbs of the nation's largest city. However, after receiving almost simultaneous commissions in 1953 to provide a plan for St. John's Abbey and University in Minnesota and to partner with the Italian engineer Pier Luigi Nervi and French architect Bernard Zehrfuss on the UNESCO complex in Paris, the practice expanded rapidly, both nationally and internationally. By the early 1960s, Breuer's office was running an international practice, as much involved with networks as with singular designs, and Marcel Breuer & Associates soon had an office in Paris for the vast project of the Flaine ski resort (see French portfolio).

Many US companies, such as IBM, also had an increasingly international presence, and the Torin Corporation of Connecticut, one of Breuer's most loyal clients, was a burgeoning business that would involve Breuer in designs for company buildings in Britain, Germany, Belgium, and Australia, as well as in California and Connecticut, Torin's home base. From the Paris office Breuer and his associates took on a variety of projects, not only in France but also in the Netherlands, where a much-acclaimed department store project, De Bijenkorf (1956)—part of the rebuilding of Rotterdam after its near-total destruction in World War II—was to be followed by the US embassy in The Hague (1959) and the headquarters of the Van Leer Company at Amstelveen (1948). Work in the United States was also increasingly public and corporate, as Breuer turned away from the modest middle-class houses that had been the mainstay of his practice in the 1940s and early 1950s and began accepting only upscale house commissions from much wealthier clients. Just twenty years after his arrival in the United States at the tail end of the Depression, Breuer had a portfolio of school buildings, public libraries, university buildings, factories, and department stores across the country and more than one beachhead elsewhere. In the late 1940s, he even considered accepting a position in Buenos Aires, and an exploratory trip resulted in an innovative project for a small-scale beach restaurant club, El Ariston, at Mar del Plata, Argentina (1948). In the following decade he would be considered for a project that would create a master plan for Bogotá and for draft projects for real estate developments along the Venezuelan coast, none of which came to fruition. In the 1960s and early 1970s the French office prospered, and by the 1970s Breuer's was one of numerous American firms that joined the call for projects in western Asia, with unrealized projects in Iran and Afghanistan.

Throughout the decades, the success of the St. John's project yielded other religious work, from the Annunciation Priory of the Sisters of St. Benedict on the plains outside Bismarck, North Dakota (1955–63) and the engineered bravura of St. Francis de Sales Church at Muskegon, Michigan (1967), to a convent at Baldegg outside Luzerne (1968–72), as well as unbuilt projects for a cathedral in Vermont (1972) and a new parish church outside Rome (1968). The scale of his projects in the United States too became even larger toward the end of his practice, with monumental civic as well as landscape designs for the Third Power Plant and Visitor Center at Grand Coulee Dam in Washington State (1967–75) and the Atlanta Public Library, the last major building Breuer had in the works when he retired from the practice due to illness. If in office buildings Breuer developed a system of precast concrete "egg-crate" façades, adaptable to program and terrain but semantically closely related, he equally developed a sculpturally expressive set of individual designs for institutional and religious buildings that involved equally continuous collaboration with engineers, always in a quest for ever bolder structural forms. By the time he retired in the mid-1970s amid the controversy over New York's Grand Central Terminal, Breuer's work was largely abroad, the economic downturn of the 1970s having made New York City a veritable ghost town for projects by New York architects. His alliance with local real estate had failed, but his international influence was a product of a network of corporations and friendships that spanned the globe.

1 Breuer at IBM La Gaude, France, ca. 1961
2 Third Power Plant, Grand Coulee Dam, Washington State, USA, 1967–75, aerial view
3 Detail of façade
4 Perspective rendering
5 Façade panel drawings, 1968
6 Overall view of the plant
7 St. Francis de Sales Church, Muskegon, Michigan USA, 1964–66, overview of church with annex parish building at left
8 Interior toward chancel
9 Undated perspectival section drawing
10 View of main façade
11 St. Paul's Cathedral (unexecuted), Burlington, Vermont, USA, 1966, perspective rendering
12 Perspective rendering
13 Olgiata Parish Church, Rome, Italy, 1968–70, perspective rendering
14 Floor plan drawing
15 Atlanta Central Public Library, Atlanta, Georgia, USA, 1977–80, section drawing
16 Detail of entrance façade from corner
17 Perspective rendering
18 View of main stair
19 Annunciation Priory of the Sisters of St. Benedict Bismarck, North Dakota, USA, 1958–63, plan
20 Aerial view of complex
21 Bell banner and cloister arcade
22, 24 Construction photographs
23 Ariston Club, Mar del Plata, Argentina, 1948, view of completed building
25 Recreational apartments (unexecuted), Tanaguarena, Venezuela, 1958, perspective rendering
26 El Recreo Urban Center (unexecuted), Caracas Venezuela, 1958–60, detail perspective drawing
27 Recreational apartments, Tanaguarena, perspective rendering
28 El Recreo Urban Center, perspective rendering
29 Proposal for a hotel (unexecuted), Bāmiān, Afghanistan, 1974
30 Proposal for a hotel (unexecuted), Kabul, Afghanistan, 1974
31 Torin Corporation Technical Center, Torrington, Connecticut, USA, 1971, floor plan drawing
32 Torin Corporation Administration Center, Torrington, Connecticut, USA, 1965–66, view from road showing Torin symbol
33 Elevation drawing
34 Torin Corporation, facility at Nivelles, Belgium, 1964–65, precast concrete panel detail drawings
35 Construction photograph of precast panels
36 Torin Corporation, facility at Penrith, NSW, Australia, 1973–76, elevations and section drawing
37 Main façade
38 Torin Corporation European Divisions, factory at Swindon, UK, 1964–71, entrance detail
39 Mundipharma factory and headquarters, Limburg, Germany, 1973–75, elevation drawing
40 Perspective rendering
41 De Bijenkorf department store, Rotterdam, Netherlands, 1956, view of model
42 View of corner toward the Coolsingel
43 United States Embassy, The Hague, Netherlands 1954–58, overall view
44 Van Leer office building, Amstelveen, Netherlands, 1957–58, office interior
45 Aerial view
46 Convent of the Sisters of Divine Providence, Baldegg, Switzerland, 1967–72, site plan drawing
47 Aerial view of convent
48 Interior of chapel
49 View of kitchen courtyard
50 Staehelin House, Feldmeilen, Switzerland, 1956–59, floor plan drawing
51, 52 Exterior detail
53 Breuer at conference table, 1960s
54 Marcel Breuer & Associates group portrait, 1978. Left to right: Hamilton Smith, Mario Jossa, Herbert Beckhard, Tician Papachristou, Breuer, Robert F. Gatje
55 Breuer at drafting table, 1970s

1

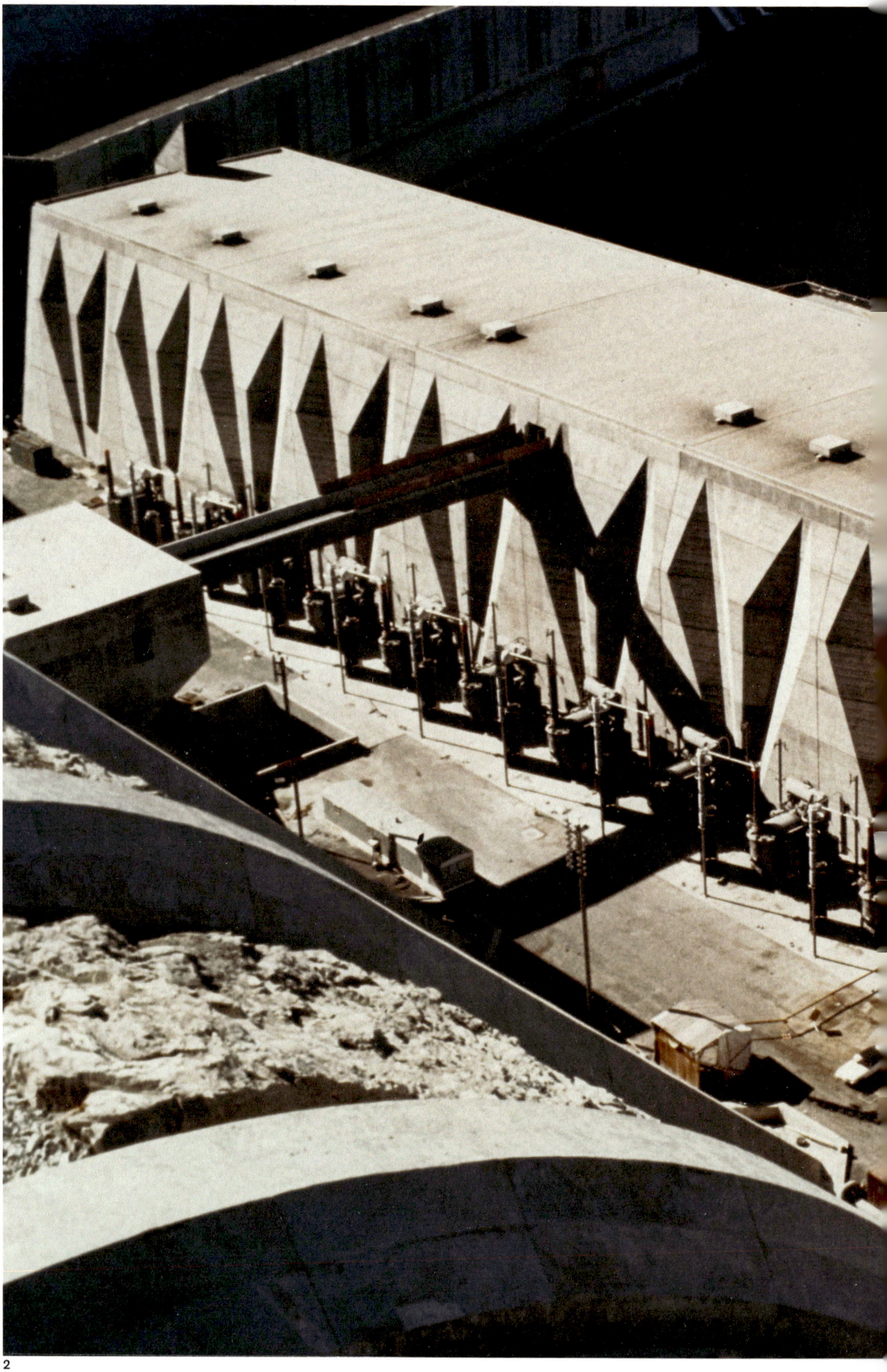

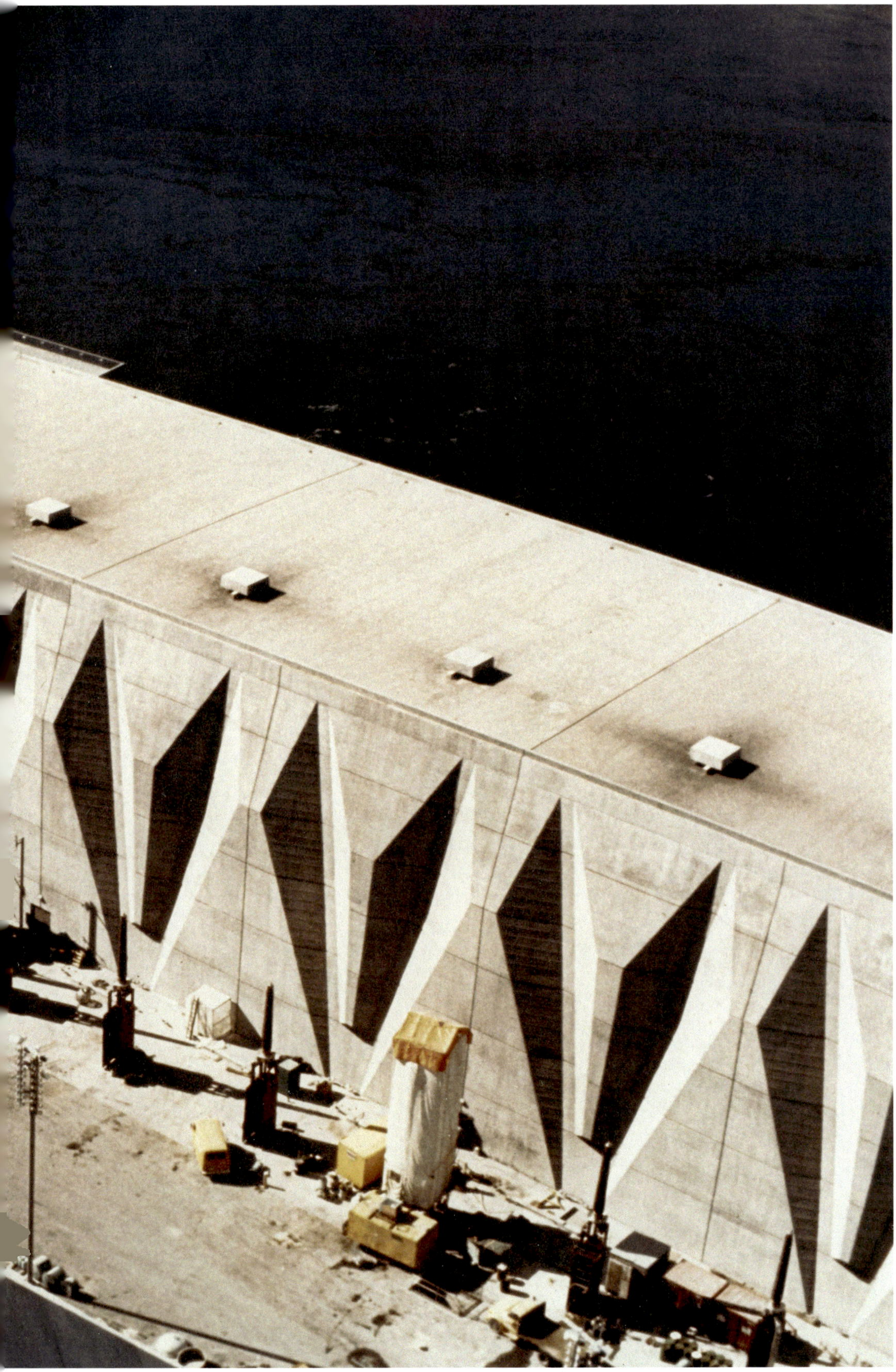

3

4

323

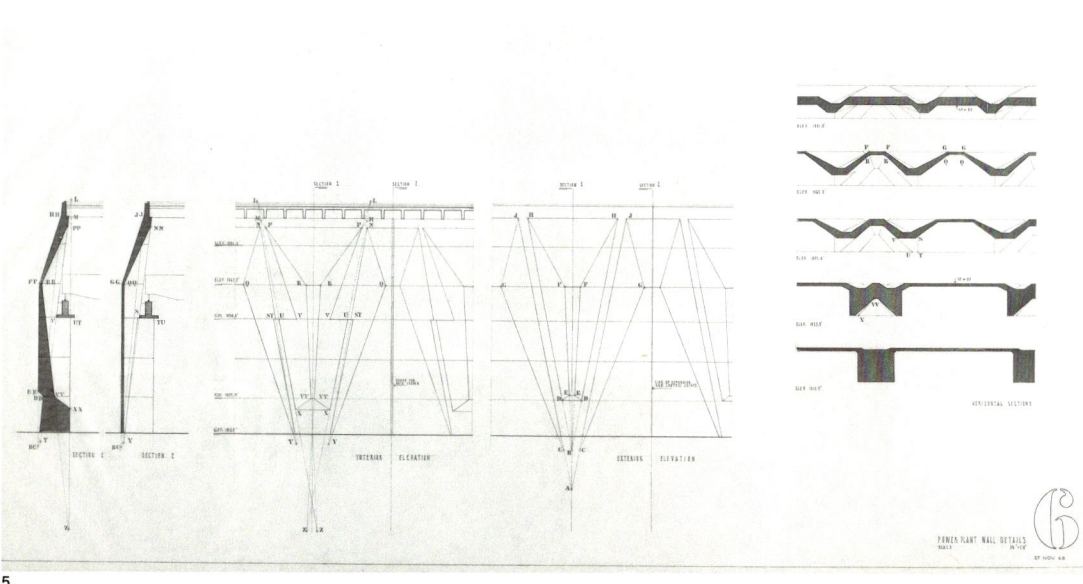

5

6

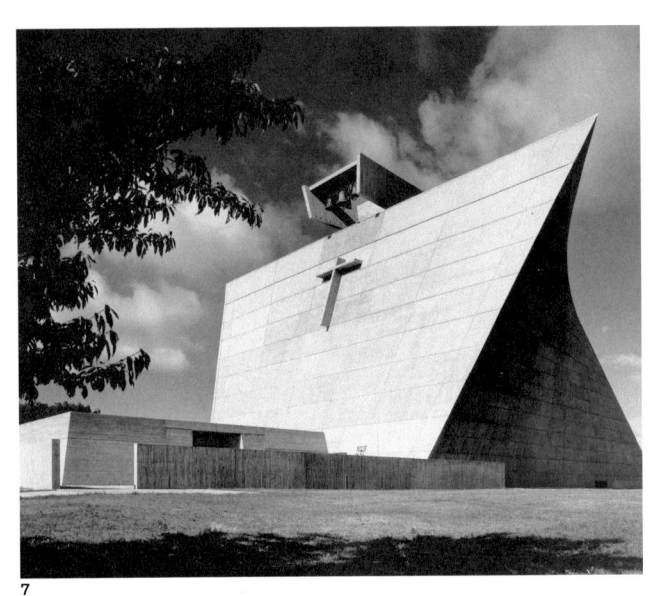

VI GLOBAL BREUER

7

8

9

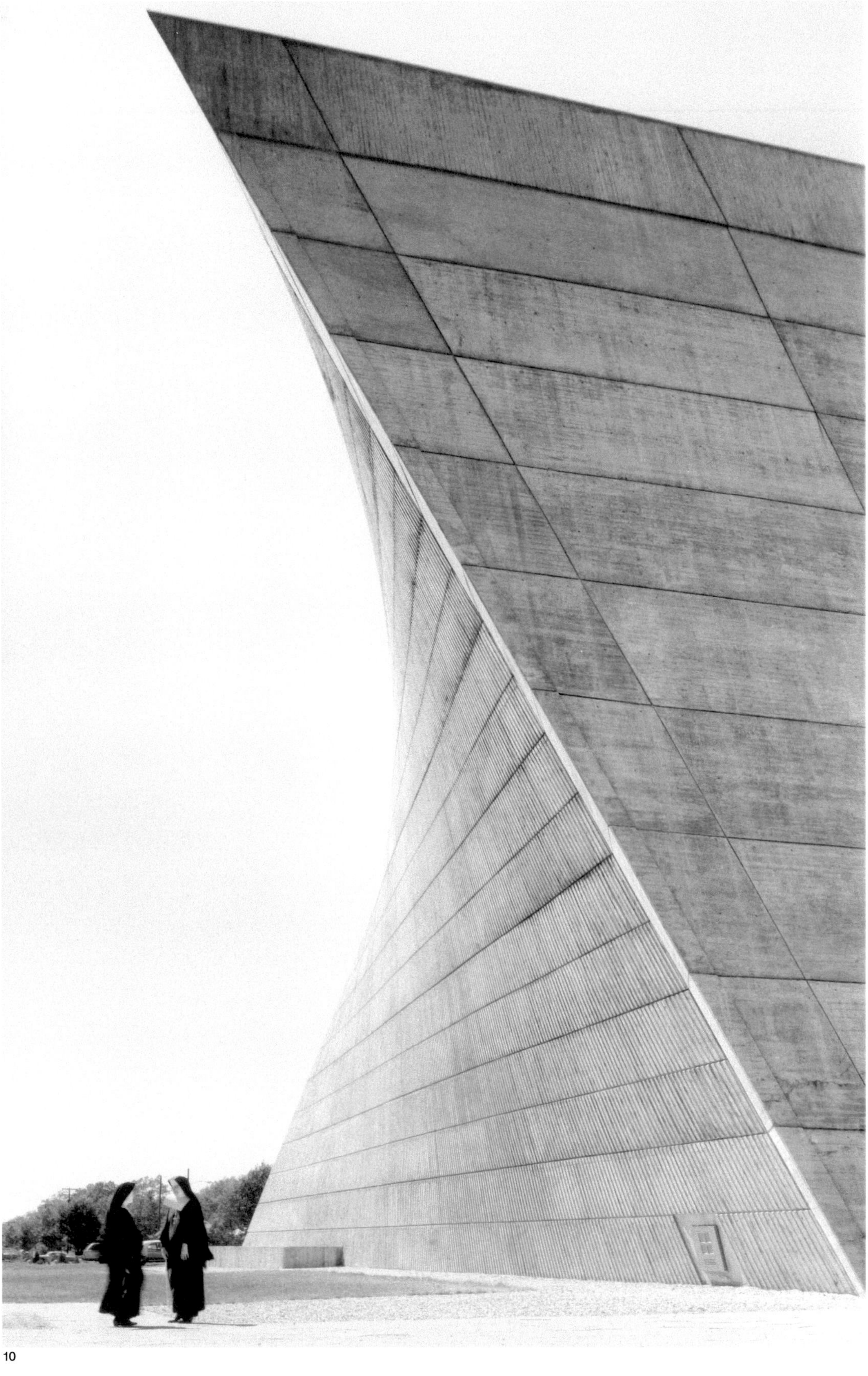

326   VI   GLOBAL BREUER

11

12

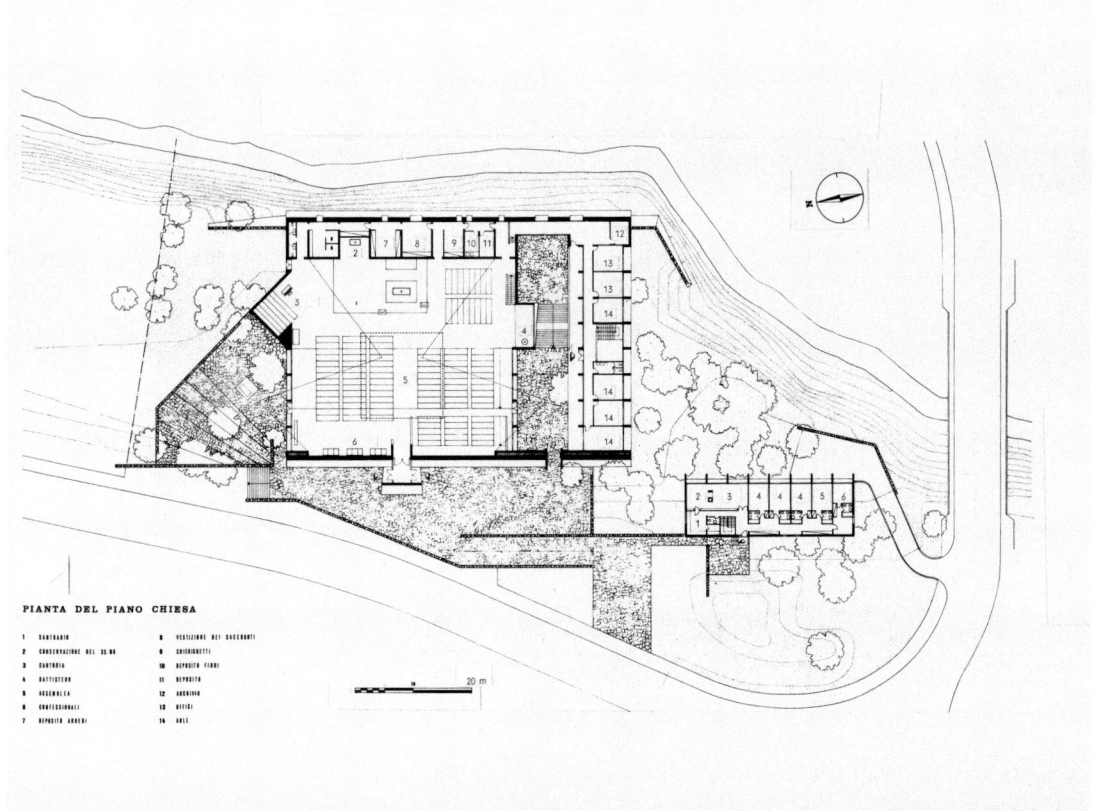

13

14

PIANTA DEL PIANO CHIESA

1 SANTUARIO
2 CONSERVAZIONE DEL SS MO
3 SAGRESTIA
4 BATTISTERO
5 ASSEMBLEA
6 CONFESSIONALI
7 DEPOSITO ARREDI
8 VESTIZIONE DEI SACERDOTI
9 CHIERICHETTI
10 DEPOSITO FIORI
11 DEPOSITO
12 ARCHIVIO
13 UFFICI
14 AULE

328 VI GLOBAL BREUER

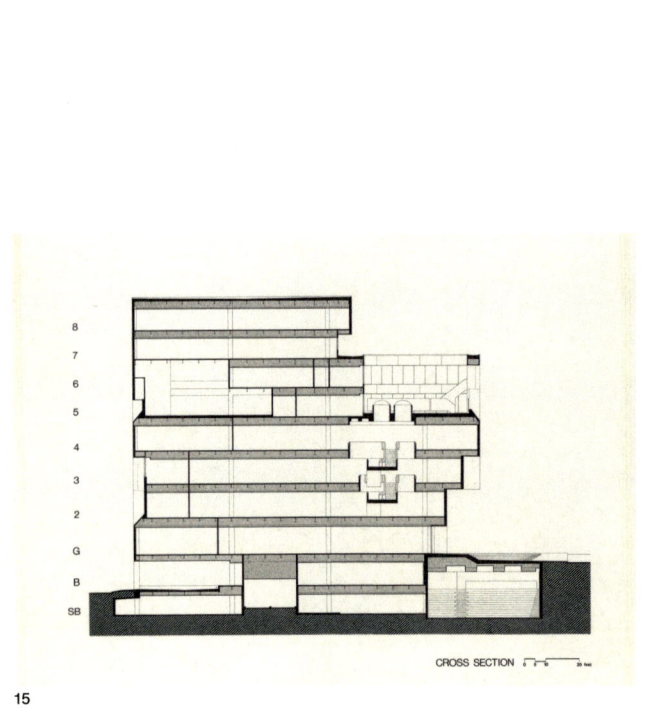

15

16

17

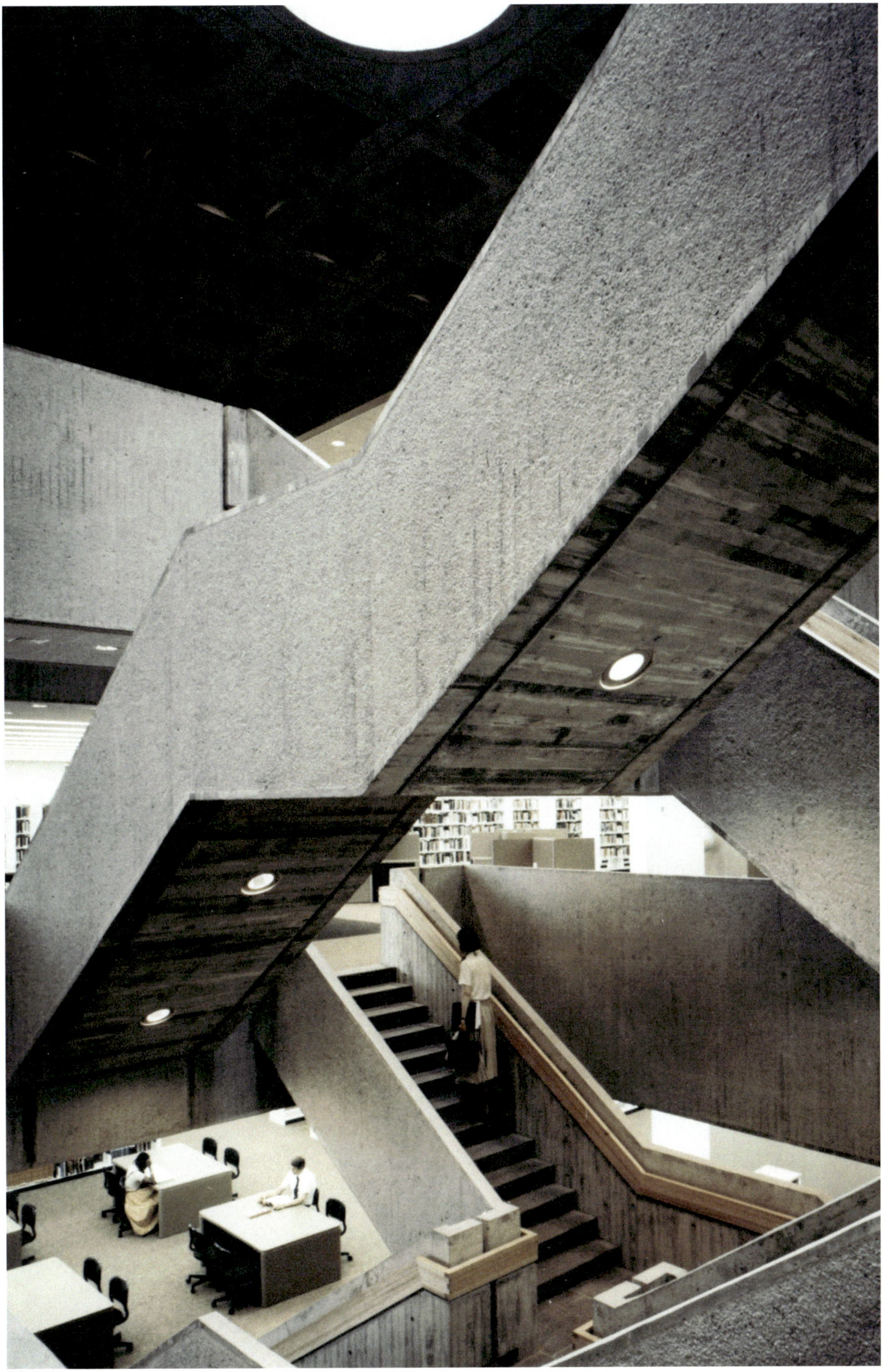

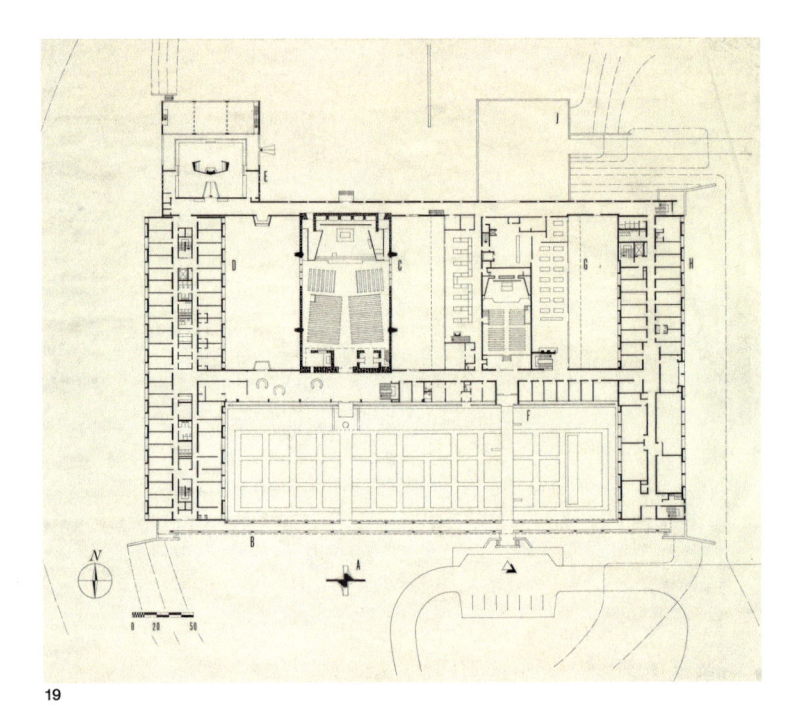

VI GLOBAL BREUER

19

20

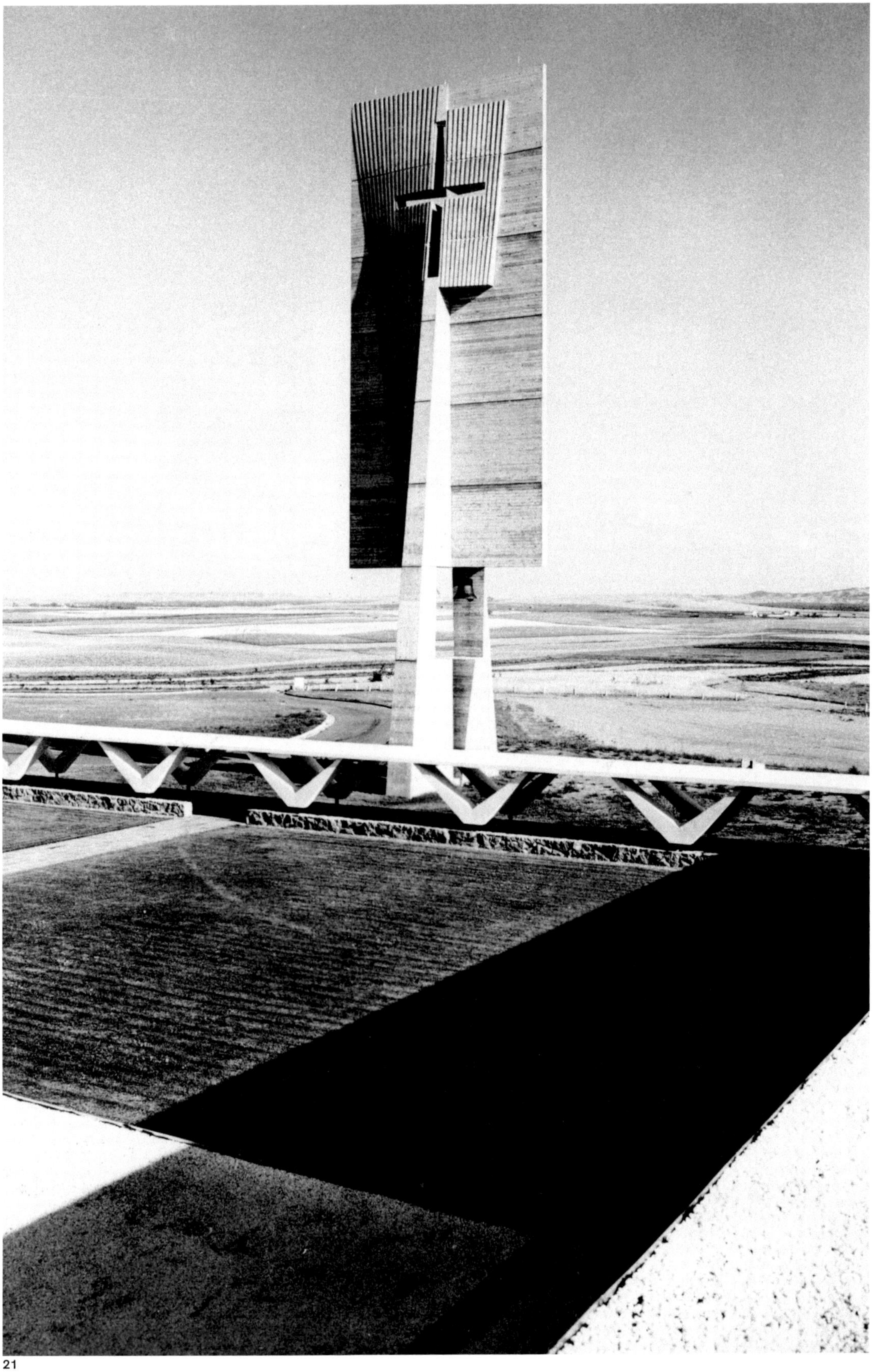

332　　　VI　GLOBAL BREUER

22

23

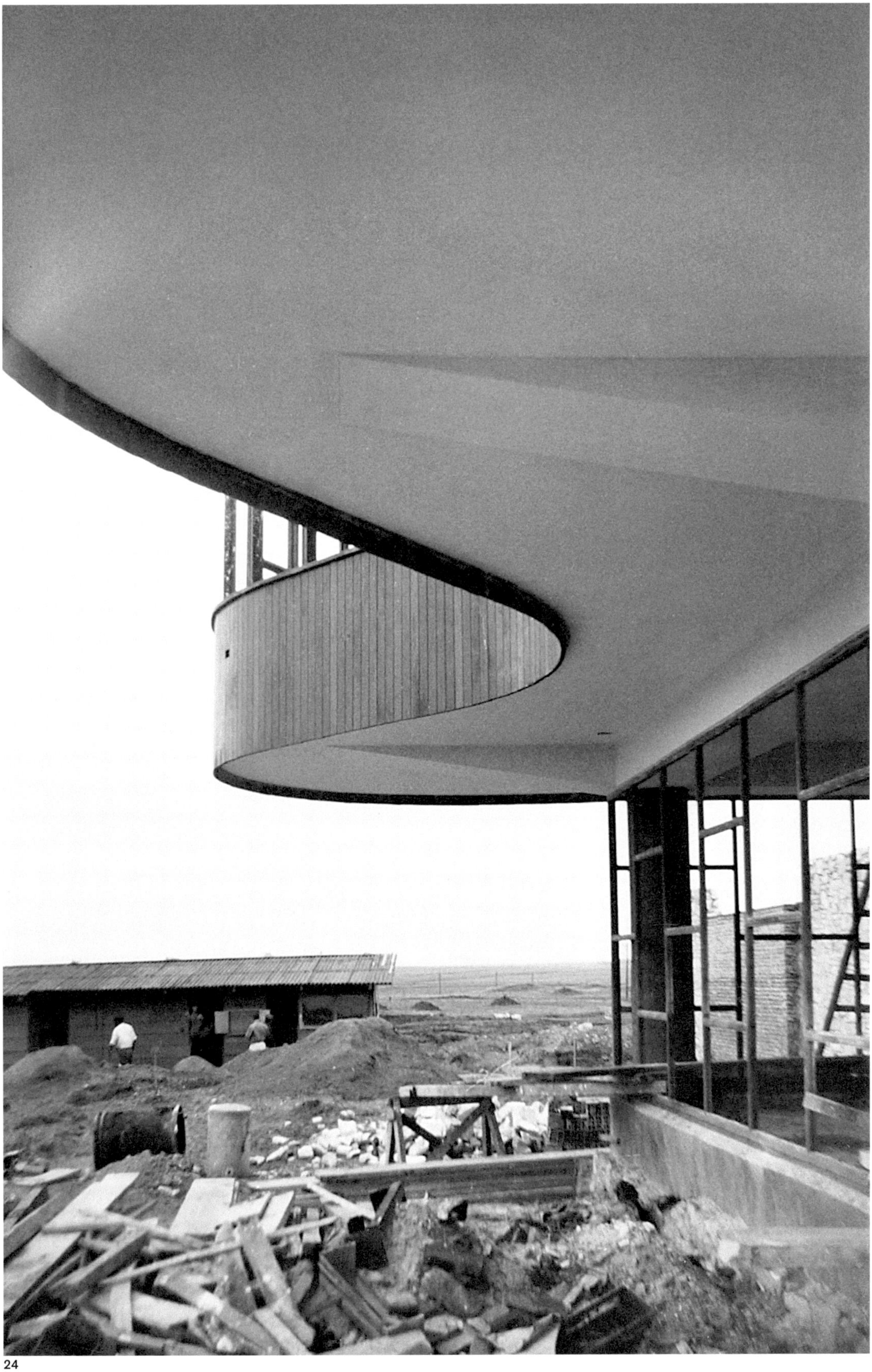

334 VI GLOBAL BREUER

25

26

27

28

29

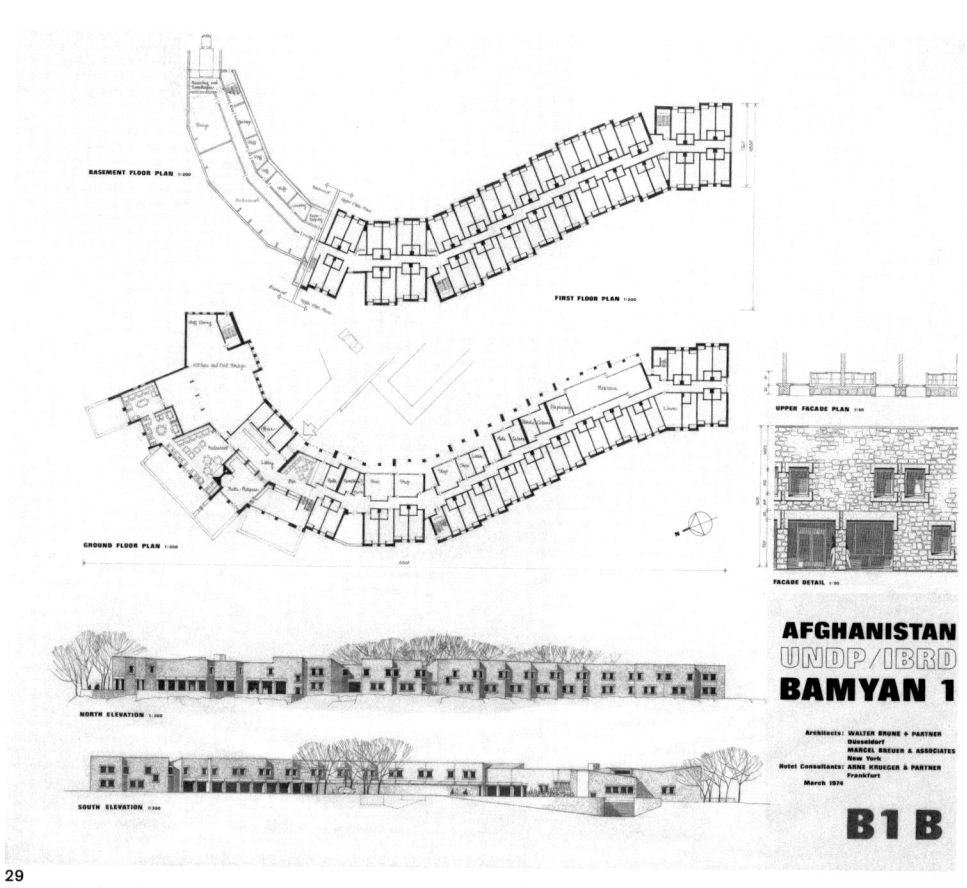

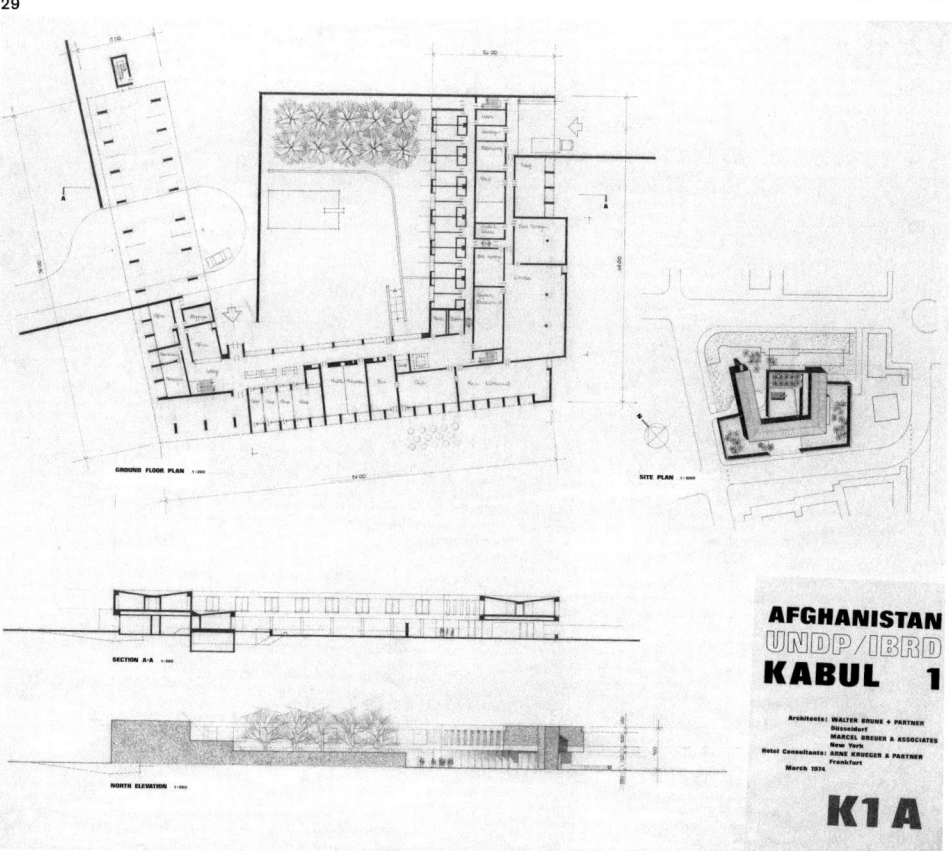

30

336 VI GLOBAL BREUER

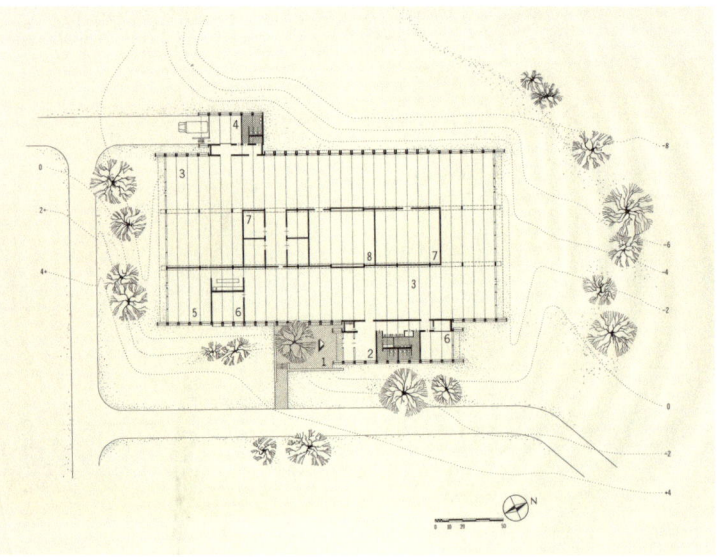

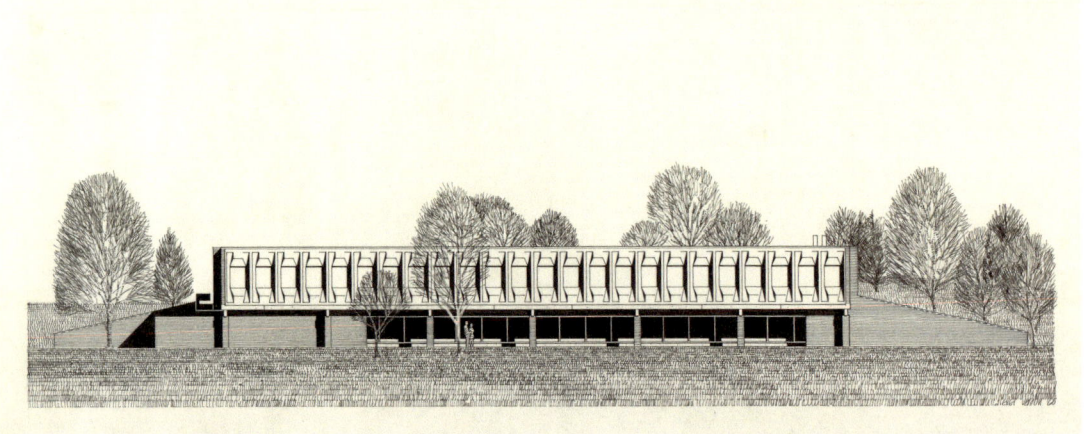

31

32

33

34

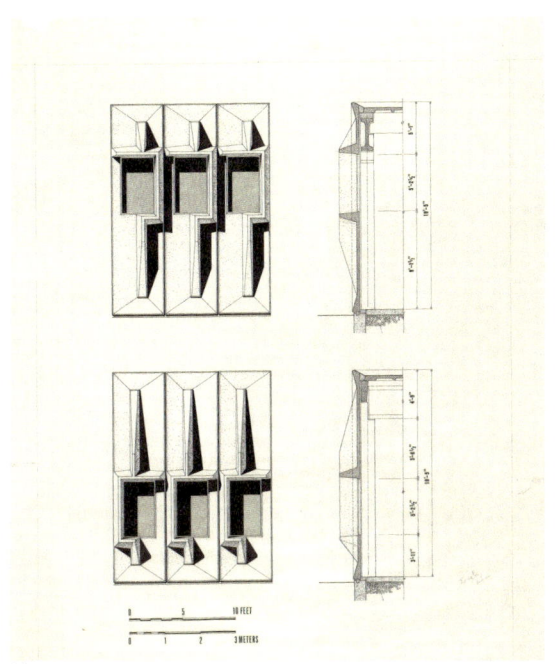

35

36

37

38

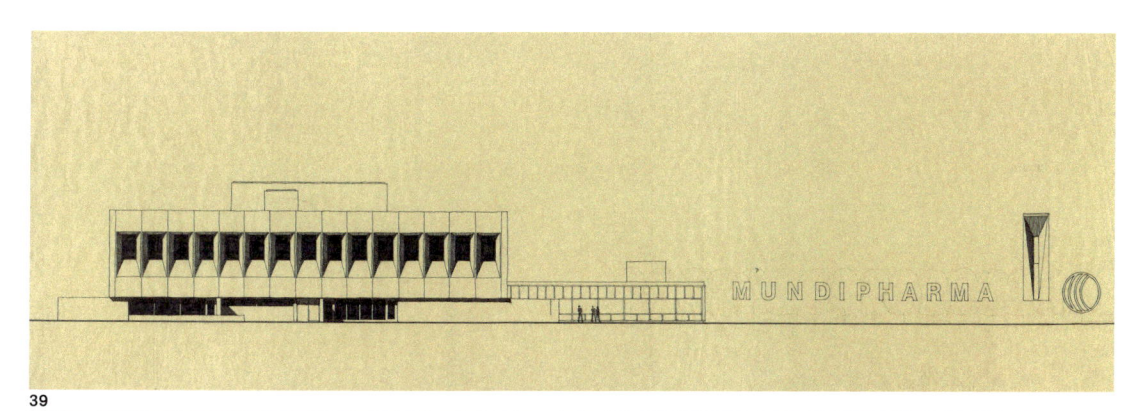

39

40

340 VI GLOBAL BREUER

41

42

43

44

45

46

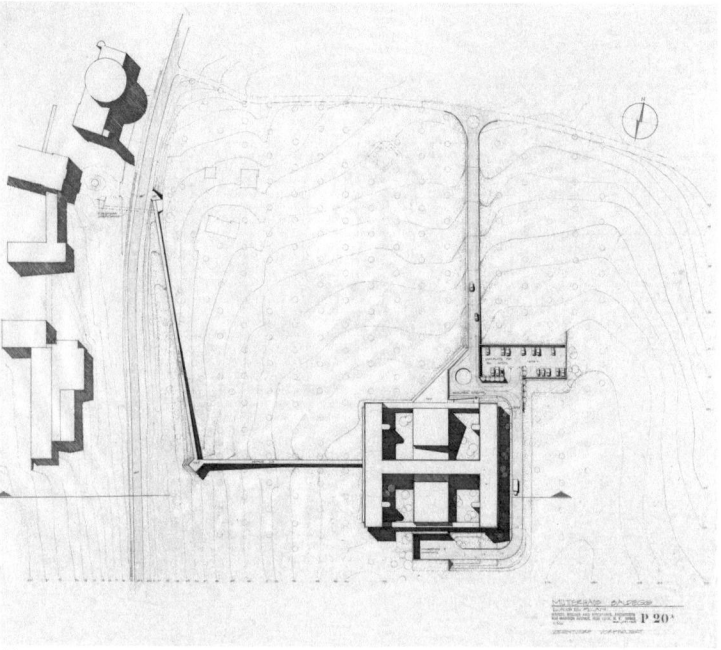

47

48

49

VI GLOBAL BREUER

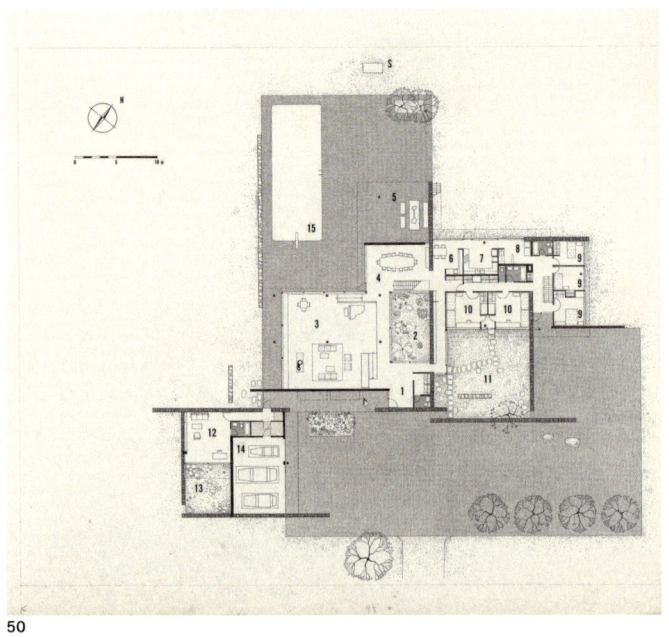

50

51

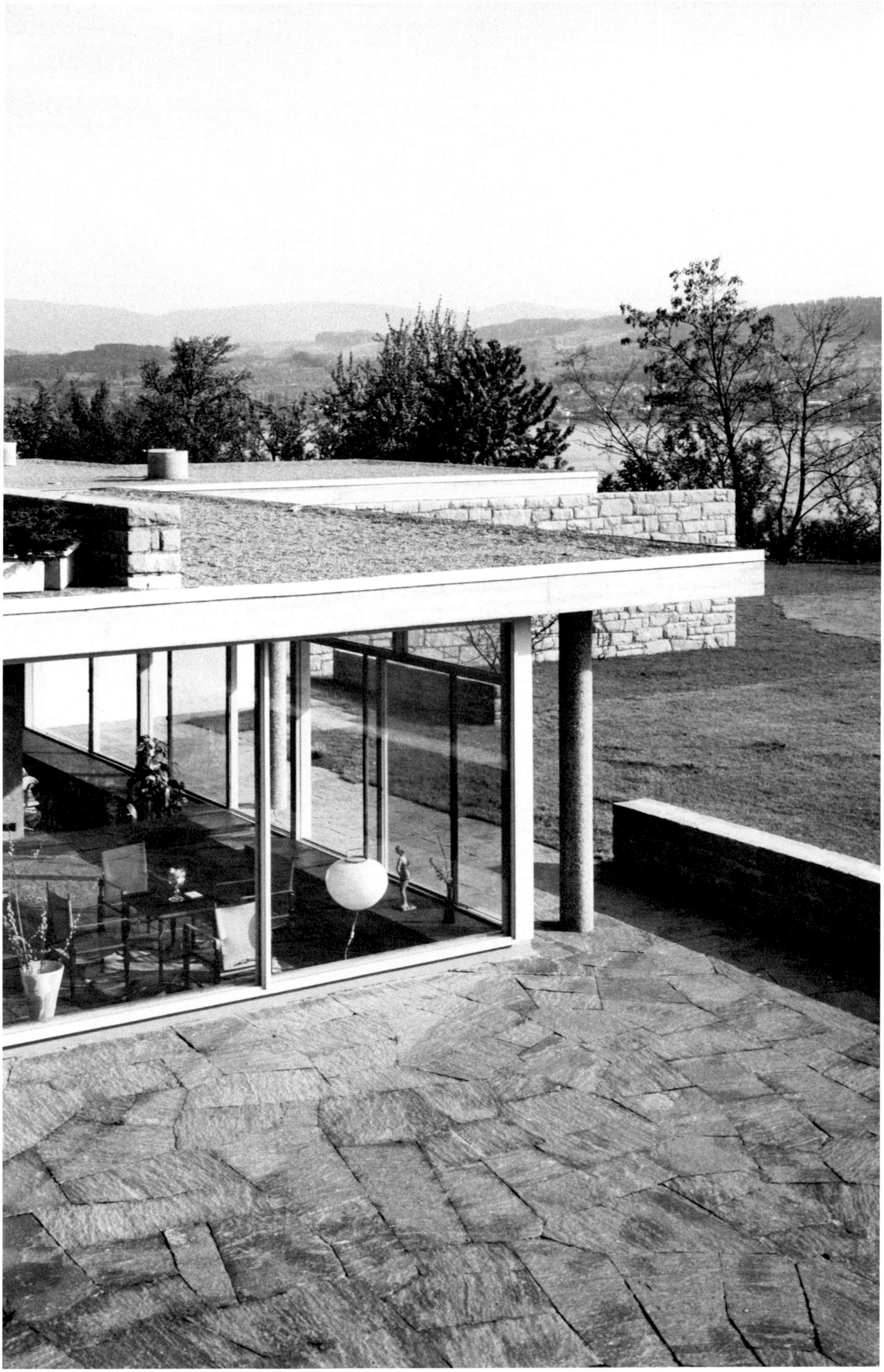

VI GLOBAL BREUER

53

54

55

1 Martin Bush, typed letter to Marcel Breuer, July 22, 1963

13210

401 Main Library

July 22, 1963

Mr. Marcel Lajos Breuer
201 East 57th Street
New York 22, New York

Dear Mr. Breuer:

    Syracuse University is currently engaged in a large undertaking aimed at making the papers and manuscripts of prominent architects available to teachers, scholars, and practitioners of learned professions. Moreover, in the University's School of Architecture interest is keen in the history, development and current trends in the field. To promote, guide, and assist this interest the University is endeavoring to acquire and preserve the official correspondence and files of creative individuals such as you.

    This is especially true because of the impact your work has had during a most remarkable career. We hope, therefore, to establish a Marcel Lajos Breuer Manuscript Collection at Syracuse University in recognition of your outstanding past and future achievements. This material would be a boon to our School of Architecture and to historians and the University and scholarly world as well. Scholars for generations to come will be able to gain a better understanding and fresh appreciation of your career in all of its various aspects.

    The type of material we are looking for includes letters and general correspondence, any records or files of a non-personal nature, designs and sketches, and manuscripts of articles, essays, or books (whether published or unpublished). At Syracuse your papers would be housed in a large air-conditioned area especially arranged for this purpose. In addition, they would be processed and then permanently shelved. Naturally, the use of material placed here would be governed by an agreement made between the Library and the donor. We hope this request will sufficiently interest you in our work and that we shall hear from you in the near future.

                                              Sincerely,

                                              Martin H. Bush
                                              Deputy Administrator
                                              of Manuscripts

MHB:db

Postface:
The Marcel Breuer Digital Archive at Syracuse University

Lucy Mulroney

On Monday, July 22, 1963, Martin H. Bush, deputy administrator of manuscripts, sat down at his desk in the Carnegie Library at Syracuse University to draft a few outgoing letters. He began each piece of correspondence with the same explanatory greeting:

> Syracuse University is currently engaged in a large undertaking aimed at making the papers and manuscripts of prominent architects available to teachers, scholars, and practitioners of learned professions. Moreover, in the University's School of Architecture interest is keen in the history, development, and current trends in the field. To promote, guide, and assist this interest the University is endeavoring to acquire and preserve the official correspondence and files of creative individuals such as you.[1]

On this day, the creative individuals to whom Bush was writing were none other than the modern architecture masters Richard Neutra, Pietro Belluschi, and Marcel Breuer.

Breuer, the youngest of the three architects, was the first to respond to Bush's letter. He said he was very honored by Syracuse's interest and would offer all the cooperation possible. However, he warned that "the task will not be simple. There will have to be a selection made from thousands of drawings and thousands of letters, dependent upon how far you wish to go in your collection. My own time will be most limited as I am fully occupied with my practice, and with my many travels."[2]

Bush's letter reached Neutra while he was traveling in Europe on a lecture tour. Neutra lamented, "Working for individual clients of flesh and blood is a much more gratifying, revealing, and informative experience then [sic] writing and speaking to listeners whom one does not really learn to know through their applause.... I am honestly puzzled myself about what so many people are interested in or why they should listen or read of my ideas."[3] Neutra seemed equally puzzled by the university's interest in his papers. Nonetheless, this modest modernist reflected upon the potential value of his "written, sometimes sketchy material." Noting that he was in failing health, Neutra saw the potential of partnering with Syracuse, since he felt unable to process and coordinate his archive himself.

Bush's letter also reached Belluschi while he was abroad—away on vacation in Italy. Belluschi replied that he was intrigued by the offer to establish his papers at Syracuse but couldn't quite fathom how it would be accomplished from a practical point of view. He wrote, "The prospect of having to go through a 40-year record covering perhaps hundreds of thousands of items, all badly in need of orderly selection, scattered coast to coast ... fills me with dismay."[4] Belluschi explained that he was in the midst of one of the most active periods of his career. There wasn't a minute to spare. Moreover, he had an enormous amount of material. His projects numbered in the thousands, and most of his nonpersonal correspondence, he thought, "would be burdensome and irrelevant."[5]

Despite their reservations, all three men began sending materials to Syracuse University within a few years, and their correspondence with Bush hints at the ambitious acquisitions program in which the Syracuse University Library was engaged in the 1960s. Earlier in July 1963, Bush had written very similar letters to the radical artist William Gropper, photojournalist Margaret Bourke-White, and pioneer conceptual artist Marcel Duchamp to ask if each of these creative individuals would be willing to establish their papers at Syracuse. Like Neutra, Belluschi, and Breuer, Gropper and Bourke-White donated their papers to the university. Duchamp wrote back from Spain explaining that, "as a rule, I tear up all my correspondence and keep nothing.... I am therefore very sorry to be unable to help you."[6] Before the end of the decade, Syracuse would solicit the papers of Constantinos Apostolou Doxiadis, Louis Kahn, Morris Lapidus, William Lescaze, Robert Moses, George Nelson, Walter Dorwin Teague, and Minoru Yamasaki. In the summer of 1964, Bush wrote to Chancellor William Tolley, who led the university from 1942 to 1969, saying, "Recently Marcel Breuer gave me the first quantity of his papers, drawings, and miscellaneous material for a Marcel Breuer Manuscript Collection at Syracuse University. Since Mr. Breuer is regarded as an architect's architect, we now have the makings of one of the nation's finest architecture collections. With the exception of Gropius and Mies Van Der Rohe, most other noted American architects have agreed to give Syracuse their material."[7]

Syracuse University's acquisitions program developed in the context of the exponential growth of the university as a result of the GI Bill and Chancellor Tolley's desire to transform Syracuse into a nationally significant research institution. Between 1945 and 1949, enrollment rose from 5,716 to 19,698, and the university's research collections grew in lockstep with the expanding student body.[8] During the 1950s and 1960s, the library's holdings increased by 280 percent, a rare books department was established, and the art collection grew to approximately 12,000 objects.[9] The timing of the university's acquisitions efforts was also significant. It was a crucial moment in the race for twentieth-century manuscript collections. Two of the most important institutions for contemporary archives had only recently been established. The Archives of American Art, then in Detroit but later incorporated into the Smithsonian Institution, was founded in 1954, and the Harry Ransom Center, then called the Humanities Research Center, was founded at the University of Texas in 1957. Thus, the acquisition of the archives of living artists and designers posed rich opportunities—especially for institutions that did not have large endowments to purchase collections.

In his study of the discourses of twentieth-century art and visual culture, *What Was Contemporary Art?*, Richard Meyer explains that typically it was only after their death, when artists could no longer produce new works, change styles, or issue new statements, that art historians could begin scrutinizing, cataloging, and assessing the significance of their work.[10] However, what we witness in Bush's letter-writing campaign is a librarian forging the canon of modernism and historicizing individual practitioners in the present tense. Early on Bush decided not to curate Breuer's work. He wrote to Breuer, "We do not intend to be selective. Because of the importance of your work, we want to preserve everything related to your life and your career. We would rather have your material shipped to Syracuse University than see any of it discarded."[11] Once the materials arrived at Syracuse, the staff at the library worked amicably with Breuer's firm, providing reference services, helping facilitate an appraisal of the donation, and timing the press release on the acquisition of Breuer's archive to coincide with the opening of the Whitney Museum in order to achieve maximum publicity. Although Breuer was careful to send only noncurrent files to Syracuse (his first donation in 1964 included no records after 1953), there was nonetheless a steady stream of requests from the firm to send back tubes of drawings and plans that were needed for current projects. For the first several years the archive functioned more like off-site storage than a research collection. However, from the start Bush had shared a vision with D. Kenneth Sargent, dean of the School of Architecture, to copy the entire collection "so that scholars today and those in the years to come will be able to use everything in connection with [Breuer's] architectural work."[12]

Living artists make living archives, and Breuer's archive was indeed a living entity, with tubes of drawings coming and going. It was also unfinished, and the university was keen to see it become the comprehensive record of Breuer's work. In an internal memorandum from 1967, Bush explained,

> Since Marcel Breuer still is a very active architect, he has told me on many occasions that he will only add to his collection when he finds that he no longer needs material for a certain year. With luck, he might bring his collection up to, let us say, 1957, but this is a decision he is not ready to make.
>
> His commitment to Syracuse University does include all of his material, but [it] will not be turned over to us until his death or upon his retirement. There are no restrictions on the collection other than the usual copyright and the courtesy of asking to reprint a photograph.[13]

In 1971, Syracuse was still encouraging Breuer to transfer his files from 1953 to 1957 to the archives.[14] Finally, in December 1972, Breuer sent eighty-one tubes of drawings, and he instructed the library to inquire annually about additional donations.

Paradoxically, it was after Breuer's death that the archiving of his work became complicated. Upon Breuer's death in 1981, his widow, Constance Breuer, donated a significant amount of material to the Archives of American Art, much of it directly related to the materials already held by Syracuse. Then, in 1987, the year after Gatje Papachristou Smith (the successor firm to Marcel Breuer Associates) dissolved, ninety-seven linear feet of additional material was added to the collection. In the 1990s, Breuer's prior partners Hamilton Smith and Herbert Beckhard sent Breuer-related materials still in their possession to Syracuse to be added to the archive. The last significant donation came in 1994, when Constance Breuer transferred to Syracuse a cache of previously unknown sketches, furniture drawings, and partnership agreements.[15]

During these years, the library gave researchers access to the Marcel Breuer Papers, although the collection was only partially processed. Efforts were made to preserve the collection and make it accessible. In the 1990s, the blueprints and drawings were transferred to acid-free tubes, which were stacked horizontally in a honeycomb configuration designed by the library's head of preservation, Peter Verheyen.[16] Collection-level bibliographic records and an electronic finding aid were created for the archive, enabling scholars to discover it, though not necessarily showing them how they might navigate it, since archival series and subseries had not yet been formally established. An initial print finding aid created from the donation accession inventories and descriptions by visiting scholars served as the most detailed guide for the collection until 2009, when the university garnered the first of two National Endowment for the Humanities preservation and access grants to process and digitize the Breuer holdings. The proposal developed by Sean Quimby, then director of the library's Special Collections Research Center, encompassed both the full processing of Breuer's papers and the development of a multi-institutional digital edition of Breuer's corpus, today known as the Marcel Breuer Digital Archive (MBDA). This online repository fulfills Martin Bush's original vision of a comprehensive, accessible collection of Breuer's work.

The principle of *respect des fonds*, or principle of maintaining original order, is fundamental to the final form that an archive takes. According to the standards set forth by the Society of American Archivists, "The records created, assembled, accumulated, and/or maintained and used by an organization or individual must be kept together ... in their original order, if such order exists or has been maintained. They ought not to be mixed or combined with the records of another individual or corporate body."[17] Upholding this standard can be particularly challenging in the processing of design collections such as Breuer's. Not only do the size and diverse materials of the collection pose challenges, but conceptually the collection is hybrid. It comprises both the personal papers of an individual as well as the legal, financial, and administrative records of that person's offices and partnerships. As Quimby writes in the grant proposal, "the Syracuse Breuer collection documents each step of the design process for many of the architect's projects: proposals, initial sketches, client correspondence, meeting minutes, presentation drawings, site plans and surveys, working drawings, specifications, contracts, construction photographs, brochures, publicity and more."[18]

    The development of the Marcel Breuer Digital Archive was an ambitious seven-year project. The first phase included processing the physical archive, conducting a census of Breuer materials held by other institutions in the United States and Europe, and developing a web portal for the first half of Breuer's career (1901–52). The second phase of the project enhanced portal functionality and added material from the latter half of Breuer's career (1953–81).

Archivist Michael Dermody arranged and rehoused the physical collection, which totaled 684 linear feet of material, and created a detailed finding aid. Following standards for processing architectural records, Dermody organized the Marcel Breuer Papers into seven primary series: personal papers, professional papers, faculty papers, sketchbooks, furniture records, and project records.[19] The conceptual framework of the digital archive differs from that of the physical collection. The physical collection is organized around Breuer as the first level of organization and then is subdivided by series that correspond to particular activities, with the design files organized by project, since this was how Breuer and his firm originally maintained their records.[20] By contrast, the digital archive is more modular and takes the digital object as its basic level of organization.[21] Each digital object is accompanied by detailed metadata derived from the original archival material, and each object is associated with a project so that researchers can browse and search the archive in a fluid but meaningful way.[22] The goal of the project was to capture the full complexity of Breuer's practice, as well as to provide highly detailed object-level metadata, including medium (blueprint, correspondence, photograph) and view type (elevation, aerial, axonometric), for scholars to use in navigating the digital archive.

The architecture historian Teresa Harris, whose essay appears in this volume, was the project coordinator from 2009 to 2015, and she worked in tandem with Dermody, making selections for digitization as he processed the physical archive. Harris conducted a census of Breuer materials held at the Houghton Library, Harvard University; Harvard Art Museums/Busch-Reisinger Museum; Francis Loeb Library, Harvard Graduate School of Design; Archives of American Art, Smithsonian Institution; Stiftung Bauhaus Dessau; the Archive of the Institute for the History and Theory of Architecture; the Archive of the Vitra Design Museum; the University of East Anglia Library; and the Whitney Museum of American Art. Each of these institutions contributed materials to the digital archive, making the final product a nearly exhaustive representation of Breuer's creative process and professional network.[23]

In his letter of support for the initial grant proposal, Barry Bergdoll wrote that "the Breuer project could open not only a new generation of Breuer scholarship, it could open a whole new set of questions about the profile and issues of American modernism from the 1930s through the late 1970s."[24] As this volume attests, Breuer remains a vital subject of critical inquiry. And one wonders how Breuer would have reacted to the digital archive's exposition of his practice. Perhaps he would have been amazed by the end result of a task that (as he rightly forewarned in 1963) would not be simple.

As Bergdoll anticipates in his letter, the impact of the Breuer archive extends beyond scholarship on Breuer and even beyond the history of architecture and design. Among the questions and issues that the Breuer project opens are those about the historical consequences of how institutions have collected, and continue to collect, the material of the present. Syracuse University Libraries' ambitious efforts to acquire the papers of living architects, artists, and designers during the 1960s reveals how the work of archivists and curators not only influences humanities scholarship but is itself a form of interdisciplinary and collaborative scholarship. Martin Bush was not simply amassing material for the university; he was articulating the formation of a canon—historicizing the contemporary and discerning who and what was worthy of collecting. The subsequent archival decisions about how to organize, describe, digitize, preserve, and provide access to the archival record determine what will be available to scholars in the future, as well as how materials dispersed across the globe might be linked. As new technologies enable us to broaden access to the archival record, they also allow for discontinuous and multivalent relationships to come to light, thereby opening up new approaches to thinking about how history is written.[25] The Marcel Breuer Digital Archive at the Syracuse University Libraries offers a dynamic interplay of the contemporary and historical. The archive, to borrow from Alexander Nagel and Christopher Wood, is "a strange kind of event whose relation to time is plural."[26]

1 Martin Bush, typed letter to Richard Neutra, July 22, 1963; Martin Bush, typed letter to Marcel Breuer, July 22, 1963; Martin Bush, typed letter to Pietro Belluschi, July 22, 1963, all in Administrative Files, Special Collections Research Center, Syracuse University Libraries.
2 Marcel Breuer, letter to Martin Bush, July 25, 1963, Administrative Files, Special Collections Research Center, Syracuse University Libraries.
3 Richard Neutra, letter to Martin Bush, August 15, 1963, Administrative Files, Special Collections Research Center, Syracuse University Libraries.
4 Pietro Belluschi, letter to Martin Bush, August 12, 1963, Administrative Files, Special Collections Research Center, Syracuse University Libraries.
5 Belluschi corresponded with Bush about his papers for several months, and since many of his projects were still active, he found it difficult to select what to send to Syracuse. In November 1963, Belluschi wrote to Bush, "In a few months I hope to retire from MIT and feel that at that time I shall be able to devote the necessary energies to

the task of collecting that which may be of interest to future historians." He did not retire until 1965. Pietro Belluschi, letter to Martin Bush, November 4, 1963, Administrative Files, Special Collections Research Center, Syracuse University Libraries.

6 Marcel Duchamp, handwritten letter to Martin Bush, August 4, 1963, Administrative Files, Special Collections Research Center, Syracuse University Libraries.

7 Martin Bush, typed memorandum to Chancellor William Tolley, June 26, 1964, Administrative Files, Special Collections Research Center, Syracuse University Libraries.

8 According to Meg Mason, university archivist, "The resulting 'GI Bulge' called for more housing and classrooms. Temporary buildings sprang up around campus and in surrounding areas. New academic programs were developed and social rules were changed." Meg Mason, *Our Doors Opened Wide*, exhibition brochure, 2016, Special Collections Research Center, Syracuse University Libraries.

9 William Freeman Galpin, John Robert Greene, and Karrie A. Baron, *Syracuse University: The Tolley Years, 1942–1969* (Syracuse, NY: Syracuse University Press, 1996), 62–63, 83, 174.

10 Richard Meyer, *What Was Contemporary Art?* (Cambridge, MA: MIT Press, 2013), 2.

11 Martin Bush, typed letter to Marcel Breuer, March 11, 1964, Administrative Files, Special Collections Research Center, Syracuse University Libraries.

12 Martin Bush, typed letter to Marcel Breuer, October 18, 1963, Administrative Files, Special Collections Research Center, Syracuse University Libraries.

13 Martin Bush, typed memorandum to Howard Applegate, May 2, 1967, Administrative Files, Special Collections Research Center, Syracuse University Libraries.

14 Philip Mooney, typed letter to Marcel Breuer, April 8, 1971, Administrative Files, Special Collections Research Center, Syracuse University Libraries.

15 In Constance Breuer's possession were also some photographs, audiotapes, and correspondence, which were donated to the Archives of American Art. With the assistance of the scholar Isabelle Hyman, she determined which materials fit best with those already held by each institution. While the original donation came without restrictions, there were concerns about companies making knockoff furniture from the drawings, so a restriction was placed on that material.

16 Today the blueprints and drawings are stored in this same manner in the library's high-density temperature-controlled storage facility. Verheyen published the results of this project in *Book and Paper Group Annual* (Washington, DC: American Institute for Conservation of Historic and Artistic Works, 2003).

17 *Describing Archives: A Content Standard*, 2nd ed. (Chicago: Society of American Archivists, 2013), accessed online at https://www2.archivists.org/standards/DACS.

18 Sean Quimby, "Marcel Breuer, Architect: Life and Work, 1922–1955," National Endowment for the Humanities Preservation and Access Humanities Collections and Resources Grant Proposal, 5, Administrative Files, Special Collections Research Center, Syracuse University Libraries.

19 Marcel Breuer Papers Finding Aid, Special Collections Research Center, Syracuse University Libraries, accessed online at https://library.syr.edu/digital/guides/b/breuer_m.htm. As Waverly Lowell and Tawny Ryan Nelb explain, "The universe of design records includes personal and family papers; personal papers such as faculty papers, creative writings, lectures and patents; business records such as administrative and marketing materials; and project records including reports, correspondence, drawings, photographs, models, videotapes, and electronic records." Waverly B. Lowell and Tawny Ryan Nelb, *Architectural Records: Managing Design and Construction Records* (Chicago: Society of American Archivists, 2006), xi.

20 The identification of Breuer's projects follows Isabelle Hyman, *Marcel Breuer, Architect: The Career and the Buildings* (New York: Harry N. Abrams, 2001).

21 The object types are derived from Lowell and Nelb's description of the types of records that are produced during design and construction projects. Lowell and Nelb, "Types of Project Records," *Architectural Records*, 37–68.

22 The original plan was to organize the MBDA around projects, not objects. However, the number of objects associated with a project could exceed five hundred (and the objects themselves could be multipart, for example, a multipage letter with an enclosed brochure). Therefore, projects were determined to be too unwieldy to serve as the basic unit of organization for the digital archive. Since the object types outlined in Lowell and Nelb's work relate specifically to design projects but not to other types of records found in the archive, such as personal papers, faculty papers, and office records, the MBDA treats those subseries as projects.

23 In January 2015, Teresa Harris accepted the position of curator of Avery Classics at the Avery Architectural and Fine Arts Library at Columbia University. The historian and archivist Sebastian Modrow completed the census of materials from the second half of Breuer's career and coordinated the project through to its completion in 2016.

24 Barry Bergdoll, letter to Sean Quimby, July 30, 2008, reproduced in Sean Quimby, "Marcel Breuer, Architect: Life and Work, 1922–1955," appendix 7.7, 54, National Endowment for the Humanities Preservation and Access Humanities Collections and Resources Grant Proposal, Administrative Files, Special Collections Research Center, Syracuse University Libraries.

25 Critical assessments of the assumptions that underlie the writing of history might be productively put into dialogue with archival practices and the potential of digital archives to make scholars rethink these paradigms. As Keith Moxey writes, "the colonial project, with

which the Western idea of history coincides, is coterminous with modernism.... Art history cannot easily abandon its investment in an idea of time embedded in a concept of history structured around a Hegelian narrative that leads from antiquity, through the Renaissance, and on to modernity. There is little space in this scheme for other forms of temporality. As a modernist enterprise, art history is inextricably linked to a notion of teleology and is therefore irreconcilable with an idea of heterochrony (many times existing at the same time)." Keith Moxey, *Visual Time: The Image in History* (Durham: Duke University Press, 2013), 2.

26 Alexander Nagel and Christopher S. Wood, *Anachronic Renaissance* (New York: Zone Books, 2010), 9, quoted in Meyer, *What Was Contemporary Art?*, 17.

Acknowledgments

The idea for this book emerged toward the end of a stimulating semester-long course co-taught by the editors at the Syracuse University School of Architecture. The course was an experiment in which students worked together to produce an exhibition and brochure, their ideas having been critiqued by a group of invited outside scholars and joined in as well by Syracuse architecture faculty and librarians. Our first thanks go to all those who participated in these discussions—in particular contributors Lucia Allais, John Harwood, and Teresa M. Harris and students Hilary Barlow, Patrick Clare, Aimee Hultquist, Marcus Johnson, Douglas Kahl, Nilus Klingel, Kristopher Menos, Paloma Riego del Mar, Melissa Santana, Scott Schwartzwalder, Michael Silberman, Simon Taveras Jr., and Daley Wilson. Mark Robbins, then dean of the School of Architecture, had conceived the idea for a course, invited us to co-teach it, and provided support as the idea of a workshop and exhibition planning became part of the pedagogical approach. Faculty members Jon Lott and Brett Snyder designed the exhibition and its catalog, which helped us see Breuer's drawings and photographs with new clarity.

One impetus for the course was the work happening in parallel at Syracuse University Libraries to create the Marcel Breuer Digital Archive (MBDA), now an invaluable online resource; a full list of those involved in the project can be found there. Sean Quimby conceptualized the digitization project, secured National Endowment for the Humanities funding to create the digital archive, and invited us to join the advisory committee. Teresa M. Harris managed the project, saw it through to completion, and generously shared the deep knowledge of the collection that she formed along the way. Lucy Mulroney has stewarded the MBDA project in its later stages and shares here her insights into the constitution of the architectural holdings of the Syracuse University Libraries. Michael Dermody and Nicolette Dobrowolski provided research support.

Barry Bergdoll had begun research in the Breuer papers in the Syracuse library many years earlier and is indebted to staff members, some now retired, including Katherine Manwaring, Mark F. Weiner, Carolyn A. Davis, Peter Verheyen, and David Boda. Patricia Waddy and Mark Linder were frequent hosts and interlocutors over the years.

The authors who contributed to the volume generously shared their insights with us and with one another, as did Robert Gatje, whose firsthand knowledge proved invaluable to some of our authors. Columbia University student Megan Anne Kinkaid provided research assistance with the copious illustration program in its early stages, and Michael Abrahamson at the University of Michigan heroically completed that work, wrangling authors and working with staff at several repositories to secure image files and publication permissions. Maureen Creamer Bemko copyedited text with clarity and care.

Lars Müller embraced this project and helped us orchestrate the relation between text and image, resulting in a handsome layout designed by Martina Mullis.

The research, illustration program, and publication of the book have been generously supported by the Graham Foundation for Advanced Studies in the Visual Arts, which awarded the project a production and presentation grant. We are also immensely grateful for the financial support and trust of Elise Jaffe + Jeffrey Brown, and of Lauren Pack and Rob Beyer, which greatly improved the quality of the publication. At the University of Michigan A. Alfred Taubman College of Architecture and Urban Planning, Linda Mills helped us manage the project budget, in concert with colleagues at Storefront for Art and Architecture.

We thank all of these colleagues and collaborators who have patiently retained their faith in a project that has developed over a decade from start to finish, and we thank them especially for their intellectual contributions in generating and publishing new perspectives on Breuer's work.

—Barry Bergdoll and Jonathan Massey

Biographies

Barry Bergdoll is Meyer Schapiro Professor of Art History in the Department of Art History and Archaeology at Columbia University and curator in the Department of Architecture and Design at the Museum of Modern Art, New York, where from 2007 to 2013 he served as Philip Johnson Chief Curator of Architecture and Design.

Jonathan Massey is Professor and Dean at the Taubman College of Architecture and Urban Planning at the University of Michigan. The author of *Crystal and Arabesque: Claude Bragdon, Ornament, and Modern Architecture* (2009), Massey is also a member of the Aggregate Architectural History Collaborative, and coeditor of its book, *Governing by Design: Architecture, Economy, and Politics in the 20th Century* (2012).

Lucia Allais is Assistant Professor in the History and Theory of Architecture at Princeton University. She is a member of the Aggregate Architectural History Collaborative and an editor of Grey Room.

Kenny Cupers is Associate Professor of History and Theory of Architecture and Urbanism at the University of Basel. He is the author of *The Social Project: Housing Postwar France* (2014) and editor of *Use Matters: An Alternative History of Architecture* (2013).

Teresa M. Harris is Curator of Avery Classics at the Avery Architectural & Fine Arts Library, Columbia University. She served as project coordinator of the Marcel Breuer Digital Archive for the Special Collections Research Center at Syracuse University Libraries.

John Harwood is Associate Professor of Architecture at the Daniels Faculty of Architecture, Landscape, and Design at the University of Toronto. He is the author of *The Interface: IBM and the Transformation of Corporate Design, 1945–1976* (2011), a member of the Aggregate Architectural History Collaborative, and an editor of Grey Room.

Laura Martínez de Gueren͂u is Assistant Professor of History and Theory of Architecture at IE University. She is co-author of *Mies van der Rohe: Barcelona 1929* (2017) and editor of *Rafael Moneo: Remarks on 21 Works* (2010).

Lucy Mulroney is Senior Director of the Special Collections Research Center at Syracuse University Libraries. Her book *Andy Warhol, Publisher* is forthcoming from the University of Chicago Press.

Guy Nordenson is a structural engineer and Professor of Structural Engineering and Architecture at Princeton University. He is the author of *Seven Structural Engineers: The Felix Candela Lectures in Structural Engineering* (2008) and a collection of essays, *Patterns and Structure* (2010).

Timothy M. Rohan is Associate Professor in History of Art & Architecture at the University of Massachusetts, Amherst. His book, *The Architecture of Paul Rudolph* (2014), is the first monograph about one of the most important modernist architects of the mid and late twentieth-century. He has also edited *Reassessing Rudolph* (2017), a volume of essays about the architect by different scholars. His latest research concerns modernist interiors.

Index

Page numbers appearing in italics refer to photographs and illustrative matter.

Adams, Fred, 195, 308
advertising, 295, 297, 302–304, 307, 308–315, 317n48
Afghanistan, 318, *335*
Anderson, Lawrence, 188
Annunciation Priory of the Sisters of St. Benedict (Bismarck, ND), 236, *305*–*306*, 318, *330–331*
anthropomorphism, 296–297, 301, 305, 307
Aquitaine resort (France), 252, *270–271*
architectonic, 121, 138
architects, consultants vs., 84–90
The Architects' Collaborative (TAC), 15, 87
Architects' Journal, 156, 164, 172
architectural authorship
   agency and, 14, 83
   "author function," 109–110
   bending and folding as determination of, 97–99, 109–110
   de-authoring of form and, 95
   disputes and rights, 36, 83, 97, 110, 112
   Foucault on authorship, 83
   nature of, 7
   postwar notions of, 15, 83, 84
   See also under specific project
Architectural Forum, 241
architectural history, questions central to, 7, 14, 16
Architectural Record (magazine), 53
Architecture without Rules (Masello), 12
Archives of American Art (Wash., DC), 11, 352, 354, 356n15
Argan, Giulio Carlo, 113n32
Ariston Club (Argentina), 44, 169, 318, *332–333*
Armstrong Rubber Company (New Haven, CT)
   ancillary strategy for, 293, 308–312
   commissioning of, 117, 309
   cultural contexts, 312–313
   design for, *117*–121, 126, 236, 293
   photographs, *117, 118, 140, 141, 310, 311, 312*
Arp, Hans, 233
Arretche, Louis, 288
Art in America (magazine), 307
artwork, 64, 111, 115n80, 121, 233, 236, 299, 300, 351
Arup, Ove, 124
Associated Universities Incorporated (AUI), 185, 187
Atlanta Public Library, 318, *328–329*
Atomic Energy Commission (AEC), 186–188

Backström & Reinus Gröndel, *88,* 89
balloon frame, 41–43, 44
BAMBOOS housing, *36–37*
banners, defined, 139n31, 236, 293
Banque Lambert (Brussels), 129–130
Barets, Jean, 282–285, *283*
Barnes, Edward Larrabee, 57
Bauer, Herman, 47
Bauhaus (Dessau), 35, 36–37, 156, 229
Bauhaus (magazine), 35
Bauhaus (Weimar), 9, 14, 16, *34,* 35, 173
Bauhaus-Archiv (Berlin), 11
"Bauhaus film," *34,* 35
Bauwelt competition, 158–159
Bayer, Herbert, 39
Becker, Marion, 156–157
Beckhard, Herbert, 12, 130, *346,* 352
Beginnings of Architecture (Giedion), 58
Begrisch, Frank, 241
Begrisch, Jane, 241
Bell Telephone Laboratories, *190–191*
Belluschi, Pietro, 349, 350, 355n5
bending, as design operation, 96–100, 109–110, 115n75
Bergdoll, Barry, 355
"Berkeley Box," 191–195
BERU (Bureau d'études et de réalisations urbaines), 276–277, 282

Biedermeier period (Germany), 161
Bier, Justus, 173
"Big Education," 140, 223, 225–228
Bigeleisen, Jacob, 187–189, 195
"Big Science," 140, 185–186, 189, 198, 199, 200n12, 240–241
billboards and signage. *See* advertising
Bitter, Karl, 233
Black Mountain College (Asheville, NC), 229
Blake, Peter J., 58, 173, 174, 241, 295, 297, 307, 313–314
Bloom, Harold, 132–133
BNZ. *See* Breuer, Marcel; Nervi, Pier Luigi; Zehrfuss, Bernard
Boissonnas, Éric, 252
Bonus Act of 1958 (Highway Beautification Act), 303, 310–311, 317n41
Boslett, A., 47
Bourke-White, Margaret, 350
Brazier, Bernis E., 191, 193
Breuer, Constance, 11, 60, 352, 356n15
Breuer, Marcel
   arrival in USA, 38, 41
   death of, 8, 202, 352
   early career, 7
   first marriage, 39
   interpretive approaches to, 14
   interviews with, 39, 42, 133, 139n31
   lectures and speeches of, 40, 54, 55–56, 137, 157, 164
   photographs of, *20, 65, 83, 203, 292, 319, 346–347*
   religion and, 48, 133, 176
   residences, 12, 41, 42–43, 122, 202
   resurgence of, 7–17
   retirement of, 318
   self-promotion and, 177
   shift from residential to institutional work, 9–10, 13, 43–45, 121–122, 318
   teaching, 7, 41, 202, 229
   See also Marcel Breuer & Associates (New York City); Marcel Breuer Digital Archive (MBDA) (Syracuse University Libraries); *Marcel Breuer Papers* (Syracuse University Libraries); Walter Gropius and Marcel Breuer, Architects (Cambridge, MA)
Bristol Center Office Building (Syracuse, NY), 131, 140, *151*
Broad Museum (Los Angeles), 11
Bronx Community College, 245–249, *246, 248*
Brookhaven National Laboratory (Long Island, N.Y.), 16, 183–195, *189,* 196, 197, 198, 200n12, 201n30
brutalism, 12, 16, 37–38, 201n45, 294, 299
Building Trades Exhibition (1936), 155, 171
Bush, Martin H., *348,* 349, 351, 352, 353, 355
Bush-Brown, Albert, 188
Byrne, Barry, 46

Calder, Alexander, 64, 233, 297, 299
Camp Upton, 185–187. *See also* Brookhaven National Laboratory (Long Island, N.Y.)
Camus, Raymond, 283
Candela, Félix, 132, 202
Can Our Cities Survive? (Sert), 173, 175
cantilevers, symbolism and, 41, 97, 296
Carreras, Guillermo, 276
Cement and Concrete Association, 155, 156
Cercler, Eric, 276
"Cesca" chair, 7–8
chair design, *34,* 35–37, 87, 97–99, *98*
Chamberlain Cottage (Weyland, MA), *42*
chiaroscuro, structure and, 121, 123–124, 127–131, 133, 134, 137–138, 240
Chicago steel frame, 44
chimneys, *296,* 297, 299
Chronopoulos, Themis, 245
churches, 318. *See also specific project*

CIAM (Congres Internationaux d'Architecture Moderne)
    Functional City, 174, 175
    Gropius and, 112n15
    growth of, 112n12, 113n22
    heart of the city conference, 174
    UNESCO project, 84–87, 99
    urban design and, 157, 159–160, 164, 167, 171–172, 173, 174–175, 177–178
Cincinnati Modern Art Society, 173
Civic and Commercial Center (Colombia), *177*
Civic Center of the Future, 89, 174, 177
cladding, 38, 118–121, 137, 202, 239, 299
Cleveland Trust Company, 140, *150*
cloverleaf plan, 156, 158, 164, 168–*169*, 170
CNIT (Puteaux, F), 45, 55
Coates, Wells, 179n42
COFEBA (Compagnie Française d'Engineering Barets), 282–283
Cohen, Aaron, *246*
collective housing, 159–160, 252, 274. See also ZUP Sainte-Croix (Bayonne, F)
competitions, *157*–158, 158–159, 160, *164, 166*, 174.
    See also *specific competition*
concrete panel systems. See *specific project*
consultants, architects vs., 84–90
consumerism, 176, 302–304, 308–312.
    See also advertising
Convent of the Sisters of Divine Providence (Baldegg), *342–343*
copyright, 36, 83, 97, 110, 112
Costa, Lúcio, 81, 91–96, 114n40
Crease, Robert P., 186, 200n10
Crofton Ganes Pavilion (UK), *39*

Daily Mail, 170
Darroquy, Bernard, 287–288
De Bijenkorf Department Store (Rotterdam), 318, *340*
Dermody, Michael, 354
designers, architects as, 84–85
"design formalism," 295–298
de Waldner, C. F., 196
digital humanities, 16–17, 355, 356n25. *See also* Marcel Breuer Digital Archive (MBDA) (Syracuse University Libraries)
Diller Scofidio + Renfro, 11
Dodson, Richard, 188, 193, 201n28
Driller, Joachim, 9, 12
Duchamp, Marcel, 350
Duran, Michel, *290*
Dworschak, Baldwin, 47, 48, 133

Eames, Charles, 195
Eames, Ray, 195
Eggers & Higgins, 228, 238, 247
Egli, Ernst, 105
Egyptian architecture, 53, 57–58, 106
Eisenman, Peter, 313
Elberfeld, Germany, *36*
El Recreo Urban Center (Venezuela), *334*
engineering, integration of, 49
English architecture, 161, 171
Erps, Martha, 39
Evans, Randall, 157
Everson Museum of Art (Syracuse, N.Y.), *59*
Exhibition Building (Turin, Italy), *122,* 123, 124
exhibitions, 13, 38, 155, 157, 170–171, 173.
    See also *specific exhibition*

"Faceted, Molded Façade, The" (Breuer), 197–198
Farkas, Barron & Partners, 122, 128, 239
farmhouse architecture, 39–40
fascism, 294, 298
Fellhemer & Wagner, 195
fieldstone walls, 41–42
figuration, 296–297
films ("Bauhaus film"), *34,* 35

fireplaces, *296,* 297, 299
Flaine ski resort (France), 252, *258*–*263,* 276, 283
flow, 50–51, 60, 117, 120, 121–131
folds/folding, 48, 52, 110–111, 121–135. *See also specific project*
formalism, 132, 293–298, 313, 315–316
Forty, Adrian, 285
Foster, Richard, 245
Foucault, Michel, 83, 100, 114n42
France, 273, 275, 278–279, 282–283.
    See also *specific project*
freestone structural walls, 39
Friedrichstraße train station (Berlin), *166,* 167
From Bauhaus to Our House (Wolfe), 8
functionalism, 47, 48–49, 50, 157, 170, 296–297
"functionalization," 101–107
furniture design, 7–8, *34,* 35–37, 38, 87, 97–99, *98,* 229

Gagarin House (Litchfield, CT), *296*–297, 299
Gallo-Roman Museum (Lyon-Fourvière, F), 123
Garden, Nelson B., 191–193
garden city movement, 171–174
Garden City of the Future (model), 15, 44, 155–179
    architectural authorship of, 157
    critical reception of, 170–178
    cultural contexts, 157, 171
    design of, 157–167, 169
    health benefits of, 159, 160
    photographs, *154, 155, 162, 166, 169*
    urban design and, 150–160, 157, 164, 167–170
    Y plan form, 167, 169, 174, 176
Gatje, Robert F.
    Armstrong Rubber Building project, 117–119, 309, 310
    Brookhaven National Laboratory project, 182–184, 189–190, 193–199
    on economic logic, 121
    IBM Research Center project, 129–130, 181, 182–184, 195–199, 252
    New York University project, 232
    photograph of, *346*
    Saint John's Abbey project, 50, 51–52, 127, 128, 138n19
    Whitney Museum of American Art project, 57, 134
    writings of, 12–13, 57
    ZUP Sainte-Croix project, 276, 288
Gatje Papachristou Smith, 352
Geller chair, *98,* 99
German Building Exhibition (1931), 36
Giedion, Sigfried, 14
    monumentality and, 44, 86, 174–176, 177, 294, 298
    on "standard form," 114n46
    on UNESCO headquarters project, 96
    writings of, 41–42, 58
God's Own Junkyard (Blake), 295, 297, 313–314
Goldberger, Paul, 8
Goldstein, Israel, 224–225
Gothic architecture, 46, 49, 50, 54, 124, 130, 131
Gothic Architecture and Scholasticism (Panofsky), 50
Grand Central Terminal (New York), 8, 318
Grand Coulee Dam (WA), 50, 127, *129,* 139n26, 318, 320–323
Graves, Michael, 8, *294,* 315, 317n49
Greenblatt, Stephen, 133
Grenauer, Emily, 306
Grenet, Henri, 276
Grenet, Jean, 288
Gropius, Walter
    Architects' Collaborative, 15
    Bauhaus (Dessau) building, 35, 229
    Breuer's break with, 9–10
    Chamberlain Cottage, *42*
    on economy of high-rise building, 159
    Hagerty House, *41,* 121–122
    Harnismacher House, *38*–39, 62n4
    at Harvard, 41

housing designs, 48, 163
influence of, 133
J. Georges Peter and, 186
office with Breuer, 37, 188, 202
papers of, 62n4, 350
photographs of, *83*
residences, 122
Saint John's Abbey project, 18, 47, 48
UNESCO project, 45, 81, 85, 87, 94, 112n15, 113n18
Weissenhof Siedlung project, 38
Gropper, William, 350
Großsiedlung Siemensstadt (Berlin), *159,* 160
Großstadtarchitektur (Hilberseimer), 160
Guichard, Oliver, 274

Hagerty House (Cohasset, MA), *41,* 122
Hague, The, 318, *341*
Harnismacher House (Wiesbaden), *38–39,* 62n4
Harris, Teresa, 354, 356n23
Harrison, Wallace, 87
Harvard University, 11, 37, 41, *43,* 54, 173, 186, 354
Hassenpflug, Gustav, *36,* 160
Haworth, Leland, 188
Hays, K. Michael, 307–308, 313, 317n48
Heald, Henry T., 225–226
"heavy lightness," 38, 56, 57, 233
Hester, James, 224, 226
HEW headquarters (Wash., DC), *152–153*
Highway Beautification Action (Bonus Act of 1958), 303, 310–311, 317n41
Hilberseimer, Karl Ludwig, 160, *166,* 167, 177
Hitchcock, Henry-Russell, 38, 81, 107, 161, 164
Hochhausstadt (Hilberseimer), *166,* 167, 177
hospitals, *36,* 45, *164*–165
House for a Sportsman (exhibition), *36*
Howard, Ebenezer, 171, 172
HUD headquarters (Wash., DC), 53, 89, 127, *130,* 138n18, 140, *144–145,* 167
Hunter College, 189, 202, *220–221,* 229
Huxley, Julian, 84, 101
Huxtable, Ada Louise, 164
Hyman, Isabelle, 9, 12, 13, 167, 309, 356n15
hyperbolic paraboloid forms, 131–132

IBM facilities (Boca Raton, FL), 119, 130, *142–143,* 199
IBM logo, 308
IBM Research Center (La Gaude, F), 16
  Breuer on, 181
  commissioning of, 195
  cultural contexts, 181–182
  design of, 53, 119, 181–201, 195, 198–199, 199n6
  photographs of, *40, 116, 180, 181, 182, 196, 198, 252–257*
  Y plan form, 40, 89, 129–130, 167, 198
IBM World Trade Building (France), 140
Ideal Home Exhibition (1936), 155, *170–171*
IKEA, *312*
Institute for Architecture and Urban Studies, 313
Institute for the History and Theory of Architecture, 354
institutions
  architectural scholarship and, 14
  Breuer's shift from residential work to, 9–10, 13, 43–45, 121–122, 318
  collaboration with, 7
  Foucault's "author function" and, 83
  postwar notions of, 15–16, 100, 184–185, 294, 299–300, 302–303
  See also architectural authorship
international organizations, symbolism and, 51
International Style, 15, 38, 223, 232, 294, 299, 307
Iran, 318
Irwin, Robert, 136
Itten, Johannes, 37
Izenour, Steven, 295, 313–314

Jacobs, Jane, 177
Jasik, Stephen, 224
Johnson, Philip, 38, 57, 226, 245
Johnston-Sahlman Company, 128
John Wood the Younger, 161
Jones, Cranston, 174
Jordy, William H., 293–294
Jossa, Mario, *346*

Kahn, Louis, 57, 58, 59, 129, 202, *206*
Kaigai Bunka Tyuo Kyoku (Japan), 173
Kardos, István, 39, 42
Kaufmann, Edgar, Jr., 195
Kimball, Fiske, 227, 228
Komendant, August, 129
Kramreiter, Robert, 46

Laurenti, André, 276
Lawn Road Flats (London), 179n42
League of Nations, 82, 84, 100, 101, 114n51
Learning from Las Vegas (Venturi, Scott Brown, Izenour), 295, 313–315, *314*
Lebanon, *105*
Le Corbusier
  brise soleil, 197
  High Court India project, 299
  influence of, 38, 39, 41, 45, 53, 133, 161, 279
  Macia Plan, *166,* 167
  the Modular, 285, 296–297
  religion and, 176
  three-pointed skyscraper project, *88,* 89
  UNESCO project, 81, *83,* 85, 86, 91–96, *106,* 112n15
  Unité d'habitation project, 45, 279, 281, 285, 286, 296–297, 299, 305
  Ville contemporaine project, 159, *166,* 167, 168, 176, 177
  Ville radieuse project, 167
Lee, Richard C., 117, 309
Léger, Fernand, 44, 294, 298
Leon, James L., 128–129
Levy, Matthys, 118–119, 121, 127, 130, 136, 138n18, 139n26
lightness, 15, 35–63, 127, 131, 202, 299, 300
  "heavy lightness," 38, 56, 57, 233
Lincoln Center (New York), 11
Lipton, Thomas, 233
Living Architecture (Stierlin), 58
Lowell, Waverly, 356n19, 356nn21–22

Macia Plan (Barcelona), *166,* 167
Malraux, André, 275–276
Marcel Breuer, 1921-1961 (Breuer), 40
Marcel Breuer, Architect (Hyman), 13
Marcel Breuer: A Memoir (Gatje), 13
Marcel Breuer & Associates (New York City)
  growth of, 10, 14, 37, 43, 202
  Paris office, 12, *65,* 252, 276, 318
  photographs of, *65, 252, 346*
  successor to, 352
  writings by partners of, 12–13
Marcel Breuer Digital Archive (MBDA) (Syracuse University Libraries), 11–12, 16–17, *348*–357
Marcel Breuer Papers (Syracuse University Libraries), 9, 10–11, 195–196, 352–353, 354
Markelius, Sven, *83*
MARS Group, 156, 172
Masello, David, 12
Mazower, Mark, 100
McCarter, Robert, 11–12
McKim, Mead & White, 202, 223, 227, 248
Mead, Margaret, 103, 107, 114n59
Meinberg, Cloud, 46, 48, 50
Meister, Morris, 245–246, 248
Melnikov, Konstantin, 232–233
Melvin, Jeremy, 157
Metropolitan Museum of Art (New York), 8–9, 174

Meyer, Adolf, 35
Meyer, Richard, 351
Mies van der Rohe, Ludwig, 37–38, *60,* 97, 188, 226, 304, 350
Miró, Joan, 64, 233, 299
Mitrany, David, 101
Modern House, The (Yorke), 156
modernism
    as accommodation, 16, 274, 285, 290
    basis of modern architecture and, 158
    collapse of, 312
    contextualist pressures on, 110
    effects of corporate design processes on, 81
    in England, 41
    figuration and, 296–297
    formalism and, 296
    mid-century, 7, 8–9, 10, 11, 81, 100, 109
    postmodernism and, 8–9, 16, 294, 295, 296–297, 312–316
    preservation vs., 106
    Regency architecture and, 161
Modrow, Sebastian, 356n23
Moholy-Nagy, László, 37
monumentality, 294–295, 306–307, 313.
    See also New Monumentality
Moore, Henry, 233, 299
Morse, Philip, 186–187
Motley, James G., 190–191
Moxey, Keith, 356n25
Mumford, Eric, 174, 179n51
Mumford, Lewis, 82, 106, 165, 175–176, 299, 300
Mundipharma Factory and Headquarters (Limburg, DE), *339*
Murphy, Joseph, 46
Museum of Modern Art (MoMA) (New York), 8, 13, 37, 57, 62n4, 135, 173, 202

native tradition, 40
Nelb, Tawny Ryan, 356n19, 356nn21–22
Nelson, George, 195
nervature, 131
Nervi, Pier Luigi
    Breuer on genius of, 108, 137
    Exhibition Building project, *122,* 123, 124
    folded concrete, 18, 48, 61, 108, 109–110, 115n75, 124, 131
    Gatti Wool Factory project, 131
    Hunter College project, 202
    influence of, 108, 133, 137–138, 165
    isostatic rib systems, 49, 54
    lectures of, 54
    Palace of Labor project, *56*
    photographs of, *83*
    Saint John's Abbey project, 18, 45, 48, 49–50, 52, 53–54, 55–56, 131
    stadium architecture, 53
    thin-shell concrete structures, 131
    UNESCO project, 45, 49–50, 52, 55, 64, 81, 85, 90–96, 107–110, 122–123, 124, 126–127, 298, 300
    Whitney Museum project, 61
Nestlé headquarters (Vevey, Switz.), *88,* 89
Neutra, Richard, 47, 349–350
New Architecture (exhibition), 172
"new baroque," 120–121, 127, 130, 131, 133, 135–136
New England Merchants Bank competition, 119
New Kensington (PA), 48, 186
New Monumentality, 44, 86, 174, 175, 294–295, 298–300, 301, 316
New National Gallery (Berlin), *60*
Newsom, Carroll, 226
New York, *202–222. See also specific project*
New York University (NYU), 16, 223–251
    Begrisch Hall, 134, *214–217, 224,* 225, 229, *232–233, 235,* 236, 238, 241
    Bronx Community College and, 245–249, *246, 248*
    commissioning of, 202, 242
    critical reception of, 241–244
    cultural contexts, 242–245, 245–249
    enrollment, 224–226, 229, 244–245, 247, 251n48
    funding, 240–241, 242, 245
    growth and expansion of, 223–224, 226
    photographs, *212–219, 222, 224, 227, 230, 232, 235, 237, 238, 248*
    Silver Hall, *214, 216–217, 224–225, 227, 228–232, 230,* 241–242, 245, 247–248, 250n18
    Technology Building, 130–131, *218–219, 237–240, 238,* 241, 242–244, 247, *248*
Niemeyer, Oscar, 45, 276
"Nine Points on Monumentality" (Giedion, Sert, Léger), 44
Noël, August L., 57
Noguchi, Isamu, 64, 233
Nowicki, Matthew, 295–296, 304, 308
Noyes, Eliot, 195, 308

Olgiata Parish Church (Rome), *327*
OMA (Office for Metropolitan Architecture), 11, 89
On Growth and Form (Thompson), 201n44

Packard, Vance, 307
Palace of Labor (Turin), *56*
Panofsky, Erwin, 50
Papachristou, Tician, *346,* 352
Pei, I. M., 57, *59,* 188, 226
Peter, J. Georges, 186–187, 188
Picasso, 64, 233
pilotis, 119–120, 126, 130–131, 133, 182. *See also specific project*
Pirelli tire company (New Haven, Conn.), 311–312
Plas-2-Point House, *43*
Poelzig, Hans, *166,* 167
popular culture, 294–295, 297, 302, 307, 312–316.
    See also advertising; consumerism; *cultural contexts under specific project*
Porto Opera House (Portugal), 11
poster (imaginary film), *34,* 35–36, 37
postmodernism, 8–9, 16, 294, 295, 296–297, 312–316
Potsdamer Platz (Berlin), 158, *168–169*
prefabricated housing, 42–43, 48, 282–283.
    See also specific project
Princeton University, 229, 315

Querrien, Max, 275
Quimby, Sean, 353

Rand, Paul, 195, 308
Rauch, John, 16
Raymond, Antonin, 47–48
Regency architecture, 161
Renaissance and Baroque (Wölfflin), 120–121
research laboratories, 191–193. *See also* Brookhaven National Laboratory (Long Island)
Robbins, Mark, 10
Robert A. M. Stern Architects, *248,* 249
Roberto, Joseph J., 244–245
Rogers, Ernesto, 81–83, 300, 306
Royal Crescent (Bath, UK), 161
Rudolph, Paul, 57, 188, 294, 313

Saarinen, Eero, 14, 81, *83,* 86–87, 90, 91–96, 134, 188
Saint John's Abbey (Collegeville, MN)
    ancillary strategy for, 300–306
    bell banner, 18, *21–23,* 54–56, 132, 134, 139n31, 236, 293, 297, *301–303,* 304, *305,* 316n26
    Breuer on, 133, 139n31
    commissioning of, 10, 43–44
    comparisons to UNESCO, 123, 132
    cultural contexts, 13–14
    design for, 18, 45–57, 64, 123, 127–129, 131, 132, 137, 308
    photographs, *18–33, 55, 56, 127, 292, 301, 304, 305*
    success of, 318

Salvadori, Mario, 53–54
San Francisco Museum of Art, 173
Sarah Lawrence College, 202, *230*, 231
Sargent, D. Kenneth, 352
Sarget-Ambrine Pharmaceuticals (Mérignac, F), 252, *268*
Saussure, Ferdinand de, 313
Sayer House (Glanville, F), 252, *269*
Schwarz, Rudolf, 46, 51
Schwendler, William T., 241
Scott Brown, Denise, 16, 294, 313–315, *314*, 317n48
Scully, Vincent, 298
Seaborg, Glenn T., 201n30
Seidler, Harry, 131, 137
Selcer, Perrin, 110
Selye, Hans, 199
Semper, Gottfried, 39
Sert, Josep Lluís
    CIAM and, 112n15, 174–176
    Civic and Commercial Center project, *177*
    Garden City of the Future project, 174–176
    New Monumentality and, 44, 86, 294, 298
    UNESCO headquarters project, 81, 86, 113n18
    writings of, 173, 175
Severud Perrone Sturm Conlin Bandel, 130
Sexton, John, 223
Shand, P. Morton, 161
Sharp, Thomas, 46
Shelter in Transit and Transition (exhibition), 157, 173
Shoup, Eldon, 185
Siegert, Bernhard, 110
signs and billboards. *See* advertising
Silver, Julius, 225
Sitte, Camillo, 171
Skidmore, Owings & Merrill (SOM), 14
slab apartments, 158–160
Smith, Hamilton, 14, 50, 51–52, 59, 60, 128, 231, *346*, 352
Smith College, 229
Smithson, Alison, 8, 177
Smithson, Peter, 8, 177
South Boston Redevelopment plan, *173*–174
Soviet collective housing, 159–160
Space, Time, and Architecture (Giedion), 42
Space for Living (exhibition), 173
Special Collections Research Center (Syracuse University Libraries), 11, 353.
    See also Marcel Breuer Digital Archive (MBDA) (Syracuse University Libraries); *Marcel Breuer Papers* (Syracuse University Libraries)
Staehelin House (Feldmeilen, CH), *344–345*
Stam, Mart, 97, 99
Standard Möbel, 87
St. Anselm's Church (Tokyo), *47*
Stern, Max, 276
St. Francis de Sales Church (Muskegon, MI), 50, 131–133, *132*, 135, 139n31, 318, *324–325*
Stierlin, Henri, 58
Stiftung Bauhaus Dessau, 354
Stone, Edward Durell, 188, 294
St. Paul's Cathedral (Burlington, VT), *326*
structure, 117–139
    divergent expression of, 119
    emotional effects of, 120–121
    fold and figure, 121–135
Stuyvesant Six, *88*, 89, *98*, 99, *174*
suburbanization, 177
Sudreau, Pierre, 275
Suger (Abbot), 46
Sun and Shadow (Breuer), 107, 120, 134, 135, 176, 295, 297, 303
Swerve, The (Greenblatt), 133
Sydney Opera House, *124*, *125*
symbolism, architecture and, 44, 51, 58, 294, 296–297, 301–308

Syracuse University Libraries. *See* Marcel Breuer Digital Archive (MBDA) (Syracuse University Libraries); *Marcel Breuer Papers* (Syracuse University Libraries)
Syracuse University School of Architecture, 10–11, 349, 352

Tafuri, Manfredo, 294, 312
Taut, Bruno, 163
Team 10, 177
Telesis, 173
Thimmesh, Hilary, 46, 52
Thompson, D'Arcy Wentworth, 201n44
Thompson, Elisabeth K., 191, 193
Thonet, 97–99
Tolley, William, 350
Torin Corporation (Torrington, Conn.), 308, 317n36, 318, *336–339*
trapezoidal plans, 18, 52, 59–60, 86, 94
Tschumi, Jean, *88*, 89
tubular steel furniture, 7–8, *34*, 35–36
TVA (Tennessee Valley Authority), 101, 105, 108

Ukrainan State Theater (Kharkov), *157–158*
UNESCO headquarters (Paris), 49–55, 81–116
    ancillary strategy for, 294, 298–300
    architectural authorship of, 15, 45, 64, 83, 84, 85, 86–87, 91, 95, 97–99, 109–112, 122, 124–125
    "bending" and folding phase, 96–100, 108, 109–110, 115n75, 122–127, *125*
    CIAM and, 84–87, 99
    commissioning of, 10, 43–44, 81–82, 96, 276
    critical reception of, 53–54, 81–83, 89, 110–112, 165, 300, 306
    cultural contexts, 13–14, 82–84, 96–97, 99–100, 101–107, *102*, *104*, 110–111, 115n79, 294
    description of, 64
    design phases, 83–84, 96–100
    design process, 90–96
    flow and form of, 122–127, 129
    framing plan, 123, 124–126
    "functionalization" and, 101–107
    legacy of, 111–112, 122–123
    NYU and, 228–229
    photographs, *49*, *51*, *64–79*, *83*, *85*, *86*, *92–93*, *105–106*, *108*, *109*, *123*, *125*, *126*, *131*, *300*
    Y plan form, 45, 49, 55, 64, 86, 87–92, 113n32, 123, 124–126
Union Internationale des Architectes (UIA), 85, 112n15
United Nations, 100, 101
University of East Anglia Library, 354
University of Massachusetts (Amherst), *146–147*, 304–305
urban design, 157, 159–160, 164, 167–178
US Embassy (The Hague), 318, *341*

Van Leer Company (Amstelveen), 167, 318, *341*
Vassar College, 229–231
Venezuela, *334*
Venturi, Rauch, and Scott Brown, 16, 295
Venturi, Robert, 16, 294, 313–315, *314*, 317n48
Verheyen, Peter, 353
Viksjø, Erling, 89
Ville contemporaine (Le Corbusier), 159, *166*, 167, 168, 176, 177
Ville radieuse (Le Corbusier), 167
Vitra Design Museum (Germany), 13, 354
Voorhees, Walker, Foley and Smith, *190–191*

Walker Art Gallery (Minneapolis, MN), 56
Walter Gropius and Marcel Breuer, Architects (Cambridge, MA), 37, 62n4, 188, 202
Wank, Roland A., 195
Weidlinger, Paul
    Armstrong Rubber Company project, 118
    Breuer and, 121, 133, 137
    Grand Coulee Dam project, 129

HUD headquarters project, 130
Saint John's Abbey project, 127, 128, 137
St. Francis de Sales project, 131, 132
use of treelike forms, 45
Whitney Museum project, 59, 136
Weissenhof Siedlung (Stuttgart), 38
Werkbund exhibition (Paris), 40
Westwick, Peter J., 186
White, Stanford, 223, 227, 248
Whitney Museum of American Art (New York)
ancillary strategy for, 293, 294, 295, 306–308, 314, 317n48
Breuer on, 14, 181, 307
Breuer papers and, 351, 354
critical reception of, 37, 306–307
design for, 37, 53, 57–61, 134–137, 307–308, 311, 314, 315, 317n49
photographs, *35, 61, 135, 136, 202–211, 294*
"rebranding" of, 8–9
Wiener, P. L., *177*
Wiesenfeld, Hayward and Leon, 128, 129–130
Wilk, Christopher, 8
Wolfe, Tom, 8
Wölfflin, Heinrich, 120–121, 127, 131, 135, 138, 316n7
Wolfson House (Salt Point, NY), 122
wood-frame construction, 37, 41–43
Wright, Frank Lloyd, 47, 171
Wurster, William, 236–237

Yale University, 130–131, 140, *148–149*
Yamasaki, Minoru, 294
Yorke, F. R. S., 16, 18, *39*, 161, 172, 179n52. *See also* Garden City of the Future (model)
Young, Victoria, 13
Y plan form
bending of, 96–100
comparisons to industrial propeller, 113n32
Costa and, 114n40
double-shaped, 167, 169, 174
Garden City of the Future model, 167, 169, 174, 176
HUD headquarters, 89
IBM Research Center, 40, 89, 129–130, 167, 198
Nestlé headquarters, *88*, 89
as new international standard, 87–89
New York University, 238
photographs of, *88, 92–93*
UNESCO headquarters, 45, 49, 55, 64, 86, 87–92, 113n32, 123, 124–126

Zehrfuss, Bernard
CNIT and, 45, 55
Gallo-Roman museum project, 123
photographs of, *83*
Saint John's Abbey project, 55
UNESCO project, 45, 64, 85, 90, 91–96, 107–110, 122, 298
Zeilenbau model, 167, 168, 170, 174
Zevi, Bruno, 82, 89, 111
Zimmermann, Erich, *166*
ZUPs, defined, 16, 275
ZUP Sainte-Croix (Bayonne, F)
architectural authorship of, 274–275, 289
commissioning of, 273–274, 275–276
critical reception of, 274, 286–290
cultural contexts, 273–274, 275, 276, 278–279, 282–283, 286–287, 288
design of, 16, 174, 252, 273–291
marketing materials for, *282, 289*
photographs, *264–267, 272, 273, 275, 277, 279–280, 282, 284, 285, 286, 287, 289, 290*
refurbishment of, 286–290

Credits

Every reasonable effort has been made to identify rights holders for the images in this book. Please notify the publishers of any errors or omissions so that they can be corrected in subsequent editions.

Front cover: Hedrich-Blessing Collection, Chicago History Museum (hb30662z)
Back cover: Marcel Breuer papers, 1920–1986, Archives of American Art, Smithsonian Institution/Lucien Hervé
Quotation on cover flap: Marcel Breuer, "Notes on lectures, 1936–1948," in *Marcel Breuer, Buildings and Projects, 1921–1961,* ed. Cranston Jones (New York: Praeger, 1962), 257.

© Peter Aaron/OTTO for Robert A.M. Stern Architects: 6/26
Administrative Files, Special Collections Research Center, Syracuse University Libraries: Postface/1
Courtesy Lucia Allais: 2/14, 2/17
Architekturmuseum TU Berlin: 4/12 (Inv. No. 2809)
Marcel Breuer papers, 1920–1986, Archives of American Art, Smithsonian Institution (AAA): II/3, II/14, 2/10, 2/21, 2/23, III/13, 5/1, 5/4, 5/8, 5/11, IV/4, V/2, V/19–20, 7/1, 7/3, 7/5, 7/7–9, VI/2, VI/6, VI/13–14, VI/16, VI/18, VI/22, VI/48
AAA / Evelyne Bernheim: IV/2
AAA / Kurt Blum: VI/49
AAA / Gilles Ehrmann: II/14, II/18
AAA / Yves Guillemaut: V/9–13, V/15, V/21, 7/4, 7/12
AAA / Lee A. Hanley: I/9
AAA / Bill Hedrich, Hedrich-Blessing: I/4, I/15, I/21
AAA / Lucien Hervé: 1/15, II/1, II/11
AAA / Shin Koyama: IV/16, VI/3, VI/20–21
AAA / Robert Lautman: III/24
AAA / Joseph W. Molitor: III/3, III/5
AAA / Chas R. Pearson: 3/17
AAA / Ben Schnall: III/9
AAA / Manfred von Werthern: II/20
Max Dupain, Art Gallery New South Wales / © 2017 Artists Rights Society (ARS), New York / VISCOPY, Australia: 3/7
Bauhaus-Archiv Berlin: 1/1, 4/4
Berland-Berthon, *Les grands ensembles d'habitat des années 60: Un patrimoine du quotidien* (Bordeaux: CPAU Aquitaine, 2008), 47: 7/17
Brazier, Bernis E. and Elisabeth K. Thompson, "Laboratories for Radioactive Research," *Architectural Record* 121 (June 1957), 216–26, republished in *Buildings for Research* (New York: F. W. Dodge, 1958): 5/6–7
Breuer, Marcel, and Peter Blake, *Sun And Shadow: the Philosophy of an Architect* (New York: Dodd, Mead, 1955): II/9
Breuer, Marcel, "Stuyvesant Six: A Redevelopment Study", *Pencil Points* (June 1944), 66–70: 2/7
Bronx Community College Archives: 6/22–25
Casabella Continuita: 2/3
Daily Mail / Solo Syndication: 4/19
Departmental Archives of Bayonne, 12 W 24/2: 7/11
© Ezra Stoller / Esto: 1/2, 1/11, 1/21, 1/23, 3/22, IV/3, IV/6–11
© Fondation Le Corbusier / ADAGP, Paris / Artists Rights Society (ARS), New York 2017: 2/2 [L4(7)39], 2/6R [L1(1)47], 2/20 (29751), 4/13 (13189), 4/15 (31006A)
Robert M. Gatje: 8/11
Habitat Sud Atlantic, Bayonne: 7/6
Harvard Art Museums/Busch-Reisinger Museum, Gift of Walter Gropius, Photo: Imaging Department © President and Fellows of Harvard College: 1/10 (BRGA.85.18)
Courtesy of the Frances Loeb Library, Harvard University Graduate School of Design: 4/22
Hedrich-Blessing Collection, Chicago History Museum: I/1 (hb30953v), I/16 (hb30955e), 1/19 (hb30955j2_pm), 3.20 (hb30662k), VI/10 (hb30662z)

Karl Ludwig Hilberseimer Papers, Ryerson and Burnham Archives, The Art Institute of Chicago: 4/16 (070383)
Historic American Buildings Survey, Library of Congress Prints and Photographs Division, Washington, DC: I/7 (HABS MINN,73-COL,2)
Jones, Cranston, ed., *Marcel Breuer Buildings and Projects, 1921–1961* (New York: Praeger, 1963): 1/8
Landesarchiv Berlin/Horst Siegmann: 1/22 (F Rep. 290 Nr. 0004316_C)
Ralph Lieberman: 8/4
Laura Martínez de Guereñu: V/22, 7/15–16, 7/18
© Massachusetts Institute of Technology, photograph by G. E. Kidder Smith: 8/8
MAXXI Museo nazionale delle arti del XXI secolo, Roma. Collezione MAXXI Architettura. Archivio Nervi: 1/20, 2/22, 3/4–5
Marcel Breuer Papers, Department of Special Collections, Syracuse University Libraries (MBDA): Introduction/1, I/3, I/5–6, I/11–13, I/17–20, 1/3–7, 1/9, 1/12–13, 1/16–18, II/2, II/4–7, II/10, II/12–13, II/19, 2/4–5, 2/9, 2/11–13, 3/1–3, 3/11, 3/13–16, 3/18, 3/21, 3/23, III/1–2, III/4, III/6-8, III/10–12, III/14–16, III/18–23, 4/1–3, 4/5–6, 4/8, 4/11, 4/14, 4/17, 4/20–21, 5/2–3, 5/9–10, IV/1, IV/5, IV/13, IV/17–18, IV/21–24, 6/2–9, 6/15–20, V/1, V/3–8, V/14, V/16–18, V/23, V/25–28, 7/2, 7/13–14, 8/5–6, 8/9–10, VI/1, VI/4–5, VI/8–9, VI/11–12, VI/15, VI/17, VI/19, VI/23–31, VI/33–40, VI/42–43, VI/46–47, VI/53–55
MBDA / Louis Checkman: V/41
MBDA / Cunningham-Werdnigg: III/17
MBDA / Gilles Ehrmann: II/16
MBDA / Bill Hedrich, Hedrich-Blessing: VI/7
MBDA / Lucien Hervé: IV/8, II/15, II/17, 3/6, 3/12, 3/19
MBDA / Pierre Joly and Véra Cardot Photographers: V/24
MBDA / Shin Koyama: I/14
MBDA / Bernhard Mossbrugger: VI/51, VI/52
MBDA / Jan Versnel: VI/44
MBDA / KLM Aerocarto: VI/45
MBDA / Ben Schnall: VI/32
MBDA / Vitra Design Museum: VI/48
Courtesy Michael Graves Architecture & Design: 8/2
Kazuyoshi Miyamoto: 1/14
© The Museum of Modern Art/Licensed by SCALA / Art Resource, NY: 4/18
National Archives of France: 7.10 (19860172/1)
Nervi, Pier Luigi, The Works of Pier Luigi Nervi (New York: Praeger, 1957): 3/9–10
New York University Archives (NYU): IV/12, IV/19–20, 6/1, 6/11–14
NYU / Dean Brown: IV/15
NYU / Irwin Gooen: IV/14
NYU / Joseph J Roberto Collection, RG11.4, Box44, Folder7: 6/21
NYU / Stanley Seligson: 6/10
Timothy M. Rohan: 8/7, 8/12
Royal Institute of British Architects Collections: 4/7 (RIBA97069), 4/9 (RIBA97079), 4/10 (RIBA97078)
Saint John's Abbey Archive: I/2, I/8, 8/1
State Library of New South Wales, [IE103271] and Jorn Utzon: 3/8
Ben Schnall: 8/3
Jean Tschumi Archives: 2/8
UNESCO Archives: 2/1, 2/15–16, 2/18–19
Venturi, Robert, Denise Scott Brown, and Steven Izenour, *Learning From Las Vegas, revised edition: The Forgotten Symbolism of Architectural Form*, figures 75 & 76, page 88 & 89, © 1977 Massachusetts Institute of Technology, by permission of The MIT Press: 8/13
Eric Sutherland for Walker Art Center, Minneapolis: I/10
Walker, Ralph, *Ralph Walker, Architect, of Voorhees, Gmelin & Walker; Voorhees, Walker, Foley & Smith; Voorhees, Walker, Smith & Smith* (New York: Henahan House, 1957): 5/5

MARCEL BREUER
Building Global Institutions

Editors: Barry Bergdoll, Jonathan Massey
Essays: Lucia Allais, Barry Bergdoll, Kenny Cupers with
Laura Martínez de Guereñu, Teresa Harris, John Harwood,
Jonathan Massey, Guy Nordenson, Timothy Rohan
Editorial Assistant: Michael Abrahamson
Copyediting: Maureen Creamer Bemko
Proofreading: Simon Cowper
Indexing: Debbie Olson
Design: Integral Lars Müller/Lars Müller and Martina Mullis
Production: Martina Mullis
Lithography: prints professional, Berlin, Germany
Printing and binding: DZA Druckerei zu Altenburg, Germany
Paper: Profibulk, 1.3, 135 gsm

Publication of this book has been supported by a grant from the Graham Foundation for Advanced Studies in the Fine Arts.

Additional support generously provided by Elise Jaffe + Jeffrey Brown, and by Lauren Pack and Rob Beyer.

© 2018 Lars Müller Publishers and the authors

No part of this book may be used or reproduced in any form or manner whatsoever without prior written permission, except in the case of brief quotations embodied in critical articles and reviews.

Lars Müller Publishers
Zürich, Switzerland
www.lars-mueller-publishers.com

Distributed in North America by ARTBOOK | D.A.P.
www.artbook.com

ISBN 978-3-03778-519-5

Printed in Germany